Isopoliteia in Hellenistic Times

Brill Studies in Greek and Roman Epigraphy

Editorial Board

John Bodel (*Brown University*)
Adele Scafuro (*Brown University*)

VOLUME 14

The titles published in this series are listed at *brill.com/bsgre*

Isopoliteia in Hellenistic Times

By

Sara Saba

BRILL

LEIDEN | BOSTON

Cover illustration: Altertümer von Pergamon VIII 1, p. 4., Library of the University of Heidelberg.

Library of Congress Cataloging-in-Publication Data

Names: Saba, Sara, author.
Title: Isopoliteia in hellenistic times / Sara Saba.
Description: Leiden ; Boston : Brill, 2020. | Series: Brill's studies in Greek and Roman epigraphy, 1876–2557 ; volume 14 | Includes bibliographical references and index.
Identifiers: LCCN 2020008668 (print) | LCCN 2020008669 (ebook) | ISBN 9789004425699 (hardback) | ISBN 9789004425705 (ebook)
Subjects: LCSH: Citizenship (Greek law) | Isopoliteia (The Greek word) | Greece—Foreign relations—To 146 B.C.
Classification: LCC KL4364 . S23 2020 (print) | LCC KL4364 (ebook) | DDC 342.3808/3—dc23
LC record available at https://lccn.loc.gov/2020008668
LC ebook record available at https://lccn.loc.gov/2020008669

Typeface for the Latin, Greek, and Cyrillic scripts: "Brill". See and download: brill.com/brill-typeface.

ISSN 1876-2557
ISBN 978-90-04-42569-9 (hardback)
ISBN 978-90-04-42570-5 (e-book)

Copyright 2020 by Koninklijke Brill NV, Leiden, The Netherlands.
Koninklijke Brill NV incorporates the imprints Brill, Brill Hes & De Graaf, Brill Nijhoff, Brill Rodopi, Brill Sense, Hotei Publishing, mentis Verlag, Verlag Ferdinand Schöningh and Wilhelm Fink Verlag.
All rights reserved. No part of this publication may be reproduced, translated, stored in a retrieval system, or transmitted in any form or by any means, electronic, mechanical, photocopying, recording or otherwise, without prior written permission from the publisher.
Authorization to photocopy items for internal or personal use is granted by Koninklijke Brill NV provided that the appropriate fees are paid directly to The Copyright Clearance Center, 222 Rosewood Drive, Suite 910, Danvers, MA 01923, USA. Fees are subject to change.

This book is printed on acid-free paper and produced in a sustainable manner.

Contents

Foreword IX

Introduction 1

PART 1
Evidence from Asia Minor, Athens, and the Islands

1 **Miletos and Lykia** 35
   The Epigraphic Record and Its Interpretation 35
   (1) *The Agreement between Olbia and Miletos* 37
   (2) *Miletos and Kyzikos* 45
   (3) *Miletos and Phygela* 48
   (4) *Miletos and Kios* 52
   (5) *Miletos and Seleukeia Tralles* 58
   (6) *Miletos and Mylasa* 64
   (7) *Miletos and Herakleia under Mt. Latmos* 67
   (8) *The Lykian League: Xanthos and Myra* 74
   Disputed Cases from Miletos 78
   (9) *Tenos* 78
   (10) *Amyzon* 79
   (11) *Histros* 81
   (12) *Unknown City (Antioch on the Maeander?)* 81
   (13) *Apollonia on the Rhyndakos* 81
   Reassessing the Use of the Award of Potential Citizenship in Miletos 82

2 **Magnesia on the Meander and Samos** 84
   The Epigraphic Record 84
   (14) *Magnesia and the Cretan Koinon* 86
   (15) *The Stele of the Founders* 89
   (16) *Magnesia and Hierapytna* 92
   (17–18) *Magnesia, Samos, and Antioch on the Maeander* 95
   (19) *Magnesia and Phokaia* 98

3 **Western Asia Minor**   101
    The Epigraphic Record   101
    (20)   *Pergamon and Temnos*   103
    (21)   *Pergamon and Tegea*   108
    (22)   *Temnos and Teos*   113
    (23)   *Skepsis and Parion*   116
    (24)   *Laodikeia on the Lykos and [---]ikeia?*   124
    Disputed Cases   125
    (25)   *Ephesos and Sardis*   125
    (26)   *Priene and Maroneia*   126
    Conclusion: Potential Citizenship in Asia Minor   131

4 **Athens**   133
    (27–28) *Athens and Priene*   133
    (29)   *Miletos*   137
    (30)   *Athens and Alabanda/Antioch*   139
    (31)   *Athens and Rome*   141

5 **The Islands**   143
    (32–33) *Keos and Eretria / Keos and Histiaea*   144
    (32)   *Keos and Eretria*   145
    (33)   *Keos and Histiaea*   147
    (34)   *Knidos and Chalke*   150
    (35)   *Tenos and Kyrene*   153
    (36)   *Lesbian League*   156
    (37)   *Mytilene and Larisa—Thessalian Confederacy*   159

PART 2
Evidence from Central Greece and Crete

6 **Central Greece: the Peloponnese and Aitolia**   165
    (38)   *Argos and Aspendos*   166
    (39)   *Messene and Phigaleia*   170
    (40)   *Aitolia and Akarnania*   175
    (41)   *Keos, Naupaktos, and the Aitolian Koinon*   179
    (42)   *Herakleia under Mt. Latmos and the Aitolians*   184
    (43)   *Chios and the Aitolians*   187
    (44)   *Aitolian League and Trikka*   190
    (45)   *Aitolian League and (V)axos*   191
    (46)   *Aitolian League and Magnesia on the Meander*   193

CONTENTS   VII

7 **Crete**   195
   Treaties between Cretan *Poleis*   197
   (47)   *Hierapytna and Praisos*   197
   (48)   *Hierapytna and the Arkades*   201
   (49)   *Hierapytna and the Hierapytnans at ?*   201
   (50)   *Axos and Tylissos*   203
   (51)   *Hierapytna and Itanos*   203
   (52)   *Hierapytna and Priansos*   204
   (53)   *Hierapytna and Unknown City*   206
   (54)   *Eleutherna and Latos*   206
   (55)   *Lyttos and an Unknown City*   208
   (56)   *Hierapytna and Latos*   209
   (57)   *Lyttos and Olous*   210
   (58)   *Latos and Olous*   210
   Treaties between Cretan and Non-Cretan *Poleis*   212
   (59)   *Allaria and Paros*   212
   (60)   *Mylasa and (mostly) Unknown Cretan Cities*   215
   Conclusions   216

   PART 3
Asylia *and* Isopoliteia

8 *Asylia* and *Isopoliteia*   221
   (61)   *Teos and the Three Syrian Cities*   222
   (62)   *Teos and Eranna*   227
   (63)   *Teos and Biannos*   228
   (64)   *Teos and Mallia*   229
   (65)   *Teos and the Arkades*   229
   (66)   *Teos and Hyrtakina*   230
   (67–68) *Kos and Kamarina; Gela/Phintias*   232
   (69)   *Tenos and Phokis*   235
   (70)   *Tenos and Phaistos*   236

   Conclusions   238

   Appendix 1: The Origins of Potential Citizenship   245
   Appendix 2: Polybios and Potential Citizenship   255
   Bibliography   260
   Index Locorum   282
   Index of Concepts and Greek Terms   287
   Index of Places   289

Foreword

This book has been long in the making. I started this project in 2008, when I came to Germany as a Postdoctoral Research Fellow of the Humboldt Foundation (Kommission für Alte Geschichte und Epigrafik, DAI Munich). Several years, jobs, and fellowships later, the manuscript is being published. I thank Brill and its editors for their support.

This book was made possible by generous grants from the Humboldt Foundation and the Gerda Henkel Foundation (which also supported the final phases of editing), as well as the grant of Bavaria at the Ludwig-Maximilians-Universität to support women in research.

I have presented portions of this work on many occasions. The list of institutions and colleagues who have hosted me is too long to include here, but I thank them all. A special thank you goes to the DAI Munich and, at the Ludwig-Maximilians-Universität, the Department of Ancient History directed by Professor M. Zimmermann; both institutions have graciously hosted me.

Two scholars have read these pages multiple times: Kent Rigsby and Denise Demetriou. To them I am grateful and deeply indebted for their constructive criticisms and advice. Gary Reger also has greatly helped me to improve this book. A thank you goes also to the anonymous reviewers. Although we do not always agree, I sincerely thank them. After all, debate is the beating heart of scholarship. A special thank you goes to Prof. Enrica Culasso, who many years ago introduced me to epigraphy and whose influence has accompanied this work as well. Jennifer Palinkas has edited and greatly improved the language of this book.

Friends and family deserve a note: Gil Renberg, Ludwig Meier, Chiara Lasagni, Werner Tietz, Molly Richardson, Rachel Meyers, Claudio Biagetti, Marco Maiuro, Filiz Dönmez-Öztürk (a dear friend whose untimely death has made the field a lesser place), Simon Malloch, Pierangelo Buongiorno, and Victor Walser. They have all contributed in some way to this book, sometimes simply because they are good friends.

Finally, family: Albrecht and the liebe kleine Lucia who complicate my life and work but make me laugh every day.

Introduction

There is an institution in the Hellenistic world that scholars call *isopoliteia*; the Greek term, however, appears rather infrequently in the ancient record. The form of *isopoliteia* I investigate here created a relationship between two *poleis*, or sometimes between a *polis* and a federation, allowing citizens of one to take up citizenship in the other. This type of arrangement is attested only between the late 4th century BC and ca. 100 BC; it is, evidently, a creation of the Hellenistic world that died away in the decades when Roman power came to dominate the Aegean and western Asia Minor. *Isopoliteia*—or, as I call it here, potential citizenship—clearly served as an important instrument in interstate relations, alongside *asylia*, *sympoliteia*, and inter-state arbitration. While recent scholarship has studied these other institutional tools, *isopoliteia* remains relatively neglected;[1] indeed, no monograph has been devoted to it since 1975,[2] despite new evidence of previously unknown inscriptions.

Isopoliteia, as an institution and diplomatic tool widely used for several centuries, deserves a fresh look. How was it used? Who used it, when, and where, and who benefited from its award? Further, what can the institution of *isopoliteia* tell us about the political and diplomatic mentalities and attitudes of Hellenistic *poleis*? These questions direct the study that follows.

I think of this book as a work in the history of institutions—the type of contribution that is well described by the concept of *Grundlagenforschung*. A study of *isopoliteia* still requires some introduction, not least because of the peculiar history of the scholarship previously devoted to it: after the publication of the only existing monograph on the topic and its reviews, scholarly opinion came to a standstill.[3] Further, with a few notable exceptions, current scholarship has adopted the understanding of *isopoliteia* as an unconditional and unlimited grant of the greatest 'good' possessed by a *polis*, namely, its citizenship, to all citizens of the partner city that had signed an agreement. This all-encompassing tool could (possibly) have opened the door to an uncontrolled flow of people from one city to another, thereby depleting the citizenry of one community to the full advantage of the other. Moreover, scholars have tended

---

1 For *asylia*, see RIGSBY 1996, on inter-state arbitration see AGER 1996 and MAGNETTO 1997. Several contributions have been devoted to *sympoliteia*: for a general and short review of these sources and other bibliography on institutional themes see SABA 2009/10.
2 W. GAWANTKA 1975 remains the only monograph that has been completely devoted the topic.
3 GAWANTKA 1975; GAUTHIER 1977/8, pp. 373–378 with further references esp. to the work of J. and L. Robert.

to believe that the grant of *isopoliteia* automatically conferred onto the citizens of the partner city other crucial rights, such as intermarriage (*epigamia*) and the right to own properties (*enktesis*). These oversimplified views constitute the more extreme interpretations of *isopoliteia*; scholars have also presented more nuanced views. Nonetheless, I argue that this grant should *not* be taken literally or at face value: Yes, *isopoliteia* entailed a concession of citizenship, but not as a ready-made and open grant. *Isopoliteia* was the concession of the *option of switching citizenship*, i.e., one had to give up his citizenship in order to take up a new one. To do so, one had to follow a certain procedure—each city had its own—and we cannot exclude that individuals could fail in this process because they did not meet the set requirements. This outline, however, merely describes the content of this tool. Grants of *isopoliteia* must have been implemented, but we do not know how often. The evidence is clear that cities used *isopoliteia* as a tool to advance their diplomatic goals, whatever these might have been, and its effects were visible on the 'loftier' diplomatic and political level well before they had any effect on the actual citizenry and life of a *polis*. In other words, even if this sounds like a paradox, *isopoliteia* was in the first place a grant from one community to another as a political entity, not to its people.

In what follows I devote my attention to this first, institutional level, while touching only lightly on the possible secondary effects of the grant, namely, the individual attempts to implement it and the effects of such implementation, which are rarely attested in the historical record. There are two reasons for my focus. First, I am more interested in the diplomatic process than in the unattested implementation of this tool. The diplomatic process gives insights not only into the mentality of Hellenistic diplomacy and its zeitgeist, but also into several issues that, through the use of this specific tool, communities tried to address—in other words, their policies. The second reason for my focus depends on the evidence at our disposal. *Isopoliteia*, as I define it, is attested in interstate treaties. I study these treaties here with their more or less detailed clauses, but from them I am careful not to draw unwarranted conclusions that would be purely speculative. Clear and direct proof of implementation is *de facto* nonexistent.

Isopoliteia and the Individual

Two uses of the word *isopoliteia* point to two unrelated acts in the Greek world: *isopoliteia* granted by a *polis* to an individual and an institutional arrangement between two communities. In what follows I describe briefly the individual version (*isopoliteia* granted by a *polis*) and present evidence possibly indicating implementation of the institution on an individual level with some examples. Also, I explain why grants *ad personam* differ from institutional grants, and why my study here looks only at the latter. Then I will introduce some of the problems and issues I want to explore in institutional *isopoliteia* by means of a few examples.

As I noted above, by looking at potential citizenship as a diplomatic, interstate tool, the aspect tied to the possible impact on the population becomes secondary here. I have studied this 'secondary' issue in a separate work devoted to the grant of *epigamia* in its relation to potential citizenship.[4] The right to intermarriage could indeed have far-reaching consequences on individuals, their families, and, at large, the structure of society, but the existing evidence sets clear limits to the investigation. Adding the right to intermarriage to an overarching grant of potential citizenship was a policy decision that we can detect and partly analyze in context. The actual consequences, however, tend to remain obscure.

In general, if one wants to consider the topic of the practical consequences of the institution of *isopoliteia* on individuals I envision two possible approaches. One way to approach the issue would be to consider how members of a community would benefit from the actual object of this grant, namely, citizenship (and the additional grants such as, for example, *epigamia*). The other would be to consider grants *ad personam* to see if any can be traced back to intercity concessions of potential citizenship.

The first approach entails the risk of forgetting that the grant of potential citizenship only gave people the option of switching citizenship, not of adding a new citizenship package to an already existing one. Only by going through a procedural process could a lawful member of a grantee city switch citizenship status. The data set preserved is rather unhelpful when we attempt to quantify the number of individuals who took up this option. The evidence is too scarce to even make an educated guess. Did only a few people try to utilize the grant—or did many? A potential citizenship grant could certainly impact lawful members of the signing communities, especially when additional grants such as *epigamia* and *enktesis*—to name only the most common—were included. We lack, however, the means to measure this impact. More or less detailed clauses regulating various aspects of the grant can be attached to concessions thus pointing to issues that preoccupied a city. A city first tried to address these issues, as the evidence I collect here shows, through the concession of potential citizenship within a diplomatic framework. States deployed *isopoliteia* to cultivate relationships with other states. Isopolity, first and

---

4 See SABA 2011.

foremost, operated on this level, as reflected by the evidence; hence my focus here on potential citizenship as a diplomatic tool.

Only two pieces of evidence may attest to individuals using—in different ways—a concession of potential citizenship. I treat the evidence below, but a brief mention is useful here. At the beginning of the 2nd century BC, Zenon, son of Zenon from Kyrene, was awarded a (no longer preserved) grant by Tenos, as we learn from *IG* XII.5 814. According to the text he enjoys citizenship right "… like all other Kyreneans …," L. 5. Before breaking off, the decree states that this man was "speaking and doing well (good things)" for Tenos, LL. 7–8, which is the reason for the grant. We know nothing else of the grant or whether it was utilized, however. My focus here is on possible historical contexts and scholarly interpretations for this document. In brief: scholars like to think that this text is proof for the implementation of a grant of potential citizenship. I do agree that the decree is an indirect piece of evidence for an isopolity relationship, but I do not believe that Zenon had ever implemented the grant. Instead the document stresses the existing tie that Tenos had with Zenon by way of the community to which he belonged.

The second piece of evidence worthy of consideration relates to the case of Epikles. A citizen of (V)axos living in Amphissa, Epikles could have his citizenship status certified by his mother city, even if he probably had never lived there, and through it claimed recognition of certain rights in the Aitolian city where he dwelled. These benefits were possible because Aitolia seems to have had an *isopoliteia* agreement with (V)axos.[5] Epikles used this interstate agreement to improve his and his family's condition in some way; precisely how, however, remains unclear. The letter of the (V)axian authorities (LL. 9–12) recognizes Epikles's status: πολίτας ἰὼν ἁμὸς αὐτός τε κα[ὶ τ]ὰ τέκ[να αὐ]τῶ Ἐρασ[ιφῶ]ν [καὶ] / Τιμῶναξ καὶ θυγάτηρ Μελίτα, and asks the Aitolian *koinon* for certain benefits [καλῶς οὖν π]οιη(σ)εῖτε φροντίδ/δοντες ὅπαι εἴ τίς κα ἀδικῇ α[ὐτώς, κω]λύηται ὑφ' ὑμίων [καὶ κοι]/νᾶι καὶ ἰδίαι, ἁ δὲ κοινοπολι[τείας] ἀϊδία ὑπάρχῃ ἀν[αγραφά]. Namely, the (V)axian authorities ask the Aitolians to extend to Epikles and his kin a form of personal *asylia* and that a copy of the *koinopoliteia* be inscribed.[6]

We learn from this text, as exceptional as it is, that people in fact used the legal framework—if *koinopoliteia* truly was an expression indicating a federal grant of potential citizenship—and that such agreements could ameliorate their condition. This piece of evidence is, however, unique and quite complex in interpretive terms because we do not know much about Aitolia's legal intricacies in regulating potential citizenship(s).

---

5   See *StV* III 585 = *I.Cret.* II.v 18A = no. 45.
6   For this text see *infra* p. 192.

INTRODUCTION   5

One last and important point pertains to (citizenship) grants *ad personam*. Some of these grants indeed contain the word *isopoliteia*. I need to stress that grants *ad personam* fundamentally differ from the Hellenistic institution because their concession happens outside the institutional framework necessary for the application of the institutional tool that I study here. More importantly, they have different diplomatic intensity and have different targets. Ultimately, a grant *ad personam* recognizes an individual who has distinguished himself in some way that is considered advantageous to the grantor. The grant of potential citizenship (*isopoliteia* as an institution) is a political act of a city directed to another city—or federation. Both grants can become political platforms to further and strengthen relations, but each creates a particular type of tie.

Grants *ad personam* that use the term *isopoliteia* in place of the more usual *politeia* are widely attested. It is important to note that all these grants come from central Greece, which suggests to me that the use of this word in citizenship grants is regional (Peloponnese and central Greece). Moreover, in these concessions, which can be easily found in bulk through a PHI search, the grantee is first and foremost awarded proxeny. Citizenship, called *isopoliteia*, appears alongside other concessions as an additional grant.[7]

The practice of granting citizenship was as old as the concept of citizenship and, certainly, this practice and the institutional tool have common traits. Nonetheless, the concessions *ad personam* cannot teach us anything about the institution because the two operate on different institutional levels and have different goals and applications.[8]

My focus is therefore on the institution of potential citizenship and its essential traits in interstate agreements.

Who Used Potential Citizenship?

The surviving evidence shows that primarily *poleis* used the diplomatic tool of potential citizenship: small or big *poleis*, rich or poor, close or distant—it did

---

7 CARLESS UNWIN 2017, pp. 131–132 discusses *proxenoi* and their role and lists grants that could be given to them. She comments on citizenship in n. 25: "it appears that *isopoliteia* was effectively the same as a normal grant of citizenship" and corroborates her statement by quoting GAUTHIER 1985. She is right and, with her footnote, shows modern scholars' tendency to attach a 'technical meaning' to the term *isopoliteia*. In grants of citizenship *ad personam*, whether citizenship is the main grant or an additional one, *isopoliteia* means citizenship.

8 GAUTHIER 1972, pp. 347–375 similarly specifies that attention must be devoted to interstate treaties and that grants *ad personam* should be excluded from a study of the institutional tool, as they cannot tell us anything about it.

not matter. What mattered was that at the time of the concession the parties involved in the exchange of potential citizenship were politically, economically, or strategically relevant to each other. The grant of *isopoliteia* was overwhelmingly exchanged bilaterally. Even in the few cases where unilateral concessions are attested, a clear expectation of reciprocation appears.[9] Federations also used *isopoliteia*, granting it to *poleis* or even to another federation.[10] How did federations use grants of *isopoliteia*? For an answer, we can look to the *koinon* of the Aitolians, which preserves the most numerous testimonies of *isopoliteia* involving a federation. This evidence further forces us to address complex problems concerning citizenship, such as the problem of dual citizenship, its role within federations, and the relation of this system of 'double citizenship' to *isopoliteia*. Aitolia seems to have granted *isopoliteia* at both civic and federal citizenship levels. It is possible that *isopoliteia* supplanted the construct of dual citizenship in newly established federations, as for example in the Lesbian league attested in the 2nd century BC.

The key to understanding *isopoliteia*, to my mind, is to view it as a grant from one community to another community: no king or dynast ever promoted it, despite claims to the contrary. Its concession was never influenced by reigning powers; it established relations or actual alliances between *poleis*.[11]

When and Where was *Isopoliteia* Used?

The geographical and chronological distribution of ancient material that survives gives a very clear indication of the dates and popularity of the grant of *isopoliteia*. This tool was used everywhere in the Greek world from the 4th to the 1st century BC. The evidence is mainly epigraphic. Literary sources rarely seem to refer to *isopoliteia* and, when they do, it is difficult to determine whether they mention awards of potential citizenship or are concerned with some other institutional tool such as *sympoliteia*.[12] That we have only (*de facto*) epigraphic evidence, however, is no surprise and finds close parallels in the

---

9   Notably in the grant of potential citizenship by Temnos to Teos (*SEG* XXIX 1149 = no. 22).
10 See for example the agreement between Aitolia and Akarnania (*IG* IX² 1 3A = no. 40).
11 The well-known dossier preserving Antiochos's concessions to Teos and this city's reply (no. 61) has fostered the opinion that kings could influence such concessions. But Antiochos was not involved in Teos's decision to propose to offer the grant to three Syrian cities. Another text that has been used to suggest possible royal influence on the concession of the grant is that concerning the case of Arsinoe and Nagidos, on which see *infra*, pp. 25–26.
12 See Appendix 2.

evidence for other institutional tools typical of the Hellenistic age. The most famous example is the institution of foreign judges, who are known to us from epigraphic material only. Closest to the case of *isopoliteia* are perhaps *asylia* and *sympoliteia*; both are better and longer attested than *isopoliteia*, but the testimonies are mostly inscriptions and only sparse references appear in literary sources.

While a substantial amount of ancient material comes primarily from Asia Minor and Crete, the rest of the evidence for *isopoliteia* is scattered across the Mediterranean and to the east. Potential citizenship was indeed a widely used and internationally recognized diplomatic tool. Secure evidence for it dates between the 4th and the 1st century BC. One can discuss (if not fight over) its earliest attestations,[13] but it is accurate to say that cities started to use potential citizenship in its most developed form consistently from the 4th century BC until ca. 100 BC, when the last known agreement that includes potential citizenship was passed.[14] Did *isopoliteia* end about 100 BC? The answer is yes, largely because of the changed historical conditions that, with the coming of Rome, further limited or made redundant an active foreign policy as it was practiced by cities in the preceding centuries.[15] But this is not a story of decadence. Rather, it is an account of the development of a tool that communities had at their disposal for use in international relations. Specific historical contexts, diplomatic activities, and opportunities shaped *isopoliteia* and other instruments. If we do not understand what these instruments were and how communities used them, it becomes impossible to follow developments in Hellenistic diplomacy and politics.

How was *Isopoliteia* Used?

The diachronic and geographical approach to the material that I have adopted has indicated that, by and large, we can identify two main ways in which the grant of *isopoliteia* was used. First, *isopoliteia* could regulate or establish diplomatic contacts and build actual, long-lasting relationships that do not seem to have had an immediate impact or reflect particular current events. In this way, *isopoliteia* could be defined as an 'aspirational diplomatic tool.' Second, *isopoliteia* could instead have had more pragmatic, immediate traits. It often figures

---

13 See Appendix 1 on the origins.
14 *I.Cret.* I.xvi 5 = CHANIOTIS 1996, pp. 358–376 no. 61 = no. 58.
15 See for example MACK 2015, esp. pp. 270–277, who discusses the changed political situation in the Greek world in his work devoted to *proxenia*.

within military agreements and could regulate political or policy issues that we can often assess or define in their general area of impact. It may be accurate to call this way a 'mediating form' of isopolity.[16]

If we apply these descriptions to the evidence, it becomes clear that the cities of Asia Minor, the islands, and Athens favored the first type of *isopoliteia*. They tended to grant this award to regulate or establish diplomatic contacts with other (distant or close) communities that were somehow significant to them from a political point of view, whether at the local or at the international level.

The second use (or type of) *isopoliteia*, which is mostly but not exclusively attested in Crete,[17] is almost always found in association with military alliances. It seems to have been used as an instrument to further cement alliances and contributed to their success.[18]

By way of illustration I offer here examples for each type of *isopoliteia*. My aim is to use these examples as case studies to show 'how' *isopoliteia* was employed.[19] For this reason, I will not immediately discuss their proper

---

16 In the past, I have tried to give 'names' to these types of awards of potential citizenship, but I have decided against all of my attempts. The two suggestions here should clarify how I define these two modes of granting isopolity, but I will not use these terms as labels. Here I argue for a more flexible interpretation of the use of potential citizenship; I fear that, by giving a name to a specific use, I will only encourage the application of new fixed and rigid interpretive categories.

17 Examples for this use of potential citizenship, although isolated, are also attested in Asia Minor and in central Greece, such as the peace treaty between Miletos and Herakleia under Mt. Latmos, *Milet* I 3 150 = no. 7, and the agreement between Skepsis and Parion, J. and L. Robert *BE* 1972 371 = no. 23. For central Greece see the curious agreement between Aitolia and Akarnania, *IG* IX² 1 3A = no. 40.

18 Strictly speaking, this use of potential citizenship is diplomatic too. I sometimes use the adjective 'diplomatic' to describe the first type of use of isopolity, but I clearly recognize that the second use also pertains to diplomacy.

19 Any study of the history of ancient institutions that hopes to reach results requires evidence that contains as many details as possible and often, in the process, a few texts (or a single one) end up assuming the role of example or even 'manifesto' for a certain institution. For *isopoliteia* the choice of this example is not unequivocal. Some scholars prefer Cretan documents, but, after considering all existing evidence for *isopoliteia*, I decided against agreements from Crete as exempla. This evidence is certainly detailed and meaningful, in some aspects more than the evidence coming from other areas. Indeed, Cretan texts often contain many details important to the students of Cretan antiquity, but the texts reflect societal and economic worries that are deeply tied to that region. In other words, although Cretan *poleis* used and understood this tool like other communities in the Greek world, they used it to address issues that are specific to the region. They do not represent broader patterns that can be discerned in *isopoliteia* agreements from other areas.

INTRODUCTION

historical and legal contexts, but instead reserve that for the chapters that follow. I use Milesian documents to illustrate the first 'type' of *isopoliteia*, which aimed to forge long-term diplomatic relationships with other states in 'peaceful' times. For the second 'type,' I present a text from the Peloponnese. My choice may seem anomalous because the majority of texts with the second type of potential citizenship come from Crete. But the inscription I discuss here is to my mind more representative because it not only illustrates well the way in which the second type of *isopoliteia* was used, but also shows many of the peculiarities of this tool. In the discussion that follows, I supplement this material with other documents to demonstrate that isopoliteia was not a unidirectional and single-use tool, but rather that its strength came from its flexibility.

(a)   Isopoliteia *as Long-Term Diplomacy*

In 218/7 BC Miletos and Seleukeia-Tralles sent embassies back and forth and, at the end of this exchange, the *poleis* granted each other potential citizenship.[20] The stele preserving the documents that testify to this diplomatic exchange was found in the temple of Apollo Delphinios and has attracted substantial scholarly attention (now published as *Milet* I 3 143, text no. 5 below).[21]

---

20   On the historical context see *infra*, Miletos no. 5. I somewhat reluctantly use this text to clarify the first type of *isopoliteia* because the author of the 1975 monograph on isopolity, W. Gawantka, also started his book with it. Nevertheless, it is necessary because of the undeniably representative character of the dossier. The main point of difference between my treatment of this inscription and Gawantka's is that he considers Miletos's decree in isolation. In addition, while Gawantka knows very well the general historical context of the inscription and its implications, he does not use these elements directly in his analysis, thus depriving it of historical depth.

21   My translation of text follows, no. 5: A (Milesian decree), LL. 12–32: (…) So that the *demos* shows that it sees with favor those who have behaved piously toward the god and with benevolence toward the city and that it grants them what is of value to it, it was decreed by the Milesians that the Seleukeians be praised for their attitude and that they be put under the care of the *boule* and the *demos*, and also that we accept the honors that have been decreed by them with benevolence. (17) (Also, it was decreed that) citizenship shall be granted to the Seleukeians who live in their homeland and city Seleukeia up to the year of the *stephanephoros* Epikrates and the month Taureon. If some have been granted citizenship by decision of the *demos*, but do not live in the city of the Seleukeians, or in case citizenship is granted to anyone after this (deadline), they shall also have our citizenship after they have inhabited Seleukeia as homeland and city for ten years starting from (the time of) their enrollment in the citizen body. Those who decide to live with us as citizens and (24) partake in (our) sacred (practices) and magistracies and all the rest, in which take part all other Milesians, shall register at the seat of the *boule* every year before the 20th of the month Anthesterion (by declaring) their fathers' name and the tribe to which they belong. (27) The secretary shall report to the next assembly after the registration; the

A section of decree A (the Milesian decree) that provides numerous details on the procedure of switching citizenship status has indeed been the focus in past scholarship, to the point that scholars neglect to discuss the rest of the inscriptions in this dossier. While this section (LL. 17–33) certainly provides rare information on procedural aspects, these details have been read either as a reflection of an alleged hostile immigration policy of the Ionian city or as a sign that the concession of the grant of *isopoliteia* (in general) implies that a *polis* would open its doors for the citizen body of another community unconditionally.[22] In fact, the text does not have such a politically charged meaning. Instead, these clauses testify only to the formal procedure that was in place in Miletos for these awards and thus need to be placed in their proper context along with the rest of the inscription.[23]

It is striking that while this dossier contains two documents that testify to the same diplomatic process and use the same tool, namely, *isopoliteia*, to

prytaneis shall distribute them by lot in the tribes, which the *demos* shall indicate. Those who join the citizen body shall partake in everything else immediately but be assigned to the guard and command of the guard only ten years after their first allocation (to the tribes). If anybody lives as citizen against this decree, he shall be liable to prosecution by the *molpoi* and with the procedures that discipline matters concerning foreigners according to the laws. (…)

B (Seleukeian decree), LL. 54–64: To good fortune; it has been decreed by the *boule* and the *demos* to praise the Milesians for their benevolence and conduct which they have in regard to the people. Citizenship rights on equal footing shall be granted and they shall partake in everything in which other citizens do. Anyone of the Milesians who wants to live as citizen in Seleukeia shall be registered by the *strategoi* and the secretary of the *demos*. They shall register the applicant in the tribe to which he wants to belong. They shall also have *proedria* in all festivals and access to the *boule* and *demos* first after the sacred matters. The current elected *strategoi* shall take care of the *demos* of the Milesians and provide for those who come to our city, so that they always find the best possible conditions. (…)

22 This concession appears to be Gawantka's position in his 1975 monograph.
23 This example is one of several inscriptions providing details about the procedure of naturalization, see *infra* especially the section on Miletos. But these details pertain to procedures. I will return to the interpretation of such clauses below, but I must stress that my position is that these clauses only reveal that the local administrators were good legislators. Procedures provide the framework for possible requests from those who wanted to take up the opportunity to change citizenship. In principle, procedures do not have to be inscribed on stone, although sometimes they are. In any case, even if one wants to see these clauses as signs of a city's will to encourage implementation of the grant, which I personally do not believe, they still do not tell us how many people decided to go through the implementation process or reveal the impact on the community. In procedural terms these considerations are irrelevant, too: it does not matter whether one or 100 requests were submitted to the local authorities, the legal framework had to be in place to open the door to this possibility.

establish permanent interstate relations, these documents differ enormously from each other in tone, attitude, and, I argue, purpose. For this reason, the decrees deserve to be studied 'in parallel' as we can profit from a comparison of the different provisions they list and their wording. In general, the exchange of potential citizenship between two communities catalyzes diplomatic contacts between them and helps promote stronger relationships. The grant is reciprocal, and the communities do not seem to have any particular interest in seeing the grant implemented. Seleukeia adds a notable feature to this flexible instrument with provisions that are meant to create a privileged temporary status for foreigners (Milesians) in town. This addition appears to be almost an appendix to the award, but its addition stresses that with *isopoliteia* cities granted the option of switching citizenship, not citizenship itself.

A few of the differences between the two decrees from Miletos and Seleukeia emerge on an initial reading of the texts. The dossier preserves the Milesian decree first. It begins by mentioning a Seleukeian embassy, which reached Miletos to reply to the mission that (at some unknown point) had started the diplomatic discourse (and appears in decree B, LL. 49–52).[24] Miletos must have initiated the contact, formally or informally, and, while there is no attempt to conceal this detail, the dossier is not concerned with this aspect. Decree A, LL. 5–11, by Miletos, starts with a summary of the content of the Seleukeian embassy and emphasizes some aspects of it, details that are not part of decree B, passed by Seleukeia-Tralles. Decree A refers briefly to the benevolent attitude described in detail (κατὰ μέρος) in B (LL. 7–8) that Seleukeia claims to have for Miletos. However, the grant of potential citizenship, which represents the core of decree B, does not figure at all in decree A's opening

---

[24] In *BE* 2015 650 Hamon commented on a short article I published on this inscription, SABA 2014. While his corrections to the translation are welcome, he misconstrues (following WILL 1995) the diplomatic situation; surely it was Miletos that initiated the exchange (and not Seleukeia as Hamon thinks): the *Prytanis* mentioned in B8ff as having travelled to Seleukeia and promoting Miletos' case was Milesian (MÜLLER 1976, p. 36 n. 30 with more bibliography and WILL 1995, p. 312, n. 24). A parallel can be found in TZIAFALIAS and HELLY 2004 (*SEG* LV 605) = no. 37 where Bacchios son of Kaikos from Mytilene is honored by the city of Larissa (2nd century BC). Bacchios pushes the case for conceding grants to his hometown, Mytilene, among which is potential citizenship. This honorary decree provides indirect evidence for one or possibly two grants of isopolity, but it singles out the work of a particular individual as catalyst for major concessions. Decree B in the Miletos-Seleukeia dossier attests that Miletos started the diplomatic contact that Seleukeia duly continued with the sending of a seemingly prestigious embassy (and to which Miletos replied—decree A). Miletos tended to grant potential citizenship by replying to a first concession, which in this case came from Seleukeia-Tralles: the city was not accustomed to granting potential citizenship first.

summary, or at least not explicitly. Instead, it emphasizes the provisions that Seleukeia approved for the Milesian Apollo (LL. 8–11 and again LL. 12–13). But, if we turn to decree B, while the Seleukeians had voted several honors to this god, these provisions constitute an appendix to the concession of potential citizenship (LL. 64–66): sacrifices for this city's main god, Zeus Larasios immediately follow (LL. 67–69). In decree B, Seleukeia grants *isopoliteia* to Miletos. The text includes short provisions on the procedures that those who intend to switch status had to follow. These Milesians, Seleukeians-to-be, says the text, would partake in "everything" immediately (LL. 56–57). Short enrollment clauses complete this section, requiring that new citizens register with the *strategoi* and the secretary of the *demos* and be enrolled in a tribe of choice (LL. 57–60). Another key provision recommends that the *strategoi* take care of the *demos* of the Milesians and especially of those Milesians who are in town.

The main body of Miletos's decree (decree A) starts by honoring the Seleukians and accepting their award of *isopoliteia*. Miletos then reciprocates the grant: the Milesians devote more space to the procedural aspects of the enrollment process (LL. 17–33 versus LL. 56–60 of the Seleukian grant). Unlike the Seleukeian decree, which shows actual concern with Milesian citizens in Seleukeia who would not exercise their potential citizenship rights, the Milesian decree spares to the topic only a line (LL. 15–16) with a brief provision favoring Seleukeians citizens who did not intend to take up the option of becoming Milesians.

The procedure to switch citizenship is described in detail: Miletos establishes different residency requirements for different categories of individuals (LL. 18–29) that had to be fulfilled before they could switch citizenship.[25] The applicants had to register at the seat of the *boule* by an annual deadline providing their patronymic and their tribe membership. The secretary then had to report at the next assembly and the *prytaneis* were responsible for the distribution of the new citizens in the tribes chosen by the *demos*. A restriction clause that follows specifies that new citizens were not eligible to be top officials in the defense of the city until ten years after their enrollment in a tribe. Finally, the last provisions are concerned with the institutional agents that will punish those who abuse the granted citizenship rights.

Although Seleukeia's enrollment clauses are less detailed, its decree *in toto* reveals that the city valued its relationship to Miletos, especially in the provision concerning additional measures to accommodate the temporary presence of Milesians in town. Seleukeia sealed its interest in a long-lasting relationship with Miletos with the concession of *isopoliteia*. Seleukeia was

---

25   See SAVALLI 1985, p. 407.

likely not interested in an implementation of the grant, but it certainly valued the presence of Milesians in its territory by assuring their protection even without becoming citizens. The Milesians responded to this award of *isopoliteia* by reciprocating it. Miletos's long and detailed clauses have been interpreted as reflecting the city's immigration policy, namely, that it tried to limit the number of newcomers by establishing strict enrollment procedures. This assessment is not accurate. I argue instead that these provisions are the result of the city's procedural and archival practice.

The provisions attested in the Milesian *isopoliteia* agreements, including the one just presented, describe procedural matters and forms of control that each city must have had in place and that are rarely attested in inscriptions. Cretan epigraphic evidence offers a parallel for such detailed enrollment clauses in the agreement between Hierapytna and Praisos,[26] while an inscription from Lykia, the agreement between Xanthos and Myra, contains extremely detailed evidence for the procedure of switching citizenship.[27] All cities had their own rules and procedures; that inscriptions do not list these details does not mean that a *polis* opened its doors unconditionally to all citizens of a partner city. The expectation that cities dwell on procedural aspects routinely on stone only ascribes to these records a task they did not have.[28]

In his 1975 monograph, Gawantka scrutinized the presence or absence of enrollment clauses in documents, and their possible meaning. His interpretations form the basis for most current claims on *isopoliteia*, some of which I wish to challenge. To clarify my own position, a brief review of his approach on this point is necessary.

Gawantka perceives a direct relationship between the geographical distance that separates the parties in a bilateral agreement of *isopoliteia* and the amount of detail on the enrollment procedures contained in these agreements.[29] I call

---

26 *I.Cret.* III.iv 1 = CHANIOTIS 1996, pp. 185–190 no. 5 = no. 47.
27 *SEG* XLIV 1218 = no. 8.
28 This issue is linked to the topic of archives and their use in antiquity. The evidence for archives is limited. We know they existed and that inscriptions were not the only way to preserve written records. Texts engraved on stone sometimes were shorter versions of the 'originals.' Inscriptions could also simply contain references to laws or other provisions that were registered elsewhere in detail. Details on procedures of different kinds must belong to specific legislative acts. See for example *infra* the case of the reference to the law on grants that appears in the concession of *asylia* to Alabanda by Athens. A reference to laws often sufficed: details were not repeated each time a standard procedure was required. On archives in Athens and the use of writing for archival purposes, see esp. SICKINGER 1999; more recently, see the collection edited by M. FARAGUNA 2013 with further bibliography.
29 GAWANTKA 1975, pp. 78–79 relying on Milesian and Cretan evidence.

this the 'geographic theory'. In addition, he claims that the stronger of two closely neighboring cities in an agreement of *isopoliteia* would have carefully regulated the conditions upon which new citizens could be enrolled in its citizenry. According to Gawantka, the stronger city feared that potential citizens would flock to it, leaving their weaker community behind. I call this prospect 'fear of implementation'.

While proximity must have impacted the terms of an agreement, or even sometimes prompted it, the presence and type of enrollment clauses can hardly have depended exclusively on proximity. Each *polis* must have had its own documentary practice, which would affect the types of document cities produced and the selection clauses included in the agreements, as demonstrated by the documents from Miletos (Gawantka used these documents as one of his two case studies). Several agreements from Miletos that include potential citizenship contain enrollment clauses. These clauses are already detailed in the 4th century BC only to become even more specific in the 3rd and 2nd centuries BC. However, these are standardized clauses and appear in extremely different contexts. They do not attest to a fear of implementation related to the communities' proximity to one another.[30]

From the Miletos-Seleukeia dossier, we learn that the diplomatic initiative originated somehow in Miletos, and the grant of *isopoliteia* in Seleukeia. It seems that Miletos may have desired to see some other consequences to its diplomatic activity, but exactly what remains unclear. Instead, Miletos obtained a highly valued concession (*isopoliteia*) that it needed to reciprocate. Miletos did reciprocate, yet, despite of the length of the provisions that are an administrative corollary to the concession, Miletos's focus is elsewhere. The city was probably concerned with cultic ties, as indicated by its emphasis on

---

30 See *infra* on Miletos. Gawantka's thesis mainly relies on the later agreements Miletos signed with Seleukeia-Tralles (*Milet* I 3 143 = no. 5), Mylasa (*Milet* I 3 146 = no. 6), and Herakleia under Mt. Latmos (*Milet* I 3 150 = no. 7). Although these cities were neighbors, the treaties they concluded with Miletos have distinct background contexts and differing requests brought forward by the parties. In addition, while these treaties contain nearly identical enrollment clauses, these similarities must be due to Miletos's documentary praxis that develops as early as the agreement that Miletos stipulates with Olbia *Milet* I 3 136 = no. 1. Gawantka's second case study comes from Crete. He compared agreements between Cretan *poleis* to agreements that Cretan *poleis* made with communities outside the island. He rightly notes that the first agreements generally provide more details on the issues at stake. However, each type of agreement regulates completely different sets of problems: internal politics and policies present distinctly local concerns that differ from foreign policy. Scholars hold that Cretan piratical attacks triggered the second type, or that they were responses to *asylia* requests. See *infra* on Crete and CHANIOTIS 1996, pp. 101–104.

INTRODUCTION 15

rituals relating to the cult of Apollo Delphinios, as well as the kinship relation that the two cities spelled out differently in their texts (I will address this kinship below).

The use of the reciprocal concession of *isopoliteia* in this decree is part of the structure and development of its diplomatic discourse, but, as odd as this statement may sound, *isopoliteia* is not the focus of this discourse; *isopoliteia* rarely is. By granting it, accepting it, and reciprocating it the two *poleis* could pursue their own goals. Although these goals remain largely unclear to the modern reader, they are articulated with a diplomatic language that was meant to trigger clear and predictable responses.[31]

Diplomacy has many faces. Another text that helps to clarify how cities could make use of potential citizenship as part of their diplomatic initiatives is the Athenian recognition of *asylia* for Alabanda/Antioch in 201/0 BC.[32] This text gives me the opportunity to focus on the interpretive directions that scholarship has taken and that need to be reevaluated before arriving at the second part of this study, where I offer textual analyses that are more technical and less concerned with general themes. In the decree, the Athenians praise the Antiocheans for their exemplary behavior (LL. 14–20), and propose that it should be resolved that Ἀντιο/χεῦσιν καὶ πολ[ιτείαν] κατὰ τὸν νόμον τὸν περὶ τῶν δωρεῶν κ[ε]ί(με/νον (LL-22). Scholars who have discussed this text have largely avoided labels or institutional definitions for the grant of *politeia* here, except for M.J. Osborne who has called it *isopoliteia*. Institutional definitions are important (although not always possible), as they provide scholars with categories that help establish a general interpretive framework. Osborne, who has made a notable contribution to the study of Greek citizenship, offers a detailed comment that deserves to be cited in full because it brings out several theoretical points that need to be addressed:

> it is clear that the Athenian grant here is in effect an act of *isopoliteia* (as opposed to being a straightforward grant of citizenship). In other words, the grant is 'potential' rather than actual. But the term *isopoliteia* is not used in Athens, only the term *politeia*—and the latter clearly has the connotation of the former in circumstances such as these here. (…) it may be that in the Hellenistic period such a grant of *politeia* was a normal concomitant of a recognition of *asylia* on the part of the Athenians. Indeed, the emphatic qualification of the grant by reference to the standing law on gifts may well have made reference to this very point.

---

31 On the diplomatic language in the Hellenistic period see JONES 1999.
32 *IG* II³, 1 1178 (RIGSBY 1996, pp. 330–332, no. 162) = n. 30.

> In these circumstances, it is not in the slightest degree surprising that the procedural clauses and the enrollment clause are lacking in this decree. For the citizenship is merely potential, and there is no question of it being implemented without some further action. (...) The grant of *politeia* in the decree here is essentially intended to give weight to the recognition of *asylia* for Chrysaorean Antioch, and for practical purposes it is doubtless to be regarded (and surely was regarded by the Athenians) as purely cosmetic.[33]

Osborne begins his comment by distinguishing between *politeia* and *isopoliteia* and ends by referring to the latter as an honorific grant that is "purely cosmetic." This comment takes us to the very core of an old discussion on *isopoliteia* that has long tried to determine whether *isopoliteia* was an 'honor' (i.e., useless) or an actual serviceable grant with practical consequences (i.e., useful). This modern problem was a non-issue in the Greek world, which did not evaluate tools/grants on the basis of their usefulness.

Osborne says that the main divide between *isopoliteia* and *politeia* is the fact that the first is "potential rather than actual." But, as Gauthier and J. and L. Robert remind us, all concessions of citizenship are potential at first. Indeed, any grant of citizenship, no matter whether it targets individuals or groups, has to be implemented before becoming 'actual.' Dual citizenship (as we understand it) in Greek antiquity did not exist; thus a grant of citizenship is not 'actual' until the grantee sets about implementing it.[34] Citizenship grants may differ procedurally and in meaning according to their target and mode of concession, but these differences do not make a grant more or less 'actual' than another. The difference between a concession of citizenship (to an individual

---

33 Osborne 1981(a), vol. II, pp. 184–185.
34 O. Picard 2012, p. 342 remarks on the topic: Having observed that no Greek city ever prohibited individuals from having more than one citizenship, and asking why that might be so, he proposes that the possession of more than one citizenship was, for the ancient Greeks, inconceivable.

An example can help clarify further this point: in the Arsinoe-Nagidos dossier (*SEG* LII 1462), LL. 19–20, Thraseas's father, Aetos, is said to be Ἀσπένδιος καὶ ἡμέτερος πολίτης i.e., an Aspendian who is (also) a citizen of Nagidos. Savalli 2012, p. 40, n. 5 rightly notes that further evidence on Aetos shows that these two *ethnika* were not the only ones he was entitled to use. It could be claimed he had more than one citizenship, but in truth he was an active citizen of one *polis* only. The key point is that *ethnika*, often taken as signs for more than one citizenship, do not always have a binding, legal meaning: Savalli 2012, p. 42. The evidence shows that such 'collections' of citizenships remained for a long time limited to certain social groups and that, even among those groups, they were exceptional: see again Picard 2012, p. 342.

or a group of people) and the Hellenistic institution of *isopoliteia* must not be sought in the legal capacity of individuals to switch status. Rather, from an institutional point of view, we must consider the city's (grantor's) goals and the relationship that this concession was meant to establish between the involved parties. Related to this issue is Osborne's comment on terminology, namely, the use of the word *politeia*: the linguistic habit he attributes to Athens is, in truth, common to the entire Mediterranean and we cannot distinguish among the types of concessions included in the term. Still Osborne sees rightly that the implementation of a grant of potential citizenship required taking different steps.

Here it is useful to review briefly the terminology used for grants of potential citizenship: The grant normally appears as an exchange or concession of citizenship, πολιτεία, to a community. Sometimes a conditional clause or a relative clause indicating the 'potential nature' of the grant, i.e., that it entailed the option to switch citizenship for individuals, appears along a so-called *metechein*-clause.[35] The meaning of the *metechein* clause should not be overstated: communities used it to avoid listing common aspects of civic and religious life in which each lawful citizen could partake. The clause has no specific legal value and we should not ask of it information it cannot give, such as, for example, whether it implied additional grants or other provisions. Such additional provisions would most likely have been stipulated separately from the grant of potential citizenship because all potential citizens (viz., citizens of the city being awarded potential citizenship) had access to them whether or not they switched their citizenship.[36]

---

35 Examples of the *metechein* clause: *Milet* I 3 142 = no. 3, LL. 14–17 Μιλησίους καὶ Φυγελεῖς πολίτας εἶναι / παρ' ἀλλήλοις καὶ μετέχειν ἱερῶν καὶ ἀρχείω[ν / κ]αὶ τῶν ἄλλων τῶν ὑπαρχόντων ἐμ Μιλήτ[ωι / καὶ] Φυγέλοις; *Milet* I 3 141 = no. 4, L. 34 τὴν δὲ πολιτείαν δεδόσθαι Κιανοῖς and LL. 37–38: ἵνα δὲ τοῖς προαιρουμένοις Κιανῶν μετέχειν τῆ[ς] / πολιτείας γίνηται τὰ ὑπὸ τοῦ δήμου δεδομένα; HERRMANN 1979, pp. 242–249 (*SEG* XXIX 1149) = no. 22 Teos and Temnos, LL. 13–15: δεδόχθαι τῆι βο[υλῆι] κα[ὶ δήμωι εἶ]/ναι πολιτείαν Τηίοις ἐν Τήμνωι ἐφ' ἴση[ι κ]αὶ ὁμοίαι [καὶ μετουσί]/αν πάντων ὧν καὶ τοῖς ἄλλοις πολίταις μέτεστιν. The *metechein* clause, however, does not have to be included. An example of a grant of potential citizenship without this type of clause, but with a clear expression to signal its potential nature is J. and L. ROBERT *BE* 1972 371 = no. 23, LL. 10–12: πολί/την δὲ εἶναι τὸν Παριανὸν Σκηψίων ἐὰν θέ/[λ]η, καὶ τὸν Σκήψιον Παριανῶν ἐὰν θέλη.

36 To compare the difference between an extension of the rights included in the *metechein* clause to those included in the additional grants, see for example *AvP* VIII.1 5 = no. 20, LL. 15–19: ἔμμεναι Ταμνί[ταισι ἐν Περ]/γάμω πολι[τ]είαν καὶ Περγαμήν[οισι ἐν Τάμνω] / μετεχόντ[ε]σσι ὧν καὶ οἱ ἄλλο[ι πολῖται μετέχοι]/σι καὶ γᾶς καὶ οἰκ[ία]ς ἔγκτησιν ἔμ[μεναι τῶ Ταμνί]/τα ἐμ Περγάμω [κ]αὶ τῶ Περγ[αμήνω ἐν Τάμνω. The debate about who could use the additional grants, by which I mean grants of the rights to ownership, intermarriage, *isoteleia*, and others, is to my eyes rather sterile (Gawantka's *Teileffektivierung*,

Finally, these agreements sometimes include enrollment clauses that contain procedural details for changing citizenship. As I noted above, (1) neither the presence nor absence of an enrollment clause, nor its type, indicates the actual probability of execution of the grant of potential citizenship and (2) the absence of procedural details describing a city's control mechanisms does not imply that the city automatically accepted new citizens into its citizen body without further scrutiny.

Ancient documents—from all cities, not only Athens—rarely use the term *isopoliteia* and, when they do, they deploy it abstractly. Documents typically use it to refer to an already conceded grant, to announce the plan of granting it, or to highlight a coming stipulation. Examples for the use of the word *isopoliteia* include the peace treaty between Herakleia under Mt. Latmos and Miletos, the agreement between Pergamon and Temnos, or even the isolated document from Lykia with which Xanthos and Myra exchange potential citizenship.[37] It is clear that in the Hellenistic period the term *isopoliteia* can describe, among other things, the institution of potential citizenship. But, because the actual concessions of the grant do not include the term, the prescriptions and details concerning the grant in the enactment formulae move from an abstract to a more pragmatic, legal level.[38]

The other question that Osborne raises pertains to the relationship between grants of *asylia* and *isopoliteia*. Indeed, because this issue has some weight in the interpretation of potential citizenship, I devote a separate section to it below. Both awards appear in the text from Athens, namely, in LL. 20–21 (citizenship) followed by the recognition of *asylia* in LL. 21–23. These two tools were related, but, on the basis of the existing evidence I argue that one was not dependent on the other. The evidence shows that although the two grants can appear together, they do not do so in a systematic way. For example, the order of the grants is not standard: sometimes *asylia* is granted after *isopoliteia* had been conceded, but sometimes *isopoliteia* follows *asylia*. Moreover, *isopoliteia* figures in *asylia*'s concessions, but *asylia* never appears as an additional grant

---

esp. GAWANTKA 1975, pp. 29–39). Relying partly on problematic evidence, Gawantka concludes that each community established different rules in these cases. Although his evaluation is certainly plausible, CHANIOTIS (1996, p. 103) presents a more likely theory. The latter points out that additional rights established *de facto* a privileged status for the grantees by giving them access to pragmatic benefits as listed in the agreements. The granting of access to these rights did not depend on potential citizenship but rather accompanied it; see for example SABA 2011, pp. 93–108 on intermarriage.

37   *Milet* I 3 150 = no. 7; *AvP* VIII.1 5= no. 20; *SEG* XLIV 1218 = no. 8.
38   I know of only one exception, in the agreement between Xanthos and Myra *SEG* XLIV 1218 = no. 8, L. 13.

in treaties of *isopoliteia*.³⁹ This circumstance slightly weakens Osborne's proposed Athenian practice of granting them together, which, he suggests, was codified in a law. I think instead that this law περὶ τῶν δωρεῶν regulated the enrollment and other procedural aspects of this and other types of grants, thus making it unnecessary to list them separately.⁴⁰ Such matters were regulated with great precision at all stages; the absence of enrollment clauses on stone does not indicate that this concession had a "cosmetic role." Rather, here the reference to the law was deemed sufficient. In this text the grant was used to strengthen the concession of *asylia* to Antioch and diplomatic discourse in general.

(b) War and Peace: the Second Type of Isopoliteia

The second type of *isopoliteia* usually appears in stipulations of military agreements or in treaties that foreshadow urgent social or political situations. In these cases, the grant appears alongside and equal to other concessions. Together, they are meant to influence the relationships between the communities that sign the agreement on a very concrete ground, as for example by allowing intermarriage.⁴¹ One text that exemplifies this use of the tool of *isopoliteia* is the agreement between Messene and Phigaleia (*IPArk.* 28 = no. 39), which Aitolian prosopography allows us to date to the 240s BC. I have purposely chosen a text from a region other than Crete to describe this second type of isopolity. Not only do I prefer to be cautious with Cretan evidence, but also this agreement from the Peloponnese allows me to cast my net broadly so that I can address other issues, such as the language of *isopoliteia*, the involvement of third parties in agreements, and the meaning and value assigned to such an award. In brief, this decree offers many thematic threads to the student of *isopoliteia*.

---

39   See *infra* the section devoted to *isopoliteia* and *asylia*.

40   A similar instance can be found in the peace treaty between Miletos and Herakleia under Mt. Latmos (*Milet* I 3 150 = no. 7), L. 53: after Miletos's enrollment clauses, we find the statement that all other matters related to appointment to offices were to be regulated according to the *nomos bouletikos*. This example shows that, for brevity's sake in an already very detailed agreement, provisions concerning additional matters could be dealt with by referring to existing laws.

41   I devoted a separate study to the relationship between *isopoliteia* and one of the concessions that is relatively frequently found with it, namely, *epigamia*: see SABA 2011. Here the social aspect of this institutional tool appears with force. If we move away from the technicalities resulting from the 'diplomatic' use of *isopoliteia*, we see that this tool must have impacted cities beyond the simple definition or redefinition of political ties.

The stele containing this document is broken in two places; unfortunately, the left upper side and the bottom part are missing, but the surviving text preserves important information on the use of *isopoliteia*.[42]

The agreement concerns the neighboring *poleis* of Phigaleia and Messene. This decree reveals immediately to the reader that the *chorai* and their borders were a main concern for the two communities: LL. 12–15 refer to contested land that perhaps caused or contributed to the controversy between them, which the Aitolians tried to mediate. The Aitolians attempted to broker an agreement meant to stop the claims of both cities while respecting the terms of the relationship that Messene and Phigaleia had at the time with the Aitolian league (details about this relationship remain unclear to us).

A quick review of the content provides a first 'list' of the thematic threads I referred to above: first comes Messene's decree, LL. 1–21, which had been prompted by the joint embassy of Aitolia and Phigaleia: the Phigaleians seem to play a passive role. The Aitolian ambassadors speak in keeping with a decree of the *koinon* recommending that the Messenians solve their conflict with the Phigaleians. LL. 9–19 paraphrase the decree of the Aitolians and specify, LL. 10–12, that the Messenians and Phigaleians are to grant to each other *isopoliteia* and *epigamia* and to establish a *symbole* between them, LL. 12–13.[43] Interestingly, the word '*isopoliteia*' appears in L. 10; as I noted, it rarely figures elsewhere in ancient evidence. This instance nicely confirms that the word *isopoliteia* refers in theory to a future stipulation. In this case, the terms would later be defined by Messene and Phigaleia. In this agreement Phigaleia must have taken the initiative in the process that led to the mediation of the Aitolians. The text describes Phigaleia's relationship with the league as one

---

42   The Greek text, here no. 39, comes from the collection of Thür and Taeuber *IPArk*. 28; the translation is my own. LL. 1–22: Since the ambassadors and mediators of the Aitolians have come, Timaios and Kleopatros ... they gave (us) the decree of the Aitolians and spoke according to its content that we should settle our claim with the Phigaleians. Present were also those who had come from Phigaleia, Tharykidas, Onomandros, Amphimachos, ?das, Ortholaidas, Krataimenes, Ti?, Damaretos, supporting the same statement. It was resolved by the city of the Messenians that Messenians and Phigaleians shall exchange isopolity and the right to intermarriage; they shall also establish a judicial agreement that pleases both cities. The land shall be cultivated by each, (the citizens) of Messene and (those) of Phigaleia, just as we cultivate it now. On everything else we shall reach an agreement with each other, both shall swear an oath, and put on display the engraved document in sanctuaries, wherever it seems more appropriate to each city. If the Phigaleians do not stay in their friendship with the Messenians and the Aitolians, this agreement shall be void. It was resolved by the Phigaleians to do as the Messenians have decreed: (*the oath follows*).

43   For *isopoliteia* and *epigamia* see SABA 2011, pp. 93–108; on *symbole* see GAUTHIER 1972, p. 368, but see also MAGNETTO 1997, p. 234.

INTRODUCTION

of *philia*. The Aitolians intervened, brokering an agreement that the parties were supposed to seal by exchanging the right to intermarriage and *isopoliteia*. These concessions were meant to help establish stronger relations between Phigaleia and Messene and, thereby, to smooth the existing tense situation probably due to contested land.[44]

How does this use of isopolity differ from that used by Miletos and Athens? In the inscriptions I discussed above, Miletos and Athens grant an award of *isopoliteia* within diplomatic acts that, while employing *isopoliteia* as the highest possible concession, did not seem connected to any actual and urgent unresolved question. The case of Messene and Phigaleia is quite different as the relations between them must have been strained by current problems tied to the territory and its use. This situation finds many parallels in Crete. In all the examples from Crete, communities resorted to the exchange of this grant, planned or actual, together with that of *epigamia*, to directly impact the populations of the cities. The differences in the use and application of *isopoliteia* is significant: while the anticipated impact of the first type of *isopoliteia* rests on a diplomatic level, the second would affect the city at the level of social intercourse. In the text that I have just discussed, the second, more radical, effect is merely foreshadowed as the two cities have not yet granted each other *isopoliteia*. The second type foresees a direct intervention and impact in the structure of the societies that open their doors to a 'planned' mobility that involves, and perhaps begins, with the creation of families that would move across borders.

The topic of geography becomes quite relevant in the second type of concession: while a 'diplomatic' use of potential citizenship was possible despite the distance between the cities involved in the exchange, the 'pragmatic' use of it is limited to neighboring cities as it can solve the problems that only territorial contiguity generates. In brief, the difference is in the context.

Who Benefited from *Isopoliteia*?

In the preceding paragraphs, I have shown that *isopoliteia*, as a diplomatic tool, was a grant of potential citizenship awarded between communities. It was

---

44 See also SABA 2011, p. 106. Further levels of historical interpretation of this text involve Aitolia and its specific role in this agreement and demonstrate how *isopoliteia* could be used as a tool to tie to itself to cities that could not be included in its sympolity. These arguments have to my eyes little strength, but belong to a different chapter, that on federations, because they connect to a set of institutional and political issues that need not concern us now.

used throughout the Greek world, between the 4th and the 1st centuries BC. States, and less frequently federations, used this diplomatic tool in two different ways: first as an aspirational means to establish long-term interstate relations, and second, as a mediation meant to repair relationships that had deteriorated or that required either dramatic improvements or the securing of the relationship because of urgent, common interests.

The next question that must be addressed is *cui bono?* Why was *isopoliteia* used and who benefited from it?

I have argued that *isopoliteia* was first and foremost an intercity grant that was given from one community to another, not to the individuals constituting the citizen body of the partner city. This assessment holds true for both types of *isopoliteia*. It would indeed be politically counterintuitive for cities to facilitate the transfer and to accept a grant in which the 'weaker' partner subscribes itself to a process of depopulation. The evidence for the actual implementation of the grant is lacking: only one inscription survives that could testify to such an occasion directly, but even this evidence is uncertain.[45] This circumstance of course does not mean that no one ever took the option of switching citizenship, but that the actual consequences of the eventual implementation of the grant remain unknown to us.

While we cannot determine the social impact on the cities and individuals actualizing the right of *isopoliteia*, I believe that the written evidence can help us 'measure' the importance of this grant. For this purpose the indirect evidence is useful. To my knowledge very few indirect pieces of evidence for *isopoliteia* survive: these include the agreements between Kamarina and Kos (242 BC), Gela and Kos (242 BC), Magnesia and Samos (mid-2nd century BC), Samos and Antioch on the Maeander (after 167 BC), and finally Priene and Bargylia (ca. 200 BC).[46] In all these cases, the preexisting potential citizenship is expressed with the uncommon term *isopoliteia*, but, most importantly, this claim is always associated with terms that define already existing, strong connections between communities.[47] For example, all these *poleis* have *philia* or a

---

45 *IG* XII.5 814 = no. 35, more *infra*.
46 See (Kos-Kamarina) RIGSBY 1996, pp. 149–150 no. 48 = no. 67; (Kos-Gela) RIGSBY 1996, pp. 150–152 no. 49 = no. 68; (Magnesia-Samos) *IMagn.* 103 = no. 17; (Samos-Antioch) *IG* XII.6.1.6 = no. 18; (Priene- Bargylia) *IPriene* 47 or *IIasos* 607. On this topic see also SABA 2010b, esp. pp. 179–180.
47 On Kos-Kamarina, LL. 9–12, see CURTY 1995, n. 24a see also n. 24b where the same statement is (completely) restored for the city of Gela; Magnesia-Samos, esp. LL. 12–13 and 37 referred to Magnesians and Samians. In line 37 the Magnesians say that the Samians are φίλοι καὶ ἰσοπολεῖται καὶ εὖν[οι; Samos-Antioch LL. 10–20 συγγενεῖς καὶ φίλους καὶ εὖ[ν]ους καὶ ἰσοπολίτας καὶ συμ[μάχους ...] CURTY 1995, n. 29; Priene and Bargylia LL. 4–5 assert that the demos of Priene was φίλος, εὖνους καὶ ἰσοπολίτης.

kinship relation in place, so that the status of *isopolites* is only added to these relationships. A possible implication is then that to be *isopolites* meant to have a privileged position and standing in another community, which differs from having, for example, fiscal privileges. A concession such as isopolity brought together two communities by establishing a tie that would be sustained over time, not because of immediately tangible advantages, but rather because a stronger relationship was in place. LL. 9–12 of the decree that recognizes *asylia* on the part of Kamarina (and Gela) for Kos are especially meaningful; the text says ἐπειδὴ οἱ Κῶιοι συνοικισταὶ ἐγένοντο τᾶς πόλιος / ἁμῶν ὑπαρχόντων τε αὐτοῖς παρ' ἁμεῖν τῶν μεγίστων καὶ / ἀναγκαιοτάτων, συγγενείας τε καὶ οἰκειότατος καὶ ἰσοπο/λειτείας. *Syngeneia, oikeiotes,* and *isopoliteia* appear next to each other and are described as the greatest and most compelling forms of relations that can exist between cities. That this description could be applied to kinship comes as no surprise, but it is extremely revealing for the less attested *isopoliteia*. *Isopoliteia* appears with two of the pillars of Hellenistic diplomacy, which prompts us to reflect upon the value and weight it had within diplomatic discourse.

Modern Terminology for *Isopoliteia*

I have tried to use the term *isopoliteia* consistently in the preceding pages, but I have also used the term potential citizenship as a synonym.[48] I have chosen to use the English term in the book instead of the Greek term, which I intend to largely abandon henceforth. I must, however, explain the reason for this choice. The definition of a concession of potential citizenship from one community to another as *isopoliteia* is primarily a modern convention. As I already noted, ancient sources rarely use the word and, when they do, they do *not* always mean this particular institution. The consequences of modern scholarship's view have been far-reaching.[49] While ancient historians are accustomed to working with modern conventions, the fact that in antiquity *isopoliteia* had multiple meanings complicates even the collection of the evidence. I would contend that this alleged *terminus technicus* can create more problems than it solves. For this reason, throughout this work I normally use the term 'potential

---

48   By 'potential citizenship' I do not intend a translation of the term *isopoliteia*—intentionally so, since a translation would not solve the problems created by using '*isopoliteia*.'

49   GAWANTKA 1975, pp. 2–3, n. 5 argues for the use of this convention, yet, although he was aware of the problems that the use of the term *isopoliteia* could create, he did not fully anticipate the negative consequences.

citizenship' instead of *isopoliteia*, even if this choice too is far from perfect. I tend to use the word *isopoliteia* when I am convinced that its use in a particular document refers to the Hellenistic institution. I hope that by proposing a possible solution to this terminological problem I can move scholars to ask themselves whether the term *isopoliteia*, when they meet it, actually refers to the Hellenistic institution or if another meaning is intended.

It will be useful to review briefly here some examples of the use of the term *isopoliteia* in ancient texts that both denote the Hellenistic institution or refer to something else.

(a)   Isopoliteia *as the Hellenistic Institution*

Ancient sources use the word *isopoliteia* to denote the Hellenistic institution as an abstract concept. The presence of this term can signal that the text in question either contains indirect evidence for potential citizenship (i.e., a reminder of old agreements) or announces a new grant of potential citizenship.

In the preceding pages, I have presented agreements where the word appears to announce the future stipulation of an *isopoliteia* agreement. For example, this use of the term *isopoliteia* can be seen in the agreement between Messene and Phigaleia where, LL. 10–12,[50] the text reads: ἦμεν τοῖς Μεσσανίοις κα/[ὶ τοῖς Φια]λέοις ἰσοπολιτείαν καὶ ἐπιγαμία/[ν ποτὶ ἀλλ]άλως ... The agreement is brokered by the Aitolians who recommend that the cities, among other things, establish an agreement that includes *isopoliteia*, which, however, the *poleis* will have to regulate later.

In the peace treaty between Miletos and Herakleia under Mt. Latmos, the following statement appears in LL. 10–13:[51]

> ἐπειδὴ Ἡρακλεῶται φίλοι καὶ ἀσ/τυγείτονες τῆς πόλε(ως) ὑπάρχοντες ψήφισμα καὶ πρεσβευτὰς ἀποστείλαντες ἠξίωσαν / τὸν δῆμον συνθέσθαι πρὸς αὐτοὺς ὑπὲρ τῆς ἰσοπολιτείας καὶ τῶν ἄλλων φιλαν/θρώπων ...

The ambassadors from Herakleia explicitly asked the Milesians to establish *isopoliteia* between the cities. Miletos obliged Herakleia but, in the Milesian decree, the text uses the common terminology for a grant of *politeia*.[52] The only inscription that attests to the use of this term beyond its abstract meaning, but also within the concession itself, is the agreement between Xanthos

---

50   *IPArk* 28 = no. 39.
51   *Milet* I 3 150 = no. 7.
52   L. 34: ... εἶναι πολίτας Μιλησίους Ἡρακλεωτῶν καὶ Ἡρακλεώτας Μιλησίων ...

and Myra.[53] But here too the term is used in the first lines to 'announce' the grant and thus refers to the institution.

There can be no doubt that the term *isopoliteia* in these texts refers and describes the Hellenistic institution. However, when the technical part (namely, the actual concession) requires attention, cities resort to the term *politeia* and the usual formulae with which this concession is given.

(b) *The Other Meanings of* Isopoliteia

The dossier testifying to the difficult relationship between Arsinoe and Nagidos in Kilikia in the second half of the 3rd century BC can exemplify the use of the term *isopoliteia* in texts with a different, noninstitutional meaning: here the word must have referred only to 'equality of rights' and did not imply an exchange of potential citizenship.[54] This well-known epigraphic dossier contains part of a letter that Thraseas, *strategos* of Kilikia in the 230s or 220s, addressed to the citizens of Arsinoe along with a second document, the decree of the Nagideis, which ratifies his requests in support of Arsinoe's claim. At the heart of the controversy was the land claimed by the Nagideis as their own, but which the Arsinoeis needed to support themselves and to be recognized as an independent community. Thraseas endorsed Arsinoe's claim, thus obliging the Nagideis to officially grant the contested territory to Arsinoe. The key point, however, is that the Nagideis did not recognize Arsinoe's status as a *polis*. In his letter to Arsinoe, written after the Nagideis had acknowledged his requests, Thraseas stated that, since the Arsinoeis had now been given the means to be a *polis*, they had to fulfill the requirements that this status entailed and to take up the responsibilities attached to it.

In L. 35 of the decree, the striking assertion that the Arsinoeis were ἰσοπολῖται Ναγιδέων appears. This phrase has led scholars to assume that the decree contains *de facto* a grant of potential citizenship, which, however, is simply impossible. Not only the form of the document, which I have examined elsewhere, but also its content should discourage us from classifying it as an *isopoliteia* text. Rather, the use of the term ἰσοπολῖται means that the Arsinoeis will have to be considered (in the future) as having the same rights as the Nagideis, i.e., they belonged to a community that was a *polis*. With it, and its associated clauses, Nagidos marked new legal boundaries by establishing rules for cult-related expenses, access to court, and the administration of festivals in general. At the same time, it stressed the subordinate status of Arsinoe by unilaterally

---

53 *SEG* XLIV 1218 = no. 8, LL. 13–15: ὑπάρχειν ἰσοπο/λιτείαν Ξανθίοις καὶ Μυρεῦσι ἐπὶ τοῖσδε ...
54 *SEG* XXXIX 1426. On this dossier and the interpretation of the grant see SABA 2012, pp. 159–170 with references to the extensive bibliography on this text.

envisioning for the Arsinoeis the option of assuming a status comparable to that of the Nagideis. In order to gain that option, however, the Arsinoeis first had to establish and adopt their own laws, pay for their own sacrifices, and so on. In brief, Arsinoe had to become independent or, in more drastic terms, it had to become a *polis*.[55]

One of the consequences of this reading is that it forces us to reflect upon the ambiguity of the term *isopolites*. Another example of its use can provide clarification: in ca. 200 BC the city of Bargylia enacted a decree to honor foreign judges from Priene.[56] In LL. 3–4, *I.Priene* 47 calls the *demos* of Priene εὔνους καὶ ἰσοπολίτης and then, in LL. 17–19, the three foreign judges are declared citizens of Bargylia. Does this last provision have a connection with the claim that the *demos* of Priene was ἰσοπολίτης? It certainly does not, as grants of citizenship to individuals were conceded independently from interstate relations. Besides, if we want to push the interpretive limits, the term ἰσοπολίτης could be considered ambiguous. It could indeed refer to a previous agreement of potential citizenship, which is not otherwise attested, or it simply could refer to the fact that the *demos* of Priene had a recognized status on the international scene. It must be the former here. By offering this example, however, I am arguing that this text shows the difficulties embedded in this question and the ambiguity of the terminology.

Another text that preserves an additional instance of the term *isopoliteia* with a noninstitutional meaning comes from Crete.[57] The text dates to the 2nd century BC and preserves part of the word *isopoliteia*, LL. 3–4, and an oath, LL. 11–26. From these lines we gather that Hierapytna granted *isopoliteia* to the κατοικόντες Ἱεραπύτνιοι [...]. Multiple interpretive problems concern these lines, but to discuss the problem of *isopoliteia*, it is enough to refer to the controversy of the identification of the κατοικόντες Ἱεραπύτνιοι. Chaniotis speaks of an external community of Hierapytnans that moved to some other territory because of a previous treaty and, he suggests, probably reached an agreement with the rest of the Hierapytnans after the situation in the community had changed.[58]

---

55 In my 2012 article I even proposed the possibility that a grant of *isopoliteia* could be established in the future: Nagidos in fact says that once Arsinoe becomes a *polis*, its citizens will have a status comparable to Nagideis.

56 *I.Priene* 47 now *I.Iasos* 607 (McCabe Priene 2), see *infra* p. 97.

57 *I.Cret.* III.iii 5 = CHANIOTIS 1996, pp. 432–439 no. 74 = no. 49.

58 CHANIOTIS 1996, esp. p. 438 supports the thesis that these *katoikoi* had created a community within the territory of Arkadia, with which Hierapytna had an agreement that allowed Hierapytnans to live there without taking up citizenship (see *katoikein*, i.e., *I.Cret.* III.iii 1b = CHANIOTIS 1996, pp. 217–221 no. 14 = no. 48). For more on this text and its ties to *I.Cret.* III.iii 5 = CHANIOTIS 1996, pp. 432–439 no. 74 see the commentary for no. 49 below.

Chaniotis suggests that "Durch die Isopolitie wurde ihnen (i.e., the *katoikoi*) die Möglichkeit offen gehalten, dorthin (to Hierapytna) zurückzukehren."[59] But these settlers had never ceased to be citizens of Hierapytna. The key here is to rethink the meaning of *isopoliteia*: it cannot be the option to switch citizenship, because these *katoikoi* were already *Hierapytnioi*.[60] I believe instead that *isopoliteia* here does not indicate the Hellenistic institution but rather signals an 'equality of rights' for the Hierapytnans who lived outside their *polis* of origin and for those who still lived in the town proper (*isopoliteia* may have this sense also in the agreement between Nagidos and Arsinoe).[61] The word *isopoliteia* appears again in the Cretan oath, L. 20, with a strongly abstract meaning that refers to a text identified as an *isopoliteia* document. Thus, it points to the document that had been inscribed in three copies to be exhibited, LL. 4–8, but has no technical meaning.

These examples show that *isopoliteia* does not always refer to the institution that granted the possibility to change citizenship to the citizens of an entire community. The institutional framework of the agreements of Nagidos-Arsinoea and of the κατοικόντες Ἱεραπύτνιοι and their signing partners does not allow for any exchange of citizenship. Instead the term *isopoliteia* refers to the establishment of 'equality of rights,' which is not tied to citizenship but rather 'replaces' it to some degree. *Isopoliteia* is *not* always used as *terminus technicus* in inscriptions, but rather has multiple meanings. To avoid confusion, we must be ready either to abandon a modern convention or to specify each time what we/the text means by *isopoliteia*.

Scholarship and Potential Citizenship

After the above discussion of the nature, terminology, and use of potential citizenship, it is time to turn briefly to previous scholarship and its contributions. I must begin with the work by Szanto (1892) and conclude with Chaniotis (1996). Gawantka (1975) remains, however, the only author who devoted a complete study to this tool. All other scholars marginalized studies of potential citizenship in their research that was otherwise always devoted to various other themes. This circumstance prompts another consideration, namely, that

---

59   CHANIOTIS 1996, p. 438.
60   GUIZZI 2000/1, p. 367 says indeed "Se i *katoikontes* fossero puri e semplici cittadini di Hierapytna in territorio straniero, una simile concessione non avrebbe senso." Therefore, he speaks of 'due entità distinte,' but cannot elaborate for lack of evidence.
61   SABA 2012, pp. 159–170.

because isopolity relates to very different topics, such as, for example, to citizenship (Szanto), *symbola* (Gauthier), Hellenistic Crete (Chaniotis), and many other themes, *isopoliteia* could contribute to their understanding, or *vice versa*.

E. Szanto's 1892 study devoted to Greek citizenship and, in substantial part, to "Isopolitie," continues to be relevant today. Although at the time a much smaller body of evidence existed, the validity of his definition of isopolity as concession of potential citizenship has been generally confirmed by further evidence that has been added to the corpus.[62] Szanto's work has remained the starting point for further research on this tool.

Philippe Gauthier's 1972 book on *symbola* provides a short, valuable treatment of interstate agreements that include grants of *isopoliteia*. In the closing chapter of his work, he treats also the topic of potential citizenship. There he focuses on the relationship and affinity between *isopoliteia* and *symbola*, and asks the following, central question: "Les conventions d'isopolitie ne constituaient-elles pas, sur certains points et d'une manière différente, l'équivalent des *symbola*?"[63] He further proposes that scholarship move away from theory and toward the actual applications and practical implications of potential citizenship. Gauthier's study remains essential to the understanding of many Hellenistic institutions.

Gawantka's 1975 volume asks all the right questions on the nature and use of potential citizenship, but the work has obvious limitations. The deficiencies have been pointed out by J. and L. Robert and Ph. Gauthier.[64] In their criticisms of Gawantka's study, these authors have rightly stressed the very abstract and overtly theoretical character of Gawantka's research, his conclusions based on modern interpretive categories, and his reliance on rigid models and definitions. His work remains, nonetheless, an important contribution and has informed decades of scholarship; indeed, it has been so influential that subsequent scholarship has only worked within the parameters that Gawantka established.

Chaniotis's 1996 collection of Hellenistic treaties among Cretan cities profoundly differs from the other studies. Significantly, this scholar engages

---

62   SZANTO 1892, pp. 67–103; GAUTHIER 1985, pp. 149–150 on this definition and its weak points.
63   GAUTHIER 1972, p. 349. In a way, the measures for the temporary presence of privileged foreigners directly contrast with the idea of potential citizenship, as Gauthier notes on pp. 372–373. The comparison between the granting of *isopoliteia* and the granting of judicial agreements, which are far more limited in scope, helps to illustrate how a grant of potential citizenship could affect a city's foreign policy.
64   See GAUTHIER's review 1977/8, pp. 373–378 with further references esp. to the work of J. and L. Robert.

directly with rich and difficult epigraphic material in which numerous attestations of *isopoliteia* are preserved. His contribution mostly concerns Cretan studies and epigraphy, but his ability to set this institutional tool in context has provided a good example of the need to start 'from the ground.' His commentary on the assembled corpus invites an extension of similar research for other regions. Part of my work on isopolity compares some of his results and observations with my own results that have come from a wider geographical context.

The Goal of this Research

Institutional tools seem destined to be relegated to a secondary position in scholarship that often deals with broader topics and relies on old studies for *Grundlagenforschung*. Often these older studies are of excellent quality and require only small updates following new discoveries. However, the marginalization of institutional tools such as *asylia*, *sympoliteia*, foreign judges, and *isopoliteia*, needed to be revisited: not only because substantial epigraphic evidence now exists, but also because their essential concepts need to be refined (I am referring here to the concept of citizenship, for example).

General observations should not become axioms or truths, and for this reason I decided to organize this work around the existing individual pieces of evidence. But this is *not* a corpus. More or less recent editions of the texts collected here have quelled any urgent need for new editions of them, but a fresh look at their content is necessary. The varied use of this tool, despite its universal practice, makes every concession a unique case. This versatility is both a strength and a weakness—and the latter because scholars often seek shortcuts and unequivocal definitions that are unsuitable to the evidence. For this reason, I offer an individual commentary to each surviving inscription that testifies to potential citizenship. These inscriptions are often not cited in full, although I consider each from the first to the last line. Simply copying all texts seemed like a useless exercise that would also give the wrong impression to the reader: the evidence for this study is of an epigraphic nature, but this work is historical.

Each inscription in this study reveals a different historical situation, more or less transparent to us, that may have triggered or created the opportunity of exchanging or granting potential citizenship. As I just noted, Gawantka's work has done much to outline the main characteristics of this tool, but a truly satisfactory definition of potential citizenship must rely on all available evidence. I have arranged the material geographically, but this arrangement might also have traced an interpretive trajectory. Nevertheless, I adhered to a strict geographical criterion and did not separate the agreements according to how I think they use *isopoliteia*. I defined two ways in which I believe this tool was used, but these are merely labels. As much as I think that labels matter, they are the result of interpretive work. I would like to think that this book not only provides my interpretation and reading of this tool (as a historical work), but also becomes a useful tool for other scholars (*Grundlagenforschung*).

In the first part of the book (Chapters 1–5), I consider texts from Miletos, then from Magnesia and Samos, and then from Asia Minor, Athens, and the Islands, excluding Crete. Crete requires a separate space (Chapter 7) and is here 'sandwiched' between central Greece (Chapter 6) and the thematic section on *asylia* (Chapter 8) which itself includes many texts involving Cretan cities. The areas that I study in the first part constitute a somewhat homogenous field for the use of potential citizenship: most preserve agreements in which *isopoliteia* appears as a tool adopted to facilitate or reinforce ties that cities could often trace back to their distant past. It is rare to find potential citizenship mentioned within agreements that refer to emergencies tied to war or territorial controversies. It is worth asking if one of these areas could be the birthplace of potential citizenship: not only because of the number of inscriptions and the wide spectrum of its application, but also because it preserves some of the earliest examples of *isopoliteia*.

In the second part (Chapters 6–8), I study the evidence from central Greece, Aitolia, and Crete, where the second type of potential citizenship was widespread. Aitolia uses both types, even seemingly mixing them, as for example in an agreement with Chios. Aitolia, however, also encouraged other communities to use this tool, as we have seen in the agreement between Messene and Phigaleia. The consequent attitude of Aitolia toward this instrument can be traced in its use of the award of potential citizenship as a tool to shape its foreign policy, while the federation adopted and used a dual citizenship-system. On Crete, both types of potential citizenship are attested: the first was mostly used to respond to foreign communities and the second to help regulate internal (mostly) territorial problems.

An exception to the geographical arrangement of the material is the part devoted to the relationship between *isopoliteia* and *asylia*; this relationship, however, is more apparent than real (Chapter 8). These terms do appear together, but without a set chronological or hierarchical order. After the conclusions, I add two appendices on the origins of potential citizenship and on the testimonies coming from literary sources.

The individual texts collected here—each previously well-published—deserve a fresh and systematic analysis. My study of them contributes to the debates on the Hellenistic *polis*, Hellenistic diplomacy, and, more specifically, these institutions. Previous scholarship has focused productively on several aspects of city policies and diplomacy,[65] but the bibliography has lacked a work devoted to potential citizenship within a discussion of institutions, diplomacy, and diplomatic language. The tool of potential citizenship can only have been the product of a certain society and political culture: namely, the mid-4th to the 1st century BC, through the early and late Hellenistic ages, when, as Ma noted,[66] cities learned to deal (often very effectively) with new powers and to move into new political and diplomatic spaces. Thus, I hope, too, to clarify some ways in which diplomacy and its language worked and to capture part of the spirit of the Hellenistic period.

---

[65] See SABA 2010(b) in *Dike* on the rich and expanding bibliography on Hellenistic institutions.

[66] MA 2002.

PART 1

Evidence from Asia Minor, Athens, and the Islands

∴

CHAPTER 1

Miletos and Lykia

The Epigraphic Record and Its Interpretation

According to the surviving epigraphic evidence, Miletos signed at least seven agreements that include concessions of grants of potential citizenship with neighboring communities or with which the town shared colonial ties. The chronology of the agreements reveals two main moments of stipulations, at the end of the 4th century BC and in the last decades of the 3rd century BC. The gap of—roughly—a century may be due to chance or to a period when Miletos used the tool less frequently, which, however, would be difficult to explain.

In six out of the seven certain instances of this tool, Miletos appears to adopt the award of potential citizenship to create, expand, or confirm long-term diplomatic relations (i.e., it adopted mainly what I describe as the first type of isopolity). Further, the details concerning the most technical aspects of the concession of the award were expressed with an increasingly standardized language.

The seventh known instance of a grant of potential citizenship from Miletos appears in the peace treaty that Miletos signed with Herakleia under Mt. Latmos, thus ending a (possibly) long state of war. It is therefore noteworthy that Miletos, with its seven certain treaties, covered the entire spectrum of possible uses of the grant of potential citizenship. The number of testimonies, their chronology, and the flexibility with which the tool was used leaves us wondering whether this *polis*, or more generally Asia Minor, began the practice of granting the option to switch citizenship to another community.

In the conclusion to this section, I include five documents that, at one point or another, scholars have identified as concessions of potential citizenship involving Miletos. These problematic pieces of evidence could confirm Miletos's extensive use of potential citizenship, but they may also be the result of a modern scholarly interpretation based on this city's attested practice of granting the award. Most of these fragmentary texts seem to be instances of grants of isopolity, identified on the basis of preserved kinship or/and colonial claims. Such claims were very common in the diplomatic language of the Hellenistic age, however, and cannot be considered certain evidence for the presence of any specific concession in a text.

Historically, the *communis opinio* considers the Milesian evidence as proof for the existence of a general plan to jump-start the city's political life and international presence after its liberation in the late 4th century BC. Later agreements (3rd century BC) that contain potential citizenship are generally interpreted as testimonies of Miletos's will to expand its political influence in Ionia and beyond. These interpretations are plausible, but I will only generally state that this city made flexible and expert use of this institution by granting, accepting, and reciprocating it to support its economic, diplomatic, and even military interests in favorable and unfavorable circumstances. More detailed historical assessments follow in the comments devoted to individual inscriptions.

On an interpretive level, we must confront the question that Gawantka has raised concerning the possible implementation of the grant. Gawantka used the epigraphically attested names of new citizens in the 3rd and 2nd centuries BC from Miletos[1] to estimate the grant's implementation rate and the impact that this institution had on the intake of newcomers. However, this evidence cannot be considered representative because it is too limited.

In this section I include an 'intruder' as well: the agreement between the Lykian cities of Xanthos and Myra (here no. 8). I deviate from my geographical criterion because the content of this text finds several close parallels in the provisions attested in Milesian treaties that best emerge if treated in sequence. The historical context of the agreement between Xanthos and Myra is difficult to reconstruct, and the text is rather late (2nd century BC) and isolated. Yet its detailed provisions show that isopolity was widely and internationally understood and adopted. Because of its peripheric provenance and because the decree was enacted later than the high point of *isopoliteia*, this agreement can be seen as a case for the reception and late usage of *isopoliteia*.

---

1 For example, *Milet* I 3 34–90.

(1) The Agreement between Olbia and Miletos

Rhodes and Osborne describe the stone that preserves the agreement between Olbia and Miletos as a "stele with moulding at the top and bottom, found in the Delphinion at Miletos." The inscription is now preserved in the Pergamon Museum (Inv. no. 678).

Edd.: *ed. pr. Milet* I 3 136; [*Syll.*³ 286; Tod 195; Rhodes and Osborne *GHI* 470–473 no. 93; *StV.* III 408].
Cf.: Herrmann *Milet* VI 1, *Nachträge*, pp. 170–171.

  Τάδε πάτρια Ὀλβιοπολίταις καὶ Μιλησ[ί]-
  οις· τὸμ Μιλήσιον ἐν Ὀλβιηπόλει ὡς Ὀλ-
  βιοπολίτην θύειν ἐπὶ τῶν αὐτῶμ βω-
4 μῶν καὶ εἰς τὰ ἱερὰ τὰ αὐτὰ φοιτᾶν τὰ
  δημόσια κατὰ τὰ αὐτὰ καὶ Ὀλβιοπολίτας. εἶναι δὲ καὶ ἀτελείας Μιλησίοις καθάσσα καὶ πρότερον ἦσαν· ἐὰν δὲ θέληι
8 τιμουχιῶμ μετέχειν, ἐπὶ βουλὴν ἐπίτω
  καὶ ἀπογραφεὶς μετεχέτω καὶ ἔστω
  ἐντελής, καθότι καὶ οἱ ἄλλοι πολῖταί
  εἰσιν. εἶναι δὲ καὶ προεδρίαν, καὶ εἰσκη-
12 ρύσσεσθαι εἰς τοὺς ἀγῶνας καὶ ἐπα-
  ρᾶσθαι ταῖς τριακάσιγ, καθάσσα καὶ
  ἐμ Μιλήτωι ἐπαρῶνται. ἐὰν δέ τι συμβό-
  λαιον ἦ(ι) τῶι Μιλησίωι ἐν Ὀλβίαι, ἰσχέτω δί-
16 κηγ καὶ ὑπεχέτω ἐμ πενθ' ἡμέραις ἐπὶ
  τοῦ δημοτικοῦ δικαστηρίου. εἶναι δὲ
  [ἀ]τελεῖς πάντας Μιλησίους, πλ(ὴ)ν ὅσοι
  ἐν ἄλλη(ι) πόλει πολιτεύονται καὶ ἀρχείω(μ)
20 μετέχουσιγ καὶ δικαστηρίων. κατὰ ταὐτὰ δὲ καὶ Ὀλβιοπολίτας ἐμ Μιλήτωι (ἀ)τε-
  λεῖς εἶναι, καὶ τὰ ἄλλα κατὰ τὸν αὐτὸν
  τρόπον Ὀλβιοπολίταις ἐμ Μιλήτωι ὑπαρ-
  χειγ καθότι καὶ Μιλησίοις ἐν Ὀλβιηπόλει.

Text by Rhodes and Osborne *GHI* 471–474 no. 93.

Transl.: This is customary to the *Olbiopolitai* and the Milesians. A Milesian shall sacrifice in Olbia on the same altars just like an *Olbiopolites* does and attend the same public religious celebrations as *Olbiopolitai* do. The

Milesians shall be exempt from taxes, as (they were) before; but if one wants to hold an office (be a *timouchos*), he shall go to the council, be listed in the city records and pay taxes like the other citizens do. They shall be granted *proedria*, called in as competitors in the contests and curse solemnly during the "Thirties," just like they do in Miletos. If a Milesian has a dispute in Olbia, he shall have (the right to) a trial and present his claim to the public court within five days.[2] All Milesians shall be exempt from taxes, except those who live as citizens in another city and hold (there) an office and deal with the local court. According to the same principles, the *Olbiopolitai* shall be exempt from taxes in Miletos, and everything else shall be arranged for the *Olbiopolitai* in Miletos in the same way as it is for Milesians in Olbia.

In the *editio princeps* Rehm dates the treaty to a year before 323 BC based on paleographical considerations and because he regards Miletos's liberation as the *terminus post quem* for the approval of the document.[3]

According to the *communis opinio*, once freed, Miletos tried to end its long isolation by establishing a φιλία agreement with Sardis and by exchanging grants of potential citizenship with, respectively, Olbia, Kyzikos (no. 2), and Phygela (no. 3). It is, however, important to remember that Miletos did not always initiate these agreements.

The most common approach to the treaty that Miletos signed with Olbia considers the colonial relationship between the cities as the shared foundation on which they built this agreement.[4] Indeed, the initial lines, LL. 1–2, refer to τάδε πάτρια Ὀλβιοπολίταις καὶ Μιλησ[ί]/οις, to provide a solid, 'ancestral' background to the document. However, we must account for the fact that the text lacks any *direct* reference to that colonial tie. This omission has troubled generations of scholars to the point that some even hypothesized that this document contains in fact two treaties, with the second renewing an older

---

2   Or to a court "manned by *Olbiopolitai*," see GAUTHIER 1972, p. 359.
3   Rehm studied the paleography of Milesian evidence dating to the 4th century BC. The eponym list *Milet* I 3 122, which contains Alexander's name, L. 81, for the year 334/3 BC, was used to test the paleography of the other surviving inscriptions. The names up to Alexander were probably engraved together in his year, while the others were added yearly to the list. EHRHARDT 1987, pp. 114–116 also uses this list to establish a relative chronology for the treaties that Miletos signed with Sardis (*Milet* I 3 135), Kyzikos, Phygela, and Olbia. Moreover, he believes that the agreement with Olbia would have been possible only after it had established a democratic government (*terminus post quem*). On this basis, he suggests that *Milet* I 3 136 (no. 1) dates between 325 BC (democracy in Olbia) and 311 BC (use of αυ). See *infra*.
4   See EHRHARDT 2003, p. 3 n. 12 and IDEM 1988, pp. 74–79; PL. *NH* 5.112; on the active colonial policy of Miletos see GRAHAM 1964, esp. pp. 98–119.

agreement that should have been signed before the 4th century BC.[5] The homogeneous content of the agreement, however, does not support this interpretation, which, further, partly relies on the unjustified belief that citizens of communities tied by a colonial relationship enjoyed reciprocal citizenship rights.[6] This treaty has attracted substantial attention, yet remains without a satisfactory interpretation. I therefore question anew the nature and meaning of this grant by reassessing the historical conditions under which the treaty was stipulated, rather than focusing on the previous relationships between these cities. While the shared colonial past had certainly facilitated the connections between Miletos and Olbia in the 4th century BC, it did not shape them juridically.

Miletos (334/3–313 BC)

We mostly must rely on the epigraphic evidence to illuminate the history of Miletos between 334/3 and 313 BC. As is well known, however, this evidence can only provide information on how a community responds to historical events that remain otherwise in the dark.[7]

Miletos was in Persian hands when Alexander's expedition started.[8] Arrian offers an account of the events of 334 BC that led to its conquest. At first Miletos resisted Alexander's siege, but his forces rapidly destroyed the city's fortifications, which caused general panic and, finally, drove the city to surrender.[9] Yet, the fight that the citizens and mercenaries put up earned them Alexander's admiration and respect, which, according to Arrian, helped them to obtain separate agreements. At the end of his narrative (1.19.6) Arrian states: αὐτοὺς δὲ Μιλησίους, ὅσοι μὴ ἐν τῇ καταλήψει τῆς πόλεως ἔπεσον, ἀφῆκεν

---

5 See SEIBERT 1963, pp. 179–191; *StV* III 408.
6 The debate on this point is quite old and has found no unequivocal solution; see *infra* the discussion concerning the agreement between Thera and Kyrene, i.e., the so-called Oath of the Founders *SEG* IX 3 (= no. 15), esp. pp. 89–91. Starting from a similar position, GORMAN (2002 and 2001, esp. pp. 145–155) proposes to interpret all known 4th-century BC Milesian *isopoliteiai* as renewals of older agreements that relied on colonial ties. According to Gorman, these treaties had been signed with the intention of moving masses of citizens from the colonies back to Miletos in order to facilitate its refoundation after the Persian destruction of 494 BC. On this reading see the critical remarks by EHRARDT 2003, pp. 1–19, who envisions continuity for the site of Miletos after 494 BC.
7 On the history of Miletos, HAUSSOLIER 1902, esp. ch. 1 remains essential. More recently CARLSSON 2010, pp. 247–250 (although sometimes not as accurate as one wishes) and WÖRRLE 2003, esp. p. 123, n. 2 with bibliographical references; see BILLOWS 1990 and BOSWORTH 1988, pp. 46–52 on Alexander.
8 On the expedition and the delay with which it started: ARR. I. 17. 1–11.
9 ARR. I. 18–19. For the siege see VON GRAEVE 2000, pp. 117–129.

καὶ ἐλευθέρους εἶναι ἔδωκεν.[10] The *stephanephoroi* list *Milet* I 3 122, L. 81, records a trace of these events by including the name Ἀλέξανδρος Φιλίππου as the eponym for 334/3 BC.[11] Miletos, however, did not remain under Alexander's control for long. The Persians took the city back in 332 BC, after Alexander's departure, only to be later freed again.[12] It is noteworthy that during these years Miletos's sanctuary of Didyma underwent substantial reconstruction, after a long hiatus of activities under the Persians.[13] The *polis* became part of the satrapy of Karia under Asander son of Agathon, who seems to have imposed a garrison on Miletos.[14] The sources are silent on the status of the city until 313 BC when Antigonos's intervention started a new era for Miletos.[15]

Beyond the eponym lists, the treaty with Sardis, and the other treaties granting potential citizenship, very few Milesian documents have survived from these decades. *Milet* VI 3 1021 preserves only a handful of letters,[16] *Milet* VI 3 1065 is a fragmentary proxeny decree, and *Milet* VI 3 1023 contains an honorary decree with a citizenship grant that dates to 330–320 BC. This decree was passed for a Thyssos of Mylasa who had given part of his cargo of imported grain to be sold at a lower price in the city.[17] That the treaty with Olbia was a

---

10 For BOSWORTH 1988, p. 250: "Liberty in this instance will have been little more than dispensation from slavery, but the Milesians were at least in possession of their property and territory." On these events see also DIOD. XVII. 22.4–5.

11 This name may signal Miletos's support of the Macedonian king and his expedition, but also, as BOFFO 1985, p. 176 n. 177, says: "Le difficoltà della polis, sul piano materiale e politico, sono attestate dalla stefanoforia di Alessandro."

12 CURT. IV. 5.13. The *stephanephoroi* list confirms the difficult moment the city went through with the entry of Ἀπόλλων Διός as *stephanephoros* for 332/1 BC, L. 83, and again 330/29 BC, L. 85 see ROBERT 1946, pp. 51–64 and J. and L. ROBERT 1976, pp. 234–235.

13 STRAB. XVII.1.43 reports a statement by Kallisthenes for which after decades of silence, the oracle gave a response to Alexander predicting his victory; see BOFFO 1985, pp. 175–176; GÜNTHER 1971, pp. 21–22; and HAUSSOLIER 1902, pp. 4–7. On Didyma and the oracle see FONTENROSE 1988.

14 DIOD. XVIII. 3.1 and 40.1; XVIII 50.1; XIX. 75.1. On Asander in Karia until ca. 314 BC see J. and L. ROBERT, 1983, pp. 97–118.

15 DIOD. XIX.75.4: οὗτοι (the generals appointed by Antigonos) δὲ παραγενόμενοι πρὸς τὴν πόλιν τῶν Μιλησίων τούς τε πολίτας ἐκάλουν ἐπὶ τὴν ἐλευθερίαν καὶ τὴν φρουρουμένην ἄκραν ἐκπολιορκήσαντες εἰς αὐτονομίαν ἀποκατέστησαν τὸ πολίτευμα. *Milet* 1 3 123, LL. 2–4: Ἱππόμαχος Θήρωνος ἐπὶ τούτου ἡ πόλις / ἐλευθέρα καὶ αὐτόνομος ἐγένετο ὑπὸ / Ἀντιγόνου καὶ ἡ δημοκρατία ἀπεδόθη. On the historical context see BILLOWS 1990, pp. 109–122, for the chronology see WHEATLEY 1998.

16 In *Milet* Günther suggests that this document testifies to intercity diplomatic contacts.

17 Recent work rules out extreme outcomes for this apparently widespread crisis, PAZDERA 2006, pp. 40–41; on *sitodeia* for these years see his pp. 261–279. For other cities that suffered shortage of grain see OLIVER 2007(a), esp. pp. 15–47 with emphasis on Athens. Scholars use the stele from Kyrene, 330–326 BC (RHODES and OSBORNE *GHI*, pp. 486–493 no. 96) to prove the gravity of the situation. Useful is QUAß 1993, pp. 229–248 and the

way to ensure Milesian access to Olbian grain markets has been suggested too, but since the effective supply capacity of Olbia is unknown at this time, the theory cannot be proven.[18]

Olbia in the 4th Century BC

Writing the history of Olbia is a difficult task because of a lack of literary sources.[19] Olbia was located several miles north of the *emporion* of Berezan, on the rivers Hypanis and Borysthenes. Its location greatly influenced its history, because it necessitated that the city continuously interact with neighboring, non-Greek populations.[20] Olbia had to rely heavily on waterways to communicate with the rest of the world; the city was not only 'water-based' but had rather an extensive *chora*.[21] Archeological research has shown that the size of the *chora* fluctuated over time because of different factors, but scholars tend to consider the barbarian Skythians as responsible for Olbia's crises and the shrinking of its *chora*.[22] In the second half of the 4th century BC, many sites flourished in Olbia's territory, suggesting a phase of prosperity.[23] In this period, however, historians try to locate the uncertain (in date and content) and unsuccessful siege of the city by Alexander's general Zopyrion. Only Macrobius, who writes on the benefits of liberating slaves, testifies to this event. Macrobius uses historical examples, including Olbia, to prove his point: Olbia, says Macrobius, was under siege and, to fight off its attackers, freed its slaves, gave citizenship to foreign residents, and canceled debts. Thus, Olbia succeeded in defending itself.[24]

In spite of the problematic nature of Macrobius's passage, this siege figures prominently in discussions of the chronology of the agreement between Miletos and Olbia.[25] Ehrhardt argues that the siege was a watershed for Olbia

---

recent article by SOSIN 2002 that discusses the financial problems that could lead to such crises.

18   See WALSER 2008, esp. pp. 302–309; PAZDERA 2006 and the work by HORDEN and PURCELL 2000, pp. 201–230 and *infra*.
19   For a synthesis of Olbia's history see now MÜLLER 2010, esp. pp. 48–57.
20   See MÜLLER 2010, pp. 48–49; KRYZHIC'KIJ 2005, pp. 123–131.
21   On the *chora* in the 4th and 3rd centuries BC see MÜLLER 2010, pp. 53–55.
22   See BRAUND 2007, pp. 62–70.
23   VINOGRADOV and KRYZHIC'KIJ 1995, pp. 134–137.
24   MACROB. I. 11.33: *Ac ne putes haec in nostra tantum contigisse re publica, Borysthenitae obpugnante Zopyrione servis liberatis dataque civitate peregrinis et factis tabulis novis, hostem sustinere potuerant.* See MÜLLER 2010, pp. 54–55 on the different interpretations of this text.
25   EHRHARDT 1987, pp. 100, and 114–116, and even MÜLLER 2010, p. 55 cite this connection. The episode is highly problematic: ancient sources provide two dates for Zopyrion's death beyond the Danube, which are used to establish the chronology of the siege. CURT. 10.1.44 and JUST. 2.3.4; 12.2.6; 37.3.2 report that Zopyrion met his death by Skythian hand and/

and its form of government: the provisions that Macrobius lists would have led to the establishment of a radical democracy, which, in turn, would have made this *polis* meet the allegedly high (democratic) ideological standards of Miletos.

It is close to impossible to make sense of Zopyrion's siege and its influence on Olbia. Nawotka has noted that Olbian decrees testify to institutional developments toward democracy around 340 BC, but no testimony of a radical democracy exists. Perhaps, he suggests, because any period with a radical democracy would have been too short to register.[26]

Alexander's campaign might have harshly impacted Olbia with a siege, yet it cannot be considered a drastic and dramatic turning point. The surviving evidence speaks of a rich city that ran the risk of becoming isolated. Even Zopyrion may have abandoned the siege because the city was not a primary target. Finally, we lack testimonies for Olbia serving as an exporter of grain.[27]

Potential Citizenship

The inscription that testifies to the exchange of potential citizenship has been interpreted in many different ways, not all of them acceptable.[28] Potential

---

or because of the poor weather, along with many mercenaries. We read of the reaction of Alexander when informed of the event, but exactly when that happened is a matter of discussion. For Curtius, Alexander received the letter on his way back from India around 325/4 BC. For Justin, the king was informed around 330 BC, when he also learned of the deaths of Agis and Alexander Molossus. LANDUCCI-GATTINONI 1992, pp. 93–96 notes that scholars tend to accept Curtius. However, the other date for Zopyrion's death and Olbia's siege (331 BC) is not *seit langem überholt* as EHRHARDT 1987, p. 100, n. 100 claims. Lack of clarity obscures also the length of the siege, e.g., BRAUND 2007, p. 69 "... an attempt has been made to connect the inscription (*Kallinikos's*) with the brief siege of the city by Macedonian forces under Zopyrion"; DUBOIS 1996, p. 28: (speaking of defensive walls) "... ces fortifications de la partie occidentale de la cité sont peut-être celles qui ont empêché le general d'Alexander Zopyrion de prendre la cité après un long siege, en 331." The evidence suggests that Zopyrion abandoned the siege voluntarily. JUST. 12.2.6; 37.3.2, reports that shortly before dying, in order to move against the Skythians, he brought together an army of 30,000 men from Thrace: BERVE 1926, p. 164 "Zahl natürlich übertrieben." This account, however, prompts the concern that, had he wanted to, or if Olbia's siege had been crucial to Alexander's plans, Zopyrion could have found manpower to take Olbia.

26 NAWOTKA 2004, pp. 239–240. Or, maybe, because it never happened.
27 PAZDERA 2006, p. 122 on Olbia: "Über Kontinuität und Mengen in der zweiten Hälfte des vierten Jahrhunderts ist nichts überliefert." See also MÜLLER 2010, esp. pp. 169–190.
28 For example, BELIN DE BALLU 1972, pp. 68–72 believes that this document only renewed an old agreement. He thinks that the radical measures that Olbia adopted to resist Zopyrion gave Miletos the right to reject/renegotiate the old treaty—given the new members of Olbia's citizen body.

citizenship, however, appears nowhere clearly in this document.[29] The text opens with a reference to the ancient relationship between Olbia and Miletos, LL. 1–2 (a colonial tie, however, never appears) and grants Milesians in town the right to participate to religious events, LL. 2–6. An indirect reference to the option of switching citizenship follows in that the inscription ties the legal status of individuals to the form of taxation and to their eventual role in the local administration. More precisely, Milesians were *ateleis* in Olbia, but any Milesian who wanted to hold an office had to become *Olbiopolites*, and *enteles*, just like all other citizens, LL. 6–11.[30] The direct connection between the form of taxation and the legal status of the Milesians in Olbia appears again in LL. 17–20, where the text mentions anew the concession of the right to *ateleia* for all Milesians, except for those who held an office in another city. Moreover, LL. 20–22 specifically state that this taxation model applies to *Olbiopolitai* in Miletos as well, while a general 'everything else' in LL. 22–24 follows to confirm the reciprocation of all other grants. This last sentence shows the prominent role that the concession of the exemption from taxes (and, I suggest, commercial interests) has in this document. The text singles out this point along with participation in religious events, undoubtedly another thematic focus, while a general expression summarizes all other provisions (LL. 22–24). After a new and additional reference to festivals and religious events, LL. 11–14, the agreement establishes provisions to expedite judicial matters for Milesians who were in Olbia temporarily (and *vice versa*), LL. 14–17.

Milesians had a special status in Olbia (and *vice versa*): participating in religious ceremonies in a foreign city was an exceptional privilege. But they also had access to local courts, where a procedure could be initiated only within strict, set time limits. All these advantages for Milesians in Olbia (and *vice versa*) make sense if the cities wanted to facilitate the temporary presence of foreigners in their territories and sustain commercial relationships. The emphasis that the text places on taxes cannot be ignored. *Ateleia* was not an easily given grant and, even in this agreement, it stops working for those who would take up an office in the partner city (or anywhere else).[31] In other

---

29   GAUTHIER 1972, p. 358.
30   On *ateleia* (and its implementation) see RUBINSTEIN 2009, pp. 115–139; see CHANIOTIS 1986, pp. 159–160 on the meaning of *enteleia* in this agreement. The text does not specify whether *ateleia* was complete or intended to free Milesians only from certain types of levies, as commercial interests that seem to be central to the agreement suggest. It is possible that a previous agreement, perhaps referred to in LL. 6–7 (although admittedly the wording would be unusual), had been previously stipulated to regulate *ateleia*.
31   In Milesian interstate treaties *ateleia* rarely appears, exceptions include the interstate treaties with the Latmioi, the Magnesians, and the Pidaseans: *Milet* I 3 148–150. From Olbia we have concessions of *ateleia* to individuals but no relevant parallels in interstate treaties.

words, if a citizen of Miletos or Olbia would decide to become an active member of the other city's administration, he had to attend to the formalities tied to switching citizenship and start paying taxes like everybody else. Switching citizenship is among the possibilities envisioned in this document, but it was included among all possible scenarios, not because it was a priority.

Holding an office and being involved in legal practices in another town are again directly tied to taxation and, through it, to one's status. In the past, scholars read this clause, LL. 18–20, as a reference to the other *'isopoliteia'* agreements subscribed to by Miletos at the time, thus promoting the possibility that Milesians would switch to one of the other partner cities.[32] But this reading is not necessary, as the clause can be considered a generic provision comparable to later Milesian agreements, i.e., with Seleukeia-Tralles, Mylasa, and Herakleia, which included provisions to regulate the possible switching of citizenship on the part of naturalized citizens or citizens living abroad.

This treaty contains *de facto* a reciprocal exchange of potential citizenship, but never mentions it clearly. Also, it contains no explicit reference to the colonial tie between Miletos and Olbia, and focuses on Milesians in Olbia, whence probably the initiative of this agreement originated.

At the time of the stipulation of the agreement, Olbia experienced a moment of prosperity, but the local authorities must have realized that the new political developments could increasingly exclude their town from Greek networks. The establishment of stronger relationships with more centrally located *poleis*, such as Miletos, must have been a priority. That the cities had a tie *ab antiquo* was a clear advantage, but not the reason for this agreement.

Olbia was an attractive partner for Miletos, too, because it offered a potentially rich market. The desire to improve the setting for commercial exchange is the most credible context for this agreement, which could have been preceded by other treaties regulating detailed aspects of the partnership. The other focus is religion: its provisions allowing Milesians to participate in city cultic activity further encouraged a Milesian presence in town, as they would be thus considered an integral part of the community.

---

32   See GAUTHIER 1972, p. 360 with bibliography.

(2) Miletos and Kyzikos

Fragment of a white marble stele that preserves traces of a relief. The stele was found in the Delphinion in 1903 and is now stored in the Pergamon Museum (Inv. n. 677). Measurements: H. 0.435; W. 0.456–0.47; Th. Not recorded. Letters: 0.018.

Edd.: *ed. pr. Milet* I 3 137 (partial ph. of the squeeze); [*StV.* III 409].
Cf.: Herrmann *Milet* VI 1, *Nachträge*, p. 171.

```
    ἔδοξε τῶι δήμωι· γνώμη συ-
    νέδρων· Φιλίσκος εἶπεν· τά-
    δε ὡμολόγησαν Μιλήσιοι
4   καὶ Κυζικηνοί, (LL. 4–11: names of the Milesian and Kyzikene
    ambassadors)
    (...) τὰς μὲν πόλεις φίλας εἶ-
12  ναι ἐς τὸν ἅπαντα χρόνον
    κατὰ τὰ πάτρια· εἶναι δὲ τὸν
    Κυζικηνὸν ἐμ Μιλήτωι Μι-
    λήσιον καὶ τὸν Μιλήσιον ἐν
16  Κυζίκωι Κυζικηνόν, καθότ[ι]
    ----------------------
```

Text by Rehm.

Transl.: It was decided by the *demos*. Proposal of the *synedroi*. Philiskos put forward the motion: the Milesians and the Kyzikenes agreed (names) that the communities shall have a friendly relationship for all times as it is customary. A Kyzikene shall be a Milesian in Miletos and a Milesian in Kyzikos a Kyzikenian ...

Paleographic and orthographic considerations date the decree to a time preceding Alexander's death.[33] According to Ehrhardt, the text was inscribed in the immediate aftermath of 334 BC because it contains a "democratic prescript" and because the language presents early morphological forms. He places the

---

[33] The text preserves a list of representatives from both cities, but prosopography is of little help. Only the family of the proposer, Phyliskos son of Anaxileus, who is also a representative of Miletos (L. 5), is known, see *Milet* I 3 137, pp. 292–293.

text second in his relative chronology, after the agreement Miletos stipulated with Sardis but before those that the city signed with Phygela and Olbia.[34]

Kyzikos

The history of Kyzikos, the supposedly splendid city located on the Propontis, is poorly known. Hasluck's work remains the main source, and we lack a proper corpus of inscriptions.[35] Additionally, sparse statements in ancient sources portray the city as a naval and commercial power that grew in strength century after century. Strabo XII.8.11 testifies that Kyzikos ἔστι δ'ἐνάμιλλος ταῖς πρώταις τῶν κατὰ τὴν Ἀσίαν ἡ πόλις μεγέθει τε καὶ κάλλει καὶ εὐνομίᾳ πρός τε εἰρήνην καὶ πόλεμον. The city had strong ties to Athens already in the 5th century BC when it was a member of the first Delian League. The relationship between these *poleis* became stormy in the 460s BC, when Kyzikos sought to abandon the Athenian sphere of influence.[36] After it successfully did so, the city enjoyed a long period of autonomy that lasted even after the peace of Antalkidas, when the Great King failed to impose a garrison on Kyzikos.[37] This condition of relative freedom must have continued up to the age of Alexander. Darius III sent troops of mercenaries led by Memnon to put the city under stricter control when Alexander set off for Asia to 'free' the Greek cities. Kyzikos, however, did not fall to Memnon: he wasted the city's territory, but fled quickly as the Macedonians, who had already taken several other cities, approached.[38] Alexander did not reach the city in person and Kyzikos retained its freedom.

Ancient sources again mention Kyzikos in reference to an unsuccessful siege of the city led by Arrhidaeus, Alexander's half-brother.[39]

---

34 EHRHARDT 1987, pp. 114–116.
35 HASLUCK 1910. Akurgal conducted the only excavation undertaken in Kyzikos, in the middle of the last century, see EHRHARDT 1988, vol. II pp. 309. *I.Kyzikos* collects inscriptions from Kyzikos and its environs, but most are funerary documents, on which see ROBERT *BE* 1980 389–423. RIGSBY 1996, pp. 341–350 treats the inviolability and panhellenic games for Kore, the *Soteria*, which the city obtained around 200 BC; for other texts from Kyzikos with commentary see in HABICHT 2005(a), pp. 93–100. On Miletos in these decades see *supra*, pp. 39–41.
36 HASLUCK 1910, pp. 165–169; Kyzikos appears in *ATL*, for example in *IG* I³ 261, L. 30; 263, L. 3; 265 L. 95, etc.; see also THUC. VIII.107. Later the city entered the Second Delian League.
37 HASLUCK 1910, pp. 168–169.
38 DIOD. XVII.7; POLYAEN. V.44.
39 DIOD. XVIII 51.52; HASLUCK 1910, pp. 172–173.

One further inscription dates to these years: *IG* II² 401.[40] This document contains an honorary decree for a Kyzikenian who helped Athens by allowing a shipment of grain from Asia sometimes between 321 and 319 BC.[41] It is possible that the struggle for power slowed down commercial naval operations in these years creating problems for the *poleis* that had previously imported grain. The inscription does not advance our knowledge on Kyzikos directly but testifies to the city's commercial activities.

Potential Citizenship

According to tradition, Miletos was Kyzikos's mother city,[42] but whether intense contact had persisted over time is unknown and, largely, immaterial.[43] As Ehrhardt has already pointed out, the Kyzikenes sent regular donations to Didyma, which do not require *per force* strong ties.

Unfortunately, the inscription preserves only the first half of the agreement that must have contained a bilateral concession of the grant of potential citizenship between Miletos and Kyzikos. LL. 13–16 refer to a common ancestral background, κατὰ τὰ πάτρια, and clearly establish this exchange of potential citizenship, but nothing more of the agreement survives after these lines. Colonial ties are not mentioned directly in what remains of the inscription. Instead, as in Olbia, a reference to ancestral customs appears, which would regulate the *philia* between the communities. The fact that *philia* appears alone in this portion of the text may signal that the strength of their relationship had diminished over time. The grant of potential citizenship follows, but its regulation is lost. The only claim we can reasonably make is that the implementation of the grant of citizenship is tied to residency.[44] The text breaks off

---

40 SCULLION 2001, pp. 116–117 has proposed new restorations, on which see GAUTHIER *BE* 2002 174 and HENRY 2001, pp. 106–108. An additional article by SCULLION 2002 in defense of his proposal has not advanced the discussion. See also BOSWORTH 1993, pp. 421–422.
41 On this PAZDERA 2006, pp. 221–229.
42 EHRHARDT 1988, p. 41.
43 See MALKIN 2012, introduction.
44 VÉRIHLAC and VIAL 1998, pp. 63–64 refer to this agreement in their discussion of *Milet* I 3 71 (which they cite as 65, LL. 7–8), ca. 232/1 BC. This example is one of the annual (?) fragmentary lists that preserve grants of Milesian citizenship to foreigners; VERIHLAC and VIAL argue that it refers to *nothoi* receiving citizenship. However, this interpretation relies only on LL. 7–8, which indicate the provenance of the father of an individual, whose name is lost, thus: Κυ]ζικηνὸς ἀπὸ πατρός. VÉRIHLAC and VIAL hold that, since there was *isopoliteia* between Kyzikos and Miletos, the descendant of a Kyzikene would be a half Milesian. We have, however, no evidence for the actual long-term legal consequences of being *isopolites* in antiquity and therefore cannot determine how this individual would be recognized. Another interpretation is possible, namely, that this man had applied for

in L. 16 where "καθότ[ι]" introduces a no longer preserved comparison.[45] This section could have referred to previous agreements, colonial ties, or others.

Our limited knowledge on the history of these communities and the preservation of the inscription hinder the formulation of any hypothesis on the motivation of these communities to establish this agreement.

(3) *Miletos and Phygela*

This fragment of a severely damaged white marble stele was found in 1905 in the fields around Miletos and is now stored in the Pergamon Museum (Inv. no. 829). Measurements: H. 0.425; W. 0.45–0.46; Th. 0.11. Letters: 0.01.

Edd.: *ed. pr. Milet* I 3 142; [*StV* III 453].
Cf.: Herrmann *Milet* VI 1, *Nachträge*, p. 176.

```
     [ἔδοξε τῆι βουλῆι καὶ] τ[ῶι] δῆμωι· Κτήσων
     [...... εἶπ]εν· ἐπειδὴ πρέσβεις ἥκουσι ἀπὸ τῆ[ς]
     [πόλ]εως τῆς Φυγελέων ἀνανεούμενοι τὴν
4    [φιλί]αν καὶ τὴν πολιτείαν τὴν ὑπάρχουσαν
     [Φυγ]ελεῶσιν ἐμ Μιλήτωι καὶ Μιλησίοις
     [ἐ]μ Φυγέλοις ἐκ τῶγ χρόνων τῶν πρότερον
     [κ]αὶ μέμνηνται τῶν εὐεργετημάτων, ὧν
8    [ε]ὐεργέτηκεν αὐτοὺς ὁ δῆμος ὁ Μιλησίων·
     [ἐ]ψηφίσθαι τῶι δήμωι τὴν πόλιν τὴν
     [Φ]υγελέων ἐπηινῆσθαι προθυμίας ἕνεκεν,
     [ἧ]ς ἔχει περὶ Μιλησίους· ὅπως δὲ ἡ φιλία καὶ ἡ
12   [ο]ἰκειότης ἡ ὑπάρχουσα Φυγελεῶσι καὶ
     Μιλησίοις διαμένηι τὸν ἀεὶ χρόνον· ἀγαθῆι
     τύχηι· Μιλησίους καὶ Φυγελεῖς πολίτας εἶναι
     παρ' ἀλλήλοις καὶ μετέχειν ἱερῶν καὶ ἀρχείω[ν]
16   [κ]αὶ τῶν ἄλλων τῶν ὑπαρχόντων ἐμ Μιλήτ[ωι]
     [καὶ] Φυγέλοις· τοὺς δὲ πρυτάνει[ς ἐπικληρῶσαι]
     [εἰς τὰς] φυλὰς τοὺ[ς ἀπογραψομένους πρὸς τὸ τῆς]
     [βουλῆς ἀρχεῖον ἐν ἑκατέραι τῶν πόλεων ...]
```

---

and received citizenship as a foreigner and that this list does not refer to *nothoi*. After all, *isopolitai* who did not take up the option of switching status, like the father of this individual, were still foreigners in the partner city.

45 On the different restorations proposed for L. 17 see Herrmann *Milet* VI 1, *Nachträge*, p. 171.

Text by Rehm.

Transl.: It was decided by the *boule* and the *demos*; Kteson son of [.] put forward the motion: since ambassadors come from the city of Phygela reminding (us) of the friendship and citizenship that Phygelans enjoy in Miletos and Milesians in Phygela from earlier times and they preserve the memory of the benefactions done to them by the Milesians, the *demos* shall decree to praise the city of the Phygelans because of their care for the Milesians. So that the friendship and the existing familial ties between the two cities remain for all times; to good fortune, Milesians and Phygelans shall be citizens of each other, they shall partake in each other's religious activities and offices and everything else that exists in Miletos and Phygela. The *prytaneis* [shall determine by lot] in which tribes [those who have registered at the seat of the *boule* in each city....]

The text belongs to the second half of the 4th century BC, broadly to the aftermath of Miletos's liberation.[46]

Phygela

Phygela was located on the Samio-Ephesian *paralia*, where it had its own harbor.[47] Both Samos and Ephesos claimed this area for themselves for centuries, but the city of Phygela managed to enjoy some autonomy even if only briefly.[48]

Phygela appears to have been autonomous around the middle of the 5th century BC, when, according to the *ATL*, it paid a tribute to Athens, and again in the 4th century BC, under much different circumstances, when coins indicate a thriving city.[49] Phygela profited from Ephesos's crisis that had been triggered by geomorphologic changes, but—paradoxically, for the same reason—Ephesos remained a constant danger. After Lysimachos's forced

---

46   In the *corpus* of the inscriptions from Miletos the text is dated to a year "vor 323 v. Chr.," but follows numerically the inscriptions that belong to the second half of the 3rd century BC. This discrepancy occurred because Rehm initially considered the paleography to indicate a lower date; Rehm corrected his view because of morphology. For EHRHARDT 1987, pp. 114–116 the morphology recommends that we date the inscription to before 317 BC, while historical events would set the upper limit to 334 BC.
47   This city has been the object of a recent and detailed study by RAGONE 1996.
48   WALSER 2008, pp. 47–87 (Ephesos); SHIPLEY 1987, esp. pp. 31–36 (Samos).
49   RAGONE 1996, p. 236, for the events of these decades see esp. pp. 353–361.

refoundation of Ephesos-Arsinoea,[50] Phygela must have retained its autonomy for a couple of decades before becoming a χωρίον in the Ephesian *chora*.[51]

The known historical events for the 3rd century BC have prompted scholars to interpret this agreement as an attempt on the part of Phygela to find a strong ally against her dangerous neighbor(s).[52] In what follows, however, I try to suggest that another interpretation may be possible.

The Agreement

This agreement must be roughly contemporary with the ones that Miletos signed with Olbia and Kyzikos, but its formulation makes it the first clearly articulated grant of potential citizenship that we have from Miletos.

The first lines record the mission of Phygela's embassy to Miletos, whose members ἀνανεούμενοι τὴν / [φιλί]αν καὶ τὴν πολιτείαν τὴν ὑπάρχουσαν / [Φυγ]ελεῦσιν ἐμ Μιλήτωι καὶ Μιλησίοις / [ἐ]μ Φυγέλοις ἐκ τῶγ χρόνων τῶν πρότερον (LL. 3–5). LL. 14–18 include the grant of potential citizenship that the text, in LL. 4–6, appears to suggest was a 'renewal.' In the lines preceding the grant, LL. 13–18, Miletos (LL. 9–13) replies to Phygela's embassy by praising it and introducing the award of bilateral potential citizenship with the wish that *philia* and *oikeiotes*, which had been perhaps determined by Miletos's former benefactions (LL. 7–8), continue forever.[53] The actual grant of potential citizenship begins with the general, bilateral exchange using the *metechein* formula, followed by a description (largely lost) of the procedure to switch citizenship. Even if these lines are fragmentary, they show that Miletos was

---

50 KIRBIHLER 2009, esp. pp. 309–311; WALSER 2008, pp. 73–76; RAGONE 1996, p. 371; ROBERT 1989, pp. 80–81; IDEM 1989, *OMS* V, pp. 377–380.

51 The city still granted its *politeia* between 310 and 290 BC *I.Eph.* VIII.1 3111. Phygela appears as a *chorion* in *IEph.* IV 1408, which Ragone dates to the "anni Ottanta del III secolo a.Cr"; cf. ROBERT 1989, *OMS* V, pp. 377–380.

52 RAGONE 1996, p. 363: "di più, si può solo ipotizzare che l'isopolitia con Mileto fosse stata ... e fosse ... per Phygela un modo per rafforzare—condividendola con una città «forte»— la sua pencolante αὐτονομία, posta sotto la perenne ipoteca di tentativi espansionistici contrapposti di Efeso e Samo." EHRHARDT 1987, p. 99: "Nach dem Ende der persischen Herrschaft und dem zunehmenden Gewicht der großen Städte konnte Ephesos schon deshalb eine potentielle Gefahr für Phygela darstellen, weil die Stadt gute Beziehungen zu Alexander unterhielt".

53 In searching for evidence of these benefactions, scholars turn to an old episode, dated 410–409 BC, when Miletos helped Phygela against Thrasyllos. This Milesian intervention cost the city many lives, according to the ancient sources, esp. XENOPH. *Hell.* I.2–3, see RAGONE 1996, p. 235.

already developing a detailed set of prescriptions for the enrollment procedure, anticipating details found in later agreements with an award of potential citizenship.[54]

Miletos's tone and the grant align perfectly with the diplomatic practice and language of the time, but it is interesting that, in its response, Miletos fails to acknowledge the preexisting *politeia* and speaks only of *philia* and *oikeiotes* only as being in place. In other words, the Ionian city moves to approve the bilateral exchange of potential citizenship by regulating it anew. Such grants, however, do not elapse. In Cretan decrees of *asylia*, for example, we see that some communities asked their Cretan counterpart to inscribe (or reinscribe) the grants as a way to confirm older concessions. For a 'renewal' I find it a bit unusual that Miletos considered it necessary to regrant a concession that, according to Phygela, had been given already. The text raises the question of whether a concession of *politeia* had already been in place—otherwise, why would Miletos acknowledge it in LL. 11–12 and then regrant it? Or were the Milesians simply regulating it anew?

Equally uncertain is whether this award of potential citizenship could have helped in a conflict with Ephesos or Samos. This concession is (or appears to be) an example of type one of isopolity. Phygela did not ask for any military help, unless such a section is now missing. Perhaps Phygela was just testing Miletos or, maybe, another reading is possible. Phygela's goal was not to search for champions in war, but for partners in business, a positive consequence of its short-lived autonomous position in the 4th BC. This assessment, however, remains speculative.

---

54   JONES 1987, p. 315 argues that this agreement records an unusual enrollment procedure for Phygela where, normally, new citizens had to also enroll in *gene*. According to Jones, LL. 17–18 contain "instructions for the enrollment of new citizens, applicable to both parties (…)." But the text is very fragmentary in this section and the reference to "both cities" has been restored. The surviving evidence of potential citizenship indicates that each partner city followed its own rules. Probably, it would be better to omit the restoration of the last two lines.

(4) *Miletos and Kios*
This stele of white marble was found in the Delphinion in 1903. Probably the stone was reworked to fit into a wall; it is now stored in the Pergamon Museum, Berlin (Inv. no. 676). Measurements: W. 0.535–0.59; Th. 0.20. Letters: 0.01.

Ed.: *ed. pr. Milet* I 3 141 (*ph.*); [*IKios* T3].
Cf. Wilhelm 1921, p. 62 n. 8 on L. 29 accepted by Robert *OMS* IV, p. 294; Nollé and Wartner 1987, pp. 361–364. Herrmann *Milet* VI 1, *Nachträge*, pp. 175–176.

Γνώμη συνέδρων τῶν αἱρεθέντων, *names follow* (LL. 2–6)
(...) εἶπαν· ἐπειδὴ
Κιανοὶ ἄποικοι ὄντες τῆς πόλεως καὶ διαφυλάσσον-
8 τες τὴμ πρὸς τὸν δῆμον φιλίαν ἀπέστειλαν ἱεροποι-
οὺς Νίκανδρον καὶ Φιλιππίδην ψήφισμα κομίζοντας,
ἐν ὧι ἀπολογισάμενοι τοὺς πολέμους τοὺς κατασχόν-
τας αὐτῶν τὴγ χώραν καὶ τὰς δαπάνας τὰς εἰς ταῦ-
12 τα γινομένας ἀξιοῦσιν εἰς τὰς φιάλας, ἃς προσοφείλου-
σιν τῶι θεῶι, ἀφεθῆναι, ὅσας ἂν δυνατὸν ἦι, καὶ οἱ ἱεροποιοὶ
δὲ οἱ ἥκοντες παρὰ Κιανῶν περί τε τούτων διελέγησαν
ἀκολούθως τοῖς ἐν τῶι ψηφίσματι γεγραμμένοις καὶ ἐμφα-
16 νίσαντες τὰ οἰκεῖα καὶ φιλάνθρωπα τὰ ὑπάρχοντα κοινῆι τε
τῶι δήμωι ἐγ Κίωι καὶ ἰδίαι τὰ γινόμενα τοῖς ἀφικνουμέ-
νοις Μιλησίων ἐμνήσθησαμ περὶ πολιτείας, ὅπως ὑπάρχ(ι)
Κιανοῖς ἐμ Μιλήτωι, προσήκει δὲ τῶι δήμωι κτίστηι ὄντι
20 τῆς ἀποικίας καὶ τὴν εἰς τοὺς οἰκείους εὔνοιαν ἐμ παντὶ καιρῶι ἀποδεικνυμένωι μὴ ἀφίστασθαι τοῦ συμφέροντο[ς],
ἀλλ' ἐπιμέλειαμ ποιήσασθαι τῶν ἀποίκων τὴμ προσήκου-
σαν· ἐψηφίσθαι Μιλησίοις ἀποκρίνασθαι Κιανοῖς περὶ μὲν τῶμ [φι]-
24 αλῶν, ὧν ἀξιοῦσι τὴν ἄφεσιγ γενέσθαι, διότι, εἰ μὲν μὴ συνέβαινε
καὶ αὐτοὺς τεθλῖφθαι διὰ τοὺς πολέμους καὶ τὰς ἀφορίας τὰς
κατασχούσας τὴγ χώραν, ἔτι δὲ καὶ ἀδύνατον εἶναι τὴν ἄφε-
σιμ ποιήσασθαι τὸν δῆμον τῶγ γινομένων ἀπαρχῶν τῶ[ι θε]-
28 ῶι διὰ τὸ τὸν νόμον τὸμ περὶ τούτων ὑπάρχοντα κωλύειν, ἐ-
π(ε)ίπαν τὸ δυνατὸν ἂν ἔπραξεν εἰς τὸ συντελεσθῆναι Κιανοῖς
τὰ περὶ τούτων ἀξιούμενα, νυνὶ δὲ ἐπιχωρεῖ αὐτοῖς ποιήσας-
[θ]αι τὴν ἀποκατάστασιν τῶν ὀφειλομένων φιαλῶν, ἐπειτὰν
32 φαίνηται αὐτοῖς κατὰ καιρὸν εἶναι. περὶ μέντοι τῶν ἐφεξῆς
οἴεται δεῖν ὁ δῆμος γίνεσθαι τὰς ἀπαρχὰς τῶι θεῶι κατὰ τὰ ὑπὸ
[τῶ]μ προγόνων συγκείμενα. τὴν δὲ πολιτείαν δεδόσθαι Κιανοῖς,
[κ]αθότι ἐμνήσθησαν οἱ ἱεροποιοί, ὅπως ὁ δῆμος φαίνηται ἐπὶ πλε[ῖ]-

36 ον τὴν οἰκειότητα διατηρῶν καὶ ἀκόλουθα πράσσων τῆι τῶμ προγό-
    νων αἱρέσει· ἵνα δὲ τοῖς προαιρουμένοις Κιανῶν μετέχειν τῆ[ς]
    πολιτείας γίνηται τὰ ὑπὸ τοῦ δήμου δεδομένα, ἐπιμελεῖσθ[αι]
    τοὺς πρυτάνεις καὶ ἐπικληροῦν αὐτοὺς ἐπὶ τὰς φυλάς, ἐὰν
40 ἀπομαρτυρῶσιν αὐτοῖς Κιανοὶ μετὰ ψηφίσματος, ὅτι εἰσὶν
    αὐτῶμ πολῖται, (...)
(an exhortation to the Kians to keep their piety and provisions on the stele's publication follow)

Text by Rehm unless otherwise noted: LL. 28–29 *lapis* ΕΠΕΙΠΑΝ, ἐπίπαν N(ollé) and W(artner) as spelling mistake due to new pronunciation; ἐπεὶ πᾶν K(awerau) and R(ehm). L. 29 N. and W. retain ἔγραψεν; ἔπραξεν W(ilhelm), R(obert) and H(errmann): "eine Kontrolle am Stein hat ergeben, daß dort in der Tat ἔπραξεν steht."

Transl.: LL. 6–41 (the *synedroi*) put forward the motion: since the Kians, inasmuch as they are colonists of the city and guard carefully the friendship with our people, sent the *hieropoioi* Nikandros and Philippides with a decree in which they recounted the wars that had plagued their land and the expenses under these circumstances, they ask to be relieved from donating the *phialae*, which they still owe to the god, as many as possible; (13) and the *hieropoioi* from the Kians spoke of these matters following the decree closely, while showing that the ties and benefactions were generally resources to the people in Kios and individually available to those Milesians who go there, (18) they raised the question of citizenship, such that the Kians should have it in Miletos, and that it was appropriate for the people who founded the settlement and who showed benevolence to their kinsmen in every circumstance not to deprive them of their advantages, but instead to make their care of the colonists. (23) Be it enacted by the Milesians to answer the Kians in regard to the *phialae*, from which they (the Kians) wanted to be exempt, that if it did not also befall them (the Milesians) to have been oppressed by wars and shortages of food on land, yet even so it would be impossible for the people to free them from the first fruits that are owed to the god because the law that exists on the matter stands in the way, since the people would have done everything possible towards accomplishing for the Kians what they had requested about these matters. Under the present circumstances, however, it is conceded to the Kians that a restoration of the donation of the *phialae* be made whenever it seems possible to them. In regard to the future, the *demos* thinks that the first fruits for the god should be given according to the way established already by the ancestors, (34) and that citizenship be granted to the Kians, just as the *hieropoioi* spoke, so that the *demos* manifestly preserves the closest relationship and acts according to the attitude of the ancestors. So that those among the Kians who choose to partake in (our) citizenship shall have what has been granted by the *demos*, the *prytaneis* shall oversee and distribute them by lot among the tribes, when the Kians have proven to them with a decree that they are really Kian citizens (...)

Rehm's unchallenged date for this decree is ca. 229/8 BC. This determination relies on prosopographical and paleographical evidence.[55]

Miletos—the Second Half of the 3rd Century BC

The history of Miletos in the second half of the 3rd century BC is poorly known.[56] One concern surrounds Miletos's claim of struggles in LL. 24–26: the most widely accepted explanation for them is that the city had suffered from Antigonos Doson's expedition. But even this hypothesis rests primarily on assumptions.[57]

In this period, the Milesian epigraphic record preserves a remarkable number of citizenship concessions to groups of people and individuals. The Delphinion has indeed revealed numerous texts that include names of individuals, and even families, who moved to Miletos and were granted citizenship during the second half of the 3rd century BC.[58] In the best-known example, the *polis* conceded *politeia* to Cretan soldiers and their families around 234/3 BC and then again in 229/28 BC.[59] According to these testimonies, after being admitted into the Milesian citizen body, these Cretan soldiers and their families were settled in the territory of Myous and assigned land that they could not sell for 20 years. Miletos was clearly trying to create a new, permanent enclave of citizens who could contribute to the defense of the town as well as to its demographic growth.[60]

---

55   HABICHT 1991, pp. 325–329 esp. on Lichas, but also *Milet* I 3 141, esp. n. 1 and p. 246.
56   The difficult task of writing Miletos's history esp. for the 3rd century BC has been undertaken recently by GRIEB 2008, pp. 245–250; GÜNTHER 1971, pp. 51–55, 92–95; HAUSOLLIER 1902, ch. 6–8.
57   LE BOHEC 1993, esp. pp. 348–349.
58   *Milet* I 3 34–99. GAWANTKA 1975, p. 80 sought to use these lists to check the implementation rate of potential citizenship, but on this attempt see GAUTHIER 1977/78, pp. 374–375.
59   See HERRMANN *Nachträge*, pp. 160–165, CHANIOTIS 1996, p. 14, and more extensively PETROPOULOU 1985, appendix 6 and pp. 128–131.
60   See also recently KÖCHE 2012, pp. 41–50.

Kios

Kios was located by the sea, on the Propontis, in Mysia. Milesian colonists founded the city in the second half of the 7th century BC;[61] the later relationship between the cities, however, is not well attested. Only sparse testimonies for the history of Kios survive, especially for the Hellenistic period, with this decree one of the main sources. In it the Kians speak of the *phialae* they had to send yearly to Apollo in Didyma, and ask for the remission of the gift.[62] The Kians emphasize their current state of financial distress due to wars, but the Milesians refuse their petition on legal grounds because, they say, a law regulating these matters hinders them from intervening, L. 28. Moreover, continues Miletos, it would have helped Kios but it suffered similar problems and thus lacked the financial capacity to do so.

The financial effort required by such donations was not insignificant,[63] and the history of Kios, although inadequately known, suggests that the claimed financial difficulties were probably real. The growth of the Bithynian kingdom caused commotion in the area, not least because its regents sought and found support for their ambitions in the Galatians already in the 370s BC.[64] The struggles taking place in this period cannot have left the Kian territory untouched.

After Lysimachos's death in 281 BC, Kios became autonomous. According to Polybios, the town fell under the rule of a tyrant named Molpagoras at the end of 3rd century BC.[65] The historian's account cannot help to reconstruct in any detail the position and policy of Kios, which was clearly located in a hotspot. This circumstance was tragically confirmed by the later events, such as the destruction of the city by hand of Philip V in 202 BC.[66] Although Kios had been tied to the Aitolian League, this friendship/protection did not stop Philip. Polybios testifies to the presence of an Aitolian *strategos* in town,[67] and associates the city with Lysimacheia and Chalchedon—these cities were allies

---

61 See also L. 7 and LL. 19–21, EHRHARDT 1988, pp. 47–48.
62 GAWANTKA 1975, pp. 156–164; GÜNTHER 1971, pp. 125–127 studies the evidence for the yearly gifts to the god on the part of the colonies. It is, however, doubtful that many Milesian colonies attended to this duty regularly.
63 See again GÜNTHER 1971, pp. 125–127.
64 VITUCCI 1953, pp. 17–19 For the Galatians see STROBEL 2006 with further bibliography.
65 POLYB. XV 21.
66 See POLYB. XV 21–24. On these paragraphs see WALBANK 1967, pp. 474–480.
67 On the alleged *isopoliteia* between Kios and the Aitolian league *infra* pp. 255–256.

and friends of the Aitolians and shared its destiny. Philip forced Lysimacheia and Chalchedon to go over to his side, but he destroyed Kios before handing the city over to his brother-in-law, Prousias, who refounded the community as Prousias by the Sea. The relevance of the later events should not be exaggerated, but these facts may validate Kios's claims as attested in *Milet* I 3 141.

The Award of Potential Citizenship

In these years Miletos incorporated a substantial number of new citizens into its citizenry, possibly in order to confront military and demographic emergencies (about which we are not well informed).[68] Still, it is unrealistic to think that the Milesians conceded potential citizenship as requested/reminded by the Kians because they anticipated and hoped for a mass migration of people from Mysia.

Kios initiated the diplomatic mission and contact with Miletos by sending an embassy comprised of two *hieropoioi*, not 'standard' ambassadors but rather representatives from the religious sphere. In this context, they would remind Miletos of citizenship (LL. 18–19) and, first and foremost, the remission of the sacred gift. The *hieropoioi* then stressed the colonial tie between Kios and Miletos and referred to their relationship of *philia*.

The text is undoubtedly built around the question of the *phialae* and their remission, to which the grant of citizenship appears to be subordinated. The concession of potential citizenship is unusually unilateral as neither of the two parties shows any interest for its reciprocation. The Milesians, after denying the first Kian request pertaining to the *phialae*, move to define the terms of the grant of potential citizenship. The conditions and procedures for switching citizenship, LL. 34–41, are clearly articulated, with LL. 39–41 preserving the important detail of the necessity of proof of Kian citizenship status for those who intended to become Milesians. Gawantka has suggested that this requirement would deter Kians from moving: in order to obtain proof of their status, citizens would have had to make their intention known to others in their own town.[69] Savalli has rightly pointed out that this interpretation is problematic.[70] Other documents attest to similar requests that must have been normal forms of control for *poleis*. Additionally, it could be interpreted as a different formulation or, perhaps, an older way to address the problem of naturalized citizens

---

68   See *Milet* I 3 33a–50 and *supra*.
69   See GAWANTKA 1975, p. 159, n. 148.
70   SAVALLI 1985, pp. 407–408, n. 153a.

from potential isopolity partner cities who wanted to acquire Milesian citizenship, as we know from later agreements.[71]

At the end of the decree, LL. 42–47, Miletos returns to the question of the *phialae*, even if indirectly, by exhorting Kios to keep its piety toward the god in order to enjoy further benefactions from their relationship. The theme of the *phialae* is central to the diplomatic mission, if not the reason for it: the request of the grant of potential citizenship is not the focus of this document, but it serves Kios's diplomatic and political goals.

An 'historical' reading of this text is possible, too, but with the *caveat* that because it relies on incomplete background evidence, it remains highly hypothetical. Miletos was not interested in a bilateral grant, which, in fact, Kios did not even offer. It is possible that Kios was exploring political alternatives along with trying to obtain the remission of the due *phialae*: Bithynian and Macedonian powers, not to speak of the Galatian danger, loomed over Kios. Perhaps in this way Kios tested Miletos's readiness to offer help, in any form.

I exclude that Kios ever considered mass migration as a way to solve its problems. Instead, I do not rule out a connection between the Milesian non-commitment policy and the fact that, not long after the stipulation of this agreement, Kios sought Aitolian friendship and alliance and even allowed a garrison in its territory.

This document testifies to a diplomatic act that was promoted and carried out by Kios using the two interconnected elements that tied it to Miletos: religion and colonial connections. Kios's mission mostly sought to achieve one result, namely, relief from a financial burden (*phialae*). Solidifying a close relationship with a major player in the geopolitics of Asia Minor (through the concession of potential citizenship) might have been on its wish list, too. Miletos listened. Granting potential citizenship, as a due recognition and diplomatic result that the Kians could have claimed to have obtained, is here set in a historical context that presents also a sense of urgency and actual political difficulties. Neither of the two types of potential citizenship can suitably describe this diplomatic act: in case one forgets, history escapes strict catogories. While Kios certainly tried to win Miletos's support, its requests were not meant to involve Miletos in any specific activity or event. Because remission

---

71   *Milet* I 3 143 = no. 5, LL. 19–23 (Miletos-Seleukeia); *Milet* I 3 146 = no. 6, LL. 26–30 (Miletos-Mylasa). Earlier but comparable in my view: *Milet* I 3 136 = no. 1, LL. 17–20 (Miletos-Olbia).

of the *phialae* would have saved Kios important financial resources, it is the focus of the requests. Kios's only hope was to obtain remission of an expensive donation. Other than that goal, Kios did not expect benefits from the mission it sent to Miletos. The embassy included the reminder of citizenship because Miletos could hardly have refused this concession. In other words, the certainty of potential citizenship balanced the unlikely remission of the *phialae*. The unilateral character of the concession indeed seems striking as it appears to go against standard diplomatic practice, but in truth it does not. I argue for the flexible nature of this tool: it was not only a diplomatic pleasantry, but a concession that would compensate for any unsuccessful results of a mission by establishing an even stronger tie between communities.

(5) *Miletos and Seleukeia Tralles*

This well-known and rich dossier has already been considered above in the introduction to this book because of its representative character for the tool of potential citizenship. The cities of Miletos and Seleukeia-Tralles granted and reciprocated a concession of potential citizenship by charging it with a different meaning. Building on my initial treatment of this important text, I present here an in-depth historical analysis and consideration of themes that differ from that of potential citizenship but have great relevance within the agreement.

I include below only the parts of the decrees by the two cities that relate to this study as they have otherwise been published in *Milet* I 3 143.

A

[- - - ca. 20 - - - ἐμφανίζο]ν̣τες π̣[ερὶ τῶν πρότερον ὑπαρ-]
[χόντων ταῖς πόλεσιν ἀμφοτέραις] πρὸς αὑτὰς φιλανθρ[ώπων, καὶ]
[νῦν ? Σελευκεῖς διὰ προγόνων ο]ἰκείως χρώμενοι τῶι δήμ[ωι τῶι]
4   [Μιλησίων διὰ τὴν ἀπὸ τοῦ θεοῦ] συγγένειαν τετιμήκασι τὸν δῆ-
[μον καὶ ἀπεστάλκασιν πρεσβε]υ̣τὰς (names follow LL. 5–6)
[ἐμφανιοῦντας τὴν αἵρεσιν αὐτ]ῶν κατὰ μέρος, ἣν ἔχουσι πρὸς τὸ πλῆθος
8   [τὸ Μιλησίων, καὶ βουλόμενοι] τιμᾶν καὶ τὸν Ἀπόλλω τὸν Διδυμῆ, εἰς ὃν ἀναφέ-
[ρουσιν καὶ τὴν ἀρχὴ]ν̣ τῆς πρὸς τὴμ πόλιν συγγενείας, ἐψηφισμένοι
[εἰσὶ πέμπειν θε]ω̣ροὺς τοὺς συντελέσοντας καθ᾽ ἕκαστον ἔτος πομπὴν
[καὶ θυσίαν καὶ ἄ]λ̣λας τιμὰς μετὰ πάσης σπουδῆς καὶ φιλοτιμίας·
12 [ὅπως οὖν] ὁ δῆμος φαίνηται συναντῶν προσηκόντως τοῖς προ-
[σενηνεγ]μ̣ένοις πρός τε τὸ θεῖον εὐσεβῶς καὶ πρὸς τὴμ πόλιν εὐ-
[νοϊκῶς κ]α̣ὶ μεταδιδοὺς αὐτοῖς τῶμ παρ᾽ αὑτῶι τιμίων, δεδόχθαι Μιλησίοις·
[ἐπῃ]ιν⟨ῆ⟩σθαι μὲν Σελευκεῖς αἱρέσεως ἕνεκεν καὶ εἶναι ἐν ἐπιμελείαι

16 [πα]ρὰ τῆι βουλῆι καὶ τῶι δήμωι, δέχεσθαι δὲ καὶ τὰς ἐψηφισμένας
    [ὑ]π' αὐτῶν τιμὰς μετ' εὐνοίας, δεδόσθαι δὲ καὶ πολιτείαν Σελευκεῦσι
    τοῖς νέμουσι πατρίδα καὶ πόλιν Σελεύκειαν ἕως εἰς στεφανηφόρον
    Ἐπικράτην καὶ μῆνα Ταυρεῶνα· εἰ δέ τινες κατὰ δόγμα τοῦ δήμου πολῖται
20 γεγένηνται, μὴ ἔνεμον δὲ τὴν Σελευκείων πόλιν, ἢ ἐάν τισιν μετὰ ταῦτα
    δοθῆι παρ' αὐτοῖς πολιτεία, ὑπάρχειν τούτοις καὶ τὴμ παρ' ἡμῖν πολιτείαν νεί-
    μασι πρότερον πατρίδα καὶ πόλιν Σελεύκειαν ἔτη δέκα ἀπὸ τῆς πρὸς τὸ
    πολίτευμα προσγραφῆς. ὁπόσοι δ' ἂν αὐτῶν αἱρῶνται μεθ' ἡμῶν συμπολιτεύεσ-
24 θαι καὶ μετέχειν ἱερῶν καὶ ἀρχείων καὶ τῶν λοιπῶν ἁπάντων, ὧγ καὶ τοῖς ἄλλοις
    μέτεστι Μιλεσίοις, ποιείσθωσαν τὴν ἀπογραφὴν ἐπὶ τὸ τῆς βουλῆς ἀρχεῖον ἀν' ἕ-
    καστον ἔτος ἕως τῆς εἰκάδος τοῦ μηνὸς τοῦ Ἀνθεστηριῶνος πατρόθεν κ[αὶ]
    ἧς ἂν ὦσι φυλῆς· ὁ δὲ γραμματεὺς εἰσαγγελέτω εἰς τὴμ πρώτην ἐκλησίαν μετὰ
28 τὴν ἀπογραφήν· οἱ δὲ πρυτάνεις ἐπικληρούτωσαν αὐτούς, ἐφ' ἃς ἂν ὁ δῆμος
    ἀποδείξηι φυλάς· τοὺς δὲ προσιόντας πρὸς τὴμ πολιτείαν τῶμ μὲν ἄλλων παρα-
    χρῆμα μετέχειν πάντων, φυλακὴν δὲ καὶ φρουραρχίαν συγκληροῦσθαι διελ-
    θόντων ἐτῶν δέκα ἀφ' ἑκάστης ἐπικληρώσεως. ἐὰν δέ τις πολιτεύηται
32 παρὰ τόδε τὸ ψήφισμα, εἶναι αὐτὸν ὑπεύθυνον τῆι τε ἐμ μολποῖς ἐνστάσει καὶ
    τῆι δίκηι τῆς ξενίας κατὰ τοὺς νόμους. (...) (provisions on publication follow)

B (decree of Seleukeia-Tralles)
    ἔδοξε τῆι βουλῆι καὶ τῶι δήμωι· βουλῆς γνώμη· ἐπειδὴ Μιλήσιοι φίλοι καὶ
                                                                          οἰκεῖοι
    ὑπάρχοντες διὰ προγόνων πρότερόν τε διετέλουν ἐμ παντὶ καιρῶι πρόνοιαν
48 ποιούμενοι καὶ κοινῆι παντὸς τοῦ δήμου τοῦ Σελευκέων καὶ καθ' ἰδίαν ἑκάσ-
    του τῶν ἀφικνουμένων εἰς τὴμ πόλιν αὐτῶν καὶ μετὰ ταῦτα παραγενόμε-
    νος Πρύτανις ἀνήγγελλεν, διότι τὴν αὐτὴν αἵρεσιν ἔχοντες οὐθενὸς ἀφί[σ]-
    τανται τῶν τῆι πόλει συμφερόντων ἐμ πᾶσιν οἰκείως ἀποδεικνύμενοι τὴ[ν]
52 αὐτῶν σπουδήν· ὅπως οὖν ἐπὶ πλέον αὔξηται τὰ προϋπάρχοντα φιλάνθρωπα
    καὶ οἰκεῖα ταῖς πόλεσιν ἀμφοτέραις καὶ φαίνηται τιμῶν ὁ δῆμος Μιλησίους
    ἀξίως ἐμ παντὶ καιρῶι τῆς εἰς αὐτὸν εὐνοίας· τύχηι ἀγαθῆι· δεδόχθαι τῆι
    βουλῆι καὶ τῶι δήμωι· ἐπηινῆσθαι Μιλησίους ἐπὶ τῆι εὐνοίαι καὶ τῆι προαιρέσει, ἣν
56 ἔχουσιν εἰς τὸν δῆμον. δεδόσθαι δὲ αὐτοῖς καὶ πολιτείαν ἐφ' ἴσηι καὶ ὁμοίαι καὶ
    μετέχειν αὐτοὺς ἁπάντων, ὧγ καὶ οἱ ἄλλοι πολῖται μετέχουσιν, καὶ τὸμ βουλό-
    μενον Μιλησίων πολιτεύεσθαι ἐν Σελευκε[ία]ι ἀπογράφεσθαι πρός τε τοὺς στρα-
    τηγοὺς καὶ τὸγ γραμματέα τοῦ δήμου· τοὺς δὲ καταχωρίζειν εἰς φυλὴν
60 τὸν ἀπογραφόμενον, εἰς ἣν ἂμ βούληται. ὑπάρχειν δὲ αὐτοῖς καὶ προεδρίαν
    ἐν τοῖς ἀγῶσιν πᾶσιν καὶ ἔφοδον ἐπὶ τὴν βουλὴν καὶ τὸν δῆμον πρώτοις
    μετὰ τὰ ἱερά. ποιεῖσθαι δ' ἐπιμέλειαν τοὺς ἀεὶ χειροτονουμένους στρατηγοὺς
    τοῦ δήμου τοῦ Μιλησίων καὶ προνοεῖν τῶν παραγινομένων εἰς τὴν πόλιν, ὅπως

64 πάντων τυγχάνωσι τῶν καλῶς ἐχόντων. πέμπεσθαι δὲ καὶ θεωροὺς τοὺς
[σ]υ̣ν̣τελέσοντας θυσίαν τῶι Ἀπόλλωνι τῶι Διδυμεῖ τῶι ἀρχηγέτηι τῆς οἰκει-
[ότητο]ς, ἐν οἷς ἂν χρόνοις συντελῶσιν Μιλήσιοι. ἐπὶ δὲ τοῖς ἐψηφισμένοις συν-
[τελέσαι θυσία]ν τῶι Διὶ τῶι Λαρασίωι καὶ τῶι Ἀπόλλωνι τοὺς ἱερομνήμονας
κα[ὶ]
68 [τοὺς - - - - 8/10- - - -καὶ τοὺς ἱε]ρ̣ο̣κ̣[ήρυκα]ς̣ ἐπευχομένους συνενεγκεῖν
ἀμφοτέραις
[ταῖς πόλεσι τὰ ἐψηφισμένα καὶ εἶναι] ἐπὶ σωτηρίαι καὶ εὐτυχίαι·
(provisions on publication of the decree follow)

Chronology and the Signing Partners

The accepted date for the dossier is 218/17 BC, when Antiochos III began his campaign against the usurper Achaios.[72]

The signing communities are Miletos and Seleukeia-Tralles. Seleukeia-Tralles is located in Karia, at modern Aydin, situated at a high point that dominated the surrounding fluvial plain. The city included the sanctuary for Zeus Larasios, considered the main deity both in the Hellenistic and the Imperial periods.[73]

Seleukeia-Tralles flourished only after signing the peace agreement of Apameia, when the city was given as δωρεά to the Attalids. Information about Seleukeia during the last decades of the 3rd century BC remains scanty and confused.[74] The very name of the city has been considered an indication of its political orientation: Antiochos I changed the city's original Karian name, Tralles, to Seleukeia.[75] Until a few years ago, scholars insisted that the city retained the dynastic name until 188 BC. However, a recently published list of citizens from Miletos dated to the second half of the 3rd century BC preserves the name of a man whose ethnic has been restored rather securely as "Trallian."[76] This evidence demonstrates a temporary return to the Karian name, perhaps because of a shift in regional hegemony.[77] Ma has hypothesized that Tralles

---

72 See WÖRRLE 1988, pp. 432–437 on the *stephanephoroi* list 124 and HERRMANN, *Nachträge* p. 176. For an historical account see MA 2002, pp. 54–63, and WILL 1982, pp. 20–23. On this inscription see SABA 2014, pp. 122–132.

73 RIGSBY 1996, pp. 416–417; BOFFO 1985, pp. 311–317; BEAN 1971, pp. 208–211; ROBERT *OMS* II, esp. 1186. In general, on the city see COHEN 1995, pp. 265–268.

74 For these years see MA 2002, ch. 2. For the city's strong relationship with the Attalids, see SAVALLI 2001(a), esp. pp. 82–85.

75 On the basis of *IG* IX.1² 17, L. 100 and Robert's restoration (see BOFFO 1985, p. 311 n. 189), this modification of the name dates to a year before 260 BC. See also the comment in *Milet* VI 3 1058; MA 2002, esp. p. 48.

76 *Milet* VI 3 1058, L. 6 Διονύσιος Ἰατροκλείους Τρα[λλιανός].

77 MA 2002, p. 57. THONEMANN 2003, pp. 101–102 dismisses this evidence also relying on a note by HABICHT 1989, p. 94. Habicht suggests that the Abderite Sosikrates son of

was forced to return to dynastic denomination around 223 BC, after Achaios's intervention but before his usurpation around 220 BC.[78] It is uncertain how Seleukeia-Tralles positioned itself in these years. This treaty can only inform us of the fact that the town was back in Seleukid hands in 218/7 BC, whether or not legitimate.

The Agreement

As I noted in the introduction, the two decrees contained in this dossier differ greatly from each other in tone and attitude and thus deserve a 'synchronic' study.

Before 1988, the *communis opinio* held that this bilateral grant of potential citizenship showed the Trallian intent to use Didyma to prove its loyalty to the Seleukids.[79] Following Wörrle's work on chronology, this dossier and other treaties containing potential citizenship have been considered Miletos's way to extend its influence in the region by taking advantage of the weakened Seleukid control.[80] An abbreviated form of my textual analysis that recapitulates the content of this inscription can also help to better set the agreement within its complex historical background.

Decree A, LL. 5–11, begins by summarizing the content of a Seleukeian embassy comprised of five men.[81] This summary emphasizes aspects of decree A that differ from decree B, passed by Seleukeia-Tralles, thus revealing the different interests of the two signing cities. Decree A dwells on the provisions Seleukeia voted for Apollo (LL. 8–11 and again LL. 12–13), but it never directly mentions the grant of citizenship that forms the core of decree B. The Seleukeians voted sacrifices to Apollo, but in their decree, they are an appendix to the concession of potential citizenship (LL. 64–66), and, immediately afterward (LL. 67–69), appear the sacrifices for their main god, Zeus Larasios.

The question of the initiative of the agreement is relevant too: the Seleukeian embassy travelled to Miletos in response to the exhortation by a certain Prytanis. This man, thought to be a Milesian, was clearly lobbying for

---

Agathon of *IG* XII.9 218 is the Sosikrates of *Milet.* VI 3 1058, L. 2 (although, as Habicht stresses, without the patronymic). Even if correct, and because *IG* XII.9 218 dates to the first half of the 3rd century BC, the evidence does not necessarily conflict: the same Sosikrates could be attested in *IG* XII.9 218 and *Milet* VI 3 1058 (dating to the second half of the 3rd century BC). I favor the hypothesis that the city briefly returned to the Karian name, at least until conclusive evidence appears for or against this conclusion.

78 On Achaios, see MA 2002, pp. 54–63.
79 See, for example, EHRHARDT 1987, p. 104 with other references.
80 FERNOUX 2004, pp. 117–118 with reference to HERRMANN 2001, esp. p. 112.
81 The group included members of excellent local families, see SHERK 1992, p. 252 who identifies Menodoros with the *stephanephoros* of *ITralles* 26.

Miletos and initiated the contact (decree B, LL. 49–52). He went to Seleukeia to speak; decree B preserves his words following a καὶ μετὰ ταῦτα (L. 49), which must refer to the previous good relationships between Miletos and Seleukeia that were διὰ προγόνων.[82] Prytanis's words echo the Milesian grant of citizenship to the Kians,[83] and respond to the known diplomatic code of the time.

In the introduction I argued that a parallel reading of the two documents reveals that the two cities emphasize different aspects of the same diplomatic contact: the Milesians stress the religious aspect, but the grant of potential citizenship constitutes the core of the Seleukeian text. But I also noted that other themes present in this dossier and their analysis can illuminate the interpretation of the document as a whole.

Kinship

One aspect that deserves attention is the way the two cities presented their kinship connections. L. 4 of decree A, in a restored part of the text, includes a claim of existing 'kinship' from the god: for the Seleukians it is *oikeiotes*, for the Milesians *syngeneia*. In his work on kinship, O. Curty points out that kinship could not have originated from a colonial tie between Miletos and Seleukeia-Tralles since such a past connection did not exist. Rather, he suggests that the *kinship from the god* reflects a Milesian diplomatic plan, without, unfortunately, further elaboration. More controversial is Curty's assertion that in this treaty *syngeneia* and *oikeiotis* are synonyms.[84]

The complexity of the theme recommends caution, but I believe that here kinship must be also read in light of the general tone of the dossier. Each city clearly perceives key topics differently, and I believe kinship should be included here: while from a philological point of view Curty could be right, the content of the dossier makes the use of different terms suspicious. Synonymy alone cannot account for the differences.

The Milesian decree follows a rhetorical scheme that emphasizes the yearly sacrifice to Apollo. In decree A, the god and his cult assume an importance and visibility lacking in decree B. For the Milesians, the fact that kinship (*syngeneia*) originates from the god confirms the centrality of this deity. Exact synonymy is not the point; the Milesians talk of *syngeneia* because the strongest tie could only come from Apollo. For Seleukeia, by contrast, additional colonial ties or mythological common roots must be added to the tie for it to be considered

---

82 On Prytanis see *supra*, p. 11 n. 24.
83 *Milet* I 3 141 = no. 4, LL. 19–23 and 44–47.
84 CURTY 1995, no. 55, who in IDEM 1999, esp. pp. 187–189, argues for his thesis *contra* WILL 1995, pp. 299–325.

the strongest. In other words, Seleukeia and Miletos differed in their perception of kinship because they perceive Apollo Didymaios and, therefore their relationship, differently.[85]

Previous interpretations of this dossier may be valid within their context, but they remain unsatisfactory. Gawantka devotes a few pages to the dossier, but focuses mainly on the Milesian enrollment clauses.[86] He uses these clauses to support his theory on the relationship between geographical distance and precision of enrollment formulae, viz., between the contrasting financial/economic strength of the signing partners and the provisions for potential citizenship. For Gawantka, the detailed Milesian clauses confirm this city's superiority, therefore justifying its 'fear of implementation.'[87] As I noted above, geographical proximity must have affected one partner's perception of the other as well as the possible consequences to their agreements. However, adopting *isopoliteia* did not involve mass movements but rather it could establish a stronger relationship that could become the foundation for further initiatives. Geography impinged the use of this tool only in association with other, preexisting issues (especially territorial ones). In these instances, *isopoliteia* served as a means toward an end (i.e., an agreement). We should not try to read between the lines of texts that do not attest to such situations only because we need to find a practical 'use' for this grant.

Why did these cities decide to grant each other potential citizenship? As I argued in the introduction, this document is almost a manifesto for the diplomatic use of potential citizenship. It shows how the same tool could be perceived differently, even within the same agreement. Here it catalyzes diplomatic contacts between two communities and helps promote a stronger and long-term relationship. The grant is reciprocal without apparent interest for its implementation. Seleukeia demonstrates that it valued the temporary presence of foreigners in town. Miletos might have liked to see more practical (?) consequences from this exchange, but exactly what consequences remains unclear.

---

85   SAMMARTANO 2007, p. 230 argues for different natures of *syngeneia* and *oikeiotes*: "… il concetto manterrà intatta questa funzione specifica nel linguaggio diplomatico ancora fino alla fine dell'età ellenistica, ove i richiami alla *oikeiotes* si riferiscono sempre a relazioni instaurate in anni recenti o che comunque vengono rinnovate nell'attualità, anche tra città non necessariamente imparentate, come nel caso famoso delle relazioni tra Delo e Roma."
86   GAWANTKA 1975, pp. 14–22.
87   GAWANTKA 1975, pp. 78–80.

(6) *Miletos and Mylasa*

The dossier preserving the two decrees from Miletos and Mylasa is inscribed on a stele of white marble with intact frame, now stored in the Pergamon Museum (Inv. no. 675). Measurements: H. 1.74; W. 0.55–0.58; Th. 0.215. Letters: 0.005.

Based on Wörrle's work on the *stephanephoroi*, the accepted date for this decree is the year 215/4 BC. Here I reproduce a few lines of the text from *Milet* I 3 146, excluding the detailed enrollment clauses that are virtually identical with those of *Milet* I 3 143 = no. 5.[88]

12   ... βουλόμενός τε ὁ δῆμος ὁ Μυλασέων ἐπὶ πλέον αὔξεσθαι
     [τὰ] παρ' ἑκατέρων φιλάνθρωπα πεποίηται μετάδοσιν πᾶσι
     [Μ]ιλεσίοις πολιτείας τε καὶ τῶν ἄλλων τῶν ὑπαρχόντων
     παρ' αὐτοῖς τιμίων·

     ἔδοξε τῆι βουλῆι καὶ τῶι δήμωι· γνώμη ἀρχόντων εἰσγραψαμένω[ν]
60   αὐτῶν· ἐπειδὴ Μιλήσιοι φίλοι καὶ οἰκεῖοι ἐξ ἀρχῆς ὑπάρχοντες τοῦ δή-
     μου πᾶσαν σπουδὴν καὶ ἐπιμέλειαν δι[α]τελοῦσιν τῆς πόλεως ποιού-
     μενοι οὐθένα καιρὸν παραλείποντες τῶν εἰς τὸν δῆμον χρησίμων· ὅπω[ς]
     οὖν καὶ Μυλασεῖς φαίνωνται τήν τε οἰκειότητα καὶ τὴν φιλίαν τὴν
64   ὑπάρχουσαν ταῖς πόλεσιν ἀμφοτέραις ἐπαύξοντες καὶ τῶμ παρ' αὐ-
     τοῖς τιμίων τε καὶ ἐνδόξωμ μετάδοσιμ ποιούμενοι Μιλησίοις, ἀγαθῆι
     τύχηι· δεδόχθαι Μυλασεῦσιν· ἐπηνῆσθαι τὸν δῆμον τὸμ Μιλησίων εὐ-
     νοίας καὶ φιλοστοργίας ἕνεκα τῆς πρὸς τὴν πόλιν· καὶ δεδόσθαι πᾶσι Μι-
68   λησίοις πολιτείαν καὶ μετουσίαν ἱερῶν καὶ τῶν λοιπῶν ἁπάντων ὧγ
     καὶ Μυλασεῖς μετέχουσιν καὶ ἔφοδον ἐπὶ τὴμ βουλὴν πρώτοις μετὰ τὰ ἱ[ε]-
     ρά·

Transl.: A, LL. 12–15: Since the *demos* of the Mylaseans wants to increase as much as possible the benefactions from both sides, it grants citizenship to all Milesians and all other existing honors they have. (For the translation of LL. 24–33 see *supra Milet* I 3 143 = no. 5)

B, LL. 59–70 It was decreed by the *boule* and the *demos*; proposal of the *archontes*, who presented it. Since the Milesians, who are friends and kin to the *demos* from the beginning, continuously show all possible regard and care for the *polis* by not overlooking anything useful for our people in any circumstance, and so that the Mylaseans clearly show that they (want) to increase the existing friendship and kinship ties between both

---

88   See Herrmann *Milet* VI 1, *Nachträge*, p. 176.

poleis and want that the Milesians partake in honors and recognitions given by them, to good fortune; be enacted by the Mylaseans to praise the *demos* of the Milesians because of their benevolence and affection for the *polis*. Also, to all Milesians shall be granted citizenship and participation to the sacred matters and all the rest, in which the Mylaseans partake and access to the *boule* first after the sacred matters.

Mylasa

Strabo describes Mylasa as a city of Karian origin located in a fertile plain near a mountain of white marble, which was used to embellish the town.[89] The geographer then notes that Mylasa played a central role in the region for centuries.[90] J. Crampa's publication of the inscriptions from the sanctuary of Labraunda has contributed greatly to modern knowledge of Mylasa's history.[91] Even if the epigraphic evidence does not specifically illuminate the events of the end of the 3rd century BC, when Mylasa signed the treaty under consideration, these texts provide insight into the general context and political atmosphere of this otherwise poorly-known period, especially the decades between 242/1 and 220 BC.[92] The dossier contains the letters between Olympichos and Philip V on the status of Mylasa and on this city's rights to Labraunda. From these texts it is possible to learn that, thanks to the recognition of the Macedonian king in 220 BC, Mylasa had become in effect autonomous and freed from the garrison that probably Seleukos II had stationed in town.[93] Thus the city acquired rights, and, importantly, full financial control over the important suburban sanctuary of Labraunda, which had been under the rule of its powerful priests for decades.

For the years following these events, the evidence is scarce. According to Schmitt, it is unlikely that the city remained under Macedonian influence through 201–197 BC.[94] Still, even if one accepts a renewed Seleukid presence and influence in the area, we have no reason to assume any change in Mylasa's status.

---

89   STRAB. XIV.2.23.
90   STRAB. XIV.2.23–24; REGER 2010.
91   STRAB. XVI.2.23 reports that the city had two main sanctuaries, an urban sanctuary for Zeus Osogos and a suburban sanctuary for Zeus Labraundos, on which see BOFFO 1985, pp. 234–243.
92   See REGER 2010, p. 49.
93   Seleukos II must have imposed the garrison around 246 BC, see BENCIVENNI 2003, ch. 9 and HEUSS 1995, pp. 298–310. Olympichos was to withdraw the garrison soon afterward but he retained it with the excuse that it protected the freedom and democracy of the *polis*, see *ILabraunda* III.i 8, LL. 13–15. See also MA 2002, pp. 150–174.
94   SCHMITT 1964, pp. 243–245.

The Treaty

Scholars associate this agreement with *Milet* I 3 143 = no. 5, although, if we exclude the identical Milesian enrollment clauses, these two documents otherwise have very little in common.

The differences are striking and begin with the very act of the diplomatic initiative: *Milet* I 3 146 reports a Mylasian initiative, while, in the dossier between Miletos and Seleukeia (no. 5), the initiative is Milesian. Another important difference pertains to the grant of potential citizenship: Seleukeia favors a Milesian temporary presence in town (LL. 62–64), while Mylasa's intent is wholly diplomatic as indicated by the general tone and the agreement's only additional grant, *proedria*. Mylasa made a greater effort than Seleukeia in planning the celebration of sacrifices and rites that were meant to guarantee the success of the agreement (LL. 71–78).[95] The different outcomes for which the two cities prayed is also noteworthy: the Seleukians's sacred representatives prayed for safety and good fortune (L. 69). In Mylasa (LL. 88–89), the prayers are ὑπὲρ ὁμο/[νο]ίας καὶ σωτηρίας τῶμ πόλεων ἀμφοτέρων. Ascribing a political meaning here may be an overinterpretation of the text, but the inclusion of the concept of *homonoia* cannot escape our attention. The term normally indicates a (lost) status of harmony and agreement within a community, so that the text may refer to political unrest, of an unknown (to us) nature and intensity.[96] Finally, the most significant difference between the dossiers of *Milet* I 3 143 = no. 5 and 146 = no. 6 is that in *Milet* I 3 146 Miletos and Mylasa do not seem to pursue different goals.

The dossiers share similarities as well. As I noted above, the second half of the decree of Miletos in *Milet* I 3 146 contains enrollment clauses that are virtually identical to *Milet* I 3 143. This correspondence, however, only suggests that the clauses list standard control procedures of the city of Miletos. Finally, Seleukeia and Mylasa both sign the agreements to 'increase' either benevolence or honors (and so on) in order to strengthen their relationships with Miletos, with which they have friendship and kinship.

---

95 On the question of whether Mylasa had a cult of Apollo Didymaios see GEORGOUDI 1998, p. 351 and FONTENROSE 1988, p. 118 esp. n. 20.

96 See GAWANTKA'S comment 1975, p. 120, esp. n. 64. See also DÖSSEL 2002, pp. 179–196; ERSKINE 1990, pp. 90–95; THÉRIAULT 1996, pp. 5–13; De ROMILLY 1972, pp. 199–209.

That this dossier supports the thesis of a Milesian plan to expand its influence in the area is possible, but far from certain. Instead, I must draw attention to Reger's work that suggests that we shift our focus from Miletos to Mylasa in the search for similar interests. Reger has pointed out that Miletos and Mylasa shared a common enemy in Herakleia under Mt. Latmos.[97] Perhaps for this reason, the cities sought to establish a stronger relationship as they could become politically and, potentially, even militarily, significant partners in a near future.

(7)   *Miletos and Herakleia under Mt. Latmos*

This stele of bluish marble was found in the Delphinion in 1903 and is now stored in Berlin (inv. No. 670). The first editor described the writing on the stone as disorderly and rough with letters whose forms vary within the text. Measurements: H. 3.015; W. 0.76–0.80; Th. 0.22–0.18. Letters: 0.012.

Edd.: *ed. pr. Milet* I 3 150; [*Syll.*³ 633].
Cf. Herrmann *Milet* VI 1, *Nachträge*, pp. 185–189.

(Names of Milesian officials) εἶπαν· *vacat* ἐπειδὴ Ἡρακλεῶται φίλοι καὶ ἀστυγείτονες τῆς πόλε⟨ως⟩ ὑπάρχοντες ψήφισμα καὶ πρεσβευτὰς ἀποστείλαντες ἠξίωσαν

12 τὸν δῆμον συνθέσθαι πρὸς αὐτοὺς ὑπὲρ τῆς ἰσοπολιτείας καὶ τῶν ἄλλων φιλανθρώπων, καὶ οἱ πεμφθέντες ὑπ' αὐτῶν Θεόδωρος Αἰνέου, Ἀρχέδημος Δελφίνου, Μαί-

ων Ὑψικλείους ἐπελθόντες ἐπί τε τοὺς ἄρχοντας καὶ τὴν βουλὴν καὶ τὴν ἐκκλησίαν

ἐξέθεντο τὰ κατὰ μέρος, ἐφ' οἷς ἠξίουν τὴν σύνθεσιν, τοῦ τε δ[ή]μου ποιησαμένου τὴν ὑ-

16 πὲρ τούτων ἀναφορὰν ἐπὶ τὸ μαντεῖον τὸ ἐν Διδύμοις ὁ [θ]εὸς χρησμὸν ἐξήνεικεν ἀπο-

φαινόμενος ἄμεινον ἡμῖν ἔσεσθαι συνθεμένοις πρὸς Ἡρακλεώτας, *vv.* δεδόχθαι Μιλησί-

18 οις·

---

97   REGER 2004, esp. p. 169.

(LL. 18–31: cult provisions for a good outcome of the agreement; date and names of the cities' representatives)

εἶναι πολίτας Μιλησίους Ἡρακλεωτῶν καὶ Ἡρακλεώτας Μιλησίων, ὑπάρχειν δὲ αὐτοῖς εἰς ἅ-
παντα τὸν χρόνον τὸν αὐτὸν ἐχθρὸν καὶ φίλον, μηθὲν ὑπεναντίον πρασσόντων τῶν δή-
36 μων τῆι πρὸς Ῥοδίους συμμαχίαι. εἶναι δὲ καὶ ἀμνηστίαν ὡς ἑκατέροις τῶν προγεγενημέ-
νων ἐγκλημάτων κατὰ πόλεμον καὶ ἰδίαι καὶ δημοσίαι, πλὴν εἰ περί τινων ἐγκλημάτων
δίκαι ὑπάρχουσιν γεγραμμέναι ἢ δικαστήριον κατέγνωκεν καὶ εἰ κατά τινων ἀπαγωγαὶ
γεγόνασιν ὑπὸ ἀρχόντων ἐπὶ δημοσίοις ἀδικήμασιν. ἐὰν δέ τις ἴῃ πολέμιος ἐπὶ πό-
40 λιν ἢ χώραν ἢ φρούρια τὰ Μιλησίων ἢ τὰς προσόδους αὐτῶν καταλύῃ τὰς Μιλησίων, βοηθεῖν
Ἡρακλεώτας Μιλησίοις παντὶ σθένει· κατὰ ταὐτὰ δὲ καὶ ἐάν τις ἴῃ πολέμιος ἐπὶ τὴν Ἡρακλεωτῶν πόλιν ἢ χώραν ἢ φρούρια ἢ τὰς προσόδους αὐτῶν καταλύῃ, βοηθεῖν Μιλησίους Ἡρακλε-
ώταις παντὶ σθένει· *vacat* τοὺς δὲ βουλομένους Ἡρακλεωτῶν μετέχειν τῆς ἐμ Μιλήτωι πολ[ι]-
44 τείας καὶ ἱερῶν καὶ ἀρχείων καὶ τῶν λοιπῶν, ὧν καὶ τοῖς ἄλλοις μέτεστι Μιλησί{ων}οις, ἀπο-
γράφεσθαι ἀν' ἕκαστον ἔτος πρός τε τοὺς πρυτάνεις καὶ τοὺς ἡρημένους ἐπὶ τῆι φυλακῆι τά τε αὐτῶν ὀνόματα καὶ ἧς ἂν ὦσιν φυλῆς καί, εἴ τισιν ὑπάρχουσιν γυναῖκες καὶ τέκνα,
καὶ τὰ τούτων ὁμοίως ὀνόματα, ποιουμένους τὴν ἀπογραφὴν ἐν τῶι μηνὶ τῶι Ἀνθεστη-
48 ριῶνι. γίνεσθαι δὲ αὐτῶν καὶ τὴν ἐπικλήρωσιν ἐν τῶι αὐτῶι μηνὶ ὑπό τε τῶν πρυτάνεω[ν]
καὶ τῶν ἡρημένων ἐπὶ τῆι φυλακῆι, ἐπικληρουμένων αὐτῶν πρὸς μέρος ἐφ' ἑκάστην
φυλήν· εἶναι δὲ αὐτοῖς τῶν μὲν λοιπῶν πάντων παραχρῆμα τὴν μετουσίαν, φρο[υ]-
ραρχίας δὲ καὶ φυλακῆς τῆς κατὰ πόλιν καὶ φρουρικῆς μετεῖναι αὐτοῖς διελθόντων

52 ἐτῶν δέκα, ἀφ᾽ οὗ ἂν ἕκαστοι ἐπικληρωθῶσιν· τὰ δὲ ἄλλα τὰ περὶ τὸν κλῆρον
τὸν ἐν ἀρχαιρεσ[ί]-
αις ὑπάρχειν κατὰ τὸν βουλευτικὸν νόμον. εἶναι δὲ καὶ Μιλησίων τοῖς
βουλομένοις ἐν Ἡ-
ρακλείαι πολιτεύεσθαι τὴν ἀπογραφὴν ποιησαμένοις πρὸς τοὺς ἐν Ἡρακλείᾳ
πρυτάνεις ἐμ μη-
νὶ Θεσμοφοριῶνι· ἀπογραφέσθωσαν δὲ καὶ οὗτοι καὶ ἧς ἂν ὦσιν φυλῆς· ὅσοις δ᾽
ἂν ὑπάρχωσιν
56 γυναῖκες καὶ τέκνα, ἀπογράφειν αὐτοὺς καὶ τὰ τούτων ὀνόματα, τοὺς δὲ
πρυτάνεις ποιεῖσ-
θαι αὐτῶν τὴν ἐπικλήρωσιν ὁμοίως ἐν τῶι αὐτῶι μηνί· εἰ δέ τινες Ἡρακλεωτῶν
μὴ ᾠκήκασιν
μήτε ἐν τῆι ἑαυτῶν πατρίδι μήτε ἐμ Μιλήτωι ἕως μηνὸς Ἀρτεμισιῶνος τοῦ ἐπὶ
τοῦ θεοῦ τοῦ
μετὰ Φιλίδαν, μὴ εἶναι αὐτοῖς προσγραφῆναι πρὸς τὸ πολίτευμα τὸ Μιλησίων,
ἐὰν μὴ πρότε-
60 ρον οἰκήσ(ωσ)ιν Ἡράκλε(ι)αν ἢ μετοικήσωσιν ἐμ Μιλήτῳ ἔτη πέντε. *vacat*
ὁμοίως δὲ καὶ εἴ τινες Μιλησίων
μὴ ᾠκήκασιν μήτε ἐν τῆι ἑαυτῶν πατρίδι μήτε ἐν Ἡρακλείαι ἕως τοῦ
προειρημένου χρόνου, μὴ
εἶναι προσγραφῆναι τούτοις ἐν Ἡρακλείαι, ἐὰν μὴ πρότερον οἰκήσωσιν ἐν
Μιλήτωι ἢ ἐν Ἡρα-
κλείαι ἔτη πέντε. καὶ ἐάν τινες ὕστερον πολιτογραφησθῶσιν ἐμ Μιλήτωι ἢ ἐν
Ἡρακλείαι, τούτοι[ς]
64 μετεῖναι τῆς παρ᾽ ἑκατέροις πολιτείας οἰκήσασιν πρότερον ἐν ἧι ἂν π[όλ]ει
προσγραφῶσιν
ἔτη{ι} δέκα. ἐὰν δέ τινες παρὰ τήνδε (τὴν) συνθήκην μετέχωσι τῆς πολιτείας,
εἶναι αὐτοὺς ὑπε[υ]-
θύνους ἐμ Μιλήτωι μὲν τῆι τῆς ξενίας δίκη(ι) καὶ τῆι ἐν μολποῖς ἐνστάσει, ἐν
Ἡρακλείαι δὲ τῆι τῆς ξενίας δίκηι.

Text by Rehm.

LL. 10–18: Since the Herakleians who are friends and neighbors of the *polis* and have sent a decree and ambassadors thought it appropriate to ask that the *demos* reach an agreement with them on *isopoliteia* and the other benefactions, and that those sent by them, namely, (Theodoros son of Aines, Archedemos son of Delphinos, Maion son of Ypsikles), having gone to the *archontes*, the council, and the assembly, explained in detail the terms, under which they wanted to establish an agreement, and since the *demos* consulted the oracle of Didyma on these matters, the god gave a response showing that it is to our advantage to reach an agreement with the Herakleians. (*vacat*) Be enacted by the Milesians (...)

LL. 34–39: (it has been decreed that) the Milesians shall be citizens of the Herakleians and the Herakleians of the Milesians, they shall have the same enemy and friend for all times, both shall never act against the alliance with the Rhodians. An amnesty for the preexisting claims arisen in war on private or public issues shall be proclaimed, except if there are legal written actions already in progress on some claims or a tribunal has passed a judgment or arrests have been issued by the *archontes* against somebody on account of public misdeeds.

LL. 39–43: If anybody goes against the city, territory, or fortresses of the Milesians as an enemy or takes away their revenues, the Herakleians shall help the Milesians with all their strength. According to the same principles, if anybody goes against the city, territory, or fortresses of the Herakleians as an enemy or takes away their revenues, the Milesians shall help the Herakleians with all their strength.

LL. 43–67: Those of the Herakleians who want to partake in citizenship, sacred matters, offices, and all the rest, in which Milesians do, shall register each year at the *prytaneis* and those in charge of security their names and the tribe to which they belong. Also, if they have wives and children (they shall also register) their names, they shall submit the request in the month Anthesterion. (48) In this same month the *prytaneis* and those in charge of security shall distribute them in equal parts in each tribe by lot. They shall partake in everything else immediately, but to the *phrourarchia*, the guard of the city, and that of the fortress they shall have access only 10 years after they have been assigned to the tribes. (52) Everything else that concerns the lot for the offices shall be regulated according to the *nomos bouleutikon*. Those of the Milesians who want to live as citizens in Herakleia, shall register to the *prytaneis* in Herakleia in the month Thesmophorion. They shall register themselves and the tribe to which they belong. Those who have wives and children shall also register them and their names; the *prytaneis* will proceed to distribute them (in the tribes) in the same month. If any of the Herakleians has not lived in his hometown or in Miletos by the month Artemision of the year of the god after that of Philidas, he shall not be allowed to register in the Milesian citizenry, unless he lives for five years either in Herakleia or in Miletos as a foreigner. (60) Equally, if any of the Milesians has not lived in his hometown or in Herakleia for the above stated period, he shall not be allowed to register in Herakleia without living first in Miletos or Herakleia for five years. In case somebody has acquired later citizenship status in Miletos or in Herakleia, they shall be allowed to take part in the citizenship of each of the two cities, provided they have lived in the city whose citizenship they have been granted for 10 years. If anybody lives as a citizen contrary to this agreement, he is liable to prosecution according to the procedures that discipline the matters concerning foreigners in Miletos by the *molpoi*, and in Herakleia, instead, according to the procedures that discipline the matters concerning foreigners.

While scholars seem to agree on the absolute chronology for this text (between 186 and 182/1 BC), the relative chronology of the document within the context of other important examples from this area remains a subject of debate. In particular, in 1989 M. Errington proposed a new date for the peace treaty that Miletos (and Herakleia) signed with Magnesia on the Meander (and Priene) (*Milet* I 3 148), based on the relationship of that text with our inscription (no. 7).[98] Errington redated *Milet* I 3 148 to the 180s BC. Errington not only highlighted the weakness of the old *communis opinio* that dated the text to the year 196 BC, but also noted an inconsistency that had curiously gone unnoticed before, namely, that Miletos and Herakleia collaborate in war in *Milet* I 3 148 but are bitter enemies in no. 7 (*Milet* I 3 150). According to Errington, this important detail makes it necessary to date no. 7 before *Milet* I 3 148.[99] Errington's view quickly became the *communis opinio* and replaced Rehm's date for *Milet* I 3 148, namely, 196 BC.[100] M. Wörrle, who at first supported Errington's thesis, proposed in 2004 to return to Rehm's hypothesis. Wörrle argued that if we direct our focus to no. 7 (*Milet* I 3 150), the point concerning the collaboration between Miletos and Herakleia becomes subordinated to other considerations, especially the issue of Myous's former territory, which had probably been one of the central motives of the war between the two communities.[101]

98 *Milet* I 3 148. For a detailed summary of the debate see LAFFI 2010, pp. 78–79, n. 7.
99 I simplify here the complex questions that Errington has treated well in his work. One point of weakness in his contribution is, perhaps, that in order to argue the case for the new date of *Milet* I 3 148 he moved quickly from the big picture to the details (and *vice versa*) such that the latter, when they are not of a technical nature, are lost to the reader.
100 ERRINGTON 1989, pp. 279–288.
101 WÖRRLE 2004, pp. 45–57, but see HABICHT 2005(b), esp. pp. 137–141 who defends Errington's date.

It is difficult to reconstruct the history of this area at the beginning of the 2nd century BC: as Wörrle noted in his contribution, the literary record is not helpful and, although important inscriptions survive, the epigraphic evidence include significant lacunae.[102] Errington and Wörrle have convincingly argued their cases and shown the weak points of each other's thesis. The persuasiveness of each scholar's argument underscores the uncertain sequence of events in these years. However, despite Errington's compelling and well-argued arguments, Wörrle's considerations on the facts around Myous's territory prompt me to question the view that the peace between Miletos and Magnesia predates the agreement between Miletos and Herakleia. At the same time, however, Habicht has stressed that Rhodes's role in *Milet* I 3 148 can hardly make sense before 188 BC. Wörrle is right to note that there is no easy solution for establishing the relative chronology between these two texts—or the date of *Milet* I 3 148—but, at least, the absolute chronology for our agreement (no. 7) is quite securely anchored in the years between 186 and 182 BC.

The Award of Potential Citizenship

The agreement between Miletos and Herakleia[103] uses the word ἰσοπολιτεία, L. 12, to describe in abstract terms the agreement to be established by the two cities, while the grant that follows uses the normal and current language of *politeia*. This document is a συνθήκη, i.e., a treaty between two cities involved in a local conflict that they hope to solve through diplomacy, probably with the intervention of Rhodes (LL. 34–36).[104] After agreeing on the necessity of establishing the treaty, the two cities go on to regulate controversial issues and set peace conditions: a general amnesty was declared, except for judicial actions already underway or directed to judge crimes against the states (LL. 36–39). Moreover, the cities establish that they will offer defensive military help to one another (LL. 39–43).[105]

The section on potential citizenship, which *de facto* helps to seal the peace, begins in L. 43 and ends in L. 67. LL. 43–65 describe enrollment procedures in both cities through rather standard clauses and specify which offices are available to newcomers and which are not. The text includes provisions for

---

102 WÖRRLE 2004, pp. 44–45.
103 A German project has started an investigation of Herakleia. Its predecessor Latmos (STRAB. XIV 1.8), and the *chora* were studied in the 1970s and the results are in publication. For a short overview of the history of Latmos see PESCHLOW-BINDOKAT 2005, esp. pp. 4–5; for the Hellenistic city see WÖRRLE 1988, pp. 428–448.
104 This conflict may have required arbitration later, see AGER 1996, no. 108.
105 Wörrle 2004, p. 53 notes the association between potential citizenship and military clauses, but I must remind the reader that this feature is quite exceptional for Asia Minor.

Milesians and Herakleians living abroad, as well as for naturalized and future citizens of both communities.[106]

The focus of this treaty is not potential citizenship, but rather the peace process and the provisions meant to regulate the issues that probably had led to war or directly connected to it: LL. 67–77 establish rules for moving possessions from one territory to the other, LL. 78–87 deal with unresolved border disputes (also the area of Myous), LL. 87–99 regulate official behavior toward runaway slaves, and LL. 99–105 deal with ferry fares. Finally, the text preserves a full oath (LL. 105–117) that refers to the peace agreement between Miletos and Herakleia. The oath is unrelated to the grant of potential citizenship, to which parties never swore.

The provisions listed in this long treaty testify to a chaotic situation and to a joint effort to end the war. I share Gawantka's view that this document testifies to the attempt these cities made to establish friendly and fair terms for a peaceful coexistence, but I disagree that no supervising organ was designated to check on the peace process.[107] I would instead argue that the reference to the Rhodians in L. 36 certainly signals a form of external control to the peace process and its implementation.

More important for the grant of potential citizenship and its meaning is that neither city presents clauses to facilitate the temporary presence or, in general, to encourage real economic exchange between Miletos and Herakleia: the war was over but peace probably still at a distance.[108]

The main function of the exchange of potential citizenship in this peace treaty is clearly and undisputably diplomatic: the grant seals the envisioned peace and the peace process that might have been quite fragile. It is worthy of note that before accepting Herakleia's offer, Miletos decided to consult its main god, thus delaying the diplomatic process. Only after a favorable response did the city agree to the signing of the peace treaty and to the settlement of the different issues that this long document lists. The order in which the provisions for *isopoliteia* and the other issues appear is of some interest: *isopoliteia* comes first, not because it was most urgent, but rather because it served as the foundation for the proposed diplomatic solutions. *Isopoliteia* seems to open doors: it was the starting point for a peace and normalization process. The byproduct

---

106 Similar clauses can be found in the Milesian decrees contained in the dossier of Miletos-Seleukeia *Milet* I 3 143 = no. 5, LL. 19–23, and Miletos-Mylasa *Milet* I 3 146 = no. 6, LL. 25–30.

107 GAWANTKA 1975, esp. p. 150.

108 By contrast, Errington interprets the declaration of the first lines that the Herakleians were φίλοι καὶ ἀστυγείτονες as a sign that the relationship had been already somewhat normalized. This understanding, however, openly contradicts the rest of the agreement.

of this concession could certainly have been an exchange of wares and people: increasing contacts between populations could have reinforced and, perhaps even accelerated, the peace process.

(8)   *The Lykian League: Xanthos and Myra*
SEG XLIV 1218 describes the stone on which this text of the agreement between Xanthos and Myra is inscribed as a "rectangular limestone stele with moldings above and below; found in the Letoon." The stele remains at the Letoon (Letoon Inv. 6071). I use the text of the *ed. pr.*

Ed.: *ed. pr.* Bousquet and Gauthier 1994; [SEG XLIV 1218].
Cf. Migeotte 2004, no. 7, pp. 30–31, LL. 1–38 with French translation.

    ἐπὶ ἱερέως τοῦ Ἀπόλλωνος Πτολεμαίου, τῆς δὲ
    Ῥώμης Δαιδάλου, πρὸ πόλεως δὲ Ἀρταπάτου,
    Ἀντίγονος Ἀντιγόνου Ἰοβάτειος καὶ Σύμμα-
4 χος Λυκίσκου ἀστικὸς καὶ Λυκίσκος Εὐέλθον-
    τος καὶ Ἀμύντας Δημέου Σαρπηδόνιοι καὶ Εὔ-
    νομος Πυρρίχου Ἰοβάτειος, οἱ αἱρεθέντες ἄνδρες
    ὑπὸ τοῦ δήμου συγγράψαι καὶ εἰσενεγκεῖν κα-
8 θότι ὑπάρξει ἰσοπολιτεί(α) Ξανθίοις καὶ Μυρεῦσι,
    τάδε συνεγράψαμεν ἔχοντες τὴν κυριείαν
    μετὰ τῶν ἀπεσταλμένων παρὰ Μυρέων ἀν-
    δρῶν, Πλειστάρχου τοῦ Πλειστάρχου, Ἀργαίου
12 τοῦ Σατύρου, Δεξιφάνου τοῦ Τανδασιος,
    ἐχόντων τὴν κυριείαν, ὑπάρχειν ἰσοπο-
    λιτείαν Ξανθίοις καὶ Μυρεῦσι ἐπὶ τοῖσδε,
    ἐφ' ὧι ὅσοι ἂν βούλωνται Ξανθίων ἐν Μύ-
16 ροις προσγράφεσθαι πρὸς τὸ πολίτευμα
    οἴσουσιν γράμματα παρὰ τῶν ἀρχόν-
    των πρ(ὸ)ς τοὺς Μυρέων ἄρχοντας καὶ μεθέξου-
    σιν πάντων καθότι καὶ οἱ ἄλλοι Μυρεῖς μετέ-
20 χουσιν καὶ χρηματίζουσιν ἐν ἧι ἂν φυλῆι ἢ
    δήμωι βούλωνται, καὶ οἱ πρυτάνεις προσγρα-
    φέτωσαν αὐτοὺς εἰς φυλὴν καὶ δῆμον ἐπά-
    ναγκες παραχρῆμα· κατὰ ταὐτὰ δὲ καὶ ὅσοι
24 ἂν Μυρέων βούλωνται προσγράφεσθαι πρὸ[ς]
    τὸ ἐν Ξάνθωι πολίτευμα οἴσουσιν γράμ-
    ματα παρὰ τῶν ἀρχόντων πρὸς τοὺς Ξαν-
    θίων ἄρχοντας καὶ μεθέξουσιν πάντων κα-

28 θότι καὶ οἱ ἄλλοι Ξάνθοι μετέχουσιν καὶ χρη-
   ματιοῦσιν ἐν [ἧ]ι ἂν φυλῆι ἢ δήμωι βούλωνται
   καὶ οἱ πρυτάνεις προσγραφέτωσαν αὐτοὺς
   εἰς φυλὴν καὶ δῆμον ἐπάναγκες παραχρῆμα.
32 ὅσοι δ' ἂν μετὰ τήνδε τὴν σύνθεσιν Ξάν-
   θιοι ὄντες προσγράφωνται πρὸς τὸ πολίτευμα ἐν ἑκατέραι τῶν πόλεων, μὴ ἐξέστω
   αὐτοῖς λαβοῦσι γράμματα προσγράφεσθαι,
36 ἐὰν μὴ ᾠκηκότες ὦσιν ἐν τῆι πόλει ἢ τοῖς
   περ[ι]πολίοις, ὅθεν ἂν φέρωσιν τὰ γράμματα,
   ἔτη τρία. ἐξέστω δὲ καὶ διορθώσασθαι τήνδε τὴν σύνθεσιν κατὰ τὸ κοινῆι συμφέρον
40 (πρεσβευσαμένα)ις ταῖς πόλεσι πρὸς αὐτάς.
   (ἀναγραφῆναι δὲ τ)ήνδε τὴν σύνθεσιν εἰς
   (στήλας λιθίνας δ)ύο καὶ ἀνατεθῆναι τὴμ
   (μὲν μίαν ὑπὸ) Ξανθίων ἐν τῶι ἱερῶι τῆς Λητοῦς,
44 (τὴν δὲ ἄλλη)ν ὑπὸ Μυρέων ἐν τῶι ἱερῶι τῆς[109]
                    Ἀρτέμιδος

LL. 7–39: (LL. 1–7 offices/priesthoods and names) those chosen by the *demos* to compose and introduce (the proposal) according to which *isopoliteia* shall be in place between Xanthioi and Myrioi. We wrote (the proposal) that follows, being plenipotentiary, together with the men sent by the Myrioi, (LL. 11–12: names) who are also plenipotentiary (ambassadors). *Isopoliteia* shall be in place between Xanthioi and Myrioi according to the following conditions: those among the Xanthioi who want to be registered in the community in Myra shall bring a document (γράμματα) (enacted from their) *archontes* to Myra's *archontes* and shall partake in all things in which the Myrioi do and be included either in a *phyle* or in a *demos* of their choice. The *prytaneis* must register them in a *phyle* and a *demos* without delay. According to the same rules, those among the Myrioi who want to be registered in the community in Xanthos (as citizens) shall bring a document of (their) *archontes* to those of the Xanthioi and partake in all things in which the Xanthioi do and be included either in a *phyle* and in a *demos* of their choice. The *prytaneis* must register them in a *phyle* or in a *demos* without delay. As far are those who, having

---

109 LL. 40–44: the mason did not engrave several letters at the beginning of each of the last four lines, but rather painted them later. The painted letters have disappeared but can be restored because they belong to standard formulae.

become Xanthioi (or Myrioi) after the establishment of this agreement, are inscribed (as citizens) in each community, they cannot obtain the document to be registered (in the other city), unless they have lived in the city or the *peripolioi*, from which they receive the document, for at least three years. It shall be possible to modify this agreement to common advantage by means of exchange of embassies. (...)

Gauthier published and commented on this text in 1994. Most of his results must be retained,[110] including his proposed chronology. The presence of the priest of the goddess Rome, LL. 1–2, should be the main dating criterion of the inscription (*terminus post quem*). The (evolving) *communis opinio* indeed holds that this cult was introduced in Lykia after 167/6 BC. However, Gauthier argues for a slightly later date, 150–120 BC, when the general peaceful situation allowed Lykian cities to assert their autonomy within the league.[111]

The focus of this document is indeed isopolity. In the *editio princeps* Gauthier notes that the text is an example of the underrepresented category of *reine Isopolitievereinbarungen*, thus citing Gawantka.[112] The text describes the concession of the grant and the procedure to switch citizenship with long and detailed enrollment clauses,[113] in a quite straightforward way that, *pace* Gauthier, is not unparalleled in its more unusual provision.[114] In LL. 15–18 and LL. 24–27, the text prescribes that applicants seeking inscription as citizens in the register

---

110 A few revisions are necessary. SCHULER 2010, pp. 77–81 published the *ed. pr.* of a new inscription from Patara's territory that prompts us to reconsider the nature of the priesthoods listed also in the prescript of *SEG* XLIV 1218. GAUTHIER 1994, p. 323 identified all as civic priesthoods, but Schuler holds that the first two are league priesthoods and the third, *pro poleos*, describes a civic, eponymous sacred office; see REITZENSTEIN 2011, esp. p. 75. LL. 3–12 also deserve a short note: the inscription testifies to three civic subdivisions—*Iobateoi, Sarpedonioi*, and *astykoi*—that the *communis opinio*, see WÖRRLE 1999, p. 359 and GAUTHIER 1994, pp. 326–328, has long held to be tribes. However, a new text (albeit an ineditum from Xanthos mentioned in *SEG* LV 1502, *app. crit.*) specifies their nature in this way: τοῦ δήμου Ἰοβατείου. Their exact function remains unclear.

111 GAUTHIER 1994, p. 324 and 347, see also BEHRWALD 2000, pp. 49–115.

112 GAUTHIER 1994, p. 328. This 'category,' however, does not quite stand alone: cities often regulate other aspects of the relationship through '*isopoliteia* treaties.'

113 GAUTHIER 1994, pp. 326–328 translates the enrollment clauses, LL. 20–21 and 29, as if καί rather than ἤ had joined the terms for deme and tribe, as it instead appears in LL. 23 and 31, but see the comment by WÖRRLE 1999, p. 360 esp. n. 25. Had this translation been correct, one could conclude that like in many other areas of the Greek world, in Lykia too, tribes and demes coexisted, with the second a subunit of the first. This translation, however, is not accurate: the text prescribes that those who intend to switch citizenship should enroll either in a tribe *or* in a deme.

114 GAUTHIER 1994, pp. 333–334.

of the partner *polis* had to present to the officials of their new city a document enacted by the officials of their native/old community. This procedure is not unknown: the treaty between Miletos and Kios lists a similar requirement and, most likely, evidence from Crete preserves analogous prescriptions.[115]

Further comparisons with Milesian texts are possible and Gauthier has already commented on them in detail. Still the most relevant analogy deserves mention because it pertains to these communities' concern for the use of the grant on the part of naturalized citizens.[116] In Lykia the new citizens had to wait three years before they could switch citizenship, as long as they resided in their new community during this time, LL. 32–38.[117] Similarly, in Miletos new citizens had to wait for five or 10 years before being able to take advantage of a newly signed *isopoliteia* agreement.[118]

Finally, the text includes a renegotiation clause, LL. 38–40, allowing changes to the treaty at any time, provided such changes were agreed upon by means of embassies.[119]

Reading *Isopoliteia*

This agreement preserves rather standard provisions for a grant of potential citizenship. Although this institution must have been well known in this part of the Greek world in the 2nd century BC, as a document Bousquet and Gauthier 1994= *SEG* XLIV 1218 (no. 8) is too isolated to allow any hypothesis on why it was signed or on its wider institutional implications for Lykia. Because the two communities involved were members of the same league, its procedural 'normality' stands out. Except for the disputed example of the stipulation of potential citizenship among the members of the Lesbian *Koinon* in its foundation act, this text is the only known case of two members of the same league signing an agreement of *isopoliteia*. Obviously, this has not gone unnoticed in scholarship.

Gauthier remarks that our document impacts the way in which we see 'federal citizenship' in Lykia. The known evidence for federal citizenship and its advantages date to Lykia's imperial period, while any evidence for the Hellenistic age is utterly lacking. This treaty then could signal that member *poleis* of the

---

115 See *Milet* I 3 141 = no. 4, LL. 39–41; see *infra* on Crete with my commentary to *I.Cret.* III.iv 1 = CHANIOTIS 1996, pp. 185–190, no. 5 = no. 47.
116 GAUTHIER 1994, esp. pp. 337–338.
117 They could live either in the city or in the "*peripolia*," on which see SCHULER 1996, esp. pp. 45–49.
118 Details in GAUTHIER 1994, esp. pp. 337–338 and in the chapter devoted to Miletos's evidence on potential citizenship.
119 See GAUTHIER 1994, esp. p. 343.

koinon at this time did not enjoy the privileged status that membership seems to have entailed later.[120]

One striking feature of this agreement is the absence of any indication of the reason behind its signing.[121] Diplomatic niceties are absent from this text, which is instead a register of the agreed upon procedures for switching citizenship. Even if this characteristic alone has no probationary meaning, it could be a sign that cities, in this period, worked as separate units within the *koinon*, at least in the area of citizenship.

Disputed Cases from Miletos

As I noted in the brief introduction to the section on Milesian evidence, the epigraphic record preserves five texts that have been considered grants of potential citizenship.

Apart from the extremely fragmentary agreement between Miletos and an unknown city (Antioch on the Maeander?), I am skeptical of these identifications. The arguments that favor *isopoliteia* are often extremely fragile and rely either on fragmentary lines that recall similar wording in other texts or on kinship claims. If correct (in other words, if these texts include concessions or exchanges of potential citizenship), the result would be that Miletos tried to extend its diplomatic net quite widely by adopting *isopoliteia*.

(9)   *Tenos*
A stele of white marble broken on all sides (measurements: H. 0.58; L. 0.43; Th. 0.08) preserves a text engraved in four columns.[122] Scholarly attention has focused on col. III, LL. 44–48, with Graindor's restoration thus:

44 Ὄκιμβις· / ἐπὶ τούτου / Τηνίοις / ἐμ Μιλήτωι / (48) ἀτέλεια π[ο]λ[ιτεία?].

Even if the inscription contains a list of Tenian eponymous archons we cannot establish its exact chronology.[123] Graindor notes that columns II through

---

120   GAUTHIER 1994, p. 347; LARSEN 1968, pp. 5–26. Too little is known about the institutions in this region for the Hellenistic period. I prefer to avoid general assumptions on the theme of federal citizenship, but, for example, REITZENSTEIN 2012, p. 153 argues that Lykians had citizenship in more than in one city in the league on the basis of later evidence from the imperial period.

121   GAUTHIER 1994, p. 336 suggests that the detailed clauses and the absence of any other indications mean that this agreement had been signed to be implemented.

122   Edd. GRAINDOR *MB* 15, 1911, 253; *IG* XII *Suppl.* 312. Cf. ROBERT *OMS* I, pp. 204–209.

123   Col. I, LL. 1–4: οἵδε ἦρξαν / ἀπὸ Τιμησίωνος / διιστά[μεν]ο[ι] / κατ᾽ ἐνι[αυ]τόν·
      On Tenos see ÉTIENNE 1990; on the history of the island in the early Hellenistic period see REGER 1992, pp. 363–387.

IV are older than column I, which was engraved by a different hand. The most likely hypothesis is that columns II through IV were engraved in ca. 300 BC and column I in the mid-2nd century BC.[124]

The last fragmentary line of column III preserves only a few of letters of a last word that has been restored ambitiously, but not impossibly, as *politeia*.[125] Following this restoration, scholars have suggested that the document testifies indirectly to a grant of potential citizenship to the Tenians by Miletos. Gawantka comments: "höchst unsicheres indirektes Zeugnis für eine einseitige Verleihung."[126] I can only share his view, except to note that the seemingly unilateral character of the grant is also an educated guess.

(10)   *Amyzon*

Two adjoining fragments from a marble anta with letters of the 3rd century BC preserve a very fragmentary text whose interpretation is highly controversial.

The text I include here is complete and relies on the *ed. pr.* by J. and L. Robert.[127]

    τὸν μὲν στεφα[νηφόρον μετὰ τῶν προσεταίρων εὔ]-
    ξασθαι τῶι τε Ἀπόλλ[ωνι τῶι Δελφινίωι καὶ τοῖς]
    ἐντεμενίοις θεοῖς - - - - -
4   Μιλησ[ί]οις ἐπιτελέ[σαι θυσίας καὶ προσόδους]
    ἱερῶν τὰς νομιζο[μένας - - - - - - -]
    ΣΑΒΑΕΙΣ καὶ ΥΜ [- - - - - - - - - - -]
    τού[τ]ων ἐγγόν[οις - - - - - - - - - -]
8   Λ- - καὶ τῶν [- - - - - - - - - - - - -]
    - - - ΥΛΑΚ [- - - - - - - - - - -]

---

124 Column III must have been engraved during the period when Miletos signed agreements of potential citizenship with Olbia, Kyzikos, and Phygela. REHM, *Delphinion* (*Milet* I 3), p. 293 suggests that the alleged grant to Tenos belongs to the same years and Milesian political plan. As GAUTHIER 1992 also demonstrates, this hypothesis is extremely problematic. In particular see GAUTHIER 1992, p. 116 n. 20, where he admits a date between 313–300 BC for *ateleia*, but also suggests that the concession of *politeia* (?) could be much earlier, around the end of the 5th century BC. For parallels, he cites two examples: the grant of Athens to Samos, *IG* I³ 127, 405 BC, on which see the appendix *infra*, and the grant used by the city of Antandros to honor the Syracusans, XENOPH. *Hell.* I.1.26, in 410 BC, which, however, attests only to a concession of citizenship to those Syracusans who actually helped the city of Antandros. See also GAWANTKA 1975, pp. 173–174.

125 A very intriguing restoration for line 48 has been suggested to me anonymously, namely, ἀτελεία π[ά]γ[των]. This restoration would eliminate the grant of potential citizenship and specify the type of tax exemption that had been awarded.

126 See GAWANTKA 1975, p. 213 (his no. 36).

127 *Ed. pr.* J. and L. ROBERT, *Amyzon* 1983, pp. 215–217 no. 15 (ph.). PONTANI 1997, pp. 5–8 offered a new edition with difficult restorations; the most recent edition is in Herrmann *Milet* VI.3 1050; cf. Brixhe *BE* 1998 388.

J. and L. Robert published the text in their work devoted to Amyzon. Literary sources mention this town only to describe it as a 'minor' city.[128] Amyzon supported itself through the temple of Artemis, which probably existed already in the 6th century BC and had been declared inviolable at some point.[129]

The text is very fragmentary, with its content and context obscure. J. and L. Robert suggest that it preserves a Milesian decree and compare especially L. 4 (prayers to Apollo) to other *isopoliteia* decrees from Miletos, namely, the examples stipulated with Seleukeia-Tralles and Mylasa, and the peace treaty with Herakleia.[130] The Roberts suggest another similarity between this text and the agreements that Miletos signed with Seleukeia and Mylasa: the restoration of L. 9 could include part of the attested Milesian clause to exclude new citizens from the most delicate military offices.[131]

Is this example then another decree by Miletos granting *isopoliteia*? This proposal is daring and highly uncertain: the apparent order of the clauses within the text is already quite unusual for a document testifying to a grant of potential citizenship. In the treaties that Miletos signed with Seleukeia and Mylasa, for example, the clause on the exclusion of new citizens from these offices appears in sections that establish the procedures to switch citizenship, while the mention of the *stephanephoros* and sacrifices come last. The order differs in the agreement with Herakleia under Mt. Latmos, where several clauses divide these two elements. This circumstance, however, is not a strong argument. L. 7 of the text from Amyzon instead may carry more weight as an argument against isopoly: this line indeed preserves a reference to descendants, ἐγγόν[οις, which is difficult to contextualize in a grant of potential citizenship. Unless we assume that the city had granted additional honors for Amyzonian ambassadors and their descendants, honors that are otherwise unattested in the other known Milesian grants, the reference is difficult to accommodate. Finally, Pontani's suggestion that LL. 6 and 7 contain *ethnika* of two Karian places would result in another unparalleled clause that hardly fits within the context of a concession of potential citizenship.[132]

The text seems to me only the end of an agreement of unclear nature completed by honors *ad personam*.

---

128   J. and L. ROBERT 1983, introduction and pp. 25–29.
129   RIGSBY 1996, pp. 335–338.
130   J. and L. ROBERT 1983, p. 216.
131   For example, *Milet* I 3 143 = no. 5, LL. 29–39.
132   L. 5/6 [Μεσ]σαβεῖς καὶ Ὑμ[εσσεῖς] Pontani, on which HERRMANN *Milet* VI 3 1050 comments thus: "In welchem Zusammenhang diese beiden nicht näher lokalisierbaren Orte hier erwähnt sein sollen, ist unklar."

(11) Histros

L. Robert joined two fragments of a stele that can be dated to first half the 3rd century BC and interpreted its fragmentary beginning as that of an agreement of potential citizenship possibly between Histros and Miletos. This identification relies on kinship claims, which are extremely common in the 4th century BC,[133] and on its similarity to other potential citizenships that Miletos signed with its colonies.[134] The eventual concession is completely lost and any further consideration would be highly speculative.

(12) Unknown City (Antioch on the Maeander?)

Milet I 3 144[135] is a fragmentary text that probably dates to the same decades as *Milet* I 3 143 = no. 5 and 146 = no. 6. The fragments of the stone preserve only the final part of two decrees that must have constituted a dossier like the agreements Miletos signed with Seleukeia-Tralles and Mylasa. The partner community is an unknown city that has been identified tentatively as Antioch on the Maeander.[136] Antioch's proximity reinforces this identification, but certainty remains elusive: identification relies on the name of a month that appears in L. 2 of the second decree (... τ]οῦ Διοσκουριῶνος μ[ηνὸς ...) and the name of what must have been the primary god of the town in L. 3 (... τ]ῶι τε Διὶ τῶι Ὁμοβουλίωι).

But the grant of potential citizenship is no longer recorded on stone and this text cannot be considered a secure piece of evidence.

(13) Apollonia on the Rhyndakos

The inscription that preserves Apollonia's attempt to reconstruct its Milesian origins in an embassy to Miletos contains only the first part of the decree.[137]

133　ROBERT *OMS* I, pp. 99–101. The text is interesting in this regard because it preserves both 'types' of kinship, *syngeneia* and *oikeiotes*, to describe the kinship relationship between Miletos and Histros. One is tempted to read the terms as synonyms.

134　*Milet* VI 3 1051: Μι[λησίων] / Ἔδοξε τῆι βουλῆι καὶ [τῶι δήμωι, γνώμη ἐπ]ιστατῶ[ν, ὁ δεῖνα] / Ἀναξιθέμιος εἶπεν· ἐπε[ιδὴ Ἰστριανοί, φίλ]οι καὶ συγγ[ενεῖς ὄντες] / τοῦ δήμου, διαφυλάσ[σοντες τὴμ προϋπ]άρχουσαν [αὐτοῖς πρὸς] / τὴμ πόλιν οἰκειότητα [καὶ φίλιαν, ἔν τε] τοῖς πρότερο[ν χρόνοις] / διετέλου[ν] εὔ[νου]ς ὑ[πάρχοντες κοινῆι] τε τῶι δήμ[ωι τῶι Μιλη]/[σίων καὶ ἰδίαι ------]. Histros was located on the west coast of the Black Sea on the homonymous river, where Miletos founded it around 650–600 BC: EHRHARDT 1988, pp. 71–72.

135　*StV* III 538; HERRMANN *Nachträge*, pp. 177–178.

136　See J. and L. ROBERT *BE* 1970 502 referring also to the observations by ROUSSEL 1916, pp. 185–187. On Antioch see COHEN 1995, pp. 250–253; STRAB. XIII.4.15.

137　*Milet* I 3 155, Herrmann *Nachträge* pp. 193–194. The text dates to the middle of the 2nd century BC according to paleography; it is now stored in Berlin (Inv. no. 728). A summary of the debate on the historicity of Apollonia's claim appears in Herrmann *Nachträge*

The stone breaks off just before the expected list of the actual provisions and requests of this city.

It is Gauthier who suggested, very cautiously, that the inscription includes potential citizenship, together with the claim of kinship and colonial relations.[138] This proposal remains, however, only a hypothesis.

Reassessing the Use of the Award of Potential Citizenship in Miletos

The publication of the rich dossier of Milesian inscriptions at the beginning of the 20th century confirmed the working definition of potential citizenship established by Szanto in 1892. Szanto's work followed more than an intuition and the evidence has demonstrated his good understanding of the Greek legal mentality.

Miletos made wide use of the institution, which may have helped to increase its popularity in Asia Minor. The town mostly used potential citizenship in diplomatic contexts that probably aimed at building long-term relationships. The inclusion of the grant in the peace treaty that Miletos signed with Herakleia under Mt. Latmos (and also in less clearly defined diplomatic situations, such as, for example, that pertaining to Kios and Mylasa), shows that the Ionian community used this tool to its full potential. The idea that this institution was used as an instrument to replenish Miletos's citizen body cannot be supported. The analysis of the historical background to the Milesian treaties containing grants of potential citizenship indicates that demographic needs cannot have been the reason for their stipulation, but rather a more complex set of motivations emerges. These motivations connect to the political and also, in general, socio-cultural landscape of the Hellenistic world at large. Agreeing to a treaty that would depopulate one's city (i.e., the partner city) is quite counterintuitive, although isopolity certainly encouraged mobility.

---

pp. 193–194: ROBERT, *OMS* IV, pp. 292–294 argues that Apollonia was a Milesian colony, *contra* SEIBERT 1963, pp. 197–200. For EHRHARDT 1988, p. 47 the town was a Milesian refoundation, while ABMEIER 1990, pp. 6–16 holds that Apollonia had recently been an Attalid colony that based the story of its Milesian origin on another nearby Milesian site, Miletouteichos. See CURTY 1995, no. 58 on *syngeneia*. Briefly on this text and the language of diplomacy, to echo Jones's expression, in JONES 1999, p. 64.

138 GAUTHIER 1972, p. 361, n. 41. Gawantka does not include this text.

Potential citizenship is best described as a seal to agreements related to matters of shared political, diplomatic, commercial (perhaps), and religious interests. This assessment is valid even when the grant is the main focus of an accord, as for example it happens in the treaty between Miletos and Mylasa. Following a recent suggestion by G. Reger, this diplomatic exchange may foreshadow a joint force against a common enemy, Herakleia under Mt. Latmos. If confirmed, this use would once more show the diplomatic force of this instrument in cementing or creating relationships that may define alliances and change the political balance of a region.

Finally, despite the temptation to consider Miletos the cradle of *isopoliteia*, no direct evidence exists to support this hypothesis.

CHAPTER 2

Magnesia on the Meander and Samos

The Epigraphic Record

The largest known *asylia* dossier comes from Magnesia on the Maeander. The city launched its campaign for the recognition of the games for Artemis as crown games and for the inviolability of city and sanctuary in ca. 207 BC.[1] One, or perhaps two, of the three inscriptions that may attest to the use of potential citizenship on the part of this city belong to or could be related to this dossier. A fourth text preserves indirect evidence for an exchange of potential citizenship between Magnesia and Samos (no. 17). Finally, scholars classify an agreement between Magnesia and Phokaia (no. 19), as 'isopolity,' but I hold that this document contains no such grant.

Magnesia does not seem to have used this grant extensively: this statement, however, does not rely on the quantity of the surviving evidence, but rather on its *quality*. Two out of the four treaties that may preserve this grant, concern Magnesia's diplomatic relationship with Crete, with which it claimed to have colonial ties and where potential citizenship was routinely used. More precisely, these two documents testify to Magnesia's attempt to establish anew or to strengthen an existing relationship with Crete. One agreement (*I.Magn.* 20 = no. 14) comprises a 'fictional' document allegedly promoted by the Cretan *koinon* with the Thessalian colonists upon their departure to found Magnesia, the second (*I.Cret.* III.iii 3C = no. 16) contains the response of Hierapytna to a diplomatic Magnesian mission that was probably directed at several Cretan cities. The first text (*I.Magn.* 20 = no. 14) is significant because it shows how Magnesia drew from a repertoire of shared 'historical' memories to create anew a solid diplomatic foundation for future agreements with Crete. The text also accomplished its goal by adding a list of several privileges for the founders of Magnesia, including *politeia*, which would cement the idea and feeling

---

[1] *IMagn.* 18–87; for the *asylia* dossier see RIGSBY 1996, pp. 179–279. For the date of the quest(s) see now SOSIN 2009 who argues against Kern's theory that Magnesia's first attempt to obtain this privileged status failed in 221/0 BC. Excavations in the agora, where the dossier was inscribed in a perimeter wall, took place at the beginning of the 20th century, see HUMANN 1904; excavations have been recently resumed, see BINGÖL 2005, pp. 165–170. On the sanctuary see STRAB. XIV.1.39; RIGSBY 1996, pp. 179–182; BOFFO 1985, pp. 196–203.

of belonging to a single, once closely connected community. For this reason, the agreement is often associated with and compared to the well-known oath of the founders from Kyrene (*SEG* IX 3 = no. 15), which some scholars have argued grants potential citizenship, too (to the Thereans). In what follows I argue against this view, because it reflects the unqualified and ahistorical use of the concept of *isopoliteia*, as I noted above in the introduction.

Two texts from Magnesia normally considered as containing a grant of potential citizenship include agreements that Magnesia signed with neighboring communities, namely, Samos (*I.Magn.* 103 = no. 17) and Phokaia (*I.Magn.* 7b = no. 19). The latter, however, is not an award of isopolity: it testifies only to other types of concessions for Phokaians and to participation in 'everything' (with the *metechein* clause) for those Phokaians who lived in Magnesia. In this agreement *politeia* does not appear. By contrast, the term does not appear in the agreement with Hierapytna (*I.Cret.* III.iii 3C = no. 16), which also records a *metechein* clause, but where the word must have been forgotten. *I.Cret.* III. iii 3C = no. 16 is a Cretan decree passed by the city of Hierapytna that uses the language and forms of Cretan decrees. I cannot therefore discard the idea that this agreement concedes isopolity even if the word *politeia* does not appear.

The surviving evidence from and for Magnesia testifies to a sporadic, rather late, historically and geographically confined use of this tool; potential citizenship seems to have been a limited experience for Magnesia.

Samos was one of Magnesia's partners in isopoly (*I.Magn.* 103 = no. 17). For this island a general policy regarding the use of potential citizenship is difficult to determine. The available evidence amounts only to two indirect testimonies that suggest that in Samos potential citizenship was a better known and probably more widely used diplomatic tool than we can appreciate. Samos deserves a separate treatment because, these two pieces of evidence aside, a 5th-century BC agreement with Athens (*IG* I³ 127 see appendix 1) probably foreshadows this practice. This agreement may indicate that in this geographical area the tool may have been first forged and used first.

(14) Magnesia and the Cretan Koinon

The inscription covered three blocks, but the third block and thus the end of the text, is lost. The historical value of the text may be minimal, but it is a very impressive piece of evidence for the perception of history and past on of a Greek, Hellenistic city, and for this reason the text deserves to be cited almost in full.

πα[ρ]ὰ τοῦ κοινοῦ τῶν Κρητῶν·
[ἔ]δοξεν Κ[ρ]ηταιέων τῶι κοινῶι συνελ-
[θ]ουσᾶν [τ]ᾶμ πολίων πασᾶν ἐς Βίλκω-
4   να ἐς τὸ ἱε[ρ]ὸν τῶ Ἀπέλλωνος τῶ Βιλ-
κωνίω, ἁγουμένων Γορτυνίων ἐπὶ
κόσμω(ι) Κύδαντος τῶ Κυννίω· ἐπειδὴ Μάγνητες οἰκεῖοί ἐντι καὶ φίλοι Κρη-
8   ταιέων πάντων, ἔδοξεν δέ τισιν αὐτῶν ἐς τὰν Ἀσίαν ἀποικίαν στείλασθαι,
ὑπάρχειν Μάγνησιν πᾶσιν οἰκειότατα
καὶ φιλίαν ἀγήρατον καὶ ἐμ πρυτανεί-
12   ωι σίτησιν, καὶ εἰσάγουσιν καὶ ἐξάγουσιν ἀτέλειαν εἶμεν ἀσύλει καὶ ἀσπονδεὶ κατὰ πᾶ-
σαγ Κρήταγ καὶ ἔγκτησιν καὶ πολιτείαν,
δόμεν δὲ αὐτοῖς ἀποπλέουσιν ἑκάστα[μ]
16   πόλιν ἀργυρίω τέσσαρα τάλαντα κα[ὶ σῖ]-
τομ πεπονημένον καὶ ἱερεῖα ὅσ' ἂν θέ[λω]-
[σ]ι̣ν [α]ὐ̣[τ]οὶ εἰς θυσίαν, [π]ροπέμψαι [δὲ]
αὐτοὺς μέχρι εἰς τὰν Ἀσίαν ταῖς μακραῖς
20   ναυσὶν καὶ συμπέμψαι αὐτοῖς τοξό-
τας εἰς πεντακοσίους ἄνδρας, προ-
πέμψαι δὲ καὶ ἀσπάσασθαι αὐτοὺς καὶ
ἄνδρας καὶ παῖδας καὶ γυναῖκας καθ' ἁ-
24   λικίαν καὶ τοὺς ἱερεῖς καὶ τὰς ἱερείας·
(…) provisions on the publication of the stele follow

Text from *I.Magn.* 20.

Transl.: From the *koinon* of the Cretans. It was resolved by the Cretan *koinon* when all the cities came together to Bilkon to the sanctuary of Apollo Bilkonion, according to the way the Gortynians reckon when Kydas son of Kynnios was *kosmos*. Since the Magnesians are kin and friends of all Cretans, it was decided by some of them to send a colony to Asia, and that all Magnesians have kinship (*oikeiotes*) and perennial friendship and *sitesis* in the *prytaneion*, and shall import and export free of taxes with personal inviolability and without need of agreements in all of Crete, and they shall have the right to ownership and citizenship, to those who sail each city shall give four silver talents and grain produced with toil and as many sacrificial animals as they want to sacrifice. (They) shall escort them up to Asia with great ships and up to 500 archers shall go with them as well, they shall escort and say goodbye to the men, youths, women according to age and priests and priestesses. (...)

This text completes the Cretan part of the general narrative of Magnesia's foundation as it is attested in *I.Magn.* 17. This part of the Magnesian dossier on *asylia* tells of the long stop made by Thessalian colonists on the island before they moved on to Asia Minor where they founded Magnesia.[2]

The decree under consideration should have been enacted in the 7th century BC by an organization (the Cretan *Koinon*) that did not exist until the middle of the 3rd century BC and, even then, did not encompass all of Crete.[3] Although the content of this decree is 'fictional,' it deserves consideration because it is the product of Magnesia's historical thinking and it contains a few other interesting elements.

In the past, scholars have associated the decree with Magnesia's need to defend itself against Cretan piracy,[4] but its inclusion in the *asylia* dossier, and especially in its opening, may point to a different explanation. Another possibility, for example, is that with this document Magnesia attempted to legitimize its origins and history in view of the signing of agreements with its Cretan counterparts. Defense from Cretan piracy could have been a result of this relationship, but not the reason for it.

One striking feature of this text is the attention it devotes to language, events, and institutions as it tries to accurately reproduce them.[5] Its content must be summarized: the text begins with the details of the occasion on which this text should have originated and its alleged date (LL. 1–6), then continues with the definition of the relationship between Magnesia and the Cretans

---

[2] MERKELBACH and STAUBER 1998, pp. 180–186; on the language see CHANIOTIS 1999(b), p. 69; on Magnesia's foundation, its traditions, and the ties with Crete see BIAGETTI 2010, pp. 42–64 and PRINZ 1979, pp. 111–137, with *testimonia* 83–93; see also PIERART 1974, esp. pp. 7–12.
[3] CHANIOTIS 1999(a), pp. 287–299 and IDEM 1996, pp. 29–36 with previous bibliography.
[4] For example, PERLMAN 1999, pp. 132–161.
[5] See again CHANIOTIS 1999(b), pp. 61–64 and p. 69.

(one of familiarity and friendship)[6] and the story of the planned expedition to Asia Minor (LL. 7–24). Within the second section, LL. 11–14 preserve honors and privileged conditions that the Magnesians were to enjoy in Crete for all times: *sitesis* in the *prytaneion*, the right of import/export secure and free of taxes, the right to ownership, and, the text adds, *politeia*. This list has been proven to be anachronistic from an institutional point of view for the 7th century BC. However, the reader has the impression that this list's main goal was to reproduce the general Cretan practice of grant-giving and, in this pseudo-institutional framework, *politeia* had to be included. It would take a leap of faith or, better, a much different mindset, to consider this document a basis for renewals of grants. Conceptually, this text was more than a simple attempt to create a precedent: as part of a historical narrative that starts in *I.Magn.* 17, this document serves to legitimize the colonial history, i.e., the roots, of this *polis*. It preserves the memory of the historical and sacred foundation of Magnesia, or its cultural heritage, with contemporary terminology. Calling the text a forgery belittles the historical process of how an important community of Asia Minor represents itself.

In this context, the alleged and popular *comparandum* to the Magnesian-Cretan text, the stele of the founders from Kyrene (*SEG* IX 3 = no. 15), deserves discussion and, with it, the theme of the weight that colonial ties carried in Hellenistic diplomacy.[7]

---

6   See SAMMARTANO 2008/9, whose interpretation of the Magnesian quest I do not always share.
7   *SEG* IX 3; M&L 5; DOBIAS-LALOU 1994, pp. 243–246 (I use this latest edition of the text). This document is often compared with *I.Magn.* 20 = no. 14, but GRAHAM (1960) 2001, p. 94 notes: "The Magnesian document confines itself to specifying privileges and illustrating the great cordiality (the role given to Crete) at the time of the foundation. We have seen that the ὅρκιον is quite different; it concerns itself almost entirely with the necessary arrangements for the establishment of the colony, and there is no attempt to show any cordiality on part of the mother city. The Magnesia inscription shows how a forgery of this kind was made to gain present political advantage." I believe a comparison is possible, especially if we stop looking for modernly perceived historical truths and consider these documents as products of communities that elaborated anew their shared historical past while reinterpreting it. This study is not the place for a theoretical discussion on 'intentional history', for which see GEHRKE 2014, but I must note that this heuristic tool could be useful to understand how here Kyrene and Thera and, above, Magnesia made use of their 'own' histories within an institutional and official framework. The 'oath of the founders' deserves consideration on its own right here because it contains an unusual grant of citizenship that, starting from CHAMOUX 1953, ch. IV up to the most recent study, e.g. CRISCUOLO 2007 *vel* 2003, has been considered a grant of potential citizenship. GAWANTKA 1975, pp. 98–111 devoted substantial attention to this text, which he also seems to interpret as potential citizenship.

(15) The Stele of the Founders

The stele, found in Kyrene is now stored in the Museum of Shahat. The inscription was first published in 1925 by Ferri and has been reedited with collation by Dobias-Lalou in 1994.[8] In this document, a 4th-century BC decree, LL. 1–22, precedes a second text, LL. 23–39, that, more than an oath, lists the rules that disciplined the foundation of Kyrene when colonists left Thera in 631 BC. A brief and colorful curse against those who would not respect these rules follows in LL. 40–51. Because scholars have consistently found this text puzzling, it has even been proposed that the 'oath' was an ancient forgery.[9]

LL. 4–16 contain the following provisions:

```
               ... ἀποδόμεν τοῖς Θηραίοις τ-
   ἀμ πολιτήιαν κατὰ τὰ πάτρια, τ[ὰ] οἱ πρόγονοι ἐποιήσαν-
   το, οἵ τε Κυράναγ κα[τώ]ικιξαν Θήραθε καὶ οἱ ἐν Θήραι [μέ]-
   νοντες, κάθως Ἀπόλλων ἔδωκε Βάττωι καὶ τοῖς Θηρ[αί]-
8  οις τοῖς κατοικίξαισι Κυράναν εὐτυχΕν ἐμμένοντας το[ῖς]
   ὁρκίοις, τὰ οἱ πρόγονοι ἐποιήσαντο αὐτοὶ ποτ' αὐτός, ὅκ[α]
   τὰν ἀποικίαν ἀπέστελλον κατὰ τὰν ἐπίταξιν τῶ Ἀπό[λ]-
   λωνος τῶ Ἀρχαγέτα· ἀγαθᾶι τύχαι, δεδόχθαι τῶι δάμω[ι],
12 καταμ[ῆ]ναι Θηραίοις ἴσαμ πολιτήιαν καὶ ἐγ Κυράναι κ[α]-
   τὰ αὐτά. ποιΕσθαι δὲ πάντας Θηραίος τὸς ἐπιδαμέ[ν]-
   τας ἐγ Κυράναι τὸν αὐτὸν ὅρκον ὅμπερ τοὶ ἄλλοι πο[κ]-
   ἀ διώμωσαν· καὶ καταστᾶμεν ἐς φυλὰν καὶ πάτραν ἐς θ{ε}?[10]
16 ἐννῆα ἑταιρήιας· κτλ[11]
```

---

8   Ed. pr. FERRI Abhandlungen Ak. wiss. Berl. 1925, pp. 19–24 (SEG IX 3). For the history of the editions of the text see DOBIAS-LALOU 1994, pp. 243–244, whose edition I use here.

9   On the question of forgery see GRAHAM 1960 now as 2001, pp. 83–112 arguing for the authenticity of its content, but not its form; see also e.g., MALKIN 2003, esp. pp. 166–167. Supporters of the theory of the ancient forgery include GAWANTKA 1975, pp. 98–111, DUSANIC 1978 (who attributes to the text an historical meaning it cannot have had), and BERNSTEIN 2003, pp. 171–207 who, quite surprisingly, has returned to this old interpretation. This text was certainly not considered a forgery in antiquity. As noted above, we could think of it as an example of intentional history, see GEHRKE 2014 and already 2001, pp. 283–313.

10 Dobias-Lalou suggests that L. 15 be emended by expunging ε and reading θ as a numeral. Her translation has disappeared in her 1994 article, but she provides it in DOBIAS-LALOU 2001, p. 360 n. 11: "qu'ils s'établissent dans une tribu, une phratrie et l'une des neuf hétairies". CRISCUOLO 2003, p. 32, who accepts Dobias-Lalou's new reading, proposes πάτραν be stressed as a genitive plural, πατρᾶν, to mean "e in 9 eterie di patrai" but the position of this genitive would be peculiar and so is the translation. For these institutional subdivisions see CRISCUOLO 2003, pp. 32–34 and HÖLKESKAMP 1993, pp. 411–415.

11 Although the text has been translated many times already, I find it appropriate to give my own translation: "(We, the Kyreneans) give the Theraians citizenship according to the

Recently, L. Criscuolo has pointed out that scholars have focused on the oath but neglected the decree.[12] In her contribution she discusses the decree and offers an interpretation of the question of citizenship. But, on an institutional level, this point could be further clarified. Criscuolo's translation of the verb ἀποδόμεν is central to the interpretation of the grant: she suggests that it can mean either "assegnare" (the object is citizenship), or, she adds, "restituire." But these translations fundamentally differ: the latter would make the concession of citizenship a renewal of the 7th-century BC grant, as attested in the oath, which would be anachronistic.[13] The former translation would imply a new, 4th-century BC concession. Criscuolo also suggests that this grant of citizenship (which she calls *isopoliteia*) was limited to the Theraians in Kyrene, but adds that, because of the above-mentioned restriction, the grant's diplomatic force was limited.[14] The problem is one of terminology and, before we accept the term *isopoliteia* to define the grant, we should make an attempt to determine its nature.

A fresh look at the text may be help. LL. 4–5 preserve a Kyrenean grant of citizenship to the Theraians κατὰ τὰ πάτρια, as it was established at the time of the colonial expedition. The grant refers to LL. 30–33, in which the Theraians who would move to Libya after the first colonists had settled there, were to

ancient customs, which the ancestors established both for those who founded Kyrene leaving Thera and those who stayed behind in Thera, when Apollo decided for Battos and the Theraians who founded Kyrene that standing by the oath they would prosper. (Those very costumes) that our ancestors established for each other when they sent the *apoikia* following the order of Apollo Archeghetes; to good fortune, it was resolved by the *demos* that the Theraians have at their disposal the same citizenship rights also in Kyrene according to these provisions: that all Theraians who live in Kyrene as foreigners shall swear the same oath as the (colonists?) did. Also, they shall be included in a tribe, and a *patran* <and> into (one of?) 9 *heteriai*."

12 On the oath see for example FARAONE 1993 with bibliography.
13 The 7th-century BC grant should appear in the oath, LL. 30–33; it is impossible, however, not to note that the word for *politeia* has been heavily restored in these lines: αἰ μὲν δέ κα κατέχ[ων]/τι τὰν οἰκισίαν οἱ ἄποικοι, [τῶν Θηραίων] τὸγ καταπλέον[τα] / ὕστερον ἐς Λιβύαν [καὶ π]ο[λιτήιας] καὶ τιμᾶμ πεδέχ[εν] / καὶ γᾶς τᾶς ἀδεσπότω [ἀπολαγ]χάνεν· "if the colonists succeed in getting settled, whoever sails later to Libya among [the Therans], shall share [citizenship] and grants, and be assigned by lot land that is still available." On the anachronisms in this text, among which the concept of *politeia* stands out, see GRAHAM 2001, pp. 106–110. In L. 12 the problematic reading of two letters of led to different restorations of the verb: M&L, 5 prefer the infinitive of καταμένω, Wilamowitz cited in app. crit. of M&L 5 suggested that the verb was κατανέμω. Dobias-Lalou's last reading confirms καταμένω.
14 CRISCUOLO 2003, pp. 42–43. AGER 2001, p. 105 offers a different interpretation, according to which *politeia* was for all Theraians—who move to Kyrene, but only because she follows Gawantka's definition of *isopoliteia*.

be granted equal citizenship and even land. The 4th-century BC concession of citizenship is approved in LL. 11–13 and the text refers again to its being κατὰ τὰ πάτρια. Additionally, the text specifies that it was ἴσαμ πολιτήιαν καὶ ἐγ Κυράναι κ[α]/τὰ αὐτά. The subsequent statement, LL. 13–15, only refers to those who were to swear the oath, πάντας Θηραῖος τὸς ἐπιδαμέ[ν]/τας ἐγ Κυράναι. As Gawantka rightly notes, this phrase must invite foreign resident Theraians to a ceremony for swearing the oath. Finally, the procedure for entering Kyrene's citizen body follows and must be considered a separate matter only related to LL. 11–13.[15]

Scholars have repeatedly asked the rather pointless question of whether this is 'potential citizenship' and whether it renewed an ancestral, colonial right of citizenship. The first question points only a problem of definition, not a historical problem; it relates to terminology and historical 'sensibility.' We must recall that this grant dates to a decade when the category of the (Hellenistic) institution of potential citizenship was fluid. For this reason, using a term like *isopoliteia* that we moderns charge with a certain meaning misrepresents the historical process sketched in this text.

More serious is the question of whether this text serves as an (unlikely) renewal of a 7th-century BC concession or as a separate and later recognition. This problem not only pertains to the relationship that a mother city had to its colony, but also relates to the differences between the ancient and the modern perceptions of history. We should look at this document at face value: it is an intercity agreement establishing privileged ties between a mother city and its colony in the 4th-century BC on the basis of a shared view of their common past. In other words, I exclude an agreement between the cities that confirmed an unlikely right of citizenship *ab antiquo*. This concession is the result of human efforts like the law and institutions, which have unique developments and subproducts that cannot be anachronistically applied all periods.[16]

---

15   See GAWANTKA 1975, p. 111, whose general interpretation of the text is difficult. He considers the unilateral nature of the grant problematic and hypothesizes that Kyrene promoted the re-publication of the 7th-century BC oath so that all its terms, which Thera had broken in the 7th-century BC, HDT IV. 153, would have to be confirmed. In particular, he thinks Kyrene wanted to avail itself of the clause allowing its citizens to return to Thera after five years of difficulty. Gawantka does not follow through 'historically' and has not considered that harsh conditions for colonists and strict regulations of the relationship with the mother city at the outset of an expedition were to be expected. The case of Thera is not unique, see MOGGI 1995, pp. 27–31. Stormy relationships between colonists and *metropolis* must have not been unusual.

16   AGER'S 2001 historical approach to this text should be also briefly mentioned. If we only work with definitions and abstract categories, we run the risk of placing ancient documents in an institutional and, more significantly, in an historical vacuum. Ager, who is

(16)   *Magnesia and Hierapytna*
Limestone stele broken in two parts; the top portion is lost. The stone contains three different documents: A is inscribed on one face of the stone, B and C on its opposite side. According to M. Guarducci, different hands created these texts, with C, the most recent, inscribed in the 2nd century BC. Internal data from A and B allow us to date these texts to a year after ca. 205 BC.[17] The stone is now in the archaeological museum of Venice. Measurements: H. 0.73; L. 1.065; Th. 0.085. Letters, document C: 0.005–0.01.

Ed.: *ed. pr. I.Cret.* III.iii 3 C.

[θ]εός·
ἔδοξεν Ἰαραπυτνίων τοῖς κόσμοις τοῖς σὺν Ἀλεξάνδρωι καὶ τᾶι πόλι, Μαγνήτων
                                                                ἀποστηλάντων
πρεσβευτὰς Θεόδοτον Ἀντιόχω καὶ Ἀριστόμαχον Ἀριστοκλέος καὶ ἀ-
4   νανεωμένων τὰν πατρίαν οἰκειότατα καὶ φιλίαν καὶ ἀξιώτων τὰ γεγρ-
αμμένα παρ' αὐτοῖς Κρησὶν τίμια καὶ παρ' ἁμὶν ἀναγραφῆμεν κατὰ τὰ αὐτὰ Μά-
[γ]νησι καὶ θέμεν ἐν ἱαρῶι, ἀγαθᾶι τύχαι καὶ ἐπὶ σωτηρίαι Ἰαραπυτνίων καὶ
                                                Μαγνήτων, καὶ ἀν[α]-
[γράψ]αι τὸς κόσμος ἐς στάλαν λιθίναν Μάγνησιν ἀτέλειαν καὶ προεδρίαν κ[αὶ
                                                                  ἐπι]-
8   [γαμίαν] καὶ ἔνκτησιν καὶ θείων καὶ ἀνθρωπίνων μετοχὰν καὶ ἐσαγωγὰν κ[αὶ
                                                                  ἐξ]-
[αγωγὰν] ὑπάρχειν κατὰ τὰ ἀρχαῖα, καὶ θέμεν τὰν στάλαν ἐν τῶι ἱαρῶι [τᾶς]
[Ἀθαν]αίας τᾶς Πολιάδος. αἰ δὲ τίς κα ἀδικηθῆι Μάγνης ἐν Ἱεραπύτν[αι, δό]-
[μ]εν αὐτῶι τὸ δίκαιον καθάπερ καὶ τοῖς προξένοις. (honors for Magnesians who 'guard' the honors that had been granted, and for the ambassadors follow).

---

not always clear on the institutional aspects of this grant, does very well in seeking the reasons for the stipulation of this agreement in *interpoleis* relations contemporary to the signing of the decree. Yet she tries to find facts that we do not possess. Therefore, her attempted historical reconstruction is legitimate, but, ultimately, not as helpful as one would have hoped.

17   *I.Cret.* III iii 3A preserves the agreement between Rhodes and Hierapytna that must have ended the First Cretan War. The second text, *I.Cret.* III.iii 3B = CHANIOTIS 1996, pp. 241–245 no. 26, preserves a fragmentary agreement between Hierapytna and Lyttos, which contains an oath tied to an alliance. According to Chaniotis, this alliance probably lasted till the end of the 2nd century BC. One more point pertains to prosopography: The ambassador Theodotos son of Antiochos, L. 3, may also appear in *I.Magn.* 70, on which see Kern's comment in *I.Magn.* 20 and CHANIOTIS 1996, p. 245.

Transl.: To the god. Resolved by the *kosmoi* of the Hierapytnans those with Alexander and by the *polis*. Since the Magnesians have sent ambassadors, Theodotos son of Antiochos and Aristomachos son of Aristokles, and want to renew the traditional kinship and friendship and find it appropriate that the written honors by them for Cretans shall be inscribed also by us according to the same principles for the Magnesians and shall be set up in a sanctuary, to good fortune and to the safety of the Hierapytnans and Magnesians, the *kosmos* shall see that it is inscribed on a stone stele that the Magnesians have, just like in the past, exemption from taxes, *proedria*, right to intermarriage and to own property, the participation to everything divine and human, right of import and export, and shall set up the stele in the sanctuary of Athena *Polias*. If any Magnesian is wronged in Hierapytna, to him justice is to be given just like to *proxenoi*.

The city of Hierapytna was located in southeastern Crete, at the site of modern Ierapetra. In the Hellenistic period Hierapytna, one of the most powerful cities of the island, continually expanded its territory at the expense of neighboring *poleis*. It is commonly held that to combat the social pressure caused by overpopulation and lack of resources its inhabitants practiced piracy quite successfully. Recent scholarship has attempted to reevaluate piracy's contribution to this city's economy. These attempts have drawn attention to this old, one-sided perspective, which remains problematic, not least because we lack sufficient evidence.[18]

The unwalled Hellenistic city of Magnesia was located by Mount Thorax, on the river Maeander and its minor tributary river Lethos, along the route that went east from Ephesos toward Tralles, Nysa, and Antioch. The city prided itself on being the most ancient *polis* of Asia Minor.[19] In the Classical period Persians controlled the city, and numerous sources testify that a Persian king, probably Artaxerses I, gave it, along with other communities, to the exiled Themistokles.[20]

The 3rd-century BC epigraphic dossier on inviolability provides important clues on Magnesia and the role of its sanctuary of Artemis Leukophryne in the Greek world. After the Battle of Kouropedion Magnesia came under Seleukid and/or Attalid influence: the evidence for Seleukid presence includes coin

---

18   See the work by GUIZZI 2001, which is mostly devoted to this topic.
19   See CURTY 1995, p. 120 esp. n. 89. The claim is found in *IG* II² 1091, LL. 4–5.
20   NOLLÉ 2003, pp. 189–198 with bibliography.

emissions and a tribe named *Seleukis*.[21] In the 320s BC, after Antiochos Hierax suffered defeat and left the area, Magnesia must have come into the Attalids' sphere of influence, as a tribe named *Attalis* could indicate.[22] A Macedonian presence appears at the very end of the 3rd century BC with the well-known episode concerning the help Magnesia gave Philip V.[23] He thanked the city by granting it the territory of Myous, which later may have triggered armed conflicts.[24]

One more detail pertains to Tacitus's testimony that in AD 22 the city claimed it opposed both Antiochos and Mithridates. It is possible that the historian confuses this city with Magnesia at the Sypilos.[25]

Potential Citizenship

Hierapytna enacted this decree to address a Magnesian embassy that reminded all Cretans of the existing familiarity and friendship and requested that the (Hierapytnans) inscribed and set up a document testifying to the existing grants in a sanctuary. The text lists concessions that should have existed κατὰ τὰ ἀρχαῖα: *ateleia, proedria, epigamia, enktesis*, right of import and export, and, finally, the isolated expression θείων καὶ ἀνθρωπίνων μετοχάν or participation in the divine and human things/activities. The *metechein* formula stands alone in the text, with no mention of a grant of *politeia*: the grant had either been forgotten (LL. 7–9) or never existed, which would be hard to explain in a Cretan treaty. This formula marks the end of the central section of the decree as the provision on the setting up of the stele shows. Noteworthy is the Rechtshilfe clause that follows in LL. 10–11, which grants the Magnesians the same rights as *proxenoi*, i.e., privileged foreigners.[26]

The scope of the decree is answering what must have been a Magnesian plea that was probably directed to all Cretans, and not only to Hierapytna, reminding them of the ancestral relationship they had with Magnesia (esp. L. 4) and of grants that the Magnesians wanted to see on stone. Similar requests appear in several decrees that belong to the *asylia* dossier from Teos that I treat in the section devoted to inviolability.

---

21 *I.Magn.* 5, L. 4. For Lysimachos see MASTROCINQUE 1979, esp. p. 43, n. 150. Magnesia struck Seleukid coins until about 241 BC, when new coins appear that suggest that the city had a more autonomous status, see BOFFO 1985, p. 200 and n. 351 with bibliography.
22 WILL 1966, pp. 296–300; *I.Magn.* 89, L. 7.
23 POLYB. XVI 24, see MA 2002, pp. 77–78.
24 See WÖRRLE 2004, pp. 45–57 and MIGEOTTE 2004, pp. 629–630.
25 TAC. *Ann.* 3.62.1; see RIGSBY 1996, p. 184; BOFFO 1985, pp. 202–203.
26 CHANIOTIS 1996, p. 418 esp. n. 2009 who suggests that here the text refers to the *nomos proxenikos*.

The form and style of our document is *Cretan* and responds to a Cretan logic also in the types of concessions listed in the text, which we can compare with the numerous surviving Cretan decrees that also grant potential citizenship. I include this text in the Magnesian section because it shows that Magnesia sought contact with Cretan communities, with which it claimed ancestral ties, even if it may have been more at home in the discussion of the Cretan documents. The most original element of the decree seems to be the Rechtshilfe clause (LL. 10–11), which signals that Magnesians were considered privileged foreigners, just like *proxenoi*, and to them was extended the same protection.

Unsurprisingly, the text has been interpreted as a Magnesian diplomatic attempt to stop piracy at its source. Although we cannot exclude this interpretation, we must note that no reference to piracy or similar predatory acts appears.

Since we are in the realm of hypotheses, it can be also suggested that this diplomatic mission belonged to the Magnesian attempt to persuade Cretan cities to take back their citizens who had gone over to Asia Minor as mercenaries.[27]

Another possibility, more likely, would agree with D. Clay that the text concerns the recognition of *asylia* testifying to the Magnesian embassy to Hierapytna.[28]

(17–18) *Magnesia, Samos, and Antioch on the Maeander*

I.Magn. 103, an inscription dated to the middle of the 2nd century BC, is concerned with Samos's decision to honor a Magnesian citizen, Telestratos son of Diogenes, and, with Magnesia's permission, to publish these very honors.[29] It is

---

[27] The Magnesians must have felt threatened in the 230s and 220s BC by the waves of Cretan mercenaries that we know were directed to Miletos, *Milet* I 3 33–38. Additional and later epigraphic evidence testifies that, while trying to arbitrate a dispute between Gortyn and Knossos, Magnesia asked both cities to take back their citizens (probably mercenary soldiers) who lived in Miletos, presumably in the territory of Myous. See MAGNETTO 1997, pp. 262–271 no. 43 and AGER 1996, pp. 350–355 no. 127, who offer differing historical backgrounds and dates. On that occasion both Cretan cities agreed to take back only those people who had not switched citizenship, MAGNETTO 1997, pp. 262–271 no. 43, I. LL. 31–41, II. LL. 24–32.

[28] CLAY 1993, p. 442.

[29] *IMagn.* 103 (no. 17). The Samian decree has also been published as *IG* XII.6.1 154, LL. 1–35. The text can be summarized as follows. LL. 1–4 record the prescript and the Magnesian eponym. A Samian decree follows ordering an embassy to be sent to Magnesia, LL. 5–19, to which the actual Samian honorary decree for Telestratos is attached, LL. 19–35. The Magnesians responded with another decree honoring the Samian embassy and city, LL. 36–68, and, finally, we find the Magnesian answer to the Samian request in LL. 68–80.

in this context that we indirectly learn that an agreement of potential citizenship between Magnesia and Samos was in place.

The document refers several times to potential citizenship, although twice in restoration. The first instance, L. 8, is restored and refers to the Magnesians in adjectival form: πρεσβεία ... πρὸς / Μάγνητας, οἰκείους κα[ὶ ἰσοπολίτας καὶ φίλους ὑπάρχοντας τοῦ ἡμετέρου]/ δήμου.... In LL. 12–13, out of lacuna, the Magnesians are referred to, again as ἰσοπολίτας; while in the *IG* edition (*IG* XII.6.1 154), in L. 18 *isopoliteia* has been restored along with kinship (*oikeiotes*) and friendship. Finally, the fourth and last instance, L. 37, declares, out of lacuna, that the Samians are φίλοι καὶ ἰσοπολεῖται καὶ εὐν[οι, clearly, of the Magnesians.

This text does not tell us when or why these cities exchanged potential citizenship,[30] but it helps to understand which terms were used (and when) to describe this institution in antiquity. This text confirms that the word *isopoliteia* and its cognates in ancient texts can denote the abstract concept of potential citizenship. Additionally, it shows that in indirect evidence the terms could be associated with other concepts, such as friendship and kinship, in order to express long-lasting and diplomatically valuable relationships. This association implies that potential citizenship belonged to the same category of Hellenistic relationships that these other terms describe.[31]

Another Samian decree that testifies indirectly to a grant of potential citizenship, in this case between Samos and Antioch on the Maeander, must be mentioned.[32] The stone was found in the Heraion of Samos and dates to ca. 167 BC (no. 18).[33] It contains traces of a lost agreement between Antioch and an unknown city along with Samian permission to set up the stele preserving the treaty between them in the Heraion, just as the Antiocheis had requested. LL. 22–26 roughly summarize the content of the lost decree and, on their basis, Habicht has suggested that Antioch had established *synoikismos* with this unknown community. This connection, however, is of no concern to the Samians who only stress their willingness to show *eunoia* to Rome and a fellow city, LL. 19–20, whose people are called ... συγγενεῖς καὶ φίλους καὶ εὔ[ν]ους καὶ ἰσοπολίτας καὶ συμ[μάχους ...].[34]

---

30 See SHIPLEY 1987, p. 31.
31 For more examples see SABA 2009/10(a), pp. 179–180; on this text see *supra* pp. 22–23.
32 On Antioch see COHEN 1995, pp. 250–253. The inscription is now published as *IG* XII.6.1 6 (McCabe Samos 12); on this text see also CURTY 1995, no. 29.
33 On the date see CURTY 1995, p. 62; *ed. pr.* HABICHT 1952, esp. pp. 242–252.
34 On the relationship with Rome see FERRARY 1988, pp. 124–132. One of the hypotheses formulated to explain the kinship is that Samos had sent colonists to Antioch, but CURTY 1995, p. 63 holds that this association is unnecessary and privileges mythological roots.

In this case, too, we ignore why and when the grant of potential citizenship was established, but its mention illustrates, along with the other pillars of Hellenistic diplomacy, the close relationship between Samos and Antioch.

A final note pertains to Gawantka's comment on *I.Magn.* 103 and on another decree that the city of Bargylia enacted to honor foreign judges from Priene.[35] LL. 3–4 of *I.Priene* 47 call the *demos* of Priene εὔνους καὶ ἰσοπολίτης and then, in LL. 17–19, the three foreign judges are declared citizens of Bargylia.

Gawantka comments as follows: "Wie gering man die Wirkung des an Gesamtbürgerschaften verliehenen Bürgerrechts in dem Falle, da es nicht aktiviert wurde, veranschlagen konnte, zeigen vielleicht am deutlichsten die folgende Zeugnisse (i.e., *I.Magn.* 103 and *Priene* 47)."[36] Gawantka holds that, since citizens from *poleis* with potential citizenship in place could be still honored with a grant of *politeia ad personam*, potential citizenship was 'institutionally' weak.[37] It may be useful to return to this point: grants *ad personam* target individuals because of their deeds. In the Hellenistic period grants of citizenship for a community refer to the *polis* as a political object: personal and city-wide concessions of citizenship do not exclude each other because they have different targets and different meanings. Moreover, from a technical point of view both needed to be implemented, i.e., no one grant excluded the other procedurally. *I.Magn.* 103 awards honors to Telestratos who was a citizen of Magnesia, which, in turn, had a good relationship with Samos. But Telestratos's merits were personal and for these he was (probably) awarded the ultimate, greatest honor by Samos, namely, Samian citizenship. This honor, however, does not mean that potential citizenship between the two *poleis* was of no consequence. It was simply a grant that acted on a different political level.

Gawantka's comment depends on his approach to the material, which he sometimes looks at from the standpoint of the individual in the attempt to find practical applications for potential citizenship. Another of his comments may help to understand this point: "Die Verleihung an die Gesamtbürgerschaft richtete sich in erster Linie an die dieses empfangende Stadt als Gemeinschaft, das Ehrendekret ad personam hob den Geehrten aus der Anonymität heraus. Dieses Denken war freilich nur möglich, wenn die Isopolitie faktisch nur geringe oder gar keine Konsequenzen zeitigte, d.h. wenn der Isopolit i.e. S. (= im engeren Sinne) weiterhin substantiell als ξένος galt."[38] This remark is correct,

---

35 *I.Priene* 47 now *I.Iasos* 607 (McCabe Priene 2), dated to ca. 200 BC. Here I treat the adjective *isopolites* as unambiguous, but see my comment in the introduction.
36 GAWANTKA 1975, p. 55.
37 GAWANTKA 1975, pp. 56–57.
38 GAWANTKA 1975, p. 57.

but, to me, what Gawantka describes is the strength and not the weakness of potential citizenship. Through this concession a *polis* or a *koinon* allowed only the potential inclusion of all lawful members of the partner community, which was, alone and as a political object, the real recipient of the grant.

(19)   *Magnesia and Phokaia*

This limestone stele, damaged on all sides, was found close to the gangway of the temple of Artemis; it had been built into a Byzantine wall. When Kern wrote in 1900, the stone was preserved in the local storage room. Measurements: H. 0.07; L. 0.37–0.47; Th. 0.21. Letters: 0.012–0.015.

Edd.: *ed. pr. I.Magn.* 7b; [*Syll.*³ 941; McCabe Magnesia 157].
Cf. Migeotte 2004, pp. 622–637 with French translation.

    [τάδε] ἔδωκαν Μάγνητες Φωκαιεῦσι· ἀ[τέ]-
    [λειαν] εἶναι Φωκαιεῦσιν ἐμ Μαγνησίαι ἀπ-
    [άντων] ἐξάγοντας ὅσα ἂν ε[ἰς] τὸν ἴδιο[ν]
4   [οἶκ]ον [ἐ]ξάγωσιν, εἶναι δὲ καὶ εἰσαγωγὴ[ν]
    [καὶ ἐ]ξαγωγὴν Φωκαιεῦσιν εἰς Μαγνησί-
    [αν] καὶ ἐμ πολέμωι καὶ ἐν εἰρήνη ἀ[συ]-
    [λ]εὶ καὶ ἀσπονδεὶ καὶ ἔφοδον ἐπὶ τὸ κοι-
8   [νὸ]ν πρώτοις μετὰ τὰ ἱερά, ἐπάγ-
    [ειν] δ' αὐτοὺς τοὺς προέδρους
    [εἰ]ς τὴν ἐκκλησίαν, εἰσκηρύσ-
    [σει]ν δὲ καὶ ἐν τοῖς ἀγῶσιν εἰς
12 [πρ]οεδρίαν· ἐὰν δέ τις Φωκα[ιέ]-
    [ων ἐ]νοικῆι ἐμ Μαγνησί[αι, εἶναι]
    [αὐ]τῶι γῆς καὶ οἰκίας ἔ[γκτησιν]
    [κ]αὶ τῶν ἄλλων αὐ[τῶι μετεῖναι]
16 [π]άντων ὧν καὶ τ[οῖς Μά]-
    [γ]νησιν, τέλη τελοῦ[ντι ὅσα ὁ]
    [Μ]άγνης τελεῖ.

Text from *I.Magn.* 7b.

Transl.: The Magnesians granted the Phokaians (the following): in Magnesia the Phokaians shall be exempted of all taxes on whatever they bring out to their own *oikos*, the Phokaians shall have right of import and export to Magnesia in peace and war and shall be inviolable and without the necessity of a treaty. They shall access public organs first after the sacred matters, and the *proedroi* shall lead them to the assembly. In the festivals they shall be called in by the herald to *proedria*. If a Phokaian lives in Magnesia, he shall have the right to own land and home and everything else that Magnesians have, he shall have too. Also he shall pay taxes like a Magnesian.

Based on paleography the inscription has been dated to the 3rd century BC.

This text is one of four documents preserved on the stone, but, together with text C, which grants proxeny and citizenship to a man named Βάκχιος Θρασ[?], it is the only legible inscription. C is dated by the eponymous Minnion, who figures already in *I.Magn.* 6, but we cannot date it with any precision. Document D may provide a clue on relative chronology, as it preserves the name of the *stephanephoros* in charge, Aristagoras.[39] Even if it is unknown when he held his office, the formula shows that he held the position after Minnion became the eponymous magistrate of the town. Finally, Kern observed that the same hand inscribed the first three documents on stone, but the fourth was inscribed later.

According to Gawantka, LL. 15 to the end contain part of an expression that can be likened to a *metechein* formula. This association, in turn, would assure us that this text contains a grant of potential citizenship.[40] But L. 13 says clearly that the listed concessions have limited applicability: the Magnesian authorities clearly distinguish between the Phokaians abroad and those who lived in Magnesia.[41]

The first line of the text addresses the Phokaians as a group, but from LL. 2 to 12 the text is solely concerned with nonresidents, and from LL. 12 to 18 the text relates to those who inhabit Magnesia. Only this second group is the addressee of the alleged grant of potential citizenship.

---

39 σ]τεφανηφοροῦντος Ἀρισ[τ]α[γόρου μηνὸς Ἀνθε/[σ]τηριῶνος ...

40 GAWANTKA 1975, pp. 27–28. The *comparanda* he offers do not support this statement: the agreement between Stymphalos and Elatea, *IPArk* 18, does not contain any potential citizenship, where Gawantka read it in LL. 28–31: ... ὑπάρχειν δὲ Στυμφαλίοις ἐν Ἐ/[λατείαι ἀτέλειαν?, ἀσυλ]ίαν καὶ πόθοδον ποτὶ βουλὰν καὶ ἐκκλησίαν πρώτοις μετὰ τὰ προιερά, καὶ / [μετέχειν αὐτοὺς ἐν Ἐλατ]είαι τᾶν κοινᾶν θυσιᾶν καὶ τῶν ἄλλων τιμίων καὶ φιλανθρώπων πᾰν/[των ... see also Thür and Taubner, *IPArk* 18, p. 252: "den Stymphaliern werden ... Teilnahme am Kult in Elateia gewährt (28–30)." In this text citizenship rights are neither listed nor referred to. His second reference is to *I.Cret.* III.iii 3C = no. 16, which contains the grant (most likely) but see *supra* for the omission of the word *politeia*.

41 On Phokaia see STRAB. XIII. 582; 621; GRAF 1985, p. 402. For the city after Kouropedion see POLYB. V.77.4 who reports that in 218 BC Phokaia went over to Attalos I; the city later must have sided with Antiochos III: LIV. XXXVII. 9.1–4; APP. *Syr.* 25, on which see MASTROCINQUE 1994, p. 452; POLYB. XXI.46.7.

The document states that the Phokaians residing in Magnesia would enjoy privileges such as the right to own land and home, along with every other right enjoyed by a Magnesian had, and they would have to pay taxes like a Magnesian. (Practical) concessions for nonresident Phokaians are included too: LL. 1–4 establish that Phokaians could take to their city anything that was meant for private use without paying taxes. More importantly, they had right to import and export to Magnesia with inviolability, under any circumstance.

The distinction between nonresidents and residents is clear, but even this second group is not referred to as (potential) citizens, as the verb (*enoikein*) used in the decree demonstrates. The text does not mention any grant of citizenship, but it lists other rights that could be used in or outside the city, according to where the grantees lived. Citizenship is neither omitted nor forgotten, more simply it was not awarded. The *metechein* clause is not a standard formula implying potential citizenship, but rather a way to cover other possible, unspecified benefits that pertain to daily life. Phokaians were privileged foreigners, but not potential citizens of Magnesia.

As I noted at the start of this chapter, the quality of the evidence rather than its quantity suggests that Magnesia on the Maeander did not widely use the tool of potential citizenship. When potential citizenship is granted, it serves the narrative of the city's history within the frame of the quest for *asylia* and establishes stronger ties with Crete, which had a strong tradition of using the grant.

From Samos the indirect evidence that has survived suggests that the city used this tool probably with a certain frequency and in its 'diplomatic' application. Perhaps contiguity with Miletos influenced the way Samos used this tool.

CHAPTER 3

Western Asia Minor

The Epigraphic Record

The richest crop of testimonies of potential citizenship comes from Asia Minor: this fact should be considered more than simple chance. The section that follows contains a discussion of all surviving treaties of potential citizenship that communities in Asia Minor, other than Miletos, Magnesia, and Samos, have stipulated. I devoted separate treatments to those cities, but the treaties stemming from all communities contribute to the conclusions I have drawn on the material from Asia Minor.

Two preserved treaties from Pergamon include grants of potential citizenship: these treaties are textbook examples of the first type of potential citizenship, as I have defined it in the introduction.[1] In both cases the diplomatic function of the grant is evident and it is just as clear that the cities with which Pergamon established the agreements were politically relevant to its current geopolitical situation. No predefined power relationship is evident. Rather, these treaties show that a grant of potential citizenship was an act between cities that either had something to offer each other (from a political or economic point of view), or found themselves in situations that made strengths or former power relationships and hierarchies largely irrelevant to the agreement.[2] From Temnos we also preserve two agreements,[3] an impressive amount for an otherwise little-known city. In the documents, Temnos figures both as grantee and grantor. The agreement between Skepsis and Parion associates a grant of potential citizenship to a military agreement.[4] This case is exceptional in Asia Minor and reveals that the towns probably found themselves in a worrisome situation. P. Herrmann has stated that cities used grants of potential citizenship in peaceful situations or to seal peace treaties. His

---

[1] *AvP* VIII.1 5 = no. 20 preserves the agreement between Pergamon and Temnos; *AvP* VIII.1 156 = no. 21 preserves the agreement between Pergamon and Tegea. The examples date to the two opposite ends of the 3rd century BC.
[2] Other examples for the relative importance of power relationships in the establishment of potential citizenship include the agreements between Miletos and Seleukeia-Tralles, *Milet* I 3 143 = no. 5, and the peculiar peace treaty between Aitolia and Akarnania, *IG* IX² I 3A = no. 40.
[3] In addition to the above-mentioned treaty with Pergamon, Temnos granted potential citizenship to Teos, *SEG* XXIX 1149 = no. 22, at the end of the 3rd century BC.
[4] J. and L. Robert *BE* 1972 371 = no. 23.

observation is certainly correct, especially in Asia Minor, and contradicts the unjustified but common tendency of scholars to associate potential citizenship and military agreements.[5] The treaty between Skepsis and Parion indeed is an exceptional testimony of the use of this tool for a different, military context in Asia Minor. Although this treaty contains the most common traits of a grant of potential citizenship, a few provisions reveal that the cities had to face a possibly difficult situation.

Two uncertain cases and a recently revealed (but very fragmentary) inscription, complete the dossier of the evidence from western Asia Minor.[6]

The political (or other) relevance of the partners to an agreement that contains potential citizenship is the reason for the concession of this grant. This statement may seem like a generic and inconclusive statement, but it is necessary. It contradicts, on good grounds, old theories that assert that *isopoliteia* reflects a power relationship or was granted to replenish depopulated cities. The inclusion, in some texts, of the other pillars of Hellenistic diplomacy, such as kinship and friendship, and the use of the diplomatic language are not the 'reasons' for the grants, but accompany it. They may appear in one breath, which in turn suggests that potential citizenship was considered among the most important types of relationships that cities could establish between themselves to shape political, religious, and economic alliances.[7] Kinship claims for example appear routinely in agreements that include *isopoliteia* concessions mostly to set the pace and tone of the agreement.[8] When *isopoliteia* and other qualifications appear back to back, they express the 'degree' of the strength of the relationship that is in place or was going to be established.[9] Gawantka is right to note that kinship alone cannot be the reason for exchanging potential citizenship. However, at the same time, recognizing why such a claim was made, can either reveal something about the communities' history or, better, about their perception of their own history. In a way, when fictional, these ties are even more meaningful than when they are real because they show how far communities would push the limits of their collective memory and identity to serve their own current diplomatic and political goals.

---

5   This assessment is true for Crete only, see *infra*.

6   The two uncertain pieces of evidence are the agreements between Maroneia and Priene, *I.Priene* 10 = no. 26, and the fragmentary text of *Inscr. Sardeis* VI.6 = no. 25, which a few scholars think contains this privilege. The new inscription testifies to an exchange of *isopoliteia* between Laodikeia on the Lykos and an unknown city *SEG* LVIII 1541 = no. 24.

7   GAWANTKA 1975, esp. pp. 92–113 already made this observation but shifted his focus to legal matters that were hardly of any concern.

8   See the extreme case of the agreement between Seleukeia and Miletos *Milet* I 3 143 = no. 5 or *infra* the more standard case of Pergamon and Tegea, *AvP* VIII.1 156 = no. 21.

9   For example, see *IG* XII.6.1 6 = no. 18 (Samos-Antioch) or the *asylia* concessions of Gela and Kamarina to Teos, *IG* XII.4.1 222 and 223 = no. 67 and no. 68.

(20) *Pergamon and Temnos*

The upper part of a blue marble stele, broken into two parts that were recovered separately in the sanctuary of Athena in Pergamon, preserves an agreement of *isopoliteia*. The upper left and right side of the frame are preserved, the rest is damaged. Measurements: W. 0.355; Th. 0.13; the height is not recorded. Letters: 0.006–0.010. Allen was "unable to locate the stele" in the Pergamon Museum in 1983.[10]

Edd.: *ed. pr. AvP* VIII.1 5 (drawing); [*OGIS* 265; *StV* III 555].
Cf.: Robert *OMS* I, pp. 204–209.

[ἔγ]νω βο]υλὴ καὶ δῆμος· γνώμη στρατηγῶν·
[ἐπεὶ ὁ] δῆμος ὁ Τημνιτῶν οἰκείως διακε[ί]-
[μενος] τυγχάνει τῶι δήμωι τῶι Περγαμην[ῶν],
4   [ἀγαθ]ῆι τύχηι, δεδόχθαι τῆι βουλῆι καὶ τῶι δή-
[μωι]· ἀποστεῖλαι πρεσβευτὰς δύο, οἵτινες παρα-
[γεν]όμενοι ἐμφανιοῦσι τήν τε εὔνοιαν ἣν ἔχων
[δι]ατελεῖ πρὸς αὐτοὺς ὁ δῆμος ὁ Περγαμηνῶν
8   [κα]ὶ διαλεγήσονται ὅπως ψηφισθῆι ταῖς πόλεσιν
[ἀμ]φοτέραις ἰσοπολιτεία. ἐὰν δὲ φαίν[η]ται
[Τη]μνίταις ἐπιτήδειον εἶναι συνθεῖναι περὶ τ[ο]ύ-
[του], τοὺς ἀφεσταλμένους αὐτοκράτορας [εἶναι].
12 [αἱρε]θέντες Ἀπολλωνίδης Ἀπέλλεος, Η[...5–6...]
[Ἑρ]μίππου. ᵛ ἀγάθαι τύχαι· ἔδοξε Ταμ[νίταισι]
[κα]ὶ Περγαμήνοισι ἐπὶ πρυτάνιος τῶ μ[ετὰ Ἡρα]-
[κ]ληΐδαν τὸν Δίτα μῆννος Ἡράω, ἐν [Περγάμω]
ἐπὶ πρυτ[ά]νιος Ἀριστοκράτεος τῶ Ἱερα[—],
μῆνος Ἡράω· *vac.* ἔμμεναι Ταμνί[ταισι ἐν Περ]-
16 γάμω πολι[τ]είαν καὶ Περγαμήν[οισι ἐν Τάμνω]
μετεχόντ[ε]σσι ὧν καὶ οἱ ἄλλο[ι πολῖται μετέχοι]-
σι καὶ γᾶς καὶ οἰκ[ία]ς ἔγκτησιν ἔμ[μεναι τῶ Ταμνί]-
τα ἐμ Περγάμω [κ]αὶ τῶ Περγ[αμήνω ἐν Τάμνω. τέλη]
20 [δ]ὲ φέρην τὸν Ταμνίταν [ἐμ Περγάμω ὅσσα καὶ ὁ Περ]-
[γ]άμηνος φέρει κα[ὶ] τὸν Π[εργάμηνον ἐν Τάμνω ὅσσα καὶ]
[ὁ] Ταμνίτας φέρε[ι - - - - - - - - - - - - - - - - - -]
[σ]τείχην ἢ ἐπὶ συ[- - - - - - - - - - - - - - - - - -]

---

10   Allen 1983, p. 17 n. 29.

Text by Schmitt (*StV* III 555); LL. 19/20 R(obert) τέλη] / [δ]ὲ φέρην τὸν Ταμνιταν [ἐμ Περγάμῳ ... emended Fränkel's restoration [ψᾶφον].

Transl.: The council and the people resolved. Proposal of the *strategoi*. Since the *demos* of the Temnians happen to be kin to the *demos* of the Pergamenes, to good fortune, it was resolved by the *boule* and the *demos* to send two envoys, who, with their presence, show the benevolence that the people of Pergamon have for them and speak so that *isopoliteia* is voted for both cities. If it seems appropriate to the Temnians to establish an agreement on this, then the ambassadors who have been sent have full powers. Apollonides son of Apelles, E(....) son of Hermippos were chosen. To good fortune. It was decreed by the Temnians and the Pergamenes when Ditas was *prytanis* after Herakleides in the month of Hereos, in Pergamon during the prytany of Aristokrates son of Hiere(?) in the month of Hereos. *Vacat.* (It was decreed that) the Temnians have citizenship in Pergamon and the Pergamenes in Temnos, sharing in all the things the other citizens also share in, and there is to be the right to own land and house for a Temnian in Pergamon and for a Pergamene in Temnos. A Temnitan shall pay taxes in Pergamon just like a Pergamene does and a Pergamene in Temnos ...

The inscription has been dated to the early 3rd century BC by paleography. For Fränkel the writing indicates a date as early as the years of Lysimachos or Phileitairos.[11]

Pergamon

The text under consideration dates to the first half of 3rd century BC, when the Attalids rose to power.[12] In his brief historical account of this dynasty, Strabo rejects the belittling comments of the historians who wrote before him on the

---

11   Fränkel in *AvP* VIII.1 5 comments on paleography citing Fabricius: "Die Hasten-Ende zeigen nur vereinzelt die später übliche Verbreiterung; beachtenswert ist das frühe Vorkommen des Alpha mit gebrochenem Querstrich in Pergamon." For ALLEN 1983, p. 17 n. 29 this text "is to be dated, ..., to the beginning of the third century BC, and it is unlikely that the stone was inscribed later than the period in which Philetairos paid allegiance to Lysimachos, although it may have been earlier." MCSHANE 1964, esp. pp. 72–73 prefers Attalos I. Scholars also routinely note that the second half of the text (LL. 13 to the end) is written in Aeolic, while Pergamon's decree, LL. 1–13, is in *koine*.

12   VIRGILIO 1984, esp. pp. 31–32. On Pergamon in general see ALLEN 1983; MCSHANE 1964; MAGIE 1950. Excavations have been conducted on Pergamon's location since 1878 by the German Archeological Institute and their results are published in the volumes of *AvP*.

obscure origins of the Attalid dynasty, and instead attributes to its founder, Philetairos, an early, refined education.[13]

Philetairos was Lysimachos's treasurer, but betrayed him by taking possession of his riches and then sought Seleukid protection. Pergamon removed itself completely from Seleukid patronage after 261 BC, when the city stopped minting coins with Seleukos's portrait; Philetairos replaced Seleukos on the coins.[14] Philetairos, however, seems to have acted with great independence from the beginning of his rule over Pergamon, not least by establishing connections with communities near and far. Philetairos offered liberal financial support to other towns that responded, for example, with the creation of a festival named *Philetairea*.[15] To this time period and context probably belongs the agreement of *isopoliteia* between Pergamon and Temnos.[16]

Temnos

This town, located in the historical region of the Aeolis, is insufficiently known. Ramsay spotted its ruins at the end of the 19th century; this identification has been confirmed several times since then, even if no further systematic archaeological investigation has been undertaken.[17] The city is located in a mountainous area by Magnesia at the Sypilos, on the river Hermus. According to Xenophon, the geomorphological nature of the district favored its freedom, when most of Asia Minor came under Persian control. This setting, however, did not stop Hellenistic kings and dynasts, who were less risk adverse.[18] Temnos

---

13   STRAB. XIII.4.1–3 on which VIRGILIO 1984, pp. 21–37.
14   ALLEN 1983, pp. 23–26; MCSHANE 1964, p. 40; for the coins see WESTERMARK 1991.
15   For Kyzikos see *CIG* 3660, recently KOTSIDOU 2000, p. 204 but without text; for Kyme see MANGANARO 2000, esp. pp. 404–405.
16   ALLEN 1983, p. 17 holds that this treaty reveals the existence of pre-Attalid contacts between Pergamon and Temnos. By preferring the years of Attalos I, MCSHANE 1964, pp. 72–73 supports the thesis of the effects of a later diplomatic activity. I exclude both the earlier and later date because of the general policy that we know Philetairos followed. This policy would make his reign a favorable moment for establishing agreements such as this exchange of potential citizenship. Under Philetairos Pergamon grew to become a main player in the area. His rule seems to be a suitable historical setting for the stipulation of an agreement of potential citizenship also because, by then, Temnos was very active at the regional level. An early agreement with Temnos could have indeed benefited an emerging Pergamon. KOBES 1996, p. 183, n. 64 remarks that this date is not "zweifelfrei." In this context, it is appropriate to observe that potential citizenship was never established by or among insignificant communities as its effects would have been wasted on cities that had no standing or ambition to increase their political weight and visibility.
17   HERRMANN 1979, esp. p. 240; RAMSAY 1881, pp. 282–292; on Temnos's location see STRAB. XIII.3.5 and PL. *NH* V.32.
18   XENOPH. *Hell*. IV.8.5; see MA 2002, pp. 143–144, also his note n. 136.

was not far from Pergamon, yet, over the decades, it fell within the sphere of different royal houses. Too little is known to make any statement about the town's real status in any given year, but for the 3rd century BC, Polybios testifies that Temnos and other *poleis* passed from Attalos' I to Achaios's hands only to revert to Attalid control in 218 BC. Temnos probably came under Seleukid control in 197 BC,[19] yet a fragmentary letter by Eumenes II records that Temnos still had a relationship with the Attalids in the first half of the 2nd century BC.[20]

Temnos preserves very few inscriptions, but then no major archaeological investigation has taken place in the area either.[21] The surviving epigraphic evidence attests to Temnian attempts to establish contact with immediate and slightly removed neighbors. Temnos actively sought to make its presence felt in the region.[22]

The Agreement and Its Terms

One remarkable feature of this agreement is that it summarizes the entire diplomatic process leading to the establishment of potential citizenship between Pergamon and Temnos. LL. 1–13 testify to Pergamon's diplomatic initiative: the city sent to Temnos two envoys charged with offering to the Aeolian city the possibility to establish an agreement on the exchange of *isopoliteia* (L. 9). The ambassadors were declared *autokratores*, i.e., they were given full powers to conclude the deal.[23] The stated reason for this initiative is Temnos's familial behavior and Pergamon's desire to show its benevolence. The diplomatic language employed in the agreement is typical for this time period and suggests that Pergamon's direct request was meant to intensify the relationship it had with Temnos. Eventually, it succeeded.

---

19 POLYB. V.77; MA 2002, pp. 143–144 hypothesizes that in this year the city was again Seleukid.
20 *AvP* VIII.1 157.
21 To my knowledge, nine known inscriptions come from or pertain to Temnos. In addition to the two potential citizenship treaties with Pergamon and Teos that I discuss here, two 3rd-century BC grants of citizenship survive, to an Elean and to a Sardian citizen, ROBERT *OMS* I, pp. 436–442. To the same century belongs a document with which Temnos responded to the honors that Smyrna granted to the city and three Temnian citizens for ransoming Smyrneans who had been kidnapped by robbers, BIELMAN 1994, no. 35; ROBERT 1937, ch. IV. Two other documents preserve the memory of a 2nd-century BC arbitration between the cities of Klazomenai and Temnos, HERRMANN 1979, pp. 249–271= *SEG* XXIX 1130 and 1130 bis. Finally, individuals from Temnos were honored in Kolophon, McCabe Kolophon 8, 3rd-century BC?, and in Ilion, *IK* 3, 40, 3rd century BC, where Diaphenes son of Pollas appears as, LL. 2–3, διατρίβων παρὰ τῶι βασιλεῖ on which see SAVALLI 1998, pp. 260–261.
22 See RIGSBY 1996(b), p. 255; HERRMANN 1979, p. 240.
23 On ambassadors '*autokratores*' see BOUSQUET and GAUTHIER 1994, esp. pp. 328–332.

The second half of the document, starting at L. 13, contains part of the joint agreement on the award of potential citizenship, to which, clearly, the Temnians had agreed through their ambassadors. After the repeated dates, according to Pergamon's and Temnos's eponyms and calendars (LL. 13–15), provisions follow that are only partly preserved. Temnians and Pergamenes granted each other citizenship, πολιτεία, that in the text is accompanied by a *metechein* formula. The long clause of LL. 15–19 highlights the difference between those who intend to switch citizenship (and who will partake in everything) and those who would not (but would still enjoy the grant of *enktesis*). The grant of the additional right to ownership of house and land (L. 18) follows, along with a restored clause regulating taxes.[24]

The parties establish *isoteleia* for their citizens, which is not unusual if we compare this text with the few other known examples that preserve tax clauses. The lengthiest text on the topic of taxation, discussed in more detail below, is the agreement between Skepsis and Parion (no. 23). There too the principle of *isoteleia* is upheld, but only after the citizens of one community living in the other city or its territory have resided there at least six months.[25]

Two Milesian decrees, the early treaty with Olbia (4th century BC), and the peace agreement with Herakleia under Mt. Latmos (2nd century BC),[26] offer two chronologically and formally distinct examples of tax regulations. In the first example, Olbia and Miletos establish *ateleia* for commercial purposes, to the clear advantage of those who do not change their citizenship status (LL. 18–20). Those who switch citizenship would instead have to be considered *isoteleis*. *Ateleia* returns in the agreement with Herakleia, but it applies only to goods that had to be transported from one territory to the other and whose movements war had previously hindered (esp. LL. 67–72). Commercial interests and postwar issues are responsible for such provisions.

The first motivation, commercial interests, could apply also to the treaty between Pergamon and Temnos. After the clause on taxes, the document from Pergamon breaks off, leaving us wondering about any enrollment clauses or other formalities that a grant of potential citizenship could include.

---

24 ROBERT *OMS* I, pp. 204–209. Fränkel thought that the text mentioned the right to vote to imply actual participation in political life, which, however, potential citizenship does not grant *a priori*.

25 In this text another provision precedes the clause and establishes that lawful members of both communities had the right to ownership irrespective of residency. Perhaps these specifications refer to the critical situation in which the agreement seems to have been signed, as demonstrated by another provision on tax-exempted goods that had to be moved because of war, no. 23 LL. 20–22, see *infra*.

26 See *supra* on Miletos, *Milet* I 3 136 = no. 1 and 150 = no. 7.

To understand the stipulation of this reciprocal grant of potential citizenship, we must remember that neither town was insignificant in the 3rd century BC. Philetairos's Pergamon extended its influence to create a solid basis for a future enfranchisement from Seleukid patronage, and Temnos was a locally important city and partner that sought to exert itself in the region by establishing also contacts south of the Aeolis. The additional grants and provisions that this agreement preserves are important pieces of information to determine the character of the treaty. For example, *enktesis* to a neighboring community indicates practical interests that go beyond the simple exchange of an 'honor.' The two communities used this agreement (including potential citizenship) to create a strong political tie and to prompt or, perhaps, even to boost commercial activities.

(21) *Pergamon and Tegea*
Upper part of a stele of white marble found broken in two parts. The larger fragment was reused as building material in a wall. Its surface is weathered to the point of being often illegible. The smaller fragment of the stele was discovered by the south side of Pergamon's theater. Measurements: H. 0.50; W. 0.58; Th. 0.16; Letters: 0.010.

Edd.: *ed. pr. AvP* VIII.1 156 (drawing); [Curty 1995, no. 41, LL. 9–24; McCabe Pergamon 156; Lücke 2000, *S*33].
Cf. Wilhelm 1897, p. 50 (also in *Kl. Schr.* II, 3, p. 208).

```
4     [- - - - τὴ]ν ὑπάρχουσ[α]ν αὐτ[ῆι - - -
      [- - -]αι [π]ολιτείαν [.]ε[..].τιν[- - -]
      [- -]Π[ε]ρ[γα]μην[ῶ]ν [.......]ν ἐ[ξεῖναι αὐτοῖς μετέχου]-
      [σι πάντω]ν [ὧν] καὶ οἱ ἄλλοι Τεγεᾶτ[αι - - -]
8     [- - -π]ρο[ε]δρίαν το[ῖς] Ἀλε[αίοις ...]
      [- - -]ς [ἀ]να.....σι· [δε]δόχ[θ]αι τῶι δ[ήμ]ωι [ἐπ]αι[νέσαι]
      [μὲν τὴν πό]λιν τὴν Τεγεατῶν, διότι καὶ [μέμνητ]α[ι τῆς εἰς]
      [ἡμῶν τὴ]ν πόλιν οἰκειότητος καὶ [δ]ια[τ]ε[τήρεκε] τὴν δ[ιάθησιν]
      [ἥν τε πρέπ]ει κ[α]ὶ [δίκαι]όν ἐστιν καὶ σ[ύμφορον, στεφανῶσαι]
12    [δὲ καὶ Παναθηναί]οις χρυσῶι στεφάνωι φ[ιλοτιμίας ἕν]ε-
      [κεν καὶ εὐνοί]ας εἰς τὸν δῆμον, τὴν δὲ ἀναγόρευσιν τ[οῦ]
      [στεφάνου] πο[ήσ]ασ[θ]α[ι] τοὺς στρατ[η]γούς. ἐξουσίαν δὲ [εἶναι]
      [καὶ] πολιτε[ύε]σθαι ἐν Περ[γ]άμωι τοῖς βο[υ]λομένοις Τεγεάτ[αις]
16    [μετέχουσι π]άν[τω]ν [ὧν κα]ὶ οἱ ἄλλοι Περγαμηνοί. [ἵνα δὲ τὰ ἐν]
      τοῖς προϋπάρχουσιν [ὑπ]ομνήμ[α]σι περὶ τῆς συγγενεί[ας ἡμῶν]
      [πρὸς] Τ[εγε]ά[τα]ς κ[αὶ τ]ὸ ψήφισμα τοῦτό τε καὶ τὸ παρὰ [Τεγε]α-
      τῶ[ν] ἐνηνεγμέν[ο]ν ἐμφανῆ τοῖς ἐπιγινο[μ]έν[οις ἦ]ι καὶ
```

20 μηδὲν τῶν τοι[ού]των εἰς τὸ δυνατὸν διὰ [χρόνο]υ πλῆ-
    [θ]ος εἰς λήθην πέσηι, ἀναγράψαι αὐτὰ εἰς σ[τήλ]ην λευ-
    κοῦ λίθου καὶ ἀναθεῖναι [α]ὐτὴν εἰς τὸ ἱερὸ[ν τῆς] Ἀθηνᾶς,
    [ἣ]ν ἱδρύσατο Αὔγη. (...)
    (provisions for the publication of the stele follow)

Text by F(ränkel) with W(ilhlem)'s restorations: L. 6 F. [—]ν; S(aba) [πολιτεία]ν.

Transl.: LL. 6–23: they shall partake in everything in which all other Tegeates do ... *proedria* at the Aleian festival ... It was decreed by the *demos* to praise the city of the Tegeates because they have kept memory of the familiarity toward our city and preserved the disposition that one should most appropriately have and is just and useful, (it was decreed) to crown (them) at the Panathenaia with a golden crown because of their loyalty and benevolence toward the *demos*, the *strategoi* are in charge of the announcement of the crown. It shall be possible for the Tegeates, who may want it, to live as citizens in Pergamon and partake in everything in which Pergamenes do. So that the words pertaining to our kinship with the Tegeates, which are preserved in the memoires, this decree and that brought by the Tegeates remain for posterity and none of these things fall into oblivion because of the (length of) time, they shall be inscribed on a stele of white marble and set up in the sanctuary of Athena that Auge founded. (...)

Paleography has helped to establish the date of this text to the first half of the 2nd century BC. The cult of Athena provides another chronological reference and indicates that this document was enacted in a year preceding the death of Eumenes II (159 BC).[27] It is possible that this inscription belongs to the early years of Eumenes's reign, as the historical background to the text that I attempt to reconstruct suggests.

This agreement testifies to an exchange of potential citizenship between two communities geographically distant but connected through kinship.

Tegea was an ancient city in the central-western Peloponnese, located ca. 50 km north of Sparta, in the historic region of Arkadia. It grew on a καλὸν

---

27 ALLEN 1983, p. 126 n. 189, referring to Ohlemutz: "(Eumenes) was concerned to advance the status of Athena at Pergamon in other ways, by propagating a spurious legendary origin of the cult."

πεδίον, an unusual feature for this region, according to Herodotos.[28] The early history of Tegea is better known than later events because our main source, Pausanias, dwells first on the mythological origins of the city and then moves to the years of its membership in the Achaean League. He thus leaves a gap of several centuries that only scattered pieces of information from Herodotos, Thucydides, archaeology, and sporadic epigraphic sources can illuminate.[29]

Just as the Attalids are key to Pergamon's history and development, Sparta's proximity influenced Tegea's life for centuries. Their relationship was not consistently a state of enmity or friendship, but rather alternated between phases of collaboration and armed opposition such that one can agree with Pretzler that this tense and ambiguous relationship defined part of Tegea's identity.[30]

After the battle of Sellasia in 222 BC, which *de facto* marked the end of Kleomenes III's attempt to revive Spartan power, Tegea entered the Achaean League, which at that time included numerous Arkadian communities (following its regionally limited beginnings in 280 BC).[31] Tegea was to continue its membership in the league until the Romans put an end to this political entity in 146 BC.[32]

Within this broadly defined historical context Pergamon and Tegea may have crossed paths. The Attalids did not plan to expand their power in mainland Greece,[33] yet, their political interests brought them to that region. Livy and Polybios testify to agreements that first Attalos and later Eumenes reached with the Achaean League. These sources also record their participation in the war that Greek communities, following Flaminius's encouragement, waged against Nabis between 195 and 192 BC.[34] A little later, around 187 BC, Polybios reports that Eumenes sent an embassy to renew the alliance with Achaea and

---

28 HDT 1.66.1. On Arkadia see NIELSEN and ROY 1999. NIELSEN 1999, pp. 16–79 focuses on the region of 'Arkadia' and its ethnic identity, while ROY 1999, pp. 320–381 deals with Arkadian economies. The intense research activity that has been conducted recently in this area clarified some of the prejudices attached to this very region.

29 PAUS. VIII.45–54.3, esp. 45.2. On Pausanias's text see also PRETZLER 1999, pp. 89–129.

30 PRETZLER 1999, pp. 114–118.

31 For the Achaean League see now MACKIL 2013 with further bibliography, esp. the numerous contributions by Rizakis. Tegea's membership is attested by numismatic evidence on which see also WARREN 2007, esp. pp. 122–123 and 2008 article, pp. 91–99.

32 See CARTLEDGE and SPAWFORTH 2002, esp. pp. 80–90 on the events in the Peloponnese from 188 to 146 BC.

33 See ALLEN 1971, pp. 1–12.

34 CARTLEDGE in CARTLEDGE and SPAWFORTH 2002, esp. pp. 59–79; ALLEN 1983, pp. 76–80, and esp. ERRINGTON's 1969 Appendix 5 on Eumenes and Achaea.

to show his benevolence to the league also by offering a substantial amount of money, which, however, the *synedrion* refused.[35]

As a member of the Achaean League, Tegea must have been on friendly terms with the Attalids at the beginning of the 2nd century BC. Even if it is impossible to pin down the specific events that led to the signing of *AvP* VIII.1 156 = no. 21, the early years of Eumenes's reign remain a possible setting for the stipulation of this agreement.

Kinship

The historical background I have just sketched is a modern, hypothetical reconstruction. The document under consideration does not refer to any of it, asserting instead that the agreement rested on kinship between Pergamon and Tegea. Kinship is expressed with both known terms of *oikeiotes* and *syngeneia*, and here, too, as in the case of the kinship between Miletos and Seleukeia-Tralles, the terms are not synonyms.[36] The kinship between Pergamon and Tegea had mythological roots, which the Tegean ambassadors probably explained in their speech by referring directly to the *hypomnemata* that figures in the decree, L. 18, too.[37]

The document also contains, LL. 23–24, the prescription for the inscribing and publication of the decree in τὸ ἱερὸ[ν τῆς] Ἀθηνᾶς, / [ἥ]ν ἱδρύσατο Αὔγη. Morphologically, the relative pronoun [ἥ]ν, refers to Athena, not to the sanctuary, and it probably refers to the cult of Athena. Aleos, Auge's father and founder of Tegea, had established a sanctuary of Athena that was to be known as Athena Alea.[38] According to this inscription, once in Pergamon, Auge herself founded a cult for this goddess.[39] This text plays with accepted and shared traditions: The material that the ambassadors presented was compelling and must have been favorably received in Pergamon along with the request to exchange the award of potential citizenship.

---

35 POLYB. XXII.7–9.
36 CURTY 1995, no. 41 and *supra* my comment on *Milet* I 3 143 = no. 5. Mythology lies at the heart of this kinship: on Auge and Telephos see PRETZLER 1999, pp. 91–92, PAUS. VIII.48.7 presents different versions of the myth. This story is also depicted on the frieze of the Great Altar, see HANSEN 1971², pp. 340–341.
37 Auge, daughter of king Aleos, was raped by Herakles and became pregnant with a child who, according to an oracle, would have killed her brother. She was expelled from Tegea and gave birth to Telephos, with whom, in one version of the myth, she appeared again in the Kaikos valley as king Teuthras's bride.
38 PAUS. VIII.45.3.
39 See ALLEN 1983, p. 125 concerning the cult of Athena Nikephoria established by Eumenes II; OHLEMUTZ 1940, pp. 16–59.

Potential Citizenship

Unfortunately, we only know this text through the second half of Pergamon's decree. Its first part, which would summarize the content of Tegea's embassy, is largely lost. L. 5 (and perhaps L. 6) mentions a grant of potential citizenship (πολιτείαν) and, possibly, a *metechein* formula. Additionally, in L. 8 we can read that Tegea adds a grant of *proedria* for the Aleaia to all Pergamenes.[40]

L. 9 preserves the motion formula that introduces Pergamon's response to Tegea's embassy: LL. 9–15 praise Tegea's benevolence and attitude toward Pergamon, which, they say, was motivated by kinship (*oikeiotes*). The authorities recommend that the Tegeans be granted a golden crown at the Panathenaia, to be announced by the *strategoi*. Reciprocation of the grant of potential citizenship follows, in an abbreviated form, LL. 15–18: any Tegean who may want it, could live in Pergamon as a citizen and partake in everything just as the citizens of the town do. The text then focuses on the necessity of perpetuating the memory of the kinship between the two communities, here *syngeneia*, as attested in preexisting documents. This requirement is to be achieved by inscribing the decree and the other documents on stone.

No enrollment clause or additional concession appears, which, however, is also true for the grant between Pergamon and Temnos that adopts the same formula. Even if I can rely only on these documents, I am tempted to consider this absence of details in enrollment procedures simply as a practice of the grantees and grantors, but this view remains hypothetical. It is more important to note that, although potential citizenship is the actual 'outcome' of Tegea's diplomatic mission, the real focus of the decree is to preserve the memory and the recognition of a shared past. With the embassy, Tegea presents the historical material for a common, shared past that Pergamon receives well but probably required further elaboration. Possibly, for this reason the two cities used different terms for kinship.

---

40   NIELSEN *Inventory* 297, esp. p. 532 on the Aleaia that were celebrated for Tegea's main deity, Athena Alea. The sanctuary for this deity probably preceded Tegea's urbanization, PAUS. VIII.45–47. Early French excavations studied the sanctuary, with more recent archaeological research at the city conducted by the Norwegian Archaeological School of Athens from 1990 to 1994. For the city see "Ancient Arkadia" volume 2005 (III) (under ed. ØSTBY 2005 in the bibliography); for the sanctuary of Athena Alea ØSTBY 2002, pp. 139–147.

(22)   *Temnos and Teos*

Block of white marble found in the temple of Dionysos at Teos during the campaigns of 1963–1966. The upper part of the stone is broken; the lower portion preserves part of the frame. Measurements: H. 0.68; W. 0.51; Th. ca. 0.23. Letters: 0.009–0.12. For his 1979 publication, Herrmann could still examine the stone *in situ*.

Ed.: *ed. pr.* Herrmann 1979, pp. 242–249 (*ph.*); (*SEG* XXIX 1149).
Cf. J. and L. Robert *BE* 1980 437; Piejko 1986, p. 95.

    (names of the ambassadors LL. 2–3)
4   [διε]γνώσθη τοῦ αὐτοῦ μηνὸς ἕκτη[ι ⁶⁻⁸, γνώμη τι]-
    [μού]χων· ἐπειδὴ Τηΐων φίλων καὶ εὐνό[ων ὄντων καὶ συγ]-
    [γεν]ῶν τοῦ ἡμετέρου δήμου καὶ πολλ[ὰς ἐπιδείξεις πε]-
    [ποι]ημένων τῆς πρὸς τὴν πόλιν ἡμῶν ε[ὐνοίας ἐψηφίσατο]
8   [ὁ δ]ῆμος εἰσκηρύσεσθαι τὸν δῆμον τὸν Τη[ΐων εἰς προεδρίαν]
    [κα]ὶ στεφανοῦσθαι χρυσῶι στεφάνωι ἐν τοῖς ἀ[γῶσιν οὓς ἐ]-
    [πι]τελεῖ ὁ δῆμος τῶι τε Διονύσωι καὶ τοῖς βασιλ[ε]ῦ[σιν, διανε]-
    νόηκεν δὲ καὶ περὶ τῶν ἄλλων φιλαν[θ]ρώπων, κα[λῶς δὲ]
12 ἔχον ἐστὶν κἀκόλουθον τοῖς προεψηφ[ισμ]ένο[ις ε]ἶν[αι πολι]-
    τείαν Τηΐοις παρ᾿ ἡμῖν· δεδόχθαι τῆι βο[υλῆι] κα[ὶ δήμωι εἶ]-
    ναι πολιτείαν Τηΐοις ἐν Τήμνωι ἐφ᾿ ἴση[ι κ]αὶ ὁμοίαι [καὶ μετουσί]-
    αν πάντων ὧν καὶ τοῖς ἄλλοις πολίταις μέτεστιν, εἶνα[ι]
16 δὲ καὶ γῆς καὶ οἰκίας ἔγκτησιν καὶ ἐπιγ[α]μίαν πα[ρ᾿] ἡμῖν [Τηί]-
    οις καὶ δίκας προδίκους καὶ ἐὰν βούληται ὁ Τήϊος ἐπικλ[η]-
    ροῦσθαι ἐπὶ τὴν φυλὴν ἐπικληρωθῆναι αὐτὸν ὑπὸ τῶν τιμο[ύ]-
    χων· ἵνα δὲ καὶ Τήϊοι εἰδήσωσιν τὴν τοῦ δήμου πρὸς αὐ-
20 τοὺς εὔνοιαν, ἀποστεῖλαι δὲ κα(ὶ) πρεσβευτὰς τοὺς ἐ[πε]-
    λευσομένους ἐπὶ τὴν ἐκκλησίαν καὶ παρακαλέσοντ[ας]
    καὶ Τηΐους τὴν αὐτὴν αἵρεσιν ἔχειν πρὸς τὴν ἡμετέρα[ν]
    πόλιν. πρεσβευταὶ ἐδείχθησαν Σάτυρος Ζωΐλου, [...]
24 Θέμις Λυσίου, Ἡρογείτων Ἀθηναίου.

Text and restorations by H(errmann) unless otherwise noted: L. 4 ἐ]γνώσθη H; [διε]γνώσθη R(obert) and P(iejko); LL. 5/6 φίλων καὶ εὐνό[ων ὄντων καὶ συγ]/[γεν]ῶν H., rejected by C(urty)

Transl.: (LL. 5–23): Given that the Teians are friends, benevolent, and kin to our *demos* and have shown many times their benevolence toward our people, the *demos* has voted to invite the people of the Teians to *proedria* and to award them a golden crown in the agons that our people organize for Dionysos and the kings, and has contemplated other benefactions as well, it is suitable and consistent with what has been decreed that the Teians have citizenship among us: Be it enacted by the *demos* and the *boule* that citizenship on an equal footing be granted to the Teians in Temnos and that (they) partake in everything in which other citizens do. The Teians shall have the right to own land and a house, the right to intermarriage in our (community), and to speedy trials. Also, if a Teian wishes to be registered in a tribe, the *timouchoi* shall do so. Moreover, so that the Teians see the benevolence of our people toward them, the appointed ambassadors shall go to the assembly and ask whether the Teians are also so inclined toward our *polis*. (...)

The decree dates to the end of the 3rd or beginning of the 2nd century BC according to paleography.[41] An additional chronological indicator is the reference to the "kings," L. 10, which could refer to the Attalids or the Seleukids, but, as Ma noted, it testifies in any case to royal euergetism.[42]

Teos

The history of Teos for the 3rd century BC is poorly known, but for the first decades of the 2nd century BC we have the rich *asylia* dossier from this town.[43]

According to Polybios, in 218 BC the city abandoned Achaios's side to become Attalid,[44] and probably stayed so until Antiochos reestablished his control over the area and freed Teos from the burden of onerous, Attalid taxes.[45]

Finally, Livy testifies that in 190 BC the Romans attacked Teian ships in their harbor because they were said to transport supplies for the Seleukid army. The Roman historian does not elaborate on Teos's destiny or its status after the peace of Apameia.[46]

---

41   HERRMANN 1979, p. 242.
42   HERRMANN 1979, pp. 245–246 opts for the Attalids after Apameia. See MA 2002, p. 143. The Seleukids appear as Teos's benefactors on other occasions, but this is not hard proof to prefer them over the Attalids: HERRMANN 1965 and MASTROCINQUE 1984(b), pp. 82–85.
43   Teos's relevance increased when the *technitai* moved into their town, but their relationship with the city proved difficult, ANEZIRI 2003, pp. 86–97. On *asylia* see RIGSBY 1996, pp. 280–325; see ANEZIRI 2003, esp. p. 91 on whether inviolability could have predated Antiochos's recognition. On Teos see also ALLEN 1983, pp. 45–57. On Temnos see *supra*, pp. 00.
44   POLYB. V.77.5. BUSSI 1999, pp. 161–162, n. 9 on the city's degree of autonomy had at the time.
45   HERRMANN 1965, text I. 18 and 33, see also pp. 101–105.
46   LIV. XXXVII.27. On Teos after Apameia see RIGSBY 1996, pp. 290–293; MASTROCINQUE 1984(a), pp. 157–159 argues that the city was given to the Attalids.

The Document

Herrmann published the text in 1979, but Gawantka knew it at the time of his own publication because Herrmann had made it available to him.[47] Gawantka rightly points out that this decree must represent only one part of Temnos's diplomatic initiative: LL. 19–20 preserve Temnos's request for Teian reciprocation of the grant of potential citizenship.

A legible text starts in L. 4 with the date and the board of magistrates drafting the document, the *timouchoi*, who are here attested for the first time in Temnos.[48] LL. 5–7 provide as motivations for this grant the traditional claims of friendship, benevolence, and kinship between Teos and Temnos.[49]

The two subsequent lines grant standard honors to the Teians, and then the Temnians offer, almost as if it were an afterthought, a greater recognition, namely, potential citizenship, LL. 13–19. After the formulaic concession with the *metechein* clause follows the award of additional grants such as *enktesis* and *epigamia*. These grants are otherwise uncommon in potential citizenship agreements in Asia Minor.[50] Another advantage Teians were to enjoy in Temnos was the right to 'speedy trials,' which must be considered an exceptional measure directed to protect the interests of a particular category of foreigners.[51] All these additional concessions indeed are extraordinary and point to Temnos's intent to promote and facilitate the temporary presence of Teians in their city. The final provision on the enrollment of new citizens, LL. 17–19, closes the body of the concession and precedes a final clause stressing Pergamon's intent to show benevolence.

Temnos has not yielded very much material, especially as it has not yet been properly investigated archaeologically. For this reason, it is all the more remarkable that we possess two concessions of potential citizenship from this city. These decrees, both rather detailed, bilateral agreements, were passed at the opposite ends of the 3rd century BC. Both carefully regulate matters important to city life, but the decree for Teos seems to address more forcefully the issue of protecting and thus favoring the interests of privileged foreigners present for a short time only within its boundaries. This text includes another extremely rare grant for this area, namely, intermarriage: so far this example is the only known inscription from Asia Minor that associates potential citizenship and *epigamia*. Right to intermarriage was normally adopted to create

---

47 The text figures in the list of evidence that GAWANTKA 1975 provides at the end of his work, p. 214 no. 39.
48 On this see HERRMANN's commentary 1979, pp. 246–247.
49 HERRMANN 1979, p. 247, but CURTY 1995, p. 224, n. 3 rejects Herrmann's restoration, which I retain because it seems to agree with the general context.
50 SABA 2011, pp. 101–102 on *epigamia*.
51 See HERRMANN 1979, p. 249; on *symbola* see GAUTHIER 1972.

closer ties (and normalize tense situations) especially between neighboring cities or within federal communities: its concession was a rather well-defined institutional strategy. But here none of these circumstances apply.[52]

The document fits the general character of the (sparse) surviving evidence for Temnos: the Aeolian city tried to assert its presence in the region by establishing relations with nearby *poleis*. Teos's answer to this specific decree is unknown, but it almost certainly reciprocated the grant.

(23)   *Skepsis and Parion*

Block of white marble with a rather weathered surface, broken on its upper and lower ends. The stone was found in Kurşunlu and is now stored in the Çanakkale Museum, Inv. No. 4–2-1967. Measurements: H. 0.485; W. 0.48; Th. ca. 0.07; Letters: 0.01–0.15. According to J. and L. Robert *BE* 1972 371 the text belongs to the "haute époque hellénistique."

Edd.: *ed. pr.* Taşlıklıoğlu II. no. 1, p. 204 *(ph.)*; J. and L. Robert *BE* 1972 371; [*I. von Parion* T 62, LL. 10–24; McCabe, IMT Skam/NebTaeler 378].

```
                        ]ΙΚΑ
                    ]Ι ἤδη δύο
                  ]ας ἡμέρας ΑΓ
4                 ]ιν ὅπου ἂν δοκῆι
                  ]Ν πόλιν τὴν ἐπικα-
[λ …] ………………… ἓξ δραχμὰς ἑκάστωι
   [              ἡμ]έρας τὴν δὲ βοήθειαν ἐ-
8  [        ἐν ἡμ]έραις πέντε ἀφ' ἧς ἂν ἐπαγγ-
[είλωσιν κατὰ?] πρεσβείαν ἀποστέλλε(ι)ν ἐν δέκα
ἡμέραις ἀφ' ἧς ἂν ἡμέρας ἐπαγγείλωσι. πολί-
την δὲ εἶναι τὸν Παριανὸν Σκηψίων ἐὰν θέ-
12 [λ]η, καὶ τὸν Σκήψιον Παριανῶν ἐὰν θέλῃ· καὶ
ἔνκτησιν εἶναι τῶι Παριαγῶι ἐν Σκήψει καὶ
ἐὰν οἰκῆι ἐν Σκήψει καὶ ἂν μὴ οἰκῆι· κατὰ ταὐ-
τὰ δὲ καὶ τῶι Σκηψίωι ἐμ Παρίωι· ὅσοι δ' ἂν
16 Σκηψίων οἰκῶσιν ἐμ Παρίωι ἢ γῆι τῆι Παρια-
νῶν ἓξ μῆνας ἢ πλέον φέρειν τέλη ὅσ' ἂν Παρι-
ανοὶ φέρωσι καὶ ἂν τις Παριανῶν οἰκῆι ἐν
Σκήψει ἢ γῆι τῆι Σκηψίων ἓξ μῆνας ἢ πλέον
```

---

52   See SABA 2011, pp. 101–102 where I suggest that in this text one could see the indirect influence of grants *ad personam*.

20 φέρειν τέλη ὅσα ἂν καὶ Σκήψιοι φέρωσι· ἢν
    δέ τις χρήματα μεταβάληι φυγῆς ἕνεκεν,
    ἀτελῆ εἶναι ἕνα ἐνιαυτόν· ἐν δὲ τοῖς ἀγῶσι
    κηρύσσεσθαι εἰς προεδρίαν ἐμ Παρίωι Σκη-
24 ψίους καὶ ἐν Σκήψει Παριανούς· προσομνύ-
    ναι δὲ τὴν βουλὴν καὶ τὰς ἄλλας ἀρχὰς ἐμ Π[α]-
    ρίωι καὶ τὴν Σκηψίων βουλὴν καὶ τ[ὰς ἄλλας]
    ἀρχὰς πρὸς τῶι ἄλλωι ὅρκωι κ - - -
28 ἔτος ἐμμένειν τοῖς ὁρκίο[ις - - -
    μενοις Παριανοῖς κ[- - -
    ἄλλο ἐπὶ συντιθω[- - -
    τοῖς ὅρκοις [- - -
    τὴν βοήθειαν[- - -

Text by J. and L. Robert 1972.

Transl.: LL 6–27.... six drachmas each, days ... help ... within five days from the day in which they would announce to dispatch the embassy, within 10 days from that of the announcement ...

... (L. 10) a Parian shall be citizen of the Skepsians, if he wants, and a Skepsian of the Parians, if he wants. A Parian in Skepsis shall also have the right to ownership, whether he resides there or not, the same shall apply to a Skepsian in Parion. Those Skepsians who happen to live in Parion or in its land for six months or longer, shall pay taxes as Skepsians do, and those of the Parians who happen to live in Skepsis or in its land for six months or longer, shall pay taxes as Parians do. However, if anyone has transferred his possessions because of flight, he shall be exempted from taxes for one year. Skepsians shall be invited to *proedria* in all contests in Parion, and Parians in Skepsis; the *boule* and all other offices in Parion and the *boule* of the Skepsians and all other offices shall swear to the other oath....

The inscription under examination must have originally included (1) a treaty stipulating military aid, (2) a grant of potential citizenship between Skepsis and Parion, and (3) an oath that refers to the military treaty. Keywords in the fragmentary beginning and end of the stele help to identify the general framework of the agreement as a military alliance into which clauses concerning potential citizenship and the other additional grants are inserted.[53] The

---

53   J. and L. ROBERT *BE* 1972 371 define the document a "un traité d'assistance militaire".

fragmentary beginning of the inscription indeed records the amount of money soldiers were to receive daily, namely, six *drachmai*, a stipulation concerning how the cities had to provide military help and also the timeline for responding to a call.

Skepsis

Skepsis was located in inland Troad, separated by the river Skamander from that of the neighboring (and enemy) Kebren.[54] Skepsis must have been originally an Aeolian city but, according to Strabo, in the 5th century BC Miletos sent a contingent of colonists who brought 'democratic institutions' with them.[55]

In the 19th century travelers identified the remains of the (still) unexcavated city and later evidence has confirmed this identification.[56] The debate on the location of a former settlement called Palaiskepsis, however, is still contested.[57]

Hellenistic Skepsis is not very well known, with the events of the years 213–199 BC particularly unclear.[58] For the aftermath of Alexander's death, we have an exceptional testimony: a letter that Antigonos Monophtalmos addressed to Skepsis and in which, while informing the citizens that the *diadochoi* had reached an agreement, he affirmed his concern and care for the freedom of Greek cities. Skepsis replied to this letter with a decree that conceded all possible honors to Antigonos, but its trust was misplaced.[59] Around 310 BC Antigonos forced this community and several others to unite in a new city, which he called Antigoneia.[60] This name was short-lived: after 301 BC, Lysimachos renamed the city Alexandreia Troas, allegedly in order to honor Alexander. He also freed Skepsis from the burden of the *synoikismos* so that the city could return to its autonomous status.[61]

54　STRAB. XIII.1.33.
55　STRAB. XIII.1.52; see LEAF 1923, on Skepsis esp. pp. 280–284.
56　For a full account see RICL 1997, pp. 177–183 and also COOK 1973, pp. 345–346.
57　AKALIN 2008, esp. pp. 8–9; pp. 10–11 on the town before Antigonos's intervention.
58　KAGAN 1984, p. 22.
59　See WELLES 1934, no. 1 and now KOTSIDOU 2000, no. 214.
60　On this *synoikismos* see AKALIN 2008, pp. 1–38; for recent archaeological work on Antigoneia-Alexandreia Troas see FEUSEN 2009; see also AYLWARD 2005, pp. 36–53 on housing in the Troad in light of *synoikismos*, on Skepsis see esp. pp. 49–50. After taking over the region, Lysimachos turned this city into the financial capital of the Troad, see ROSE 2003, esp. pp. 31–35.
61　STRAB. XIII.1.52: εἶτ' εἰς τὴν Ἀλεξάνδρειαν συνεπόλισε τοὺς Σκηψίους Ἀντίγονος, εἶτ' ἀπέλυσε Λυσίμαχος, καὶ ἐπανῆλθον εἰς τὴν οἰκείαν. The Skepsians struck again their own coins, KAGAN 1984, pp. 11–29 and ROBERT 1951, pp. 11–16.

After 281 BC, Skepsis must have been under Seleukid influence, but it is more difficult to determine how it positioned itself following the events that opposed Achaios and installed Antiochos in 213 BC. It is then possible that Antiochos III and Attalos reached an agreement that freed the Troad of the Seleukids; this status could have lasted until the early 2nd century BC, when the Seleukid king reextended his power in the area.[62]

Parion

Ancient sources testify to Milesian involvement in the foundation of Parion, but it is thought that a contingent from Paros figured decisively in the success of the city's foundation, such that the city derived its name from this island.[63] Parion was a coastal town with a convenient harbor that made it attractive over the centuries.[64] Hellenistic Parion's history is poorly known, but the surviving evidence shows that, just as in Skepsis, this *polis* fell, too, to Antigonos in 311 BC. Around 295/4 BC, it must have allied with Lysimachos until his death in 281 BC. The parallel histories of Parion and Skepsis possibly continued through the years after the battle of Kouropedion.

A text from Chios attesting to this community's verdict in a dispute between Lampsakos, one of the most faithful cities to the Attalids, and Parion provides evidence to assess the city's political orientation.[65] Using this text, P. Frisch hypothesizes that Parion sided with the Seleukids at the eve of the peace of Apameia. But a conflict with an ally of Pergamon is not solid proof. Strabo, XIII.1.14 may be more useful: at some unspecified point, Parion seems to have enlarged its territory, with the support of the Attalids, by taking over part of the neighboring Priapos.[66] Clearly, however this community may have allied itself before 188 BC, Parion afterward conducted fruitful diplomatic activities.

Both cities were members of the *koinon* of Athena Ilias. It is uncertain whether Antigonos or Alexander founded it, but certainly the *koinon* had Lysimachos's support.[67] This *koinon* is only epigraphically attested and

---

62   KOSMETATOU 2003, pp. 56–58; MA 2002 pp. 89–90; RICL 1997, esp. pp. 180–181; KAGAN 1984, p. 22 and the discussion by LANZILLOTTA 1978 on TAŞLIKLIOĞLU 1971, II, pp. 206–207 on which see also J. and L. ROBERT *BE* 1972 371.
63   See EHRHARDT 1988, pp. 36–37 and LEAF 1923, pp. 80–86.
64   *I.Parion*, esp. pp. 47–55 and again pp. 62–66 with an historical outline for the Archaic and Classical city.
65   McCabe Chios 28 (*ed. pr.* VANSEVEREN 1937, pp. 337–344, n. 10) now also in *I.Parion* T 59.
66   LEAF 1923, pp. 73–76. STRAB. XIII.1.14; on Parion's progressive growth see PRÊTEUX 2009, esp. pp. 337–341.
67   On the *koinon* see ROSE 2003, pp. 61–63; BILLOWS 1999, pp. 218–219; *I.Ilion* esp. pp. XI–XV and the inscriptions nos. 1–18; see also ROBERT 1966, pp. 18–46.

we know that in the Hellenistic period it had 12 members that contributed annually to finance the Lesser and Greater Panathenaia. Other income, such as from renting sacred land, allowed this sanctuary to function as one of the "temple banks" described by Bogaert.[68] A common sanctuary with a deity that could vouch for the reliability of both partners and 'protect' their agreement may be of relevance here. Finally, I must note that, also following J. and L. Robert's chronological estimate, this treaty must have been signed after 301 or before ca. 310 BC, in consideration of Skepsis's status.

The Treaty

Before moving to the grant of potential citizenship, an additional consideration of the character of the treaty is due. Although it is a military alliance, this treaty does not have to be tied to an imminent peril but could have been a preventive agreement.

The details of the military agreement are lost to us, but in LL. 10–24 the text changes topic and regulates in great detail a grant of potential citizenship that deserves an equally detailed commentary.

LL. 10–12 contain the actual grant of potential citizenship expressed with a conditional clause whose protasis, ἐὰν θέλῃ, defines clearly the potential nature of the concession. The apodosis of the conditional clause contains *ethnika* that refer to the parties involved.

LL. 12–15 establish a reciprocal right to ownership for members of both communities.[69] I have already pointed out the relevance of additional grants to understand a city's general policy and the goals a community pursued with the concession of potential citizenship. The possible beneficiaries of these additional concessions have been debated by scholarship with differing results. Specific rules must have certainly varied from case to case, but, as Chaniotis has concluded for Crete, I assume that every citizen of a community to which the grant was directed was entitled to the benefits coming from the additional concessions, whether or not he switched citizenship.[70]

The exchange of *enktesis* contained in this document has attracted attention because it specifies that the grant was not subject to residency. Was this specification so exceptional that it needed to be clearly articulated? Or was it a necessary premise to the rules on local taxation that follow in the text (LL. 15–22)?

---

68 On Ilion see BOGAERT 1968, pp. 237–240. For the financial organization of the *koinon* see esp. *I.Ilion* 5; 6; 10 and 11.
69 See HENNIG 1994, esp. pp. 334–335.
70 See CHANIOTIS 1996, p. 103, n. 619 and pp. 109–111.

Except for Crete, where the right to ownership often accompanies a grant of potential citizenship,[71] this additional grant rarely appears in other areas. In Asia Minor *isopoliteiai* the only instances of *enktesis* can be found in the agreements between Temnos and Teos (*SEG* XXIX 1149 = no. 22), and between Pergamon and Temnos (*AvP* VIII.1.5 = no. 20) as well as in the inscription under examination. In the mainland, instead, two treaties, that between Aitolians and Akarnanians (*IG* IX 1² 1 3A = no. 40) and that involving Naupaktos, Aitolia, and Keos (*StV* III 508 = no. 41), contain a reciprocal grant of right to ownership. Finally, the very short inscription that testifies to potential citizenship between Knidos and Chalke (*IKnidos* 605 = no. 43) mentions, LL. 6–7, γᾶς ἐνων[ὰν] which means right to ownership, but without further details.

Temnos made a unilateral concession of potential citizenship along with other grants to Teos, but it sought reciprocation (*SEG* XXIX 1149 = no. 22). *Enktesis* is only one of the listed additional grants, the others being *epigamia* and the right to a speedy trial. With the grants, Temnos tried to provide favorable conditions for the temporary presence of Teians in its territory and probably cement their relationship.[72] The text of the agreement between Skepsis and Parion instead pursues a very different goal, namely, safeguarding property and disciplining propertied taxation.

The agreement between Pergamon and Temnos was established following a Pergamene embassy that had requested a bilateral exchange of potential citizenship (LL. 8–9). Although the text assumes the form of an honorary decree, the acceptance of Pergamon's proposal by the Temnians was the premise to a factual, detailed agreement (LL. 15–23) that unfortunately is only partly preserved. The text contains a grant of *enktesis* immediately followed by the regulation of taxes related to property, which strongly suggests that the text pursued practical goals (perhaps temporary presence) along with diplomatic goals.

The treaty between Aitolians and Akarnanians, ca. mid-3rd century BC, includes another joint concession of grants of *enktesis* and potential citizenship. Like the agreement between Skepsis and Parion, this document also contains a military alliance. But this comparison can prove risky: the situation in northern Greece may have been very different from that in the Troas, and we lack the ability to properly assess the difference. Aitolia and Akarnania were longstanding enemies who agreed to an alliance in dire circumstances; as it would

---

71 *I.Cret.* III.iii 4 = CHANIOTIS 1996, 255–263 no. 28 = no. 52, LL. 13–14; *I.Cret.* III.iii 6 = CHANIOTIS 1996, 273–274 no. 35 = no. 53, L. 3 restored; *I.Cret.* I.xvi 17 = CHANIOTIS 1996, 276–278 no. 37 = no. 54, LL. 11–12; CHANIOTIS 1996, 337–351 no. 59, LL. 11–13 restored = no. 56. Cretan communities also granted *enktesis* to Teos in the *asylia* documents, for which see *infra*.

72 On the peculiar concession of *epigamia* see SABA 2011.

turn out, this alliance survived only for a short time. In other words, knowledge of the general historical conditions is vital to the interpretation of the concessions contained in this piece of evidence. For the agreement between Skepsis and Parion, however, the historical context is unknown so that we must interpret the award using the detailed conditions under which it was granted. Finally, the grant of *enktesis* for Keos, and reciprocated by this community, was given by Naupaktos, i.e., an Aitolian city, which suggests that this could be a local practice.

The problems that Skepsis and Parion regulate were not unique to them, but the cities address the issues with an uncommon precision and propose solutions that must have been determined by the historical (unknown to us) circumstances.

LL. 15–20 specify that to use *enktesis* Skepsians and Parians do not have to switch citizenship or live in the partner city. Then the focus shifts from *all* Skepsians and Parians to only those who live in the partner city or its territory.[73] These individuals must start paying taxes just like the citizens of the host *polis* after a period of residency of six or more months.[74] The question to ask, although it remains largely unanswerable, pertains to the taxation system that applied to these people before the six months had elapsed. Any period of residency shorter than six months must have been considered temporary, but we do not know whether, before this deadline, owners were exempt from any form of taxation or had to pay higher taxes. It is important to consider that the general terms of this concession are distinctly marked by reciprocal generosity and, normally, in treaties such deadlines establish the end of exceptionally favorable conditions.[75]

LL. 20–22: In 1972 J. and L. Robert urged a study of the expression φυγῆς ἕνεκεν, which H. Müller addressed a few years later.[76] In his contribution, Müller interprets the sentence with this expression by assigning to almost each word a secondary meaning: χρήματα would mean "bewegliche Habe," μεταβάλλειν "transportieren," and, finally, φυγῆς ἕνεκεν would have nothing to

---

[73] Scholars have already noted the peculiar use that this agreement makes of the term *ghe* in L. 16 and L. 19 where one would expect the more usual *chora*. Recently, PRÊTEUX 2009, p. 342 has suggested that '*ghe*' has an almost religious meaning and indicates the city proper as a 'homeland.'

[74] On *ateleia* and taxation see RUBINSTEIN 2009.

[75] In several *sympoliteia* agreements, temporary housing and favorable tax conditions were given to facilitate the move of new citizens, who, after this set period, were required to start paying like all other residents, see SABA 2007.

[76] MÜLLER 1975, pp. 129–156; J. and L. ROBERT *BE* 1972 371, esp. p. 449; see also J. and L. ROBERT *BE* 1976 574 with an approval of his argument.

do with a ban[77] and would mean instead "Flucht vor dem Gegner im Kriege." This clause would agree with the militaristic nature of the text: both cities agree to welcome each other's citizens and permit them to bring in their possessions, without subjecting them to taxation for a year, double the time normally prescribed.

LL. 22–24 contain a reciprocal grant of *proedria*, which must be considered an added benefit and was meant to confirm the privileged status of the citizens of Skepsis and Parion in both communities.

The Oath and the General Interpretation of the Text

The closing lines of the inscription contain the oath that all major governing organs of the cities had to swear. This feature is common in military alliances.[78] J. and L. Robert note that the verb used in this section is προσόμνυμι and then, L. 27, the text refers to yet 'another' oath, as if the cities had to take additional vows. The focus here is undoubtedly on the military alliance.

A combination of grants of potential citizenship and newly stipulated alliances are common in Crete, where also *epigamia* and *enktesis* are routinely added to these agreements.[79] In these instances all three grants work together as diplomatic means to cement the treaties. Outside of Crete, alliances and grants of potential citizenship are rarely associated, so that scholars could rightly remark that the award of potential citizenship is a tool mainly employed in peaceful or pacified situations. Gawantka has devoted a few pages to the connection between military alliances and potential citizenship in non-Cretan *comparanda*.[80] Unsurprisingly, he could only find the treaties between the Aitolians and Akarnanians and between Miletos and Herakleia under Mt. Latmos. The latter, however, comes at the end of a war and presents a very different contexts than a (preventive) military alliance.[81]

Be that as it may, the closest term of comparison for the alliance between Skepsis and Parion is probably *IG* IX² 1 3A = no. 40, even if only superficially.[82] The heading of the document defines it συνθήκα καὶ συμμαχία—between Aitolia

---

[77] Thus still PRÊTEUX 2009, p. 342.
[78] No oath refers to potential citizenship. For example, an oath appears in the peace treaty between Miletos and Herakleia, *Milet* I 3 150 = no. 7, LL. 109–115 (but it refers to peace), and in the agreement between Phigaleia and Messene, *IPArk* 28 = no. 39. The second agreement focuses on the conditions for the use of the land between the two cities and their relationship with the Aitolians: the parties swear to keep the terms of the agreement they have reached.
[79] See CHANIOTIS 1996, pp. 101–104.
[80] GAWANTKA 1975, pp. 143–151 with a convincing theoretical analysis of this institution.
[81] *IG* IX² 1 3A = no. 40; *Milet* I 3 150 = no. 7.
[82] SCHOLTEN 2000, esp. pp. 78–83 and KLAFFENBACH 1955, pp. 46–51.

and Akarnania—and the terms of the latter are carefully listed in LL. 26–40. A weakened Epiros and the Macedonian threat must have prompted the stipulation of this agreement, with which the two partners established reciprocal *epigamia, enktesis,* and *politeia,* i.e., a grant of potential citizenship that is here, however, not specified. That two federal states are involved raises questions that directly relate to the lack of clauses regulating potential citizenship. These leagues probably never anticipated any form of implementation for these concessions.[83] In the agreement between Aitolia and Akarnania potential citizenship seals the συμμαχία; in the Troad, beyond absolving this warranty-role, the grant could be interpreted as a safety net created by the *poleis* for their citizens. This function is very unusual in Asia Minor, but there is no doubt that this text contains a testimony for the institution of *isopoliteia*.

(24) Laodikeia on the Lykos and [---]*ikeia?*

This recently found inscription has added to the existing general dossier of texts that testify to grants of potential citizenship. The first editor of the inscription, F. Guizzi, dates it to "fine II–inizio I d.C." As Hamon notes, "d.C." must be a typographical error for 'a.C.'. In any case, the date would still be too low, and Hamon instead proposes the end of the 3rd or the beginning of the 2nd century BC.

The stone preserves a fragmentary decree enacted by an unknown city in response to a request by the *demos* of Laodikea on the Lykos and reciprocates a grant of *isopoliteia,* L. 5.[84] Guizzi, tentatively restores the name of the unknown city as that of Stratonikeia, but, in his commentary to this new inscription in *BE,* P. Hamon stresses the hypothetical nature of the restoration. Hamon adds that the name as attested in the patronymic *Naukratou* is thus far unknown for Stratonikeia. This observation neither weakens nor strengthens the identification, but must be addressed.

---

83 The Aitolians signed a very similar agreement with the Cretan city of Axos *IG* IX 1² 1 193 = *I.Cret.* II.V. 18A = no. 45 at the end of the 3rd century BC. Gawantka has noted already that this is the only potential citizenship and military alliance that a Cretan city signed with a community outside the island. The text, however, is too fragmentary to be useful.

84 Block of white marble, with the right side nearly chiseled out. The reuse of the stone created two holes on the left side. The inscription was found in the gymnasium of Laodikeia and is now stored in the Museum of Denizli. The *editio princeps* is by GUIZZI 2008, no. 3 (ph); but see the text in *SEG* LVIII 1541 with Hamon's restorations as in HAMON *BE* 2010 554. In his work, GUIZZI 2008, pp. 20–22 reports the basic facts about the history of Laodikeia on the Lykos with the most relevant bibliography. Here I will not attempt to trace the historical background to this agreement given the uncertainty that surrounds even the second subscriber. Here I use the text in *SEG* LVIII 1541.

The Decree

The document testifies that the *Laodikeis* sent an embassy to an unknown city bearing a decree with which their *demos* granted, among other things, *isopoliteia*, L. 5. The text (LL. 2–6) says: [ἐπειδὴ Λαοδικεῖς κοι]/[ν]ῆι τε πρὸς τὸν δῆμ[ον καὶ ἰδίαι πρὸς ἑκασ]/[τ]ὸν τῶν πολιτῶν [*e.g.* εὖνοι καὶ φίλοι ὄντες] / [ἐ]-ψηφίσαντο ἰσοπο[λιτείαν καὶ ἀτέλει]/[α]ν καὶ προεδρίαν, στ[εφανώσαντες δὲ τὸν] / [δ]ῆμον ἡμῶν χρυσῷ[ι στεφάνωι ...). The other city reciprocates the grant and uses standard formulae (LL. 22–25): [... ἐν ἀμ]φοτέραις [ταῖς πόλεσι ---] / [.. δε]-δόχθαι· εἶν[αι Λαοδικεῖς πολίτας καὶ] / [μετέχ]ειν αὐτο[ὺς πάντων ὧν καὶ οἱ ἄλλοι ?...] / [...]ικεῖς μετέχο[υσι·.... Finally, the closing lines of the same document seem to indicate that officials were in charge of visiting *Laodikeis*, thus suggesting that the cities (or the city?) favored the temporary presence of foreigners in their territories (LL. 28–31): [ὑπάρχειν δὲ αὐτοῖς] / [καὶ] ἔφοδον ἐπὶ τὴμ βουλὴν καὶ τοὺς στρα[τη]/[γο]ὺς καὶ τἆλλα ἀρχεῖα ἐπιμελεῖσθα[ι Λαο]/[δ]ικέων τῶν εἰς [τὴ]μ πόλιν ἀφ[ικ]νου[μένων]. Further discussion of the intent and nature of this exchange between Laodikeia and the unknown city, however, cannot be offered given the fragmentary condition of the stone.

Disputed Cases

(25) *Ephesos and Sardis*

Inscr. Sardeis VII.6 is an extremely fragmentary text considered by Buckler and Robinson to be part of an agreement through which Sardis and another city, probably Ephesos, exchanged citizenship.[85] These scholars also suggested that this fragment probably belongs to the Sardian copy of the agreement between this city and Ephesos, otherwise known through the copy from Pergamon.[86]

Gawantka does not include this text in his collection because it is too fragmentary and, as Laffi notes, because he considers its date too late (ca. 100 BC) to contain an exchange of potential citizenship. This latter reason, however,

---

85   For a detailed treatment see LAFFI 2010, esp. pp. 103–105 with further bibliography. I copy here the text by Buckler and Robinson as it appears in *Inscr. Sardeis* VII.6, but their restorations must be considered *exempli gratia*:
[.... ἐὰν δέ τις Σαρδιανῶν βούληται] πολιτεύεσθαι ἐν [Ἐφέσωι],
[ἐπικληρῶσαι αὐτὸν τοὺς ἐσσῆνας ε]ἰς φυλὴν καὶ χιλιαστ[ὺν καὶ εἶ]-
[ναι αὐτῶι ἔφοδον ἐπὶ τὴν βουλὴν καὶ τὸ]ν δῆμον καὶ τέλη φ[έρειν]
4 [αὐτὸν ἴσα καὶ ὅμοια τοῖς ἄλλοις τοῖς τὴν] πόλιν οἰκοῦσιν· ὅ τ[ι δὲ ἂν δι]-
[άγηι τις διὰ Σαρδέων εἰς Ἔφησον ἢ διὰ Ἐφήσο]υ εἰς Σάρδεις δια[γωγήν]
[τούτου εἶναι αὐτῶι ἀτελεῖ ...]

86   *AvP* VIII.3 268 also *OGI* 437 on which see LAFFI 2010.

is insufficient to reject its interpretation as a piece of evidence for potential citizenship: the last known treaty of potential citizenship dates to 110/9 BC.[87] But Laffi's argument pro-*isopoliteia*, i.e., that this tool was often associated with broader agreements and especially military agreements, is equally weak because, in Asia Minor, the opposite is true.

Commenting on the text, H. Müller has pointed out that in L. 4 the verb *oikeo* appears within a sentence that, in a grant of potential citizenship, should have introduced a comparison with citizens. Instead, the verb implies only a generic reference to 'inhabitants.'[88] This term could indicate that the agreement contained special arrangements for taxation, but perhaps not a grant of potential citizenship. Still the first line would seem to suggest that citizenship rights were at stake. The contradictions in the text and its fragmentary state recommend that, for now, we consider the nature of this text undetermined.

(26)   *Priene and Maroneia*
Stele of blue marble found reused in the paving of Priene's main Byzantine church. According to the *editio princeps*, the lettering of the inscription dates to the end of the 4th century BC. The stone is now stored in Berlin, Inv. No. 16. Measurements: H. 0.92; W. 0.495; Th. ca. 0.08; Letters: 0.013.

Ed. *I.Priene* 10 and p. 308; [*IThr. Aeg.*, TE 83, pp. 114–115; McCabe Priene 62].

```
                  - - - εἶναι δὲ Μαρω-
12   [νίτα(ι?)]ς ἰσοπολιτείαν ἐν Πριή]ν[ηι], μετεῖ-
     [ναι] δ' αὐ[τοῖς καὶ τῶν ἄλλων καὶ] ἱερ[ῶν] κ[α]ὶ ἀρ-
     χε[ί]ω[ν ὅσων καὶ Πριηνεῦσιν μέτεστιν· ......]
     [.....]ΕΙ[..]Ι[..]ΛΛ[.. 10 c ... ἢν δέ] τις Μα-
16   [ρ]ωνιτέω[ν ἀδικῆι τινα Πριηνέων, ἐπαγγεῖλαι]
     [πρ]ὸς τὸγ γρ[α]μ[μ]α[τέα τῆς βουλῆς καὶ το]ὺς τι-
     μούχος [......]τῶ[ν - - -]
     κεῦ[ν] τ[ῆ]ι πό[λει [..] ΛΝ [- - -]
20   στήμ Π[ριήνη]ν [..... ἢν δέ τις Πριήνεων ἀδι]-
     κῆι τιν[α] Μα[ρ]ωνιτέ[ων ἢ τῶν οἰκούντων ἐμ Πριή]
     νηι ἢ τῶν εἰσα[φικνουμένων εἰς τὴν χώραν τὴν Πριή]-
     νέων, ἐπαγγεῖλαι ἐλ[λόγωι πρὸς τὰς ἀρχὰς· κτλ ...
```

LL. 11/ 12 εἶναι δὲ Μαρω[νίτα(ι?)]ς ἰσοπολιτείαν Hiller von Gaertringen; εἶναι δὲ Μαρω[νίτα(ι?)]ς πολιτείαν ... Saba.

---

87   *I.Cret.* I.xvi 5 = CHANIOTIS 1996, 358–376 no. 61 = no. 58 treaty between Latos and Olous.
88   MÜLLER 1975, p. 144, n. 55.

Transl.: LL. 11–23: (11) the Maroneitans shall have [*politeia*? in Priene], they shall have access to the sacred activities and the offices in which the Prieneans partake. - - - (17) if a Maroneitan harms a Prienean, he shall report to the secretary of the council and the *timouchoi* - - - (20) [if a Prienean] injures any of the Maroneitans who either lives in Priene or has come to the territory of Priene he shall notify [the authorities] in this regard (...)

Hiller von Gaertringen dates the document to the last quarter of the 4th century BC, or earlier, mainly on the basis of the Ionicisms in the language. The absence of any other internal reference and the impossibility of placing the *stephanephoros* Philon in a chronological sequence hinder more precision.[89]

Priene

The Ionian city located north of Miletos on the Mykale peninsula was never a major player in Asia Minor. Although the impressive results of the German excavations have attracted modern interest toward this town, our knowledge of its history, remains incomplete.[90]

After the liberation and the establishment of a democratic government by Alexander, Antigonos must have taken control of the area until the battle of Ipsos ended his life. The Rhodian arbitration on the contested territories between Samos and Priene testifies to the presence of a tyrant, Hieron, who ruled over Priene for about three years, after which dissidents expelled

---

89   CROWTHER 1996, p. 198 on Ionicisms.
90   WIEGAND und SCHRADER 1904; KLEINER *RE* Suppl. IX (1962), 1187–1190. For an outline of the history of Archaic and Classical Priene see SCHIPPOREIT 1998, pp. 205–210. Numerous questions on this town's history remain unresolved. One of the most important queries pertains to its 'second' foundation. Excavations have yielded a negligible amount of material dating earlier than the 4th century BC, which has suggested to some that the *polis* was moved and re-founded after 334 BC. Not everybody, however, agrees with this thesis. DEMAND 1986, pp. 35–44 has voiced her skepticism and pointed out that archaeology has only provided *argumenta ex silentio*, unsupported by written sources, see STRAB. XIV.1.12 and PAUS. VII.2.10–11. She has also benefited from SHERWIN-WHITE's 1985 work redating the engraving of the Edict of Alexander, *I.Priene* 1 to Lysimachos's years. Even if Demand's arguments have not won general acceptance, they have led to a discussion on the original (?) location of Priene, which is unknown, and on the alleged founder of the new community. The three candidates for founder include Athens (which scholarship now tends to exclude), Alexander, and the Hekatomnids; see SCHIPPOREIT 1998, pp. 193–236 who believes that Priene had been in fact relocated and rebuilt with the help of the Hekatomnids; BOTERMANN 1994, pp. 162–187 instead hypothesizes that the city was never moved and its 4th-century BC buildings were constructed with Alexander's patronage.

him. Their base of operation was located on these contested territories.[91] Democracy (?) was apparently restored and the surviving epigraphic evidence testifies to the active role of king Lysimachos in this city's affairs.[92] After his death, the area experienced alternating Seleukid and Ptolemaic influence, with the first holding on to the region longer than the second.[93] A traumatic event for the city and its territory is attested in 278 BC, when the Galatians ravaged and despoiled the town.[94]

Maroneia

In 1880 S. Reinach spotted the ruins of Maroneia in Thrace; later travelers confirmed his identification.[95] The city was located on the coastline in the northern Aegean opposite the island of Samothrace about 40 km away. Mt. Ismaros towered over the north-eastern side of the *polis*, which was built on a fertile and temperate plain. Two routes connected the town with the interior of Thrace: these routes made the community vulnerable to attacks from the north, but also opened new commercial possibilities. Excavations in the area began in 1969 and continued until 1988 bringing to light numerous testimonies that consistently date to the 4th century BC or later.[96]

The city was perhaps a Chian colony. It appears in the written sources for the first time in a fragment by Archilochos that sets the *terminus ante quem* for its foundation in the first half of the 7th century BC.[97] The chronological discrepancy between the foundation as attested in the literary sources and the excavated city has raised questions. Recently, relying mainly on numismatic evidence, a team of researchers has suggested that Maroneia had moved from an original, unknown location to a new one in the 4th century BC. These same scholars have also suggested that a possible location for Archaic and Classical

---

91 On Hieron, see MAGNETTO 2008, pp. 113–123.
92 SHERWIN-WHITE 1985, pp. 69–89. *I.Priene* 14 and 15 (WELLES, no. 44). With the first example the city grants honors to the king who rescued it from a war against local populations (?), which was taking the wrong turn. The second is an incomplete letter by Lysimachos, see CROWTHER 1996, pp. 221–224. The king was also called to judge the controversy between Samos and Priene on which see MAGNETTO 2008, esp. pp. 125–126.
93 See *I.Priene* 18 honors Larichos an official of the Seleukids; *I.Priene* 59 and 82 mention Zeuxis, Antiochos's III *epi ton pragmaton* on whom see MA 2002, pp. 123–130.
94 *I.Priene* 17.
95 PSOMA et al. 2008, pp. lvii–lix; ISAAC 1986 pp. 111–113.
96 For a history of the excavation see PSOMA et al. 2008, pp. lvii–lxx.
97 PS. SKYMNOS, LL. 676–680 is our only source on the Chian origin; for the location of the town see STRAB. VII, fr. 43, 44a. On Maroneia's foundation see MÖLLER 1996, pp. 315–324.

Maroneia is the Molyvoti peninsula, west of the later settlement.[98] Bakalakis, who first dug in the peninsula, found evidence pre-dating the 4th century BC, which he attributed to the Thasian colony of Stryme.[99] Psoma et al. propose instead to identify Stryme by Maroneia on the walled hill of Haghios Georgios, which would have later been absorbed by Maroneia.[100]

All that can be said with certainty is that at the end of the 4th century BC Maroneia enjoyed a prosperous period as an active *emporion*.[101] Philip II stormed the region in the 350s BC, probably attacking Maroneia's territory in 353 BC; Isaac, however, suggests that he did not take it until 338 BC.[102]

Important information for the Hellenistic history of the town comes from the numismatic evidence.[103] It reveals Lysimachos's presence in the area and, on the basis of a monogram ΑΓΑΘ, Psoma suggests that Maroneia briefly

---

98 PSOMA et al. 2008, pp. xlix–lii; LOUKOPOULOU and PSOMA 2008, with a discussion of the literary evidence, esp. pp. 62–63 on Maroneia, HDT. VII.108–109; DEM. L. 22. The attempt by Psoma et al. to align the archaeological and literary sources has met obstacles particularly from the conflicting pieces of information in Herodotos that cannot easily be clarified. These scholars also suggest that PL. *NH* IV.42, in which *Maronea prius Orthogurea dicta* (normally dismissed as inaccurate), is reliable. By contrast, they reject STRAB. VII, fr. 47, in which Orthagoreia was an independent town east of Maroneia at the time the latter allegedly moved; see LOUKOPOULOU and PSOMA 2008, pp. 77–78. They blame Strabo's sources for the error, primarily Herodotos who could not have known of Maroneia's move; his later sources too would refer already to the Maroneia that had been synoicized with Orthagoreia. For a discussion of this theory see SABA 2018.

99 Stryme appears on the Molyvoti peninsula on the Barrington Atlas too (51 E3) with a question mark; already ISAAC 1986, pp. 70–71 was skeptical.

100 LOUKOPOULOU and PSOMA 2008, on Stryme, pp. 62–63. See also the plan of the site of Maroneia with its different districts in PSOMA et al. 2008, p. lxxi. The authors must be right in rejecting Bakalakis's identification, but Haghios Georgios looks too close to Maroneia. HDT. VII.108–109 locates Stryme on a river, with a lake between Maroneia and Stryme; this location could be wrong. An inscription dated to AD 202 testifies that Stryme was located not far east of Traianoupolis, i.e., rather distant both from Molyvoti and Haghios Georgios. Finally, LOUKOPOULOU and PSOMA 2008, p. 76 cite LIV. XXXVIII.41 who identifies Sale, slightly west of Traianoupolis, as a *vicus Maroneitrum*, which, however, only suggests that Maroneia's interests had moved eastward.

101 Sources on the Classical city are scarce. See ISAAC 1986, pp. 117–123. PSOMA *et al.* 2008, p. 168 use the inscription from Vetren to confirm Maroneia's active role in local trade in the second half of the 4th century BC, but still identify the *emporion* of Pistiros with this city of central Bulgaria. See DEMETRIOU 2010, pp. 77–93 for the location of the *emporion* that she holds was on the coast. Also, Demetriou argues that this means that Maroneia and the other cities mentioned in the inscription could conclude fruitful diplomatic agreements with the new Odrysian regents that had replaced the assassinated Kotys in 359 BC, on which see ARCHIBALD 1998, pp. 145–150.

102 ISAAC 1986, p. 121.

103 PSOMA et al. 2008, pp. 207–254.

changed its name into Agathokleia, in honor of Lysimachos's son, but, after his execution, the town reverted to the original denomination of Maroneia.[104] This view remains, of course, hypothetical.

After the battle of Kouropedion, Seleukid and Ptolemaic kings conquered, lost, and ruled over the region. For the most part, we lack other direct evidence on Maroneia, except for a few pieces of information pertaining to the Ptolemaic garrison that probably saved the city from the Gauls. The last years before the peace of Apameia saw the return of the Seleukids with Antiochos III installing a garrison in town. The city opened its doors to the Romans, but it could enjoy renewed and longer lasting freedom only after the end of the Macedonian wars in 167 BC.[105]

An Unlikely Grant of Potential Citizenship

Priene passed this decree in an unknown year of the last quarter of the 4th century BC, granting several concessions to the Maroneitans in town, LL. 8–10.

The word *isopoliteia* was ambitiously restored in the text by the first editor, probably because of the *meteinai* (*metechein*) clause, LL. 11–13. Here, however, it is more likely that the text contained the word *politeia*. In any case, this grant is peculiar. Judging from the available space, no enrollment clause or any other detail is included. Rather the text focuses exclusively on Rechtshilfe clauses that establish legal protection for the citizens of Maroneia who either lived or were temporarily present in Priene, LL. 15–27.

These clauses are also formulated in an unusual fashion: Gauthier notes that they focus on resolving private quarrels with a swift intervention of the authorities.[106] The prescribed rapidity is central to the provision: cases had to be judged within three days, L. 25 and 29, and a delay was acceptable only if due to an official decision, LL. 30–32; otherwise those responsible for a delay were to be heavily fined. According to the text, anyone could make a delay known to the authorities. If he swore that the delay had damaged the city, the city would then fine those responsible. The money would go to the damaged Maroneitan.[107]

---

104   PAUS. I.10.3–4; STRAB. XIII.4.1. See PSOMA et al. 2008, pp. 207–211; LUND 1992, esp. pp. 195–198.
105   PSOMA et al. 2008, pp. 247–249.
106   GAUTHIER 1972, p. 244. The intentions of the Temnians in their concession to Teos, *supra* L. 17, may have been similar. There δίκας προδίκους means "speedy trials," L. 17.
107   For *katadike* as 'fine' see SCHULTHEß, *RE* X.2 col. 2456/7.

The text breaks off at this point. It is highly likely that the document did not contain provisions related to an award of potential citizenship. If a grant had been included, it would somehow have favored the temporary presence of Maroneitans in Priene, to which the rest of the decree is devoted (but from the point of view of the legal protection). Here it is useful to refer back to the question that Ph. Gauthier asked in his work on *symbola* in regard to potential citizenship, namely, "Les conventions d'isopolitie ne constituaient-elles pas, sur certains points et d'une manière différente, l'équivalent des *symbola*?"[108]

The text under consideration in a way allows us to give an affirmative response to this question, paradoxically because this agreement may have joined these two institutions to promote the intensification of exchange and foreign presence in the partner cities. If the text contained the institution of potential citizenship at all, it would therefore have been more directed to individuals than typical grants of potential citizenship.

Conclusion: Potential Citizenship in Asia Minor

The commentaries of the inscriptions included in this section epitomize my view on potential citizenship and highlight the fragility of some assertions in past scholarship. Problematic earlier views include the claim that this tool was used routinely within the stipulation of alliances, that it automatically granted the right to change citizenship, or even that it was a means to replenish the citizen body of cities going through a demographic crisis. In opposition to the last theory, but equally controversial because of how it was formulated, is Gawantka's argument that *isopoliteia* was a 'gesture,' with only one text attesting to its practical use: the hotly contested announcement of the concession of citizenship on the part of Teos for three Syrian cities (*SEG* XLI 1003 = no. 61), which I will consider below. None of these readings of potential citizenship is very convincing (at least as exclusive readings). Potential citizenship is rarely found within military alliances outside of Crete but rather this tool was most often used in peaceful situations also in order to shape future alliances. Additionally, concerning procedural matters, switching citizenship was certainly not an automatic procedure: this legal step was carefully regulated, as demonstrated by the inscriptions from Miletos and the Lykian text.

---

108 GAUTHIER 1972, p. 349.

At the same time, this tool had great diplomatic significance, on par with *syngeneia*, *oikeiotes*, or *philia*, which often appear with potential citizenship. In other words, the institution of potential citizenship was a cornerstone of Hellenistic diplomacy. However, it exhausted its potential at the end of the 2nd century BC because, unlike *syngeneia*, *oikeiotes*, or *philia*, it could have had legal implications, too.

CHAPTER 4

Athens

(27–28) *Athens and Priene*

In Classical Athens concessions of citizenship to entire communities were exceptional events prompted by equally exceptional circumstances, as the two famous cases of grants of citizenships to the people of Plataia and Samos demonstrate.

The Hellenistic evidence from Athens preserves traces of the possible use of the concession of potential citizenship. Three examples of this grant may have survived in concessions to the *poleis* of Alabanda/Antioch, perhaps to Priene, and, although the evidence is very uncertain, to Miletos. All possible recipients are cities in Asia Minor and, at least one of them, Miletos, routinely used potential citizenship.[1]

Athens's consistent attitude toward citizenship and the evidence for potential citizenship convey the impression that Athens rarely used this institution, only with communities that were extremely familiar with it and exclusively to pursue diplomatic goals.[2] In other words, Athens could reconcile a traditional and consistent approach to citizenship with the evolution of the role of grants of citizenship to communities in Hellenistic diplomacy.

---

1 In the past, scholars have considered other Athenian texts as evidence for the grant of potential citizenship, but using, in my opinion, problematic criteria for identification. For example, OSBORNE 1981(b), p. 155, n. 6, followed by RHODES 1984, p. 195, holds that *IG* II² 456, 307/6 BC, contains indirect evidence for this institution. This interpretation relies on L. 25 of the decree, which preserves an invitation to dinner to the Kolophonian ambassadors, whose compatriots are defined as *apoikoi* of Athens, LL. 7 and 14. The fact that the invitation is to *deipnon* rather than *xenia* has been used to suggest that the Kolophonian ambassadors were thought of as citizens of Athens. But *isopolitai* were not citizens, but rather privileged foreigners. On *sitesis*, see my lemma in the *Encyclopedia of the Ancient World* (2013) 11, 6272–6273. Perhaps, in this case, it was the recognition of the 'colonial' ties that prompted the invitation to *deipnon* or, perhaps, already in this period the Athenians may have begun to inconsistently distinguish between *deipnon* and *xenia*.
2 On the Athenian attitude toward citizenship see OLIVER 2007(b), pp. 273–293 and, briefly, HELLER and PONT 2012, esp. p. 11.

Priene

Two texts, *IG* II³, 1 1065 (no. 27) and *I.Priene* 5 (no. 28), are commonly considered evidence for an exchange of potential citizenship between Athens and Priene at the end of the 4th century BC or even earlier.[3] That the cities had strong ties is well known.[4] After all, Athens claimed to be the *metropolis* of all Ionian cities, as the surviving epigraphic material attests through the 2nd century BC.[5]

Contacts between Athens and Priene intensified after the middle of the 4th century BC, possibly soon after the installation of the Athenian clerouchy in Samos in 365 BC; it even survived Athens's evacuation of the island.[6] This circumstance reminds us that in diplomacy, conceptual proximity is often more effective than actual, geographic nearness.

According to *I.Priene* 45, which preserves a fragmentary Athenian decree honoring Priene for sending its contribution for the Panathenaia, the Prieneans showed awareness of their tie to Athens *ab antiquo*. Although it survives only in restoration, the decree notes a kinship relation that returns in the alleged grant of potential citizenship.[7] We cannot ignore the cultural and cultic aspect of the relationships between these *poleis*, as they were both devoted to Athena.

---

3 A third inscription, *IG* II² 566, dating to the end of the 4th century BC, was restored to attest to an old concession of Prienean citizenship to all Athenians, LL. 6–8. But already GAWANTKA 1975, p. 207 n. 3 has pointed out that this text is too fragmentary and the restorations too uncertain to support this view. For example, in WILHELM's 1974², pp. 789–790 restoration, the text grants citizenship only to the ambassadors, LL. 6–7.

4 OSBORNE 1981(a), III/IV X20, p. 129 provides a list of texts documenting this relationship; see CULASSO 2004, esp. pp. 220–222.

5 CULASSO 2004, pp. 220–222; CURTY 1995, esp. p. 128. For Athens as *the* mother city see esp. *I. Priene* 45 = *IG* II³,1 1239, dated to the 2nd century BC, and *I.Priene* 109, dated to 120 BC.

6 See SALOMON 1997, esp. pp. 81–85; SHIPLEY 1987, pp. 155–168. On the Athenian clerouchy and the attempt of this city to retain the island see HABICHT 1995, pp. 48–52 for a general overview, and CULASSO 2004, pp. 111–122 on *Ag.* XVI 111.

7 *I.Priene* 45 = *IG* II³,1 1239, LL. 3–7: ἐπειδὴ Πριηνεῖς φίλο[ι καὶ συγγενεῖς ὑπάρ/χοντες] ἐκ παλαιῶν χρόνων με[τ ... μνη]/[μονεύου]σιν διὰ παντὸς τῶν τε ἄλλ[ων εὐεργετημάτων] / [τῶν γ]εγονότων αὐτοῖς ὑπὸ τοῦ δήμου [καὶ μάλιστα ὅτι ἀ]/[νώ]ικισαν αὐτοὺς Ἀθηναῖοι μετὰ τὴν ἐπὶ [Κύρου ἀνάστασιν].

For CURTY 1995, p. 128 kinship rests on the foundation history/myth of Priene, see also CURTY 2005, pp. 112–117.

I. Priene 5 (no. 28) is the earliest known text that mentions a grant of *politeia* to Athens:[8]

       [- - -] Ν· ἔ[δοξε τῆι βουλῆι καὶ]
τῶι δήμωι· τῆι Ἀθηνᾶι τῆι Πολιάδι καθ᾽ [ἑκάστην]
πεντετηρίδα τοῖς Παναθηναίοις τοῖς μεγάλοις
4 πομπὴν καὶ πανοπλίαν εἰς Ἀθήνας ἀποστέλλε[ιν]
μνημεῖον τῆς ἐξ ἀρχῆς συγγενείας καὶ φιλίας
ἡμῖν ὑπαρχούσης πρὸς αὐτούς· εἶναι δὲ Ἀθη[ναίοις]
ἅπασι καθάπερ καὶ πρότερον ὑπῆρχεν αὐτοῖς [καὶ]
8 πολιτείαν ἐμ Πριήνηι καὶ ἰσοτέλ[ε]ιαν καὶ προεδ[ρίαν]
ἐν τοῖς ἀγῶσι, καὶ εἰσκηρύσσεσθ[αι] αὐτοὺς καθά[περ]
τοὺς εὐεργέτας· (...)[9]

The second relevant piece of evidence is *IG* II³, 1 1065 (no. 27), an Athenian decree that praises Priene and appears to mention *isopoliteia* in its very last extant lines.

          [- - - δήμου] τοῦ Ἀθ-
[ηναίων - - - ὅπως ἂν οὖν ὁ δ]ῆμος φαί-
[νηται τιμῶν τοὺς ἀποδεικνουμένους ἐμ παν]τὶ καιρῶι
4 [ἣν ἔχουσιν αἵρεσιν πρὸς αὐτόν, ἀγαθῆι τ]ύχηι δεδόχθαι
[τῆι βουλῆι τοὺς λαχόντας προέδρου]ς εἰς τὴν ἐπιοῦ-
[σαν ἐκκλησίαν χρηματίσαι περὶ τού]των, γνώμην δὲ
[ξυμβάλλεσθαι τῆς βουλῆς εἰς τὸν δῆ]μον ὅτι δοκεῖ
8 [τῆι βουλῆι ἐπαινέσαι τὸν δῆμον τῶν] Πριηνέων καὶ
[στεφανῶσαι χρυσῶι στεφάνωι κατὰ τὸν] νό[μ]ον εὐνοί-
[ας ἕνεκα καὶ φιλοτιμίας τῆς εἰς τὸν δῆμο]ν τῶν Ἀθηναί-
[ων· καὶ ἀνειπεῖν τὸν στέφανον Διονυσίω]ν τῶν ἐν ἄσ-
12 [τει τραγωιδῶν τῶι ἀγῶνι, τῆς δὲ ποιήσεως] τ[οῦ] στεφά-
[νου καὶ τῆς ἀναγορεύσεως ἐπιμεληθῆναι το]ὺς στρα-
[τηγούς. εἶναι δὲ αὐτοῖς - - -] καὶ ἰσοπο-
[λιτείαν - - -] ἐπαι-
16 [νέσαι - - -]

---

8 Curty 1995, 49; McCabe *Priene* 42.
9 LL. 6–10: (...) to all Athenians, just like before, shall be granted also citizenship in Priene, *isoteleia* and *proedria* in the celebrations, and they shall be announced just like it is done with benefactors.

Neither inscription can be dated to a particular year. *I.Priene* 5 (no. 28), L. 18 preserves the name of an Athenian *strategos* in Samos, [Di]philos, whom scholarship identifies with Diphilos of the *demos* of Aixones. His name and office may be attested in a naval inventory of 326/5 BC, which would, therefore, serve as a chronological reference for *I.Priene* 5.[10]

The date of *IG* II³,1 1065 (no. 27) uses paleographical considerations to date the inscription to the beginning of the 3rd century BC.[11]

The relationship between Athens and Priene seems to have survived the whims of politics and time, but it must have been favored also by historical circumstances. The Athenian presence in Samos could have reinforced their ties and thus, perhaps, Lysimachos's interest in both Athens and Priene.[12]

In the 3rd century BC, the Prieneans voted to send their contribution to the celebrations of the Panathenaia,[13] clearly recognizing ancient and preexisting kinship and *philia*, two of the pillars of Hellenistic diplomacy: *I. Priene* 5 (no. 28), LL. 5–6. *I. Priene* 5 (no. 28), LL. 6–10, lists the grants of *politeia*, *isoteleia*, and *proedria* that, L. 7 adds, should have been already in place (καθάπερ καὶ πρότερον ὑπῆρχεν αὐτοῖς). These lines are remarkable because they separate *syngeneia* and *philia* from the concession of *politeia*, *isoteleia*, and *proedria*, thus suggesting, if my observations on the language of *isopoliteia* are sound and can be applied to the Athenian case, too, that this grant was no 'renewal.' Rather it is a brand-new concession, a new (formal) chapter in the relationship between Athens and Priene.[14]

Scholars also cite another piece of evidence, *IG* II³,1 1065 (no. 27) as illuminating the nature of the relationship between Priene and Athens, but, in truth, this inscription cannot tell us anything other than that the relationship

---

10 Another possible restoration for the name is Sophilos, but Diphilos is usually preferred, see *PAA* 368980 (PA 4467 = ?4468) and CULASSO 2004, p. 216 n. 18; for Diphilos *strategos* in Samos in *IG* II² 1628, LL. 119–120. See also DEVELIN 1989, p. 400; but cf. CROWTHER 1996, p. 197 n. 9 on *IG* II² 1628, for whom: "the restoration of Diphilos' name is by no means assured." See also SHIPLEY 1987, p. 160.

11 There are other opinions, too. For example using a restoration of the expression κατὰ τὸν] νό[μ]ον in reference to the crown, L. 9, Wilhelm suggests that the decree was enacted before 303/2 BC, see CULASSO 2004, p. 222 n. 41. We lack decisive evidence so that, since Wilhelm's hypothesis relies only on a very heavy restoration, it is preferable to retain the *communis opinio*.

12 On Lysimachos and Athens for example see *Ag.* XVI 172 with commentary by Woodhead. AMELING 1991, esp. pp. 113–114 collects and briefly comments on the epigraphic evidence.

13 See Low 2007, p. 50 n. 64 discussing the offerings that 'colonies' had to bring to Athens on the occasion of the Panathenaia before the 4th century BC; see also GÜNTHER 1998, p. 21.

14 See the introduction, pp. 22–23.

existed.[15] Still the last five letters of *IG* II³,1 1065 (no. 27), L. 14, ΙΣΟΠΟ, are usually and understandably restored as part of the word *isopo[liteian*, therefore they require a brief comment.

Even if I am pointing to the obvious, I must note again that in the evidence we possess on the institution of potential citizenship, the term *isopoliteia* appears very rarely. When it does appear, it normally refers, as an abstract concept, to a preexisting grant (i.e., it is indirect evidence) or to a plan to establish potential citizenship. The position of the word in this particular text seems to support the second type of reference. However, *I.Priene* 5 (no. 28), is earlier than *IG* II³,1 1065 (no. 27), which presents a problem. Did the later text refer to a preexisting grant, and therefore use the term differently, or did *I.Priene* 5 (no. 27) truly grant potential citizenship? Or, perhaps, should we see this example as one of those ambiguous usages of the term that is attested in other contexts?[16] The text breaks off after these few letters, leaving an open question that simply cannot be answered at present.

(29) *Miletos*

This fragmentary text is engraved on a rectangular fragment of white-gray marble that was found, reused in the 'Derwisch-Kloster' north of the Delphinion. Measurements: H. 0.23; W. 0.23; Th. 0.88. Letters: 0.01.

Edd. *Ed. pr.* Günther 1998, pp. 29–32 (*ph*); *IG* II³, 1 1242; [*SEG* XLVIII 1998, 1415]; *Milet* V 3 1032 (Günther).

```
       ca 4 Ι τῶι δήμωι τῷ[ι Μιλησίων - - -]
       ... ΕΙΝ Ἀρίσταιχμον Τ - - -
       ... ΝΟΣ, γνώμην δὲ συμ[βάλλεσθαι τῆς βουλῆς εἰς τὸν δῆ]-
4      μον, ὅτι δοκεῖ αὐτῆι ἀναν[εώσασθαι τὴν οἰκειότητα καὶ]
       [τὴ]μ φιλί[αν] τὴν ὑπάρχ[ουσαν πρὸς τὸν δῆμον τὸν Μιλησίων]
       [κ]αὶ τὴμ πολιτείαν Ἀνδρίω[ι - - -]
       [Μ]αιανδρίωι ἡμῖν παρε[πιδημοῦσιν· τῆς δὲ στήλης ? ἐπι]-
8      [μ]εληθῆναι καὶ ἀπομισ[θῶσαι τὴν ἀναγραφὴν τοῦ ψηφίσ]-
       [ματο]ς το[ὺς] τε τει[χοποιοὺς καὶ τὸν ἀρχιτέκτονα - - -]
```

---

15 GAWANTKA 1975, p. 207, n. 3 adds this text to the entry for *IG* II² 566 noting that it is a very uncertain piece of evidence.
16 See the introduction, pp. 22–23.

> LL. 3–7: (...) The *boule* shall present to the *demos* the proposal that it seems well to renew the [kinship ties?] and the friendship existing with the *demos* of the Milesians and the citizenship to Andrios ... to Maiandrios ... with us (?) ... (provisions on the publication of the stone follow)

W. Günther dates the inscription to ca. 200 BC relying on its paleography.[17] The text is so fragmentary that it does not preserve the names of the cities involved; the cities have been deduced from the findspot, Miletos, and from the formula recorded in LL. 4–5, Athens.[18]

According to Günther, the text preserves part of an Athenian decree with which the city 're-activated' its contact with Miletos and recalled an existing *philia, oikeiotes*.[19] Next follows the term *politeia*, which Günther suggests is meant to refer to an older potential citizenship agreement between these towns that he dates to the end of the 4th century BC: "als Milet nach dem Ende der persischen Oberhoheit aus seiner Isolation heraustrat und Isopolitieverträge mit Olbia und Kyzikos abschloss."[20] Günther considers the agreement between Miletos and Phygela (*Milet* I 3 142 = no. 3) as a comparandum. There the reminder of the preexisting grant was followed by an actual, official decision to give Phygela potential citizenship. Here, however, the text breaks off and the rest of the document contains only proper names and provisions for the payment (and probably publication) of the stele.

The naming of two Milesians in LL. 6–7 is peculiar and their function within the inscription remains unknown.[21] In L. 7 only the first four letters of the verb, which most likely governs the sentence, survives: παρε[.... This verb may refer to the two Milesian men and Günther has suggested that we restore it as *parepidemeo*. I do not exclude that this concession of *politeia* applied only to Andrios and Maiandrios and that, therefore, this text cannot serve as a reminder of a grant of potential citizenship between these communities.[22]

---

17   GÜNTHER 1998, p. 29, n. 42.
18   BRIXHE *BE* 1999 465 and GÜNTHER 1998, pp. 29–30.
19   Günther restores *oikeiotes* because in Athens the term was preferred over *syngeneia*, see also JONES 1999, p. 44.
20   GÜNTHER 1998, p. 31. *Ibid.* n. 50.
21   Andrios and Maiandrios: on these names in Miletos see GÜNTHER 1998, p. 30, n. 45.
22   From about 100 BC to the 2nd century AD epigraphic evidence attests to many Milesians living in Athens, but VESTERGAARD 2000, pp. 81–107 rightly excludes that this circumstance was a direct consequence of an eventual potential citizenship grant. On Milesians, and also on foreign residents in Athens in general, see OSBORNE and BYRNE 1996.

(30) Athens and Alabanda/Antioch

In 201/200 BC Athens recognized *asylia* for Alabanda/Antioch and, before focusing on this recognition, it decided Ἀντιο/χεῦσιν καὶ πολ[ιτείαν κα]τὰ τὸν νόμον τὸν περὶ τῶν δωρεῶν κ[είμε]/νον.[23] I have discussed this document in the introduction: I consider it an instructive example of a 'diplomatic' grant of potential citizenship because of its context and because of the reference to a specific Athenian law regulating technical aspects of the grant. In what follows, I focus on the text's historical context and on its place within Athenian evidence.

Chronology and Antioch/Alabanda

The date of this text can be determined with a certain precision: the first editor, R. Pounder, has dated the decree to ca. 203 BC relying on internal data. L. 26 mentions the council of the "650" in Athens, which came into existence in 224/3 BC, when the tribe Ptolemais was created. Its membership shrank to 550 members around 200 BC with the abolishment of the two Macedonian tribes.[24] Moreover, one of the two ambassadors sent to Athens, Pausimachos son of Iatrokles, appears also in a decree found in Delphi, with which the Amphictiony grants *asylia* to Antioch.[25] This decree preserves the name of the eponym, *Philaetolos*, who cannot be assigned securely to a particular year, but probably held his office between 205 and 201 BC.[26]

It is generally accepted that these *asylia* requests date to the same year and, given the above-mentioned chronological limits, we must reevaluate the old *communis opinio* that would date the Alabanda grant to 203 BC when Antiochos was in Teos. Rigsby has argued for 201 BC based on the cycle of

---

23   Text from *IG* II³, 1 1178, LL. 20–28: δεδόσθαι δὲ Ἀντιο/χεῦσιν καὶ πολ[ιτείαν] κατὰ τὸν νόμον τὸν περὶ τῶν δωρεῶν κ[είμε]/νον· καὶ εἶνα[ι τ]ὴν πόλιν αὐτῶν καὶ τὴν χώραν καθιερωμένην τῶ[ι / Δ]ιὶ τῶι Χρυσ[αό]ρει καὶ τῶι Ἀπόλλωνι τῶι Ἰσοτίμωι καὶ ἄσυλον δ[ια]/μένειν εἰς τὸν ἅπαντα χρόνον ὅσον ἐστὶν ἐπ' Ἀθηναίοις· εἶνα[ι δὲ / α]ὐτοῖ[ς] καὶ προεδρίαν ἐν πᾶσι τοῖς ἄγωσιν οἷς ἡ πόλις τίθη[σιν / καὶ π]ρόσοδον πρὸς τὴν βουλὴν καὶ τὸν δῆμον πρώτοις μετὰ τ[ὰ / ἱερά· ἐ]πιμελείσθω δὲ καὶ ἡ βουλὴ οἱ ἑξακόσιοι καὶ πεντήκοντ[α / κ]αὶ[ὶ οἱ] στρ[α]τηγοὶ τῶν ἐπιδημούντων Ἀντιοχέων ὅπως ὑπὸ μηθε/νὸς ἀδικῶνται ... Transl.: be it resolved that the Antiocheans be granted citizenship according to the law on grants. Their city and land shall be sacred to Zeus Chrysaoreos and Apollo Isotimos and remain inviolable for all time, as far as the Athenians can assure. They shall have *proedria* in all games organized by the *polis* and access to the *boule* and *demos* first after the sacrifices. The *boule* of the 650 and the *strategoi* shall care for the Antiocheans sojourning (in Athens) so as that no one hurts them. (...)
24   POUNDER 1978, pp. 52–53; on the *Ptolemais* see HABICHT 1995, p. 182.
25   RIGSBY 1996, pp. 332–334 no. 163 now in *Choix* pp. 174–177 no. 90.
26   See RIGSBY 1996, p. 333. Still crucial for *Choix* pp. 174–177 no. 90 is HOLLEAUX 1942, pp. 144–157.

the *Soteria* in which Pausimachos successfully took part and this date is now accepted in *Choix*.[27]

We know little about Antioch/Alabanda, a town located on two hills watching over the valley of the Marsias river. The original Karian name, Alabanda, was changed into Antioch around 260 BC under Antiochos II.[28] Possibly the city reverted to its original name after the peace of Apameia or right before this treaty was signed. No extensive archaeological work has been conducted in the area, but sources indicate that the city was prosperous and played an important role in the region.[29]

The Decree

The most instructive element contained in this decree is the statement for which the Athenians δεδόσθαι δὲ Ἀντιο/χεῦσιν καὶ πολ[ιτείαν κα]τὰ τὸν νόμον τὸν περὶ τῶν δωρεῶν κ[είμε]/νον. This statement has been read as a testimony to a grant of potential citizenship from Athens to Antioch, after which the document moves to the recognition of *asylia*.

What is this grant? Pounder speaks of a grant of citizenship; Rigsby avoids labels and notes that this concession on the part of Athens was quite extraordinary.[30] Osborne instead has labeled this concession 'isopoly,' although his interpretation, in a way, is pejorative in that he sees isopoly as a purely cosmetic grant.[31] For his commentary, which I discussed extensively in the introduction, Osborne uses and refers to Gauthier's 1972 definition of potential citizenship, which, as Gauthier himself notes,[32] is "negative" and meant to stress the potential nature of the grant. For Gauthier this definition serves only as the starting point for a longer analysis of the institution, which leads him to explore the consequences to potential citizenship also by considering later additional provisions that accompany a grant of *isopoliteia*. Furthermore, in this study and others, Gauthier argues against the view that potential citizenship was an empty tool.

---

27   Formerly, it was assumed that other cities took advantage of Antiochos's presence in Teos to submit their requests to his attention. RIGSBY 1996, pp. 328–329 does not think this assumption is necessary. See *Choix* esp. p. 177.

28   On the location see STRAB. XIV. 2. 26; on Alabanda see COHEN 1995, pp. 248–250; BOFFO 1985, pp. 307–311. In its request of inviolability to the Amphictiony the Karian city speaks of *syngeneia* to "Greeks," *Choix* pp. 174–177 no. 90, LL. 12–13 … συγγενὴς ἐοῦσα / τῶν Ἑλλάνων …, on which see CURTY 1995, no. 13.

29   RIGSBY 1996, pp. 326–330; see also PACE 1996, pp. 60–65 on the coins from this city and briefly on its history. See also STEPH. *s.v.* Alabanda.

30   RIGSBY 1996, p. 332; POUNDER 1978, pp. 51–52.

31   On OSBORNE 1981(a), vol. II, pp. 184–185 see my comment in the introduction.

32   GAUTHIER 1972, pp. 347–348.

This text is extremely short and does not focus on the grant of potential citizenship, which, however, must have been regulated in detail through legislative acts that are simply referred to here. This aspect is not uncommon in Greek documents.

One reflection by Osborne worthy of additional consideration refers to the association between *asylia* and *isopoliteia* that I will consider in a separate chapter. The relationship between these two grants was not as strong as it has been suggested in the past and a dependency relationship did not exist. But that *asylia* and *isopoliteia* could be granted together as a way to reinforce the diplomatic act underway was a practice that we see attested here, too.

This text is the latest piece of Athenian evidence for potential citizenship. Priene and Athens must have used it to strengthen their relationship in the 4th century BC; the evidence from Miletos is not unequivocal. The city of Athens knew and used this tool, but probably mostly in its 'earliest' phase. If one considers the richness of the Athenian epigraphic record, however, one must concede that isopolity was certainly not among its preferred tools. The reference to a law 'on grants' is probably one of the most interesting results from this review of the Athenian evidence: that such laws existed is clear, but here we see a reference system to a set of laws at work.

(31)   *Athens and Rome*

According to modern scholarship, the literary tradition preserves two references to grants of potential citizenship involving Athens: one pertains to a possible grant to Rome, the second to Rhodes.[33] A curious section from the work of Zonaras VIII.19 has been interpreted as preserving the memory of a grant of potential citizenship to the Urbe. Within the narrative about the Roman intervention against Illyrian pirates in 229 BC, Zonaras indeed says: οἱ δὲ Ῥωμαῖοι διὰ ταῦτα παρὰ Κορινθίων ἐπηνέσθησαν, καὶ τοῦ Ἰσθμικοῦ μετέσχον ἀγῶνος, καὶ στάδιον ἐν αὐτῷ ὁ Πλαῦτος ἐνίκησε. καὶ πρὸς Ἀθηναίους δὲ φιλίαν ἐπεποιήκεσαν, καὶ τῆς πολιτείας σφῶν τῶν τε μυστηρίων μετέσχον.

The (literal) meaning of these lines is clear; their interpretation instead is difficult. The Athenians honored and thanked the Romans for their engagement by allowing them to participate in the Panhellenic games and in the Eleusinian Mysteries. According to the text, the Athenians also added also a grant of citizenship.

---

33   I discuss the second testimony in the appendix where I collect several pieces of evidence that come from the work of Polybios, pp. 169–172.

In a parallel passage, Polybios mentions the concession of the Corinthians to Rome, which Zonaras mentions, but does not refer to Athens.[34] It is impossible to know why Polybios omitted the information on Athens, but the result is that we have no corroborating evidence for Zonaras's statement.[35] A grant of *politeia* to Rome on the part of Athens would be extremely difficult to contextualize within Athens's policy of the second half of the 3rd century. Moreover, it is hard to imagine that Athens would grant its citizenship to a population (the Romans) still largely considered barbaric, especially because it hardly granted it even to Greek cities.[36]

---

34   POLYB. II. 12.8; on the Corinthians see SCHMITT 1957/8, esp. p. 9.
35   See also GAWANTKA 1975, p. 219.
36   HOSE 1999, p. 316.

CHAPTER 5

The Islands

The evidence from the islands can best be studied by grouping the existing documents in pairs. The first pair of inscriptions includes two 4th century BC documents preserving two agreements that Keos signed with two Euboian cities, namely, Eretria (*StV* II² 232 = no. 32) and Histiaea (*StV* II² 287= no. 33). Both documents refer to a turbulent time in history, when these communities sought their place on the international stage. Reciprocal potential citizenship is granted in both cases. The concession of this award seals the agreements and helps consolidate the relationships that these towns sought to establish by signing broader agreements. These texts can be considered early examples for this institution and their unusually clear historical contexts allow us (for once) to observe diplomacy at work in smaller communities within the framework of wider historical events.

The second pair of documents from the island that includes a grant of potential citizenship contains two indirect pieces of evidence: a very short summary of an agreement between Knidos and Chalke (*IKnidos* 605= no. 34) where the grant of *politeia* could be the institution of potential citizenship and a decree enacted for an individual (*IG* XII.5 814 = no. 35) that refers to an older agreement of potential citizenship between Tenos and Kyrene. The second document could be a unique piece of evidence for the implementation of a concession of potential citizenship on the part of an individual. Even in this case, however, we should be cautious in drawing too many conclusions because the text is fragmentary.

The third and last pair of texts includes two documents that testify to the use of potential citizenship in the late Hellenistic period. In one example, potential citizenship could have been used as an alternative to federal citizenship within the poorly known Lesbian *Koinon* (*IG* XI.4 1064 = *IG* XII *Suppl*. 136 = no. 36). In the second text, a Lesbian city, Mytilene, grants *politeia* to Larisa, a member of the just refounded Thessalian *Koinon* (*SEG* LV 605 = no. 37). The document suggests that another concession of potential citizenship on the part of Mytilene had been previously given to all Thessalians. These two documents show that using potential citizenship was a community's deliberate choice, one that did not impinge on its independence or standing within a larger organization. I exclude from this chapter the evidence from Crete, which is abundant and, in many ways, an exceptional case study for potential citizenship. A. Chaniotis has studied the Cretan evidence and published his conclusions, most of which I share, as I will demonstrate below in the section devoted to the evidence from this island.

(32–33)   *Keos and Eretria / Keos and Histiaea*

The two agreements from Keos must be set in a broader institutional context. To begin, three potential citizenship agreements with Kean involvement have indeed survived. Two (nos. 32 and 33) can be dated to the first half of the 4th century BC and were meant to establish a tighter relationship with two Euboian cities. Keos signed the third agreement with the city of Naupaktos (no. 41) in the 3rd century BC to extend the concession to all of Aitolia. Historically this last agreement belongs to a time when the Aegean islands pursued a defensive policy.

The number of potential citizenship grants is impressive for a small island and the historical background to each example is unusually clear. Thus, the case of Keos offers the ancient historians the rare chance to draw some conclusions on the use of this tool in the island. Keos and its authorities used the concession of potential citizenship, by granting it at a federal level, to establish connections with communities that at the time were significant either for its independence or safety. The diplomatic and political force of this concession emerged within the context of wider political dealings and must have provided a stronger and better-defined diplomatic structure for further initiatives. This 'mixed-use' of the tool of potential citizenship is apparent, as the diplomatic force it carried cannot be doubted. However, at least for the agreement with Histiaea, we must envision a broader context, maybe even an alliance.

(32) *Keos and Eretria*

Preserved fragment of a white marble stele, found in 1947 in Chora; it is broken on all sides. The stele was stored in local museum (inv. no. 15) at the time of the *editio princeps*. Measurements: H. 0.45; W. 0.21; Th. 0. 112. Letters 0.18–0.06. According to Dunant and Thomopoulos, the text is *stoichedon* with 34 letters per line and its lettering dates to the beginning of the 4th century BC.

Edd. *ed. pr.* Dunant and Thomopoulos 1954, no. 1 (*ph.*); [*SEG* XIV 530; *StV* II² 232].

Cf. Lewis 1962 who restores longer lines; Knoepfler 1997, p. 375.

```
     [- - - - - - - - - - - - - - ἐὰν ὁ Κεῖος βόληται ἐ]-
     [ν Ἐρετρίηι πολιτεύεσθαι, πρὸς τὸς στρατη]-
     [γὸς τὸς ἐν Ἐρετρί]ηι ἀπ[ογ]ραψά[σθω τὸ ὄνομα]
4    [τὸ αὐτὸ· οἱ δὲ στρ]ατηγοὶ φυλὴν κ[αὶ δῆμον δό]-
     [ντων αὐτῶι ἐν] ὧι ἄμ μέλληι πολιτεύ[εσθαι· ἐ]-
     [ὰν δὲ ὁ Ἐρετρ]ιεὺς βόληται ἐγ Κέωι πολ[ιτεύ]-
     [εσθαι, ἀπογ]ραψάσθω πρὸς τὸς θεσμοφύλακ[α]-
8    [ς τὸ αὐτὸ ὄ]νομα· οἱ δὲ θεσμοφύλακες δόντω[ν]
     [αὐτῶι φυλὴ]ν καὶ τριττὺν καὶ χῶρον.
     [Θεοί (?) ἔδοξε]ν τῆι βολῆι προσγράψαι πρ[ὸς ...]
     - - -
```

Text and restorations by D(unant)-Th(omopoulos), unless otherwise noted L. 4 [δῆμον] K(noepfler); D-Th; L(ewis) [χῶρον].

Transl.: LL. 1–9: If a Kean wishes to live as a citizen in Eretria, his name shall be registered at the *strategoi* in Eretria. The *strategoi* shall assign him to the *phyle* and *choron* in which he will live as a citizen. If an Eretrian whishes to live as a citizen in Keos, his name shall be registered at the *thesmophylakes*. The *thesmophylakes* shall assign them a *phyle*, a *tritty* and a *choron*.

This extremely fragmentary decree is considered evidence for an exchange of potential citizenship between the island of Keos and Eretria in Euboea, whose name and ethnic, however, never appear in the text out of brackets.[1]

---

1 DUNANT and THOMOPOULOS 1954, p. 318. The identification of Eretria as the second signing community is more than an educated guess, but attention must be nonetheless drawn to this point.

The date of the text deserves a longer note since it is closely related to the question of the community with which Keos establishes the agreement.

For the first editors, the analysis of paleography, *stoichedon*, and engraving indicate that the stone belongs to the beginning of the 4th century BC,[2] specifically between 393 (the battle of Knidos) and 378/7 BC (the creation of the second Athenian League). Lewis, however, relying on the same criteria, first suggested that the period for this decree's approval be placed between 390 and 340 BC. Then, after a closer analysis, he has proposed a date around 364 BC.[3]

One of the most important points in Lewis's analysis relates to the use of Keos's political unity as a chronological criterion.[4] For most of the 4th century BC Keos was a federation,[5] which at first must have looked at Thebes, although perhaps only by way of Euboea, as a political filter.[6] Eretria was a member of the second Delian League, but defected from Athens for the Thebans in 371 BC, only to rejoin the League in 357 BC.[7] The 360s BC were years of turmoil during which we know that Eretria was extremely active. An agreement with the island of Keos, which had also tried to rebel, fits well in this historical context.

Possibly, Keos stipulated two potential citizenship agreements with cities from Euboea in these years. Of the agreement with Eretria we preserve only these (fragmentary) enrollment clauses; we have lost the first part of the decree that perhaps contained additional pieces of information on the reasons for this treaty. In the surviving enrollment clauses, we can still read that the island granted "Kean" citizenship, which must have been a form of federal citizenship. The text breaks off right after listing short procedural clauses.

---

2 DUNANT and THOMOPOULOS 1954, pp. 321–322.
3 See LEWIS 1962, p. 1–5, on p. 1 where he calls this agreement "sympolity."
4 On this topic see BRUN 1989, esp. pp. 128–138 and LEWIS 1962, pp. 1–5. REGER 2001, p. 171 and later WALSER 2009, pp. 145–148 have dealt with the phenomenon of sympolity in Keos in the Hellenistic period. Whether this union meant that the cities of the island, probably with the exception of Poiessa, shared all institutions, as BRUN 1989, esp. pp. 131–132, suggests, can be questioned.
5 Most likely the federal system had been in place between 393 and 377 BC and then, again, in the 360s BC, after the island rebelled from Athens, under whose influence it had returned by 363/2 BC. See GUAGLIUMI 2005 and 2003 for the main piece of evidence for this rebellion and Athens's subsequent intervention in 363/2 BC, namely, *IG* II² 111.
6 See BUCKLER 1980, esp. p. 173.
7 For a brief history of Eretria see REBER, HANSEN, DUCREY *Inventory*, n. 370 and GEHRKE 1985, pp. 63–66.

(33) Keos and Histiaea

The second inscription attesting to ties between Keos and Euboea is preserved on a fragmentary stele of white marble; the left-hand margin is partially preserved. According to Tod, the stone is now built into the wall of a house by Tsia (ancient Ioulis). The measurements of the stone are not recorded in the existing publications; Tod asserts that the text is not *stoichedon* and that the letters are "small, simple letters of the fourth century BC."

Edd.: *ed. pr.* Savignoni *Εφ. αρχ.* 1898, 243.1; [Ditt. *Syll.*² 934]; *IG* XII.5 594 (*ph.*) + *IG* XII (9) p. 169; [*Syll.*³ 172; Tod II 141; *StV* II² 287].
Cf. Dunant and Thomopoulos 1954, pp. 316–322 on L. 6; Lewis 1962, esp. p. 1.

{*multa desunt*}
[ὅτ]αν δέ[ω]νται· ἐὰν δέ τις [τῶγ Κείων ...]
[φε]ύγηι ἐς Ἱστιαίαν ἢ τὴν Ἱστι[αιέων χώραν, μὴ]
[δε]κέσθω ἡ πόλις : ἐὰν ὁ Ἱστιαιεὺς βούληται ἐγ Κέ]-
4 [ω]ι πολιτεύεσθαι, ἐλθὼν ἀπο[γραψάσθω πρὸς θεσμο]-
[φύλ]ακας τὸ ἑαυτοῦ ὄνομα, οἱ [δὲ θεσμοφύλακες]
[δό]ντων φυλὴν καὶ τριπτὺν [καὶ χῶρον αὐτῶι·]
[ἐὰν] ὁ Κεῖος βούληται ἐν Ἱστ[ιαίαι ἢ τῆι χώραι]
8 [πο]λιτεύεσθαι, πρὸς τοὺς στρ[ατηγοὺς τοὺς ἐν]
[Ἱστ]ιαίαι ἀπογραψάσθω τὸ ὄν[ομα τὸ ἑαυτοῦ, οἱ δὲ]
[στ]ρατηγοὶ φυλὴν καὶ δῆμον [δόντων αὐτῶι ἐν ὧι ἂμ]
μέλληι πολιτεύεσθαι. ἐξαγω[γὴν δὲ εἶναι τῶι]
12 Ἱστιαιεῖ ἐκ Κέω καθάπερ τῶ[ι Κείωι, καὶ ⟨τῶι⟩ Κείωι ἐξ]
Ἱστιαίας καθάπερ τῶι Ἱστια[ιεῖ, ἐσαγωγὴν δὲ ἐς]
ἑκατέρους. καὶ τῶι ὅρκωι πρ[οστίθεσθαι ⟨ἐγ Κέωι⟩ τῶι τῆς]
βουλῆς· καὶ περὶ Ἱστιαιέωμ β[ουλεύσειν ⟨ἀγαθὸν⟩ ὅ τι ἂν]
16 δύνωνται, ἐν Ἱστιαίαι δὲ τῶι [ὅρκωι· καὶ περὶ]
Κείωμ βουλεύσειν ἀγαθ[ὸν ὅ τι ἂν δύνωνται. ἐπι]-
μέλεσθαι δὲ ἐγ Κέωι [μὲν τήν τε βουλὴν καὶ τοὺς]
[πρ]οβούλους καὶ τ[οὺς .. ca 12 .. καὶ τοὺς]
20 [ἀσ]τυνόμους τῶ[ν Ἱστιαιέων, ἐν Ἱστιαίαι δὲ τοὺς]
[ἄρχ]ο[ν]τα[ς ...]

Text by *StV* II² 287.

Transl: ... If any of the Keans seeks refuge in Histiaea or in its territory, the *polis* shall not admit him; if a Histiaean wishes to live in Keos as a citizen, he shall have his name registered at the office of the *thesmophylakes* having gone there. The *thesmophylakes* shall assign him to a tribe and a *trypty* (and a *choron*?). If a Kean wants to live as a citizen in Histiaea or in its territory, he shall have his name recorded at the *strategoi*'(s office) and they shall assign him to the tribe and *demos* where he will live (as a citizen). A Histiaean shall have the right of export from Keos just like a Kean, and a Kean from Histiaea just like an Histiaean, and (they shall have) right to import to each. In Keos the oath of the *boule* shall be sworn, namely, that the best possible decisions shall be taken about the Histiaeans. In Histiaea that the best possible decisions shall be taken about the Keans. The *boule* and the *probouloi* and the [?] and the *astynomoi* shall take care of the Histiaeans in Keos, in Histiaea the *archontes*.

This fragmentary text was found in Ioulis, one the four ancient cities on the island of Keos.[8] The document must predate the year 363/2 BC, when the (second) revolt of this city against Athens—and its League—was suppressed, as recorded in the exceptional testimony of *IG* II² 111.[9] Euboea had rebelled against Athens at an earlier date, probably around 370/69 BC, not long after the battle of Leuktra. Thebes was then the new hegemonic power in Greece, and Euboea probably sought its support.[10] It is against this broadly defined historical background that scholars interpret this grant and the other existing Kean grant of potential citizenship to Euboian cities. Namely, they are considered proof for Kean attempts to secede from the Athenian League.[11]

The reconstruction of this historical context and related hypothesis may be plausible, but the grant of potential citizenship is not as straightforward. The first surviving clause, LL. 1–3, is striking: exiles from Keos could not be taken in by the partner *polis*. This provision must have been closely tied to

---

[8] On the cities of Keos, see REGER 1997, pp. 449–455.

[9] This text is now also in RHODES and OSBORNE pp. 196–203 no. 39; for a historical commentary of this inscription see GUAGLIUMI 2003, esp. pp. 34–40; DÖSSEL 2003, pp. 147–158 with an edition of the text, translation, and short commentary.

[10] See GUAGLIUMI 2005, pp. 420–422.

[11] For Keos and Eretria see *supra*. On Histiaea/Horoi see REBER, HANSEN, DUCREY *Inventory*, n. 372, on its constitutional changes during the 4th century BC see GEHRKE 1985, pp. 73–75 and more recently LASAGNI 2010, pp. 371–390. MACK 2015, pp. 182–184 reads the text in connection with a proxeny catalogue from Karthaia, *IG* XII 5 542, as attesting to the strong ties between the involved communities and geographical areas, since his focus is on networks.

the political, internal struggle that was underway in Keos and, perhaps, more specifically referred to the pro-Athenian faction members who had been driven away by the pro-Theban party.[12] After this provision follow fairly detailed enrollment clauses.[13]

The text lists further provisions, for example, pertaining to the right of import-export. Most likely this provision only includes the absence of custom taxes for the lawful members of these communities, LL. 11–15. According to Guagliumi, this clause is relevant because it would point to the strong economic interests that led the two communities to subscribe to this agreement.[14] Even if economic interests led to the stipulation of this agreement, they were not alone responsible: the presence of the final oath, which is never a feature of potential citizenship agreements but rather to broader agreements in which potential citizenship is set, clearly indicates that this grant was framed within a larger (now lost to us) regulation of the relationship of these two cities.[15] Main governing organs of both communities had to swear the same oath relating to every future deliberation about the partner community.

Here I suggest that we read this document as part of a bigger 'plan': the two communities had just established a broader alliance that is lost to us, but required the stipulation of an oath and allowed for possible reviewing of the agreement. The cities cemented it with a concession of *isopoliteia* not unlike what we have seen in Asia Minor with the case of Skepsis and Parion.

---

12   The historical situation is well discussed by GUAGLIUMI 2003, esp. pp. 39–44.
13   The registration in the civic units that can be found in Eretria, too, see KNOEPFLER 1997, pp. 355–448 esp. p. 375.
14   GUAGLIUMI 2005, p. 423 n. 13 who at the same time notes rightly that a little later Athens achieved a monopoly of the red ruddle from Keos, *IG* II² 1128. Keos and Attica are very close to each other, but so is Euboea, and probably both served as references for the economic activities of the small island.
15   Oaths are never tied directly to potential citizenship. For example, Miletos-Herakleia under Mt. Latmos *Milet* I 3 150 = no. 7, L. 77 mentions an oath related to landed property and LL. 109–117 record the oath tied to the *syntheke*; J. and L. ROBERT *BE* 1972 371 = no. 23, LL. 24–28 contains potential citizenship within a defensive military agreement between Skepsis and Parion.

(34) *Knidos and Chalke*

The first editors of this inscription, Bean and Cook, wrote that the stone was "found at Burgaz, now in the School of Resadiye. Fragment of a stele of dark grey limestone, broken at top and bottom. (...) The inscribed surface is carefully smoothed and polished. Both right and left edges are preserved, but the stone is much worn and letters are lost on both sides."[16] In 1992 Blümel noted that the stone is lost. Measurements: H. 0.20 m.; W. 0. 28 m.; Th. 0.083 m. Letters 0.012–0.013 m.

Edd.: *ed. pr.* Bean and Cook 1952, pp. 187–188 no. 3 (*ph.*); Susini 1963/4, pp. 256–257; [*IKnidos* 605].
Cf.: J. and L. Robert *BE* 1954 228 on Bean and Cook; IDEM 1957, pp. 85–87 accepting Klaffenbach 1955, pp. 93–98 (*SEG* XIV 727); J. and L. Robert *BE* 1967 416 on Susini who was not aware of Klaffenbach's work.

    [Χα]λκεᾶται Κ[νιδίων εὐ]-
    [ερ]γέται· ἔδωκ[αν Κνίδι]-
    [οι] Χαλκεάταις ἔσ[πλον]
4   [καὶ] ἔκπλον καὶ ἐμ πολέ-
    [μω]ι καὶ ἐν ἰρήναι ἀσπον-
    [δὶ κ]αὶ ἀσυλὶ καὶ γᾶς ἐνων[ὰν]
    [καὶ] πολιτείας μετῆμε[ν]
8   [Κνίδιοι] Χαλκητᾶν ε[ὐερ]-
    [γέται - - -]

IKnidos 605 using the text as restored by Klaffenbach.

Bean and Cook date the text to the middle of the 4th century BC relying on paleography. The Chalketai and the Knidians sign this agreement, but the Knidians' name appears in the text only in restoration. Bean and Cook first thought that this text included a grant of several rights *ad personam*, but Klaffenbach restored the text as an interstate agreement and identified the second partner as Knidos because of its findspot and the (mostly lost) second text, whose content must have been analogous.[17]

---

16   BEAN and COOK 1952, p. 187.
17   BEAN and COOK 1952, pp. 187–188; KLAFFENBACH 1955, pp. 93–95 and again BEAN and COOK 1957, pp. 85–87 acknowledge and accept Klaffenbach's restoration and interpretation.

The inscription comes from the area of Burgaz, near modern Datca, where some scholars locate the old town of Knidos. Around the time of Alexander the 'capital' of Knidia should have moved westwards, to the tip of the peninsula.[18] This inscription is considered the *terminus post quem* for the move because it shows that, at least until the middle of the 4th century BC, the main center of Knidos was still located in the area of Burgaz. It is possible that at that point the most important activities of the town moved toward the sea. However, we lack conclusive evidence to determine whether the town moved.

In any case, in these decades Knidos was under Mausulos's control. According to Hornblower, Mausulos allowed Karian towns some latitude in domestic and, given this inscription, foreign policy.[19]

Chalke is a small island west of Rhodes. Strabo mentions it briefly and records that it included a temple of Apollo and a harbor; the exact location remains the subject of debate.[20] The main town was probably located on the southwestern part of the island. Reger notes that although no source calls Chalke a *polis*, this inscription suggests that it was one. Moreover, J. and L. Robert argue that this text must have been passed by an independent Chalke, before the second half of the 4th century BC—or the 3rd century BC—when an inscription from Kamiros testifies that by then it belonged to the territory of this synoikized Rhodian town.[21]

---

18   BEAN and COOK 1952, pp. 187–188 argue that the archaeological remains suggest that Knidos moved from Burgaz to Tekir. In the 1950s the available archaeological evidence from Tekir-Knidos did not date past the late Classical/Hellenistic period, while the area around Datca offered material that also pre-dated this period. Bean and Cook's theory on the relocation of Knidos found wide acceptance, for example J. and L. ROBERT *BE* 1954 228 spoke in its favor. LOVE 1973, who dug the alleged (new) Knidos-Tekir, has challenged the view. DEMAND 1989, pp. 224–237 and 1990, pp. 146–150 followed Love and finally BLÜMEL 1992, in the introduction to the volume of the inscriptions from Knidos, argues against the move. These scholars argue that the city of Knidos never moved, because of the new archaeological evidence (unfortunately not conclusive) and a new—although problematic—reading of the ancient sources; they instead locate Knidos at Tekir. More recently, scholarship has returned to the view of Bean and Cook, see BRESSON 1999, pp. 83–114, esp. pp. 83–86, with an extremely useful overview of the entire debate, IDEM 2010, pp. 436–437 and also BERGES 1994, pp. 5–16.

19   HORNBLOWER 1982, pp. 5; 14; 29; 116 who treats the economy and the origins: for Knidos as Spartan colony see HDT. I.174.2. Note also the different tradition in STRAB. XIV.2.6 for which the Knidians were Dorians from Megara. See also FLENSTED-JENSEN *Inventory*, no. 903.

20   STRAB. X.5.15; see REGER *Inventory*, no. 477; SUSINI 1963/4, esp. pp. 247–258.

21   J. and L. ROBERT *BE* 1954 228; *Tit. Cam.* 109 (*IG* XII. I. 694) and its Suppl. p. 237, n. 109 referring to FRASER 1952, pp. 193–195 who dates the text to the 3rd century BC. The inscription says that, except for Chalke, all other *ktoinai* had to register by the sanctuary of

The Text

This brief text summarizes a decree that the Knidians passed for Chalke and, after a *vacat*, the stone preserves the beginning of a second text that must have contained a similar document for Knidos on the part of Chalke. The *Chalketai* are said to be benefactors of the Knidians with no further specification. Several grants follow: right of entry and exit from the harbor area under any political situation, safely and without formal treaty; LL. 7–8 contain the concessions to own land; and, finally, πολιτείας μετῆμε[ν].[22] The sequence of the concessions does not stress the grant of citizenship, but this observation is immaterial in such a short text. Scholars tend to classify this as an award of isopolity.[23]

Gawantka does not discuss the document, but he lists it in his catalogue as no. 11 and comments on it thus: "nicht völlig sicheres Zeugnis für eine einseitige Verleihung."

His caution is understandable since this text does not provide enough details to allow us to determine its nature. Instead the inscription contains only a summary or perhaps a reminder of several grants that must have been related to commercial activities between the two islands. An award of citizenship appears with certainty and, although very unspecific, it is attested with a language that could be taken from an agreement that stipulated potential citizenship. Whether the grant was unilateral or not, it cannot be determined with certainty because the second part is lost.

     Athena; on *ktoinai* and this text see GABRIELSEN 2002, esp. p. 193 confirming a date in the 3rd century BC.

22   On the right to ownership, here *enona*, HENNIG 1994, esp. pp. 322–323.

23   HENNIG 1994, p. 323 n. 53; BLÜMEL in *IKnidos* 605 does not comment on the last line of the decree.

(35) Tenos and Kyrene

Stele of white marble decorated with a small pediment with *acroteria* and now stored in the Archaeological Museum of Tenos.[24] Measurements: H. 0.40 m.; W. 0.31 m.; Th. 0.07 m. Letters: 0.008.

Edd. *ed. pr.* Dumulin 1902, n. 18 (*facsim.*); *IG* XII.5 814.
Cf. Graindor 1907, esp. pp. 45–46 (restoration of LL. 1–5).

  ἔδοξεν τῆι βουλεῖ καὶ τῶι δήμωι· [Κ]τη-
  [σίτ]ι[μ]ος ἐπεστάτει, Κλεοστρατίδης εἶ-
  [πεν· ἐπει]δὴ Ζήν[ω]ν Ζήνωνος Κυρηναῖος
4 [ὑπαρχούσ]ης [αὐτῶ]ι πολιτείας παρ' ἡμῖν [κα]-
  [θ]άπε[ρ κ]α[ὶ τοῖς ἄ]λ[λ]οις Κυρηναίοις διὰ [τὴν]
  [οἰ]κειότητα τὴν ὑπάρχουσαν ταῖς πόλ[εσιν]
  ἔν τε τῶι ἔμπροσθεγ χρόνωι διετέλε[ι πολ]-
8 λὰ καὶ φιλάνθρωπα καὶ κοινεῖ ὑπὲρ τῆς [πό]-
  λεως καὶ λέγωγ καὶ πράττων καὶ ἰδί[αι Τηνί]-
  [ων τοῖς] ἐ[ντυγχάνουσιν αὐτῶι ...]

Text of *IG* XII.5 814.

Transl.: it was decided by the *boule* and the *demos*. Ktesitimos was *epistates*, Kleostratides put forward the motion: since Zenon son of Zenon of Kyrene, who enjoys citizenship like all other Kyreneans because of the ties of familiarity that exist between the cities, and, as he has already done in the past, he keeps on benefiting (us) both commonly in regard to the city by speaking and acting and privately [in regard to Tenians who happen to be by him] ...

Paleography has led students of antiquity to date this inscription to the beginning of the 2nd century BC. The stone was found north of the monumental sanctuary of Poseidon and Amphitrite located in the southeastern part of the island, not far from the only existing *polis* on Tenos, namely, the city of Tenos.[25] In the 3rd century BC the Tenians might have started their quest for

---

24 The local ephoria (ΚΑ᾽Εφορεια Προιστωρικων και Κλασικων Αρχαιοτητων) has kindly confirmed the location of the stele per email on 11.22.2012.
25 On the sanctuary see STRAB. X.5.11; ÉTIENNE and BRAUN 1986; ÉTIENNE 1990, p. 20. For the city proper see ÉTIENNE 1984, pp. 205–211.

asylia for the sanctuary of Poseidon and Amphitrite, and the island. Possibly, embassies attesting to a mission for the reminder of *asylia* are attested for the 2nd century BC.[26]

During the Hellenistic period Tenos came under the influence of several kings, but the otherwise strong Ptolemaic presence in the Kykladic islands is hardly attested there.[27] At the beginning of the 2nd century BC, the island became the center of the revitalized League of the Islanders, at that time led by Rhodes.[28] The League's organization and eventual restrictions imposed on its members remain largely unknown. König speaks of substantial freedom for members of the League to run their own foreign policy, citing the agreement of Tenos with the Phokians, and, for the Rhodian period, a *symbolon* with the Achaean League.[29]

Kyrene was one of the Greek cities of Libya, a rich territory that after the death of Alexander passed under Ptolemaic control.[30] The history of this *polis* in the Hellenistic period is poorly known. Here it suffices to point out that the region remained under Ptolemaic control, although not always willingly, from the middle of the 3rd century BC until after Apion bequeathed it to Rome in 96 BC.

Evidence for the relationship between Tenos and Kyrene is sparse: for the period in which this decree was enacted, it amounts to our document and to a funerary inscription testifying to the burial of a Kyrenean in Tenos.[31]

Our document refers to older contacts between these communities that, apparently, at some point established a grant of potential citizenship (LL. 3–7) between them, if one accepts Graindor's restoration. Gawantka notes that what the Tenians truly granted Zenon remains unknown, yet he seems to treat

---

26 The date is uncertain see RIGSBY 1996, p. 154.
27 ÉTIENNE 1990, p. 93; BAGNALL 1976, p. 151.
28 The sources on the League of the Islanders are scarce: Liv. XXXI.15.8 and Polyb. XVI.26.10. To those, one can add epigraphic evidence mainly represented by honorific decrees; on the League see SIPPEL 1986(a) and (b); KÖNIG 1910 must be still consulted. See also MERKER's 1970 which focuses on the Ptolemaic period, on which now see also MEADOW 2013. For the Rhodian phase see GABRIELSEN 1997, esp. pp. 56–63 and SHEEDY 1994, pp. 423–449. For the move of the seat of the *koinon* from Delos to Tenos, see GABRIELSEN 1997, esp. p. 174, n. 117; SIPPEL 1986, pp. 35–40.
29 KÖNIG 1910, p. 77.
30 See LARONDE 1987, esp. 27–36. The area never came under control of the Great King, but later Kyrenaika could not retain its independent position and became—at some, uncertain point—a Ptolemaic possession. See WILL 1960, pp. 369–390.
31 LE DINAHET-COUILLOUD 1974, p. 414 records the text of this late Hellenistic stele that has now disappeared: Δημήτριος Δημητρίου / Κυρηναῖος χρηστὲ / χαῖρε.

the text as if it testified to a concession of citizenship to Zenon son of Zenon.[32] If the decree truly implemented an older exchange of potential citizenship at the request of an individual, which I doubt, this document would be a unique example, but we cannot certainly characterize it as such, because the second half of the inscription is lost.

Étienne defines this text as indirect evidence for potential citizenship relying on Graindor's restoration. Étienne even sketches the possible occasion for its award, namely, the concession of *asylia* to sanctuary and island, comparing it to that of Tenos and the Phokians (however, I doubt *isopoliteia* was exchanged in this example).[33] This interpretation does not rest on a very solid foundation: *asylia* is unattested in North Africa, at least in the 'Greek' sense. In his comprehensive study on this grant, K. Rigsby notes that about a dozen grants of *asylia* come from Egypt, which date to the 1st century BC and are more similar to Roman *asilum*, i.e., religious immunity from civil law, than the Greek *asylia*.[34] Kyrene was a Greek city. Although its relationship to Egypt does not mean that it necessarily followed Ptolemaic Egypt in all ways, the fact that no *asylia* grant is known from this community may go against this theory.

The text does not offer many reference points for its interpretation and contextualization. In LL. 5–7 we learn that *oikeiotes* between Kyrene and Tenos is the alleged reason for the original grant. This detail, however, hardly helps us to reconstruct possible historical contexts. A small, and equally uncertain, clue could come from the famous inscription testifying to Kyrene's donation, or maybe sale at good conditions, of grain to numerous Greek communities between 330–326 BC.[35] Included among the recipients, although in a difficult restoration, appear the 'Tenians', L. 15.[36] If the restoration is correct, perhaps

---

[32] GAWANTKA 1977, p. 57, n. 37: "Hier wurde dann eindeutig ein individueller Anspruch auf das Bürgerrecht auf Grund einer Isopolitie bestätigt –wobei natürlich offenbleibt, ob dies geschah, weil der Titular ein Interesse daran hatte, es *auszuüben*, oder ob es sich ebenfalls seiner Funktion nach bloß um ein <Ehrenbürgerrecht> handelte, das ihm die Stadt verleihen wollte. Dieses Dekret wäre aber in jedem Fall der bislang einzige Beleg für eine *rechtliche* Verbindung von Isopolitie und Bürgerrechtsverleihung ad personam."

[33] GRAINDOR 1907, pp. 45–46. See *infra* no. 69 on Tenos and Phokis.

[34] RIGSBY 1996, pp. 540–544.

[35] RHODES & OSBORNE pp. 486–493 no. 96.

[36] OLIVERIO 1928 restored L. 15 as Τ[ηνέσ]σι δύο μυριάδας and was later followed by LARONDE 1987, p. 30 and MARASCO 1992, p. 13. BRUN 1993, p. 187, n. 16 rejects the restoration because of several considerations. First, he notes that, in comparison to the other recipients, the amount of grain for Tenos would be out of proportion. His second argument pertains to the ethnic, which in this form is extremely unusual and not fully supported by the reading of the stone. Brun lists a third (weak) reason to reject the restoration: citing *IG* XII 5 814 he considers it illogical to try to establish a connection between the two texts because they are too chronologically distant. But ancient diplomacy was extremely resourceful.

the grant of citizenship could be placed at that time. But this hypothesis must remain very tentative.

The unique feature of this text is that it mentions an existing intercity grant of potential citizenship within a decree concerned with an individual. The question that has been asked is whether this document testifies to (the only) case of implementation of a grant of potential citizenship—which I do not believe. The text says that Zenon is a Kyrenean, but the function of the statement is to underline the tie between communities, but then it breaks off. We will never know how many individuals decided to switch citizenship by relying on a grant of potential citizenship. Was it a common process? Was it exceptional? Even if the answer to this specific question remain elusive, the practice must have occurred and we should be ready to admit to this possibility.

(36) *Lesbian League*

Three inscribed fragments, found at different times, constitute the extremely patchy document that has been published as *IG* XI.4 1064 (and *IG* XII *Suppl.* 136).[37] This fragmentary inscription contains the 'charter' of the otherwise poorly known Lesbian League, which included Mytilene, Methymna, Eressos, and Antissa.[38] L. Robert suggested in 1929 that L. 27 of this document refers to a concession of potential citizenship among the members of the League.[39]

The document dates between 200 and 167 BC according to both paleography and a passage from Livy that says that the Romans destroyed the city of Antissa in 167 BC because it harbored Perseus.[40] The text is too fragmentary to allow an intelligible translation; a summary of its content can be helpful.[41]

MARASCO 1992, Figs. I-II-III presents excellent pictures of the inscription in his work, but these neither support nor overrule the reading of the letters preserved in L. 15. The two fragments of the stele are joint across L. 15 and most of the name of the city listed there is lost. The first letter could be a "τ," the last is surely a "ι," while the "σ" is uncertain. The proposed Τ[ηνέσ]σι is not very unlikely epigraphically, but the arguments against it are certainly valid.

37   Ravoisé and Poirot saw and copied the text in 1829; B is the biggest fragment and was found in 1903. The first editors already suggested that B could be joined with A. The inscription is now in Delos, inv. nr. Δ 547 A. C contains only sparse letters; its findspot is unknown and it is now stored in Delos, inv. nr. Δ 547B.

38   On the *koinon* see ROBERT *OMS* II, pp. 721–735, see also DIMIPOULOU 2015, pp. 312–316. The Lesbian League is attested only epigraphically for the imperial period see LABARRE 1994 and 1996, on which see GAUTHIER 1997, pp. 349–361.

39   ROBERT *OMS* I, p. 209 on L. 27.

40   LIV. XLV. 31.13; see MASON 1995, esp. pp. 402–410; LABARRE 1994, p. 426; BUCHHOLZ 1975, pp. 152–153 and ROBERT *OMS* II, p. 730.

41   See also LABARRE 1996, pp. 426–427 and ROBERT *OMS* II, pp. 731–732.

Fragment A must have contained the date of the agreement according to each city's dating system. In L. 5 appears for the first time the sanctuary of Messa, which was the religious, political, and juridical seat of the confederacy in the 2nd century BC. A restored mention of existing *philia* follows. The personal names recorded in the subsequent lines (LL. 7–14) must have belonged to the representatives of the four Lesbian cities signing the agreement.

The first 6 or 7 lines of B probably dealt with defense troops and the 'human' contribution each member city was required to send, according to its capacity, if need arose. It is Robert's opinion that L. 6 mentions additional troops and that the agreement outlines the decisional process for their dispatch.[42]

In L. 11 appears the expression οἱ ὑπὸ τῶ κοι[ν]ῶ δεδείγμενοι which is the first reference to the Lesbian confederacy. The first editors, however, have avoided restoring the word *koinon* for epigraphic reasons and, probably, because its use here would have been peculiar. L. 13 mentions "common security," which was to be attained through the exploitation, probably selling, of natural resources and the payment of dues (LL. 13–21). Provisions against cities that did not meet these financial requirements follow. L. 26 mentions "the cities without *apographas* and *symbolas* [- - -]," keywords that signal the topics treated, but they appear out of context and cannot be interpreted.

In the subsequent line, L. 27, Robert identifies the presence of enrollment clauses that he thinks would complete a grant of potential citizenship among the cities of the island. This thought led him to restore the text as we have it now.[43] From the point of view of the institutions, L. 29 is also relevant because it says that new, common (?) laws had to be enacted, but after that only numbers that refer to the cities follow. In any case, all of this was to be accomplished "for the growth and the harmony of the Lesbians" (L. 33).[44]

The last surviving section of the text pertains to justice; apparently the instrument of choice to regulate and resolve conflicts among communities included the service of foreign judges.[45] The text implies the existence of a list of cities, on which the members of the *koinon* had to agree, and from which foreign judges could be called, once the name of the city to be appointed had been drawn by lot (LL. 41–43). Provisions on the adequate escort and the location of the court, namely, Messa, follow. Judges could try mediation or (more

---

42   ROBERT *OMS* II, p. 731 assigns this meaning to συμμαχίας.
43   L. 27 [- - - ἀπογράφεσθα]ι πρὸς τοῖς στρατάγοις καὶ εἰς φύλαν ἄν κ[ε βόλληται ἐπικλάρωσθαι - -]
      It is possible that LL. 28–29 still dealt with this grant, but the text is too fragmentary.
44   [- - - εἰς? αὔ]ξησιν καὶ ὁμόνοιαν τῶν Λεσβίων καὶ περιπι[- - -].
45   See ROBERT *OMS* II, pp. 727 and 731.

likely 'and') arbitration, and their judgment was final (L. 48).[46] Nothing else could be deduced from the rest of the inscription.

How this *koinon* was organized is largely unknown and, most importantly, we ignore whether it had any form of federal citizenship in place. Labarre assumes it did, but no proof for it exists.[47] In fact, I wonder whether federal citizenship was essential in a newly born, Hellenistic confederacy, especially because another solution to share a privileged status was envisioned: namely, the citizens of Methymna, Mytilene, Eresos, and Antissa became privileged foreigners in each other's town and territory through the grant of potential citizenship. This arrangement could have been a satisfactory compromise. Judging from the length of the existing clauses, the issue of citizenship does not seem to have preoccupied exceedingly the authorities of the newly constituted federation. By contrast for example, judicial matters seem to have been treated more extensively at both the city and confederacy level. Legal rights of the *koinon* members were paramount, but citizenship status may have been a minor issue within the confederacy.

A multilateral exchange of potential citizenship among members of a newly created confederacy represents an institutional solution, one less charged than dual citizenship, which probably assumed a more organized and tighter structure and closer relationship for the cities involved.

In his introduction to his work on federal states, Larsen writes that: "it is possible, though not likely, that in some federal states a citizen possessed potential citizenship in all cities of the confederacy so that, if he wished, he could by registering transfer his active citizenship to any of them that he wished."[48] In Lesbos perhaps this form of potential citizenship was the system of choice, but, I add, it lacked any other superimposed form of citizenship. I argue that here the multilateral grant of potential citizenship served as an alternative to federal citizenship rather than as a complement to it. A twofold reason supports this position. First, the Lesbian *xoinon* never truly united and was apparently characterized by a general, reciprocal 'distant' behavior of its members.

---

46   Other epigraphic testimonies show that, at the very least, this part of the agreement was enforced, see AGER 1996, no. 92 and GAUTHIER 1972, esp. p. 344.

47   LABARRE 1994, esp. pp. 428–429 (and again in 1996). On pp. 429–430 he also provides a hypothetical reconstruction of the working institutions of the *koinon*. He believes that the expression *koinon ton Lesbion* alone assures the existence of federal citizenship. He makes some risky assumptions on the alleged potential citizenship, too: After quoting Robert's restoration in L. 27 LABARRE 1994, p. 427 asserts that: "Par consequent, les citoyens qui changeaient de residence pour s'installer dans une autre cite lesbienne se voyaient offrir les privileges du droit de citoyenneté, de possession du sol (*enktésis*) et de mariage (*épigamie*)." However, the surviving text does not testify to these grants, which were not given 'automatically.'

48   LARSEN 1968, *introduction* p. XX.

Second, a new, Hellenistic *koinon* could not rely on structures more often present in older *koina* where the ethnic and traditional common background played a central role in shaping the institutions of the confederacies.[49]

(37)   *Mytilene and Larisa—Thessalian Confederacy*
Stele of white marble broken in two joining fragments that were reused to cover a Roman gutter, found during a rescue excavation on the acropolis of Larisa. The stone is preserved in the Larisa Museum (AEML 97/12). Measurements: H. 0.208; W. 0.53–0.485; Th. 19–17.5. Letters: 0.015–0.01 in the first line; 0.005–0.006 in the rest of the text.

Edd. *ed. pr.* Tziafalias and Helly 2004-5, pp. 378–402 (*ph*); [*SEG* LV 605; Dimipoulou 2015, pp. 303–306].
Cf. Helly *BE* 2009 356.

ψαφίσματα Λασαίουν·
ταγευόντων Ἀγαθοκλείδα Ἀγαθουνείοι, Ἱππονόοι Παναγ[α]-
θείοι, Πάνθειρος Πετθαλείοι, Ἀρ[χ]ελάοι Τιμοσθενείοι, Θούρακος Πτολ[ε]-
4   μαιείοι *vvv* Ἰτουνίοι τᾶ ἑσκαιδεκότα, ἀγορανόμεντος Ἱππονό-
[ο]ι Παναγαθείοι *vvv* ὀπειδεὶ Βάκχιος ὁ Καΐκειος Μιτυλειναῖος φί[λο]ς
[ο]ὖν καὶ εὐεργέτας παργενόμενος ἐν τὰν πόλιν τὰν Λασαίουν δι[ε]-
[λέ]χθει καὶ παρεκάλεσσε τὰν πόλιν τὰν τοὖν Λασαίουν ὄσκε ἅ τε
8   [φιλ]ία καὶ αἱ τιμαὶ αἱ ὑπάρχονσαι ἀτ τᾶς πόλιος τᾶς τοὖν Λασαίουν πο[τ]-
[τὰ]ν πόλιν τὰν τοὖν Μιτυλειναίουν διαμένουνθι καὶ ὄσσα παρλελιμ-
[μέ]να εἶεν ἐν τοῦ παρελθουκόντι χρόνου ψαφιξούνθειν Λασαῖοι Μιτυλ[ει]-
[ν]αίοις [π]άντα, κοινὰ π[ο]έντες Μυτιλειναίοις τὰ ὑπάρχοντα τᾶ πόλι τὰ [πά]-
12   ντα οὖσπερ καὶ Μιτυλειναῖοι Πετθαλοῖς, καὶ τάνε ἀμφοτέροις ὑφά[γ]ει[σιν]
[ἐ]νφερέμεν καὶ ἐνεφάνιξε τὰ ἐψαφισμένα τᾶ βουλᾶ καὶ τοῦ δ[ά]μου τοὖν
Μιτυλειναίουν [τοὖμ π]ρούταμ μὲν ἐψαφισμένοι Λασαίοις εἶεν ἐμ [Μιτυ]
λ[άνα]
[τὰμ] πολι[τ]είαμ μετεχό[ντεσ]σι πάντουν τούμπερ Μιτυλειναῖοι [- - - - -]
16   [- - - - - - - - - - - - - - - - - - - -]Α καὶ τοῦ κοινοῦ [- - - - -]
[- -] ἀσυλεῖ καὶ ἀσπονδεῖ
[- -]ΛΑΝ καὶ ποτ τὸν δᾶ-
[μον -]ΙΕΠΕΙΜΑΤ[- -]

---

49   See LASAGNI 2010, esp. pp. 259–264. On the *koinon* of the Lesbians see *supra* and esp. MASON 1995, p. 401 on the loose ties between its members.

Text and restoration by T(ziafalias) and H(elly) unless otherwise noted; LL. 6–7 δι[ει]/[νέ]χθει T. and H., δι[ε]/[λέ]χθει *SEG* LV, 605 Ch(aniotis).

Transl.: LL. 5–15: ... Since Bacchios son of Kaikos from Mytilene has always spoken as a friend and benefactor when he has come to the city of the Lariseans and has urged the city of the Lariseans to preserve friendship and the recognitions on the part of the Lariseans for the city of the Mytileneans and that the Lariseans shall vote for the Mytileneans all that has been left out in the past, thus sharing with the Mytileneans everything that the city has, just like the Mytileneans do with the Thessalians, and that they take these as guidelines to both and he showed what the *boule* and the *demos* of the Mytileneans have voted for the Lariseans, namely, that they have citizenship in Mytilene and partake in everything the Mytileneans do....

The title crowning the stele found in Larisa shows that the stone preserved several documents, which, however, do not have to be part of a dossier.[50]

In an undetermined year at the beginning of the 2nd century BC, the city of Larisa honored a citizen of Mytilene, Bacchios son of Kaikos, for his friendly attitude and benevolence toward Larisa. Within this document a possible unilateral grant of potential citizenship, or perhaps even two grants, appear, LL. 11–15.

Tziafalias and Helly have shown that Bacchios is already known to Lesbian epigraphy as he can be identified with *Bacchios Ka[...* of *IG* XII *Suppl.* 3.[51] This text must belong to the same years as our document and testifies to this man's successful mission to Thessaly. Bacchios there speaks in front of the governmental organs of Mytilene announcing that the Thessalians had accepted to participate in the renewed festivities for Asklepios held by the Mytileneans and to which they must have invited numerous Greek communities.[52] The reason behind this request to Thessaly could depend on several factors, for example, a diplomatic result of the military operations of the Second Macedonian War and the (re)creation of the Thessalian Confederacy in 196 BC.

---

50   Tziafalias and Helly 2007 published three new decrees that, although engraved on the same stele, treated different topics. This characterization could also apply to our stele.

51   See Tziafalias and Helly 2004–5, pp. 392–394 for a discussion of the text of *IG* XII *Suppl.* 3 with translation and Robert's considerations in *OMS* I, esp. pp. 27–32. It is not necessary here to summarize their work because I refer to it below, especially in regard to prosopography and their detailed commentary of the text.

52   Tziafalias and Helly 2004–5, pp. 399–402.

In *IG* XII *Suppl.* 3 Bacchios presents his proposal to grant a crown to the *koinon* of the Thessalians not only because they accepted to take part in the games and sacrifices, but also because they behaved as kin and in a benevolent way toward Mytilene.[53] The link between Bacchios and Thessaly is thus securely established for a year after 196 BC. Tziafalias and Helly reasonably assume that Bacchios, in his capacity as a 'ambassador,' must have visited the most important cities of Thessaly, which, as Larsen notes, retained a rather independent position within the confederacy.[54]

From the text of the new inscription published by Tziafalias and Helly, we learn, among other things, that Mytilene grants *politeia* to Larisa. I focus on LL. 5–18, where the causal preposition ὀπειδεὶ introduces the name of the honoree, Bacchios, and his role as a friend and benefactor of Larisa. These lines also preserve the content of Bacchios's intervention: he exhorted the Thessalian city to keep its friendship (here the text has been largely but plausibly restored), listed the honors for the city of Mytilene, and then called a vote for anything else that had not been already voted in the past. In their detailed and valuable commentary on the inscription, Tziafalias and Helly suggest that this passage relates to an interruption in the diplomatic activities in Thessaly due—perhaps—to war.[55] If we follow their reconstruction, we can assume that, once peace had been reestablished, Bacchios must have gone as a Mytilenean representative to Larisa and to other Thessalian cities. He urged them to keep, or re-establish, their friendly relations with Mytilene and, LL. 10–12, to "put everything in common," just like the Mytileneans had done with the Thessalians. This last sentence is of some interest because the attention shifts from Larisa to Thessaly, perhaps meaning that Bacchios's speech was wide-reaching in its goals, and meant for a broader audience. In the subsequent lines the focus returns to Larisa with Bacchios pointing out that Mytilene had granted *politeia* to this city, L. 15. Unfortunately, the text breaks off after this statement. When it resumes, the text not only seems to be concerned with a different topic, but it is also extremely fragmentary. Before this long lacuna of 24 lines, only three lines appear. Although the lines contain keywords, such as *koinon*, and the formula *asylei kai aspondei*, without a context the words have little meaning.

The concession of potential citizenship to Larisa must have been a new initiative of Mytilene and perhaps Bacchios was seeking reciprocation on the part of Larisa and other Thessalian cities. The text, however, leaves room for

---

53 LL. 14–16: (...) ἔν τε τῶ [πρό]/[σθε χρόν]ωι διετέλειον οἰκηίως καὶ εὐνόως [ἔχον]/[τες πρὸς] τὰν πόλιν ...
54 LARSEN 1968, esp. pp. 281–294.
55 TZIAFALIAS and HELLY 2004–5, esp. p. 402.

speculation as LL. 11–13, κοινὰ π[ο]έντες Μιτυλειναίοις τὰ ὑπάρχοντα τᾶ πόλι τὰ [πά]/ντα οὔσπερ καὶ Μιτυλειναῖοι Πετθαλοῖς, may indicate that this award could have been preceded by another 'broader' grant to Thessaly as confederacy. Perhaps Mytilene had already granted its potential citizenship to the newly re-founded *koinon* and then tried to establish stronger contacts at a local level with individual *poleis*. If accurate, this hypothesis would be significant because it would demonstrate that potential citizenship could exist on two levels. This view is plausible because federations tended to have already a system of dual citizenship, and we see it already operating in Aitolia (*StV* III 508, III = no. 41).

The evidence for potential citizenship from the islands (excluding Crete) varies greatly. It includes the use of concessions between federations, between cities and federations, and even preserve the only possible evidence we may have for the implementation of an intercity concession of potential citizenship by an individual. The flexible and wide use of this tool by these communities is very instructive for students of antiquity and challenges any possible monolithic interpretation of this institution. These texts show instead that this tool had evolved over time and could be used in multiple ways to achieve multiple goals.

PART 2

Evidence from Central Greece and Crete

CHAPTER 6

Central Greece: the Peloponnese and Aitolia

Potential citizenship is rarely attested in the Peloponnese. We know of only two (hardly comparable) documents that testify to the use of this institution: the agreement between Argos and Aspendos from the second half of the 4th century BC (*SEG* XXXIV 282 = no. 38) and that between Messene and Phigaleia dated to the 240s BC (*IPArk.* 28 = no. 39). The latter also demonstrates Aitolia's involvement with an attempt to mediate a tense situation over contested land. The agreement between Argos and Aspendos was approved with the intent to reestablish a relationship between the cities that, they say, relied on *syngeneia*, which, in turn, derived from their colonial ties. The limited use of potential citizenship in the Peloponnese contrasts with its wide use by the Aitolian League. The League's involvement in the one agreement in which potential citizenship is planned for Peloponnesian communities suggests to me that the Aitolians imported this tool to the Peloponnese. Peloponnesian communities, however, appear to have largely resisted its use.

The Aitolian evidence presents one more important feature for historians, namely, a clearer historical background. I will analyse the historical context of each piece of evidence in part to challenge a recent interpretive trend that privileges the view that the Aitolians used potential citizenship as an instrument for their expansion-driven politics.[1] According to this interpretation, by bestowing this grant, Aitolia supposedly tied to itself communities that were too far away to become actual members of its federal state. In addition, the fact that the known documents from Aitolia grant almost exclusively federal citizenship has added material that must be explained within the context of the problematic discussion on the relationship between federal and local citizenship.[2]

In this chapter I argue that Aitolia uses potential citizenship like all other communities and to its full potential. Potential citizenship in Aitolia can hardly be considered an instrument meant to subtly enlarge the Aitolian *koinon*. Instead the evidence indicates that for Aitolia this award served as

---

1 See for this see *infra*, pp. 00.
2 The one notable exception is the three-way grant among Keos, Naupaktos, and the Aitolian League (*StV* III 508, III = no. 41), which includes also grants of citizenship in the *polis*, see *infra* pp. 178–180.

a diplomatic tool to be used in pan-Mediterranean diplomatic and political dialogues. On the complex and multilayered topic of dual citizenship and its relationship to the award of potential citizenship, I can draw only tentative conclusions and hypothesize that the two forms of citizenship coexisted (as well as their potential forms) and could be granted with the knowledge of all institutions involved.

(38) *Argos and Aspendos*

In the early 1980s the American excavations at Nemea recovered an inscription containing a decree that testifies to a grant of potential citizenship by Argos to Aspendos in Pamphylia.[3] Stroud 1984, pp. 194–195 describes the three fragments as being part of a gray limestone stele found built in in an ancient wall "near the southwest corner of the Temple of Zeus" at Nemea. Now the stone is stored in the Nemea Museum, I 75. Scholars have devoted limited attention to this isolated document that, however, raises important questions about kinship and colonial and political relationships between distant communities.[4]

Ed. pr. STROUD 1984; [*SEG* XXXIV 282; CURTY 1995, no. 3]
Cf. CHARNEUX *BE* 1987 604.

```
        [- - - ca 7–9 - - -]ΩN
        [Θεός. Τύχαι. Ἀλιαίαι ἔδοξε τελεί]αι, Ἀμυ[κλ]αίου ἑπομένου  ᵛ
        [..... ca 11..... ἀ]ρήτευε βωλᾶς Πο[λυ]χάρης Ἡραιεὺς Κολου-
        [ρίς· ἔδοξε τῶ]ι δάμωι τῶν Ἀργείων· Ἀσπ[εν]δίοις συγγενέ-  ᵛ
   5    [σι καὶ.....]οις Ἀργείων πολιτείαν ἦμεν ἐν Ἄργει καὶ πό-
        [τοδον πὸτ ἀ]λιαίαν πράτοις πεδὰ τὰ ἱαρὰ καὶ τὸνς Ῥοδί-  ᵛ
        ων (sic) καθάπερ κ[α]ὶ τοῖς Σολεῦσι καὶ ΕΝΣΚΛΗΙΝΣ ἐς τὸνς ἀγῶν-
        ας· καὶ τοὺς θεαρ[ο]ὺς οὕς κ[α] ἀποστέλλωντι θύσοντας τῶι Διὶ
        τῶι Νεμέαι καὶ τᾶ[ι Ἥραι τᾶι Ἀ]ργείαι προπέμπεμ π[ε]δὰ τῶν Ἀ[ρ]-
  10    γείων καὶ καλῖσθαι E [.... ca 11..... ἐπιμέλε]σθαι δὲ τὸν ἀγωνο-
        θέταν καὶ τὸνς ἰαρομν[άμονας τὸνς ἀεὶ ἀντι]τυγχάνοντας· ἐπιμέ-
        λεσθαι δὲ καὶ τὰν ἁλιαίαν [..... ca 13......]ΝΣΑΣ τὸν ἄπαντα χρόνον
        τῶν Ἀσπενδίων, αἴ τί κα δέ[ωνται·] καἴ τίς κα χράιζηι Ἀσπενδίων
        οἰκὲν ἐν Ἄργει, οἰκε[ί]τω τελώμ[εν]ος ἅπερ ὁ Ἀργεῖος, κ[αθ]άπερ καὶ Ἀρ-
```

---

3 Stroud 1984, whose edition I reproduce here, called this a treaty of sympolity, but already EHRHARDT 1987, pp. 100–102 pointed out that this text contains a grant of potential citizenship.
4 STROUD 1984, p. 217.

15 γείοις ἐν Ἀσπένδωι ἔστιν· ἀγγρά[ψ]αι δὲ τὸ δόκημα [τόδε ἐ]ν στά-
    λαι ἐν τῶι τοῦ Λυκείου ἱαρῶι καὶ Ν[ε]μέαι [κ]α[ὶ] πὰρ Ἥραι· π[ὸ]τ τὸν τελα-
    μῶνα τὸν ἐν τῶι τοῦ Λυκε[ίου] ἰα[ρ]ῶι [τὸν δᾶ]μον τῶν Ἀσπεν[δίω]ν ποτα[να]-
    γ[ρ]άψαι ⸱ ἔλεξε Εὔμελος [..... ca 11–13 ...... Ἀ]σπένδιος ΕΛ[------]
    ..... vacat 0.03 m

Text by Stroud.

Transl.: LL. 4–19: it was resolved by the *demos* of the Argives to grant citizenship in Argos to the Aspendians who are kin and ... to the Argives and access to the assembly after the sacred matters and the Rhodians, just like the citizens of Soloi. (Also, it was resolved) to invite them to the festivals/competitions. It shall also be conceded to the *theoroi*, who are sent to sacrifice to Zeus of Nemea and to Argive Hera, to be in the forefront of the procession with the Argives and to call ... the *agonothetes* and the *hieromnemonas* (pl.) in charge shall take care of (that?). Also the assembly and the (...) shall take care of the Aspendians for all time, if they need anything. And if an Aspendian wishes to live in Argos, he shall live there being taxed like an Argive, the same applies to Argives in Aspendos. This decree shall be inscribed on a stele in the sanctuary of *Lykeios* and in Nemea and by Hera. The (name) of the People of the Aspendians shall be inscribed on the *telamon* in the sanctuary of the *Lykeios*. Eumelos ... (and?) Aspendios EL(...) proposed ...

Stroud dates the document between the 330s and 255/4 BC on the basis of general historical considerations but adds: "if the lettering is a reliable criterion, we may narrow this down to *ca.* 330s–*ca.* 300 BC."[5]

The historical background to this agreement is unknown, but, as Stroud has pointed out, at the time of its signing the city of Argos must have been free to conduct its own foreign policy.[6] Scholars tend to focus on the colonial ties between Argos and Aspendos, although the connection does not figure in the

---

5 The broad chronological historical *termini* depend on the archaeological context and on the location of the Nemean games; STROUD 1984, p. 214, for the paleography of the text see pp. 212–213.

6 STROUD 1984, pp. 213–215; to the same years belongs the decree for Rhodes, MORETTI *ISE* I 40 = CURTY 1995, no. 4, (end of the 4th-beginning of the 3rd century BC). This text preserves a *syngeneia* claim that resembles the one found in this decree for Aspendos.

surviving text,[7] and on Arrian's account, the only surviving piece of narrative history we have for Aspendos in these decades. Arrian describes Alexander's conditions for Aspendos's surrender: the city had to give horses and money to pay Alexander's mercenaries *una tantum*. In exchange, Alexander would not impose a garrison on the town. Apparently, affluent Aspendos did not suffer any financial setback because of this request, which it must have met. Whether this event truly has direct bearing on this decree is open to debate, but it is routinely mentioned because it provides *a* historical context.[8]

The Award of Potential Citizenship

Aspendos may have taken the initiative in signing the treaty, if LL. 14–15 in fact testify to an already existing privileged status for Argives in their community (although this proposal may be forcing meaning upon the text). In any case, LL. 4–11 contain Argos's grant of *politeia* to Aspendos, said to be *syngenes*.[9] Aspendians had priority access to the assembly after the sacred matters and the Rhodians.[10] Finally, an invitation to competitions appears, tied to the games for Zeus in Nemea and for Hera at Argos with further honors.[11]

The text does not elaborate on the grant of citizenship by adding procedural details. Rather LL. 11–15 dwell on the status and privileges for Aspendians who are temporarily in Argos or live there as foreigners. The text orders the *aliaia* and a governmental organ (no longer specified) to help the Aspendians in

---

7   Argos is the mother city of Aspendos in STRAB. XIV.4.2; MELA I.78; see CURTY 1995 esp. pp. 8–9. On Alexander and Aspendos see ARR. I. 26. BOSWORTH 1988, p. 166; BADIAN 1966, esp. pp. 58–59.
8   See especially EHRHARDT 1987, p. 101.
9   On *syngeneia* see CURTY 1995, p. 5. Stroud restored LL. 4–5 as καὶ ἀποίκ]οις, but CHARNEUX *BE* 1987 604 prefers Habicht's οἰκεῖ]οις, which may be the better option.
10 CHARNEUX *BE* 1987 604 discusses hypotheses for LL. 6–7: for example, reports Stroud's suggestion to amend the genitive Ῥοδίων with Ῥοδίους or the article τόνς with τά or his suggestion to imply χρηματισμόνς before the genitive Ῥοδίων.
11 Stroud (p. 203) explains L. 7 ΕΝΣΚΛΗΙΝΣ either as ἔνσκλη᾽ ινς, which he prefers, or ἔνσκλη᾽ ινς ⟨ς⟩, namely as the accusative plural or accusative singular of εἴσκλησις. See also CHARNEUX *BE* 1987 604 esp. pp. 406–407.

Argos in need.[12] LL. 13–15 add to the grant by listing provisions that establish a form of *isotelia* for Aspendians living in Argos, which the text says was already in place for Argives in Aspendos.[13] Precisely when this accommodation began for the Argives in Aspendos is impossible to determine: we can only speculate whether it existed *ab antiquo*, (however, the wording makes it unlikely) or it is a new concession for which Aspendos had sought reciprocation.

Ehrhardt has elaborated on the fact that this text does not contain detailed enrollment clauses and, following Gawantka, has suggested that this absence is due to the geographical distance between the two cities. But this view makes little sense in a text that regulates guests' fiscal behavior: I hold that the inclusion or exclusion of enrollment clauses depends on the city's documentary practice. In other words, enrollment clauses existed everywhere, but in this document and in many others the clauses are not specified.

Instead of focusing on what the text does not say, I would like to concentrate on the clauses present in the text. Fiscal agreements were serious matters tied to everyday life and also to the local economy. Their inclusion suggests that Argos wanted to facilitate the temporary presence of Aspendians who would retain their own citizenship and, probably, their strong ties with their own community, by allowing them to pay taxes like Argive citizens.[14] In this agreement *politeia* is of little concern to the involved parties. Reciprocal accommodations for individuals who travelled between the two communities or lived in them as foreigners seem to be the priority, which makes the grant of potential citizenship a way to create a privileged relationship between the cities with further benefits for individuals.

---

12   STROUD 1984, p. 205 proposes that we restore the crippling lacuna of L. 12 with καὶ τὰς ἀρχὰς ἀπά]νσας, and also records Kritzas's solution [τὰς ἀρτύνας]. CHARNEUX *BE* 1987 604 p. 408 in his analysis also proposes to restore the name of the council or to interpret '*aliaian*' as a partitive genitive followed by another genitive. Other inscriptions preserve parallels to this prescription, for example in Keos the *astynomoi* are in charge of the Histiaeans *StV* II² 287 = no. 33 LL. 17–21, 360s; in Seleukeia-Tralles the *strategoi* are in charge of the Milesians in town, *Milet* I 3 143 = no. 5, LL. 62–64, 218/7 BC.
13   For the philological difficulties of the passage see CHARNEUX *BE* 1987 604, esp. p. 408.
14   See GAUTHIER 2000, pp. 109–114.

(39)   *Messene and Phigaleia*

In the introduction to this book I used this inscription to describe the 'second type' of *isopoliteia*. Here I wish to analyze its content within the context of broader agreements that had been approved in attempts to resolve tense situations with clear historical associations. Thus our discussion can move beyond abstract diplomatic dealings.

The text I cite here follows the edition by Thür and Taeuber *IPArk*. 28 (= *IG* v.2 419) = no. 39[15] and serves as the basis for the discussion below as well as the introduction:

[ἐπειδὴ παραγενόμενο]ι̣ πρεσβε[υ]ταὶ καὶ διαλ- ν
[λακταὶ ? παρὰ τῶν Αἰτω]λῶν Τίμαιος, Κλεόπατρος
[....... τό τε ψάφισ]μα τὸ παρὰ τῶν Αἰτωλῶν ἀπ-
4 [έδωκαν καὶ αὐτοὶ] διελέγοντο ὅμοια τοῖς ἐν τ-
[ῶι ψαφίσσματι, ἀξ]ιῶντες διαλυθῆμεν ποτὶ τὼ-
[ς Φιαλέας, συνπ]αρόντες δὲ καὶ τῶν ἐΦιαλείας
[παρελθόντων] Θαρυκίδας, Ὀνόμανδρος, Ἀνφίμα-
8 [χος ....]δας, Ὀρθολαΐδας, Κραταιμένης, Τί-
[........, Δ]αμάρετος τὰ αὐτὰ ἀξίων, ἔδοξε τᾶι
[πόλει τᾶι Μ]εσσανίων, ἦμεν τοῖς Μεσσανίοις κα-
[ὶ τοῖς Φια]λέοις ἰσοπολιτείαν καὶ ἐπιγαμία-
12 [ν ποτὶ ἀλλ]άλως· ποιήσασθαι δὲ καὶ συνβολὰν ἅ-
[νπερ δοκεῖ] ἀνφοτέραις ταῖς πολέοις. τὰν δὲ χ-
[{χ}ώραν? καρπ]ίζεσσθαι ἑκατέρως τώς τε Μεσανίω-
[ς καὶ τὼς Φι]αλέας, καθὼς καὶ νῦν καρπιζόμεθα.
16 [ὅσα δέ κα ἄλλ]α (?) ὁμολογήσωμες πότ' ἀλλάλως, ὀμό-
[σαι ἀνφοτέρω]ς, καὶ στάλας καταθέσθαι ἐν τοῖς
[ἱεροῖς, ὁπεῖ κ]α̣ δοκεῖ ἀνφοτέραις ταῖς πολέο-
[ις· εἰ δέ κα μὴ ἐν]μένωντι οἱ Φιαλέες ἐν τᾶι φιλ-
20 [ίαι τᾶι πὸτ τὼς Μ]εσανίως καὶ Αἰτωλώς, ἄκυρος ἔ-
[σστω ἅδε ἁ ὁμολο]γία. ἔδοξε δὲ καὶ τοῖς Φιαλέ[ο]-
[ις ποιεῖν καθ' ἅ ο]ἱ̣ Μεσσάνιοι ἐψαφίξαντ[ο. Ὅρκ]-
[ος Μεσσανίων· ὀμν]ύω Δία Ἰθωμάταν, Ἥρα[ν.....

---

15   The document, now stored in the Epigraphic Museum of Athens, was found in the middle of the 19th century in Pavlitza, on the site of ancient Phigaleia, and has been published many times. The stele is broken in two parts; unfortunately, the left upper side and the bottom part are missing. According to Thür and Taeuber, *IPArk*. 28 (*IG* v.2 419), on whose edition I rely, the text is *stoichedon* with L. 1 counting 37 letters, while LL. 2 (?) to the end contains 36 characters each. Measurements: W. 0.43; H. 0.47; Th. 0.95 m. Letters: 0.02.

24 [............]ον καὶ θεὼς ὁρκί[ως πάντας· ἦ]-
    [μὰν ἐνμενεῖν ...] ἐν τᾶι φιλί[αι τᾶι ὑπαρχώσαι?]
    [πὸτ' Αἰτωλὼς καὶ Φι]αλέας Π ....
    .... μεγ ....

Transl.: LL. 1–22: Since the ambassadors and mediators of the Aitolians have come, Timaios, Kleopatros ... they gave (us) the decree of the Aitolians and spoke according to its content that we should settle our claim with the Phigaleians. Present were also those who had come from Phigaleia, Tharykidas, Onomandros, Amphimachos, ?das, Ortholaidas, Krataimenes, Ti?, Damaretos, supporting the same statement. It was resolved by the city of the Messenians, that Messenians and Phigaleians shall exchange isopolity and the right to intermarriage; they shall also establish a judicial agreement that pleases both cities. The land shall be cultivated by each, (the citizens) of Messene and (those) of Phigaleia, just as we cultivate it now. On everything else we shall reach an agreement with each other, both shall swear an oath, and put on display the engraved document in sanctuaries, wherever it seems more appropriate to each city. If the Phigaleians do not stay in their friendship with the Messenians and the Aitolians, this agreement shall be void. It was decided by the Phigaleians to do as the Messenians have decreed: (*oath follows*)

The first aspect to discuss is the date of the text. Aitolian prosopography allows us to establish fairly accurately a date in the 240s, BC most likely to that decade's second half. Both Timaios and Kleopatros, who are here the Aitolian representatives, are known as *hieronmnemones* in Delphi for the years included between 244 and 236 BC.[16]

The agreement concerns the neighboring *poleis* of Phigaleia and Messene, located in Arkadia and Messenia in the southwestern Peloponnese.[17] The river Neda may have served as a natural boundary between the cities, but, according to K. Harter-Uibopuu, it is possible that Phigaleia's territory could have extended beyond it to reach the area of Aulon on the west coast. If correct, the

---

16 See THÜR and TAEUBER *IPArk*. 28, p. 300 n. 3 and 4. Timaios is known as *hieromnemon* in Delphi in 244 or 240 BC (see *Syll.*³ 444E and LEFEVRE 1995, p. 193; Klaffenbach's introduction to *IG* IX 1², p. LIV) and as *strategos* (in *Syll.*³ 480; *IG* IX.1².1 174). Possibly in 240 BC Timaios attacked Spartan territories with Charixenos, POLYB. IV.34.9. Kleopatros is attested as *hieromnenon* in Delphi around 236/5 BC (*Syll.*³ 461).

17 For the topography of the region see HARTER-UIBOPUU 1998, esp. pp. 51–52. On Messenia see GRANDJEAN 2003, esp. pp. 15–17.

strategic importance of Phigaleia would vastly increase, as that strip of land was a crucial crossway.[18] *Chorai* and their borders were a main concern for these two communities: LL. 12–15 refer to contested land that perhaps caused or contributed to the start of the controversy between Messene and Phigaleia that the Aitolians sought to mediate.[19] Thus the Aitolians attempted to broker an agreement meant to stop the claims of both cities while respecting the terms of whatever relationship Messene and Phigaleia had with the Aitolian League at the time.

The inscription sketches out this relationship, which is said to be one of φιλία, but does not explain it. Any interpretation must rely on the admittedly scanty historical pieces of information we have on the political positioning of the two *poleis* with regard to Aitolia. For the second half of the 3rd century BC, sources cite Phigaleia in connection with Aitolia,[20] but scholars tend to exclude that either Phigaleia or Messene were already members of the *koinon* of the Aitolians when they signed this agreement.[21] Since this document is the only text that testifies to the unclear relationship of these cities with

---

18   HARTER-UIBOPUU 1998, esp. p. 52.

19   This document does not contain arbitration, MAGNETTO 1997, pp. 230–237 no. 38. Later inscriptions may testify to a territorial controversy that could have pertained to the same land and for which arbitration was possibly called, *IG* V.1 1430 on which HARTER-UIBOPUU 1998, no. 7. On LL. 13–15, see BURASELIS 2002, p. 228; the parallel with *I. Cret.* III.iii 4, L. 11 that was originally suggested by GAWANTKA 1975, p. 67, n. 60 is only superficially sound. Even if the wording matches, the Cretan text refers to a radically different concept. But Buraselis is right when he points out that our text does not talk of "joint use of land," but of contested land whose modes of use are not defined anew in the agreement.

20   In general, on Phigaleia, see MEYER in *RE* XIX.2 col. 2065–2086; HILLER's introduction to the section of *IG* V.2 and NIELSEN, *Inventory*, pp. 527–528 on the Archaic and Classical town. SCHOLTEN 2000, esp. pp. 116–130. HARTER-UIBOPUU 1998, pp. 46–50 provides a pointed reconstruction of the historical context of *IPArk.* 28 = *IG* V.2 419.

21   The assumption that Aitolia and Phigaleia had isopolity relies on POLYB. IV.3.6 who says that Phigaleia is συμπολιτευομένη with the Aitolians (the reference is to the 220s BC). GAUTHIER 1972, p. 367 refers to WALBANK 1957, p. 234 commenting on POLYB. II.46.2 and IV.3.6, for whom Polybios used the concept of *sympoliteia* where he meant *isopoliteia* (but see *infra* in the appendix on Polybios and LASAGNI 2017). Yet no hard proof for isopolity between Aitolia and Phigaleia exists (for 240 or even later), while our document speaks of φιλία, a contradiction, for example, that MAGNETTO 1997, p. 235 notes, too. For the historical context of the years of the so-called Social War see HARTER-UIBOPUU 1998, pp. 46–50. Messene, on which see SHIPLEY *Inventory*, pp. 561–564, may have also sought Aitolian protection against its old enemies, Sparta and the Achaean League, starting from the 270s BC, but became a member of the Aitolian League only at a later, yet uncertain date. GRANDJEAN 2003, esp. pp. 73–76 discusses in detail the meager evidence for the decades between 280 and 235 BC and asserts that Phigaleia had isopolity with Aitolia; POLYB. IV.6.11 and GRANDJEAN's 2003, p. 75 on the Messenian relationship with Aitolia.

the Aitolian league for the 240s BC it seems reasonable to think (until new evidence emerges) that neither city was a member of the Aitolian League at the time. This decree only shows that Messene and Phigaleia accepted the Aitolian presence and activities as a counterweight to the expansionism of the Achaean League.[22]

In the decree we can distinguish three sections. A. Magnetto indeed says: "la prima (ll. 1–21) costituita dal decreto di Messene, la seconda dalla dichiarazione della *polis* di Figalia di farne proprie le clausole (ll. 21–22), la terza, quasi interamente perduta, dai giuramenti prestati dalle parti."[23]

Like Gauthier, Magnetto believes that the peculiar form of these grants reflects the direct involvement of the Aitolians.[24] This certainly correct view can be further explained, at least concerning *isopoliteia*. I have already argued in the introduction and elsewhere that the term *isopoliteia*, when it refers to the Hellenistic, diplomatic institution, defines the abstract concept of a grant of potential citizenship. In a text, the term can signal that the document contains indirect evidence for potential citizenship or it anticipates and describes the actual grant of potential citizenship that follows, normally by including procedural details and a more concrete '*politeia*' wording.[25] In this treaty '*isopoliteia*' does not indicate that potential citizenship has been established, but it refers to a future stipulation, whose terms were going to be defined later by Messene and Phigaleia.[26]

The Meaning of Potential Citizenship

It is not unusual to read that, with this decree, and by way of an alleged *isopoliteia* with Phigaleia, the Aitolians tried to connect Messene to their league.[27] While no hard evidence exists for a previous agreement of potential citizenship between Aitolia and Phigaleia, I must stress that this line of reasoning builds on a modern syllogism. Even if, like all syllogisms, it seems to work, we must remember that the 'domino effect' often postulated for potential citizenship (namely, that the potential citizens of one city that was tied to another community by way of *isopoliteia* were also potential citizens of the other city),

---

22   SCHOLTEN 2000, p. 122 discusses the geography of Phigaleia, see also SZANTO 1892, pp. 76–77.
23   MAGNETTO 1997, p. 233.
24   See MAGNETTO 1997, p. 234 following GAUTHIER 1972, pp. 367–368.
25   For example, *Milet* I 3 150 = no. 7, L. 12; *AvP* VIII.1 5 = no. 20, LL. 15–18.
26   LL. 10–13: ἦμεν τοῖς Μεσσανίοις κα/[ὶ τοῖς Φια]λέοις ἰσοπολιτείαν καὶ ἐπιγαμία/[ν ποτὶ ἀλλ] άλως, ποιήσασθαι δὲ καὶ συνβολάν, ἅ/[νπερ δοκεῖ] ἀνφοτέραις ταῖς πολέοις.
27   MAGNETTO 1997, p. 235 and p. 237 n. 23 for example. See *infra* on the Aitolian use of this tool.

while certainly possible on a theoretical level, is 'constitutionally' fragile. The ultimate consequences of this view of potential citizenship, i.e., that a community would lose control of its prerogative to grant citizenship and control its own grants of citizenship, are hardly acceptable. The provisions contained in a few Milesian treaties and in the agreement between Xanthos and Myra, establishing strict(er) rules for those people who had received citizenship later than the stipulation of the *isopoliteia* agreements, indicate concerned cities attempting to strictly regulate this issue.[28] In those agreements, naturalized citizens were required to endure a long wait before them, if they wanted to use the option to switch citizenship and become lawful members of the third community.

Phigaleia initiated the process that led to Aitolian mediation and therefore this agreement. The text describes the relationship that Phigaleia had with Aitolia as one of *philia*. The Aitolians brokered an agreement they hoped Messene and Phigaleia would seal by exchanging the right to intermarriage and potential citizenship.[29] The hypothesis that this agreement was an instrumental part of an Aitolian plan to extend its influence in the area is, in my view, rather weak. Aitolia already exerted influence without directly controlling these towns. If anything, this text confirms Aitolia's strong presence in the Peloponnese and is not a means to that end.

The Aitolian League

According to M. Sordi, one defining characteristic of federal states is the coexistence of federal and *polis* citizenship, which scholars define as dual citizenship.[30] The precise nature of these citizenships, whether they complemented each other or simply coexisted, is difficult to determine because the evidence is sparse and each league had particular specificities.[31]

The question of the nature of dual citizenship emerges also within the context of a study devoted to potential citizenship. One *koinon* in particular, the Aitolians, frequently used the Hellenistic institution of *isopoliteia* by granting its (potential) federal citizenship to partner communities. In only one text is a city of the *koinon* the main subject of a grant of potential citizenship: Naupaktos conceded the grant to Keos, which reciprocated it and then extended it to the

---

28 The clearest examples include *Milet* I 3 143 = no. 5, 146 = no. 6 and 150 = no. 7, and also the agreement between Xanthos and Myra, *SEG* XLIV 1218 = no. 8.
29 See also SABA 2011, p. 106.
30 SORDI 1994, pp. 4–5. LASAGNI 2011, esp. pp. 127–133 defines this problem in general. She outlines with clarity the difficulties faced and the results attained by scholarship. See also the important discussion by LARSEN 1968, pp. XVIII–XXI on this topic.
31 On this see LASAGNI 2017.

entire Aitolian *koinon* (*StV* III 508, III = no. 41). It is difficult to determine what this grant with federal citizenship entailed and its consequences, but this difficulty has enhanced the debate on the complex topic of dual citizenship.

A widespread opinion holds that the Aitolians used potential citizenship to control distant communities without annexing them.[32] The evidence, however, does not fully support the interpretation of potential citizenship as an instrument of Aitolian 'Machtpolitik.' The epigraphic material reveals that Aitolia granted potential citizenship to support broader agreements with either diplomatic or more practical goals in sight: in other words, the Aitolians used this tool to its full potential. For example, the treaty I often reference, *IG* IX² 1 3A = no. 40, which Aitolia established with Akarnania, includes a very unspecific grant of (federal) potential citizenship within a military treaty that, at its outset, tries also to regulate territorial issues between the two federations. By contrast, in the concession to the Herakleians (Funke 2000 = *FD* III 3 144 = no. 42) the grant is a means to bring forward a diplomatic contact that entails also Aitolia's intercession for Herakleia in front of the Ptolemies. These texts are but two (extreme) examples that show how the Aitolians understood and used this tool.

One hot topic in scholarship dealing with ancient federal states relates to terminology, which is often both confusing and confused. In few other contexts have scholars thrown together and used such a high number of terms drawn both from ancient and modern political and institutional language and, moreover, almost resemanticized them in a way that increases the risk of serial misunderstandings. I hope that my insistence on what I mean by potential citizenship can help lessen this problem at least for the institution of *isopoliteia*.

(40)   *Aitolia and Akarnania*

The agreement between Aitolia and Akarnania is unique because it includes an award of *isopoliteia* between two federal states. The text defines anew the boundaries between the states and then proceeds to describe the terms of a military agreement. Its details have been well studied and commented on in the past; I focus here on the agreement rather than the military alliance (i.e., I focus on the συνθήκα not on the συμμαχία).[33]

---

32   SCHOLTEN 2000 acknowledges this view too, see pp. 115–116 and pp. 189–190. GAUTHIER 1972, pp. 370–373 and pp. 248–258 focuses on the juridical aspects of the relationship between Aitolians and foreigners who were citizens of communities with which Aitolia had established *isopoliteia*; however, see *infra*. See LARSEN 1968, esp. pp. 202–206.

33   On the *symmachia*, see the comment by SCHOLTEN 2000, p. 79; DANY 1999, pp. 69–80 with previous bibliography.

Found in Thermon, the inscription is engraved on a small bronze, opisthographic stele that is now stored in the Epigraphic Museum of Athens (EM 12228). The fragment of a second copy of this agreement was later found in Olympia.

Measurements: W. 0.352–0.363; H. 0.42; Th. 0.045.

Edd.: *IG* IX^2 1 3A; [*StV* III 480; Ager 1996, pp. 105–108 no. 33, LL. 1–11].

Συνθήκα καὶ συμμαχία
Αἰτωλοῖς καὶ Ἀκαρνάνοις
Ἀγαθᾶι τύχαι. συνθήκα Αἰτωλοῖς καὶ Ἀκαρνάνοις ὁμόλογος· εἰρήναν
4 εἶμεν καὶ φιλίαν ποτ' ἀλλάλους, φίλους ἐόντας καὶ συμμάχους ἄμα-
τα τὸμ πάντα χρόνον, ὅρια ἔχοντας τᾶς χώρας τὸν Ἀχελῶιον ποταμ-
ὸν ἄχρι εἰς θάλασσαν. τὰ μὲν ποτ' ἀῶ τοῦ Ἀχελώιου ποταμοῦ Αἰτωλῶν εἶμεν,
τὰ δὲ
ποθ' ἑσπέραν Ἀκαρνάνων πλὰν τοῦ Πραντὸς καὶ τᾶς Δεμφίδος· ταύτας δὲ
Ἀκαρνᾶν-
8 ες οὐκ ἀντιποιοῦνται. ὑπὲρ δὲ τῶν τερμόνων τοῦ Πραντός, εἰ μέγ κα Στράτιοι
καὶ Ἀγραῖ-
οι συγχωρέωντι αὐτοὶ ποτ' αὐτούς, τοῦτο κύριον ἔστω· εἰ δὲ μή, Ἀκαρνᾶνες καὶ
Αἰτωλοὶ
τερμαξάντο τὰμ Πραντίδα χώραν, αἱρεθέντας (!) ἑκατέρων δέκα πλὰν Στρατίων
καὶ Ἀγρα(ί)-
ων· καθὼς δέ κα τερμάξωντι, τέλειον ἔστω. εἶμεν δὲ καὶ ἐπιγαμίαν ποτ'ἀλλάλους
καὶ γ-
12 ᾶς ἔγκτησιν τῶι τε Αἰτωλῶι ἐν Ἀκαρνανίαι καὶ τῶι Ἀκαρνᾶνι ἐν Αἰτωλίαι καὶ
πολίταν εἶμε-
ν τὸν Αἰτωλὸν ἐν Ἀκαρνανίαι καὶ τὸν Ἀκαρνᾶνα ἐν ⟨Α⟩ἰτωλίαι ἴσογ καὶ ὅμοιον.
ἀναγραψάν-
τω δὲ ταῦτα ἐν στάλαις χαλκέαις ἐπ' Ἀκτίωι μὲν οἱ ἄρχοντες τῶν Ἀκαρνάνων,
ἐν δὲ Θέρμ-
ωι τοὶ ἄρχοντες τῶν Αἰτωλῶν, ἐν Ὀλυμπίαι δὲ καὶ ἐν Δελφοῖς καὶ ἐν Δω[δ]ώναι
κοινᾶι ἑκάτ-
16 εροι (...) (new date and a strictly regulated *symmachia* follow in LL. 16–40)

Text by Schmitt *StV* III 480

Transl.: Agreement and alliance between the Aitolians and the Akarnanians.

To good Fortune. The treaty was signed in agreement by Aitolians and Akarnanians. (They establish) peace and friendship with one another, that they shall be friends and allies for the whole time, (that) the river Acheloos shall mark the boundary between their territories down to the sea. To the east of the river Acheloos the land shall belong to the Aitolians, to the west to the Akarnanians with the exception of Pras and Demphis. The Akarnanians shall not lay claim on those. As far as the limits of Pras are concerned, if the *Stratioi* and the *Agraioi* can agree on them, their decision shall stand. If they cannot agree, Akarnanians and Aitolians shall establish the boundaries by choosing 10 men each, with the exception of *Stratioi* and *Agraioi*. How they will determine them (the territorial limits), that shall be definite. They shall have right to intermarriage with one another and an Aitolian shall have the right to own land in Akarnania and an Akarnanian in Aitolia, an Aitolian shall be citizen on equal footing in Akarnania and an Akarnanian in Aitolia. The officials of the Akarnanians shall see to it that these decisions are inscribed on bronze stele in Aktion, those of the Aitolians in Thermon, both in Olympia, Delphi, and Dodona. (...)

The date of this text has been hotly contested, but Scholten's argument for a year between the end of the 260s and the 250s BC should be preferred. He has suggested that Aitolia used Akarnania as a buffer zone, hence the treaty, in a moment of weakness when Epiros could have opened the door to dangerous Macedonian attacks.[34] This alliance, however, did not last long: Polybios testifies that Aitolia and Epiros Akarnania divided among themselves a few years later.[35]

The importance of this agreement for modern knowledge of the Aitolian administrative system, the territories of Aitolia and Akarnania, and their armed forces has been amply discussed in scholarship; here I focus on the exchange of *politeia*.

---

34   SCHOLTEN 2000, Appendix B, esp. pp. 253–256. DANY 1999, pp. 70–80 summarizes the scholarly debate on the topic and concludes that the text dates to 271–270 BC which, however, appears to be too early. He offers two possible explanations for this alliance: (1) an Akarnanian attempt to assert its newly found independence or (2) an agreement that resulted from the help of Alexander II who later took his revenge by 'dividing' Akarnania with Aitolia.
35   SCHOLTEN 2000, pp. 77–83; POLYB. II. 45.1; IX.34.7.

The exchange of (potential) citizenship in LL. 11–13 comes after the parties define the terms of the agreement for establishing the northwestern boundaries between Aitolia and Akarnania. Next follows a string of grants, namely, the right to intermarriage, ownership of land, and equal citizenship.[36] Afterward, the treaty preserves the stipulations for publishing of the stone and a very detailed military agreement.

The grant of *politeia* is by no means the focus of a text that is instead concerned with much broader issues. The grant comes last in a list of other concessions including crucial rights like *epigamia* and *enktesis*. This organization suggests that, combined, these grants were meant to seal an agreement that treated highly sensitive topics, such as the definition of borders and the common defense of the territories, that needed specific solutions but also a strong relationship between the signing parties to work. This role for the grant of *politeia* strongly resembles the plan that the Aitolians had envisioned for Messene and Phigaleia. In this agreement the absence of a plan to implement *isopoliteia* is clear. Moreover, it cannot be argued that potential citizenship served as a stepping stone toward an Aitolian annexation of Akarnania.[37] This agreement suits best the mood of the time in its articulation of the

---

36   On the territory see ANTONETTI 1987, pp. 99–102; SABA 2011, esp. pp. 104–106 on *epigamia* and potential citizenship in border disputes. On *enktesis* see HENNIG 1994, esp. p. 334, n. 89.

37   GAWANTKA 1975, pp. 146–149 devoted his attention to this agreement, too; pp. 148–149 summarize well his view on it: "Bedenkt man, daß dieser Vertrag zwischen zwei ungleich mächtigen Partnern geschlossen wurde (…) und daß der gegenseitige Verleihung des <potentiellen> Bürgerrechts als solchen kaum mehr als ein deklamatorischen Charakter zukommt—das gesamte Interesse vielmehr darauf gerichtet ist, für Probleme der *zwischen*-staatlichen Beziehungen (Grenzfragen, Symmachie) Lösungen auf der Basis völliger Gleichberechtigung zu finden, dann kann man wohl annehmen, daß dieser Vertrag aus der Sicht des schwächeren Partners nicht dazu dienen sollte, einen gemeinsamen Staat zu schaffen, sondern genau zu dessen Gegenteil: die Respektierung der Gleichberechtigung und damit auch der Eigenstaatlichkeit des schwächeren durch den stärkeren Bündnispartner." Although my historical and institutional interpretation aligns in many ways with Gawantka's study, he assigns a very different value to single pieces of evidence. Gawantka indeed stresses the Akarnania's presumed concern about Aitolia's political plans, but the historical context of this agreement suggests that when the two leagues signed the agreement, they had other perceptions of themselves and other worries. In other words, at the time of the signing the problem of annexation was, even if only very briefly, not a major concern. Gawantka downplays the role of potential citizenship by assigning it a *deklamatorischen Charakter*. But this concession, along with *epigamia* and *enktesis*, was a means to create a shared foundation of interests and to bring together both abstract (potential citizenship within the *koinon*) and more concrete participation of their members in each other's territory; on *epigamia*, for example, see SABA 2011.

diplomatic and practical (defense) needs to be met, for which the exchange of *politeia*, along with *epigamia* and *enktesis*, constituted a solid foundation.

The exact nature of the type of citizenship that was granted in this document remains undetermined. The parties are two leagues that exchanged their common or federal citizenship, along with the right to intermarriage and to hold property. Do these concessions mean that Aitolians and Akarnanians could claim for themselves properties, ties, and even citizenship everywhere in Aitolia and Akarnania? What was the role of the individual communities that were part of these leagues? We cannot answer these crucial questions, however, with this agreement.

(41) *Keos, Naupaktos, and the Aitolian* Koinon

The two fragments that Broendsted found in 1811/12 by the temple of Apollo in Karthaia contain the text of a decree that I partly reproduce here; two other fragmentary documents are associated with the decree (*StV* III 508, I–II). Later, in Athens, Wilhelm identified another small fragment that contained a copy of this text (LL. 8–9). He sent its transcription to Tod, but the new fragment did not contribute very much to eliminating doubts and lacunae in the already known document.

Edd.: *IG* XII.5 532 + *IG* XII.5, *Add.* p. 321; [*StV* III 508, III].

Ἡρακλείδης εἶπεν· ἔδοξεν τῆι βουλῆι καὶ τῶι δήμωι· ἐπειδὴ ἀναγγέλλουσιν οἱ πρέσβεις οἱ ἀποσταλέντες εἰς Ναύπακτον καὶ πρὸς τοὺς συνέδρους τῶν Αἰτωλῶν
πᾶσαν εὔνοιαν καὶ φιλοτιμίαν ἐνδεδεῖχθαι Ναυπακτίους καὶ τοὺς συνέδρους
4   τοὺς Αἰτωλῶν πρὸς τὰς πόλεις τὰς Κείων, καὶ ἐψηφισμένοι εἰσὶν Ναυπάκτιοι
πολιτείαν εἶναι Κείοις καὶ γῆς καὶ οἰκίας ἔγκτησιν, καὶ τῶν ἄλλων μετέχειν Κείους ὧνπερ καὶ Ναυπάκτιοι μετέχουσιν, δεδόχθαι Κείων τῆι βουλῆι καὶ τῶι δήμωι
εἶναι Αἰτωλοῖς πολιτείαν ἐγ Κέωι καὶ γῆς καὶ οἰκίας ἔγκτησιν, καὶ τῶν ἄλλων
8   μετέχειν αὐτοὺς πάντων ὧνπερ καὶ Κεῖοι μετέχουσιν ... δειν
οις τοὺς [ἄρ]χοντα[ς τοὺς] ἐπι - - - - προ - - - -
Αἰτω - - -
εἰς Κέω - - -

Text by Schmitt (*StV* III 508, III)

Transl.: LL. 1–8: Herakleides put forward the motion: it was decided by the *boule* and the *demos*. Since the ambassadors who have been sent to Naupaktos and the *synedrion* of the Aitolians report that the Naupaktians and the *synedrioi* of the Aitolians have shown all their benevolence and respect for the cities of the Keans, and the Naupaktians have voted citizenship and right to own land and house for Keans, and that the Keans shall partake in anything else in which the Naupaktians do, it has been decreed by the *boule* and the *demos* of the Keans that the Aitolians shall have citizenship in Keos and right to own land and house, and that they shall partake in anything else in which the Keans do ...

Schmitt published this decree as *StV* III 508, III.[38] The activities of the Aitolian *strategos*, whose name is restored relying on *StV* III 508 II, L. 8, serve as an internal chronological reference to establish a date around 222/3 BC for this text.[39] Although not pinpointed to a specific date, this date is a reliable, general indication.[40]

Naupaktos and Keos

Naupaktos had been a member of the Aitolian League for about a century starting from the middle of the 3rd century BC. Its favorable geographic position on the coast of Lokris, facing the Peloponnese, made Naupaktos strategically important. It indeed grew to serve as the harbor from which many naval enterprises of the Aitolians started.[41]

Around the time when the documents here were enacted, the Aegean islands sought external support or attempted to create their own defense and support structures, mainly because of the Ptolemies' withdrawal from their

---

[38] *StV* III 508, I contains an Aitolian decree granting *asylia*, personal inviolability, to the citizens of Keos, while *StV* III 508, II testifies to existing *philia* between Keos and Naupaktos, ZIEGLER 1975, esp. p. 206. The absolute genitive ὡς Αἰτω/λῶν ὄντων τῶν Κείων of LL. 4–5 of *StV* III 508, I has been used to establish a relative chronology among the three documents published as *StV* III 508 (I-II-III). According to the *communis opinio*, Naupaktos had granted potential citizenship to Keos before Aitolia's approval of personal inviolability, because (so goes the argument) otherwise the statement ὡς Αἰτω/λῶν ὄντων τῶν Κείων of *StV* III 508 I, LL. 4–5 could not have been possible. This line of reasoning can work only if we charge this genitive absolute with a legal binding meaning it does not possess.

[39] For Schmitt (*app. crit.*): "Von den in Frage kommenden Strategen des 3. Jh.s paßt Πανταλέωνος (früher 221/1 sic!, jetzt von G. Klaffenbach 223/2 datiert) ... besser in den freien Raum als Χαριξένου (234/3?) oder Δωριμάχου (202/1?)...."

[40] REGER and RISSER 1991, esp. pp. 305–306.

[41] For the history of Naupaktos, see FREITAG 2000, pp. 67–94. Philip II gave the city to the Aitolians after killing the Achaean garrison that had been stationed there, STRAB. IX.4.7; see ROUSSET *Inventory*, esp. p. 396.

Aegean bases. The cities of Keos restored their island federation.[42] According to Reger and Risser, the cities of the island completed this process by the 240s BC, modeling their own, new federation after that of the Aitolians. This structure implies substantial freedom for each member *polis*, although federal organs determined a common foreign policy. Reger and Risser also argue that this union was created in order to deal with the Aitolian presence in the Aegean.[43] However, Scholten has demonstrated persuasively that the Aitolians operating in the area were not official representatives of the Federal State but rather individuals with their own financial interests, from which, in the long run, the *koinon* benefited, too.[44] Under the circumstances, it is likely that the Aegean communities sought protection from the Aitolians in the Aitolian League, which itself played a double role: protector and, occasionally or indirectly, aggressor.

Another detail worth mentioning about the relationship between Naupaktos and the island of Keos, although it is completely absent from our decree, is that the sources report that Naupaktos was known as the mother city of Keos.[45] This relationship, then, could also be a reason for the Kean choice to send an embassy to Naupaktos as a way to establish firmer contacts with Aitolia.

The Award of Potential Citizenship

StV III 508 I, II, and III, involving three different parties, Naupaktos, Keos, and Aitolia, have attracted much scholarly attention.[46] Decree III contains the Kean concession of potential citizenship to Naupaktos and Aitolia, along with *epigamia* and *enktesis*, in reciprocation for the grant of potential citizenship that Naupaktos had awarded to Keos. *StV* III 508, III attests that Keos had sent an embassy to both the city of Naupaktos and the *synedrion* of the *koinon* (LL. 2–3). Keos's specific requests on the occasion of those embassies are lost, but, reading the responses to Keos in the Naupaktian text (*StV* III 508, II) and in the Aitolian text (*StV* III 508, I), it can be deduced that

---

42   The history of the Aegean islands for the decades between the 260s and 200 BC is difficult to reconstruct, see REGER and RISSER 1991; REGER 1994 with further bibliography. For Aitolia and the Aegean, see FUNKE 2008 and SCHOLTEN 2000, esp. pp. 105–116.
43   See esp. REGER and RISSER 1991, pp. 312–314.
44   SCHOLTEN 2000, p. 116: "... in dealing with the Aegean collective policy seems to have been secondary to individual interests."
45   FREITAG 2000, p. 69 n. 343 with sources.
46   See FUNKE 1997, esp. p. 167; GAUTHIER 1972, esp. pp. 255–256; LARSEN 1968, pp. 203–204; SZANTO 1892, pp. 84–86.

the Keans had expected reciprocation of their declaration of friendship and had also made some other request. Naupaktos's answer (*StV* III 508, II) is fragmentary, but, on the evidence of *StV* III 508, III, we know it included a grant of potential citizenship. *StV* III 508, I, the Aitolian answer, grants personal inviolability to the Keans, which was perhaps their first and main request.[47]

Scholarship has addressed, several times, the difficult problem of the procedure for granting potential citizenship within a league, but I will revisit this problem to consider the specific issue of dual citizenship and its relationship to potential citizenship. The question here is whether Naupaktos's grant of potential citizenship to Keos (*StV* III 508 III, L. 4) included both local and federal citizenship, as some scholars have interpreted the text of *StV* III 508 I, LL. 4–5, or whether it included local potential citizenship. According to Funke, because Naupaktos was a member of the *koinon*, a grant of citizenship given by it had to include federal citizenship. Moreover, he thinks that the procedure attested in this decree (*StV* III 508, III) shows that *poleis* members of a *koinon* could not make independent decisions about citizenship grants (of any kind, I dare to suggest), but that such grants had to be ratified by the federal organs.[48] This argument is acceptable so long as we do not draw from it unsupported conclusions.

In his commentary on these texts Schmitt wrote: "Die Verleihung der Isopolitie durch die Bundesstadt Naupaktos hatte den Keern automatisch das potentielle Bürgerrecht im Ätolerbund gebracht, so daß Keos folgerichtig die Isopolitie dem gesamten Bund, nicht nur der Stadt Naupaktos verleiht."[49] But, more simply, I hold that Keos's grant of potential citizenship to Naupaktos and Aitolia (*StV* III 508, III) might have been separate recognitions and reciprocations for the grants that the Keans had obtained from those entities, i.e., from Aitolia, the grant of personal inviolability (*StV* III 508, I) and from Naupaktos the grant of potential citizenship (*StV* III 508, II–III). Such grants had to be

---

47 So also LARSEN 1968, p. 207 for example.
48 FUNKE 1997, esp. p. 167: "Jedenfalls bleibt festzustellen, dass zumindest hinsichtlich der Isopolitie das Verleihrecht des Bundes und das der Gliedstaaten nicht unabhängig und in konkurrenz zueinander bestanden, sondern offenbar durch gemeinsamen gesetzlich fixierten Rahmenbedingungen geregelt waren." LASAGNI 2011, esp. pp. 231–232, hypothesizes instead that *koinon* and *polis* could grant their citizenships independently. I expect that the *koinon* and the *poleis* would have communicated on this topic. Still, this view is tentative and, as Lasagni notes, each federation had its own specificities.
49 *StV* III 508, p. 219.

reciprocated and a concession of potential citizenship to both parties was a way to accomplish it. What matters, however, is that we do not have to deduce from the evidence of Keos's grant of potential citizenship to Naupaktos and Aitolia (*StV* III 508, III) that the Keans thought of themselves as proxy Aitolians.

Now I will address the difficult question on the nature of dual citizenship for which the interpretation of *StV* III 508 I, LL. 4–5 is crucial. The genitive absolute contained in this passage, ὡς Αἰτω/λῶν ὄντων τῶν Κείων, has been read by some as a technical-legal formula attributing to the Keans the legal status of Aitolians, which, it has been argued, they would have gained automatically through Naupaktos's grant (*StV* III 508, III, L. 4).[50] But in this text the Keans appear as foreigners, LL. 2–3, which in fact they must be as potential citizens.[51] This interpretation to my mind points to the very essence of the award of potential citizenship, which, on a substantive level implies that the formula ὡς Αἰτω/λῶν ὄντων τῶν Κείων did not have any binding legal meaning, but was used to acknowledge the privileged, but still foreign, status held by the Keans in Naupaktos and in the league.

Gauthier stated that complete citizenship in a league could be attained only through a grant given by a *polis*.[52] It remains possible, however, that federal citizenship and *polis* citizenship were two separate and different concepts that entailed different rights, even if one somehow implied the other. The available evidence in Aitolia indicates that federal and civic (potential) citizenship could be granted separately, which might have required a double procedure for their approval. If implemented, one citizenship might have given access to the other, but we know too little about the specific regulation of the *koinon* to speculate on the precise content and meaning of these separate statuses.[53]

---

50   GAUTHIER 1972, esp. p. 258 for example.
51   *StV* III 508 I, LL. 1–5 ἔδοξεν τοῖς Αἰτωλοῖς· ποτὶ τοὺς [Κε]ίους τὰν φιλίαν τὰν ὑπάρχουσαν διαφυ/λάσσειν, καὶ μηθένα [ἄ]γειν Αἰτωλῶν μηδὲ τῶν ἐν Αἰτωλίαι πολιτευόν/των τοὺς Κείους μηθαμόθεν ὁρμώμενον, μήτε κατὰ γᾶν μήτε κατὰ θάλατ/ταν, μήτε πὸτ Ἀμφικτυονικὸν μήτε πὸτ ἄλλο ἔγκλημα μηθέν, ὡς Αἰτω/λῶν ὄντων τῶν Κείων·.
52   See GAUTHIER 1972, p. 258, but he assumes that such clauses always had a legal value. In his unpublished Habilitation, which he kindly allowed me to read, Funke is also skeptical.
53   See again LARSEN 1968, pp. XVIII–XXI.

(42) Herakleia under Mt. Latmos and the Aitolians

In his book on *syngeneia*, O. Curty devotes his attention to this curious inscription that, he says, is engraved on a limestone block that was found near the Treasury of the Athenians at Delphi; it remains there today (Inv. no. 56 = 1078).[54] The text I cite relies on the recent version that was reedited and published by Funke after a new collation of the squeeze in Berlin.

[στρα]ταγέοντος τῶν [Αἰ]τωλῶν Ἀρχί[σωνος τὸ δεύ]-
[τερ]ον ἔδοξε τοῖς Αἰτωλοῖς· ἐπειδὴ Ἡρ[ακ]λειῶται
[ψά]φισμα καὶ πρέ[σβ]εις ἀποστείλαντες Μ[ε]νεκράτ[η]
4 [καὶ - - - τ]ὰν [συ]γγένειαν ἀνενεώσαντο κ[αὶ τὰ]
[ὑπάρ]χον[τ]α πα[ρ]ὰ τᾶς πόλιος αὐτῶν φιλάνθρωπα ποτὶ το[ὺς]
[Αἰτωλοὺς ἐπαύξη]σαν· δεδόχθαι τοῖς Αἰτωλοῖς· πολί-
[τας] εἶμεν τοὺς Ἡρα[κ]λειώτας τῶν Αἰτωλῶν, ἐπεὶ τυγχάνον-
8 [τι εὔ]νους τῶι [κ]οινῶ[ι κ]αί, εἴ τις ἀποστέλληται πρεσβεία
[π]οτὶ [βασιλ]έα [Π]το[λ]εμαῖον, διαλέγεσθαι ὑπὲρ αὐτῶν κατὰ
[τ]ὰς δοθ[ε]ί[σας ἐν]τ[ολ]ὰς παρὰ τᾶς πόλιος τῶν Ἡρακλειωτᾶν,
[ὅπω]ς βουλ[ήσε]τ[αι πολυ]ωρῆσαι, περὶ ὧν οἴονται δεῖν οἱ Ἡρακλει-
12 ῶται [τὸν βασιλέα] ἑαυτῶν πολυωρεῖν ὡς ὄντων ἀποίκων
[τῶ]ν Αἰτωλῶν, [κα]ὶ [τα]ῦτα ποιῶν εὐχαριστήσει τοῖς Αἰτω-
λοῖς· ἀναγ[ράψαι δὲ κ]αὶ τὸ ψάφισμα ἐν Δελφοῖς ἐν τῶι
ἱαρῶι τοῦ Ἀπόλλωνος

Transl.: When Arkison was *strategos* of the Aitolians for the [second time], it was decreed by the Aitolians: since the Herakleians, after sending a decree and the ambassadors Menekrates and … reminded of the kinship and increased the existing benefactions to the Aitolians on the part of their city; be it enacted by the Aitolians that the Herakleians are to be citizens of the Aitolians, since they happen to be benevolent to the *koinon* and, if an embassy is sent to king Ptolemaios, the embassy should tell about those things according to the instructions given by the city of the Herakleians, so that he is willing to take care of those issues about which the Herakleians think he should care, because they are a colony of the Aitolians. Acting thus, he shall please the Aitolians. The decree shall be engraved in Delphi in the sanctuary of Apollo.

---

54 *Ed. pr.* POMTOW, *Klio* 18, 1923, n. 220 [*SEG* 11 257]; *IG* IX 1², 1, 173; [MORETTI *ISE* II 77; ROBERT 1978, pp. 478]; *FD* III.3 144; [CURTY 1995, no. 15]; FUNKE 2000, pp. 506–509.

Chronology and Identification of Herakleia

The new collation of the squeeze allowed Funke to produce this edition and to discuss its date anew, arguing convincingly for the last two decades of the 3rd century BC.[55] The new date is sensibly later than the one previously accepted (i.e., 259–255 BC), which relied on the chronology of the *strategos* Arkison. Arkison appears in a decree from Delphi that grants honors to a certain *Athanion Patronos*,[56] who probably held the office of *archon* in the middle of the 3rd century BC.[57] The discovery of a text related to the Magnesian quest for *asylia* and in which *Athanion* is again attested as *archon*,[58] however, has led to a revision of the chronology of his archonship and, consequently, of Arkison's *strategia*.[59]

Additionally, Funke notes that an inscription found in Herakleia under Mt. Latmos dated to the 190s BC contains the record of an embassy that this city sent to Zeuxis, in which a man named Menekrates, just like the ambassador of our document, participated.[60] This last piece of evidence would reinforce both the new, lower date of the text and the (now certain) identification of the Herakleia of the inscription with Herakleia under Mt. Latmos.[61]

The Award of Potential Citizenship

The inscription contains an Aitolian grant of potential citizenship for the city of Herakleia, LL. 6–7. The decree begins with a reference to an embassy sent by Herakleia to Aitolia in order to confirm the existing *syngeneia* and other unspecified 'benefactions,' in an effort to increase them. Aitolia replied to this embassy by granting a unilateral concession of federal potential citizenship to Herakleia. Here, just as in the alliance with Akarnania, citizenship is not the focus of the decree, but rather the handling of Herakleia's attempt to gain coveted favor at the court of the Ptolemies with Aitolian mediation.

---

55   FUNKE 2000, esp. pp. 512–515.
56   *IG* IX 1² 172 (= *Syll.*³ 479).
57   Details in FUNKE 2000, pp. 510–511.
58   RIGSBY 1996, pp. 204–205 no. 79, L. 1.
59   FUNKE 2000, pp. 512–517, on the historical context see *infra*.
60   FUNKE 2000, p. 512.
61   L. ROBERT 1978, pp. 477–490 was able to identify Herakleia with Herakleia under Mt. Latmos because of its kinship with Aitolia, see also CURTY 1995, no. 15 and more recently PATTERSON 2004, who, however, wrongly thinks that Herakleia entered the league on the occasion of the enactment of this decree, (PATTERSON 2004, p. 349). The myth of *syngeneia* between Aitolia and Herakleia comes from the story of Endymion, Aitolos's father, who sought refuge by the Latmos, then founded the city of Herakleia.

Only meager evidence survives on the relationship among the three parties involved here. The Aitolians and the Ptolemies, who figured prominently in Karia especially in the first half of the 3rd century BC, must have shared a positive partnership.[62] At some point Herakleia came under Ptolemaic control, but the evidence for it is rather slim.[63] Our decree may signal the first effects of the Ptolemies's progressive abandonment of Karia and the Aegean area. By the time this agreement had been established, Aitolia's relationship with the Ptolemies was better than the relationship Herakleia had with them.[64] Yet, the document appears to be the result of a new Herakleian policy. Herakleia makes use of the kinship argument to initiate a diplomatic discourse with Aitolia (and 'use' this), which was probably seen as a possible 'option' to replace the waning power of the Ptolemies and thus fill the power vacuum left in the area.[65]

In these years Aitolia signed numerous agreements with other communities of Asia Minor, among which stands out the fragmentary *asylia* agreement with Miletos.[66] We do not know whether the only common ground shared by our text and the *asylia* with Miletos is the Aitolian presence, or whether the difficult state of affairs between Miletos and Herakleia, which later turned into the epigraphically well attested war, played a role too as a way to help sort out a complex situation on a local level.[67] Yet the scenario is suggestive and the early attempts of the *poleis* to find an agreement with Aitolia may imply local as well as international interests.

In this document the *koinon* of the Aitolians does not use potential citizenship to connect itself to a distant city. Rather it is a diplomatic response to advance an articulated diplomatic intervention and presence in the area.

---

62   See BAGNALL 1976, esp. pp. 89–94.
63   See FUNKE 2000, pp. 512–517; WÖRRLE 1988, pp. 434–436.
64   On Aitolian-Egyptian relations, FUNKE 2000, pp. 512–513 and SCHOLTEN 2000, esp. p. 138, n. 31.
65   FUNKE 2000, p. 517 rightly stresses that Aitolia never really pursed hegemonic plans in the area, although he also reminds us of the many inscriptions that date to the second half of the 3rd century BC and testify to Aitolian activity there.
66   *StV* III 564 dated to the last decades of the 3rd century BC: see FUNKE 2008, pp. 265–267 and IDEM 2000, pp. 516–517.
67   See *supra* my comments on *Milet* I 3 150 = no. 7.

(43) Chios and the Aitolians

The well-known decree (now in *Choix* pp. 151-156 no. 77) with which Chios thanked the Aitolians for granting it a vote in the Amphictyony, testifies indirectly to an exchange of potential citizenship between these communities that chronologically must have come just before the concession of the vote.[68]

The four fragments of the decree were found in Delphi in different years,[69] with the first part of the document found last (*SEG* XVIII 245). This part summarizes the diplomatic exchange preceding the concession of the seat with a vote in Delphi to the Chians.[70] Here I reproduce part of the text as in *Choix* pp. 151-156 no. 77:

["Εδο]ξεν τῆι [βουλῆι καὶ τῶι δήμ]ωι· πολεμάρχω[ν ἐπιμήνιος....8-10....
... Φιλίστου κα[ὶ ἐξεταστῶ]ν ἐπιμήνιος Αἰαντίδη[ς.... 8.... εἶπαν·
[ἐ]πειδὴ τὸ κοινὸν [τῶν Αἰτωλῶ]ν διά τε τὴν οἰκειότητα κα[ὶ φιλίαν τὴν]
4   ὑπάρχουσαν διὰ προγ[όνων τῶ]ι δήμωι πρὸς Αἰτωλούς, πρότερ[ον μὲν πο]-
λιτείαν ἡμῖν ἐψηφίσατ[ο καὶ] ἀπηγόρευσε πᾶσιν μὴ ἄγειν τὰ τῶ[ν Χιῶν]
μηδαμόθεν ὁρμωμένοι[ς, εἰ] δὲ μή, ὑποδίκους εἶναι ἐν τοῖς συνέ[δροις]
ὡς τὰ κοινὰ βλάπτοντας τ[ὰ] τῶν Αἰτωλῶν, ἐφ' οἷς ὁ δῆμος ἀποδεξ[άμενος]
8   οἰκείως τὰν εὔνοιαν αὐτῶ[ν] ἐψηφίσατο πολίτας τε εἶναι τοὺς Αἰτ[ωλοὺς]
καὶ μετέχειν πάντων ὧ[ν] καὶ Χῖοι μετέχουσιν, ἔγνω δὲ καὶ ἔ[φοδον]
αὐτοῖς ὑπάρχειν πρώτοι[ς] ἐπί τε τὴν βουλὴν καὶ τὴν ἐκκλησία[ν, καὶ]
παρακαλεῖσθαι αὐτοὺς ε[ἰ]ς προεδρίαν ἐμ πᾶσι τοῖς ἀγῶσιν οἷς ἄ[ν ἡ πόλις]
12   [π]οιῆι, καὶ νῦν δὲ οἱ θεωροὶ καὶ οἱ πρέσβεις παραγενόμενοι ἀνήν[γειλ]-
[αν] τῶι δήμωι τήν τε ἄλλην εὔνοιαν ἥν εἶχε τὸ κοινὸν τῶν Αἰτωλῶν [πρὸς τὴ]-
ν πόλιν, πᾶσαν προθυμίαν ἐνδεικνύμενον εἰς τὸ συντελεῖσθαι [ὅσα]
οἱ πρέ[σ]βεις ἠξίωσαν, καὶ [δ]ιότι δεδώκασι τῶι δήμωι ψῆφον ἱερομναμ-
[ονικὴν]
16   εἰς το[ὺς] Ἀμφικτύονας, [ἀ]κόλουθα διαπραττόμενοι τοῖς προυπάρχου[σιν αὐτ]-
[ο]ῖς οἰκ[εί]οις καὶ φιλανθρώποις πρὸς τὴν πόλιν· (decree with honors for the Aitolians follows and the clauses regulating the election of the *hieromnamon*)

---

68   See also GAUTHIER 1972, pp. 256-258.
69   See MORETTI II. 78, esp. p. 19 lemma.
70   On Chios in the Amphictyony, see AMANDRY 1986, pp. 218-225; on the meaning of this concession, see SCHOLTEN 2000, pp. 110-114 with bibliography; always useful is FLACELIÈRE 1937, pp. 228-233.

Transl.: It was decreed by the *boule* and the *demos*; the *epimenios* of the *polemarchoi* [Name missing] son of Philistos and the *epimenios* of the *exetastai* Aiantides (...) put forward the motion: since the league of the Aitolians, because of the familiarity and friendship of the *demos* toward the Aitolians from the time of the ancestors, first voted (to grant) us citizenship and prohibited attacking the properties of the Chians to everybody, no matter where they sailed from, otherwise they would have been indicted and brought in front of the *synedrion* as if they had damaged Aitolian property, for these reasons the *demos*, after accepting their benevolence, decreed that the Aitolians shall be (our) citizens and partake in anything in which the Chians do. It was also decided to grant them priority access to the *boule* and the *ekklesia* and to give them *proedria* in all festivals the *polis* celebrates. Now the returning *theoroi* and ambassadors report to the *demos* another (proof of) benevolence that the *koinon* had toward the city by revealing great zeal in taking to completion all the things that the ambassadors requested, and because they have granted the *demos* a hieromnamic vote in the Amphyctyony, thereby acting according to the preexisting familiarity and benevolence toward the *polis*....

The Aitolian concession of the Amphictyonic vote to the Chians allows us to date the decree to the middle of the 3rd century BC.[71] Recent scholarship has readdressed how Aitolians successfully expanded through the Aegean. Scholten's treatment of the two main views on the topic (i.e., state-planned expansionism *vs.* private Aitolian interests progressively supported by the *koinon*) is particularly illuminating.[72] Scholten holds that the Aitolian League indirectly supported private initiative of its members in the Aegean. This interpretation seems to agree with Errington's work on Chian history for the 3rd century BC. Chios established close ties with the Aitolians, without submitting to them, probably because it could serve as a safe harbor and a stepping stone to Asia Minor.[73] This decree is the cornerstone of this long-lasting alliance, but scholars have exaggerated the consequences of potential citizenship.

---

71 Chian presence in the Amphictyony lasted ca. 60 years; see in general AMANDRY 1986, pp. 218–223 in general. On the unorthodox way the Aitolians gave the vote to Chios see SCHOLTEN 2000, p. 101. L. 48 records the name of the first Chian *hieromnamon*, Gannon son of Klytomedon, under Dion's archonship; *CID* II 139 and *CID* IV 56, see SCHOLTEN 2000, p. 248. *Choix* esp. p. 154 dates the concession of the vote, and therefore our text, to 248 or 247 BC.
72 SCHOLTEN 2000, pp. 110–112; see also FUNKE 2008.
73 ERRINGTON 2006, esp. pp. 142–147.

The decisions contained in our document concern mainly the vote in the Amphictiony, but the reciprocal concession of potential citizenship figures briefly in the opening of the text as the means used by the parties to establish a firm diplomatic contact. The terms regulating potential citizenship do not appear in the text. For this reason, I do not accept Scholten's conclusion: "they (i.e., "citizens of the League") were given access to full citizenship (*ISE* II 78.8 πολίτας τε εἶναι τοὺς Αἰτ[ωλοὺς] not εἶναι τοῖς Αἰτωλοῖς συμπολιτείαν, that is, limited citizenship, as in, *e.g.*, *StV* III 495.10–11) and all the other rights and privileges due to any other Chian. These rights probably included not only exemption from harbor duties, but also special access to the Chian council and assembly."[74] Scholten's argument on Aitolian advantages deriving from this agreement is certainly sound, but his reference to *StV* III 495 = *IPark* 28 = my no. 39, LL. 10–11, is confusing. I believe that Scholten draws a distinction between federal and local citizenship (complete?) but in the process he assumes that additional rights were included in the *metechein* clause, which is not accurate.

What must have started as a request of personal inviolability on the part of Chios transformed into a politically important concession: that of the Amphictyonic vote.[75] The most interesting part of this decree, as relates to isopolity, is that it shows us the diplomatic process and passages that had led to this concession. Through the application of this tool, which the communities may have used with different intentions, they achieved the hoped for results, namely, a privileged and secure position for Chios and access to a key location in the Aegean for the Aitolians.

---

74   SCHOLTEN 2000, p. 115, n. 89.
75   GAUTHIER 1972, p. 257 reflects on judicial rights and thinks that because Chios received 'only' federal citizenship, its people would have had a weaker position in court than, for example, the Keans who had 'complete isopolity.' This view, however, if it has any validity, which I do not ascribe to it, would be circumscribed to Naupaktos-Aitolia. Finally, it must be noted that both agreements were wide-reaching in their purposes.

(44) *Aitolian League and Trikka*
Stele of limestone broken on the upper and lower part; measurements: W. 0.325–0.335; H. 0. 37 m.; Th. 0.08 m. The stone was found on the site of ancient Kalydon and, according to Schmitt, is still in the area.

Edd. *IG* IX 1² 136; [*StV* III 542].

> Ἀγα[θ]ῆι τ[ύ]χηι. Αἰτωλῶν τὸ κοι-
> νὸν Τρικκαίων τῆι πόλει ἔ(δ)ω-
> καν (!) πολιτείαν, ἀτέλειαν, ἀσυ-
> 4 λίαν, ἀσφάλειαν καὶ αὐτοῖς
> καὶ χρήμασιν καὶ κατὰ γῆν καὶ
> κατὰ θάλατταν καὶ πολέμου
> καὶ εἰρήνης. ἔδωκαν δὲ καὶ Τρικ-
> 8 καῖοι Αἰτωλοῖς κατὰ ταὐτά.
> βουλαρχούντων Φρίχου, Με-
> νοίτα, Δορκίνα, Σκορπίωνος, Κοι-
> σέα, Ἀρχεδάμου, γραμμα-
> 12 τέος Παυσίου.

Text by Schmitt.

Klaffenbach dates the inscription to after 206 BC relying on paleography; Schmitt follows suit. In this period, Trikka, and Hestiaotis in general, abandoned the Aitolian League, which they joined in ca. 229 BC.[76]

Thessaly did not remain under Aitolian control for long. The interests of its powerful neighbors and broader political forces were too great to allow this membership to continue. Moreover, this area was not traditionally Aitolian. Apparently, the rebellion that brought most of the region into the league followed Doson's death.

This complex and uncertain context does not help us to read and interpret this concise text.[77] In the past, it was thought that with this document Aitolia had established Trikka's league membership, but, institutionally, this view cannot be correct. Alternatively, it was hypothesized that the inscription reflected Aitolia's attempt to connect itself through potential citizenship to a city that

---

76 SCHOLTEN 2000, pp. 165–170, but on p. 210 he includes an earlier date: after 229 BC. The evidence on these events is scarce, for Trikka's inclusion in the Aitolian League see LIV. XXXIX. 25. 3–4.

77 Briefly on the practice of publishing abbreviated texts see RHODES 2001, esp. pp. 36–37.

had once been part of the Aitolian League.[78] In other words, the Aitolians would have tried thus to retain the close relationship and the advantages that this partnership had brought them. Trikka reciprocates the grant, too (LL. 7–8), but its true meaning is difficult to determine because of the text's brevity.

(45) Aitolian League and (V)axos

The small fragment of a stele found in 1890 in a private house located on Crete contains a possible reminder of a grant of potential citizenship that had been established between the Aitolian League and the Cretan city of (V)axos. The text dates to the end of the 3rd or beginning of the 2nd century BC.[79]

The text is very fragmentary, but preserves part of the word *isopoliteia*:

. συγγεν[ει - - -] / [.]ταδε συγ - - - / [.]ται Αἰτωλ[- - - - - - - - Αἰτ]/ωλίαν ἰσοπ[ολιτ - - -/ [.]τι κοινα δ [- - -] / ροις τοῖς θεο [- - -] / βοαθεῖν των [- - -] / κατὰ δύναμ[ιν - - -] / χόντων δὲ ο [- - -]/ τὰ ὀψώνια τετ[- - -] / τας τὰ ὀψώνια - - - κτλ

A few keywords in the text reveal the militaristic nature of this agreement and the fact that kinship was evoked in its establishment.

The relationship between (V)axos and Aitolia is also attested elsewhere, but, in the past, scholars have tried to see connections where there were none. Two inscriptions found on Aitolian soil, *IG* IX² 6, dated to 300–250 BC, and *IG* IX² 1 99, dated after 170 BC, testify to two Aitolian officials, a *boularchos* and a *strategos*, whose *ethnika* are, respectively, (L. 11) ϝαξ(ί)ου and (L. 2) Ὀαξίου. Scholars, and among them even Guarducci in *I.Cret.*, thought that these men came from Crete and had been allowed to take up offices because of the existing potential citizenship between Atolia and (V)axos. But as Lerat, Larsen, and Funke note, these men must have come from the homonymous city of Axos in west Lokris and not from Crete.[80] The strongest argument against the old 'Cretan' identification is institutional: a grant of potential citizenship does not

---

78 FLACELIÈRE 1937, p. 254, see also *StV* III 542 esp. p. 281. BURASELIS 2003, pp. 44–45, commented on this text "Of course, the expedient of *isopoliteia*, actually consisting in the bestowal of applicable citizenship rights only after movement to the territory of the community conferring them and so establishing a sort of prospective *sympoliteia*, ideally served the cases of cities and other communities far away from Aetolia, which could thus be linked with it to mutual benefit." Although the basic definition of isopolity is correct, this view cannot be shared: *isopoliteia* is not a stepping stone to *sympoliteia*, on which see GAWANTKA's 1975 in his introduction.
79 *StV* III 585 (also as *IG* IX² 1 193 = *I.Cret.* II.v 18A).
80 FUNKE 1995, p. 73 of his unpublished Habilitation, which he kindly allowed me to read; LARSEN 1968, pp. 204–205; LERAT, 1952 I, pp. 18–20.

establish participation in political life for potential citizens, unless an individual decides to use the option of changing citizenship and assume a new status.

In this context, the dossier of Epikles, *Syll.*³ 622A and B (now in *Choix* no. 120), deserves a note. According to paleography, the documents that belong to this dossier date to the last quarter of the 3rd century BC. *Syll.*³ 622A contains the fragmentary Aitolian decree presented in response to a letter of the Cretan city of (V)axos pleading the case Epikles, *Syll.*³ 622B. According to the letter by the city of (V)axos, Epikles was the legitimate son of a (V)axian man who had moved to Cyprus to fight. After his death, his son Epikles had been sold to Amphissa under unclear circumstances. Later in life he managed to buy his freedom.[81] Epikles must have then asked his mothercity, (V)axos, to certify his citizenship status to help him obtain Aitolian recognition of what the text calls *koinopoliteia*, *Syll.*³ 622B, L. 12.

It is possible that *koinopoliteia* indicates the league's federal citizenship, which must have brought with it several benefits and forms of protection.[82] A third inscription, *FD* III 3 117, was republished by Bousquet who attributed it to the Epikles's dossier.[83] If Bousquet is correct, this text would present a positive response by Aitolia to (V)axos. The text indeed states that Aitolia (?) granted π]ολιτείαν and that it would make sure they—the verb is plural—would be unharmed during their stay. Whether this text relates to Epikles's case is uncertain, but there would be no contradiction. As Gauthier has also noted, Aitolia did not use the word *isopoliteia* but rather *politeia* and, if Szanto is correct to associate *koinopoliteia* with *(iso)politeia*, we simply have confirmation of the result that Epikles had sought.

Eplikes's dossier confirms potential citizenship between (V)axos and Aitolia, whose grant was 'federal.' Epikles's case could have been somehow an exception because of his legal status, but the fact that he pursued the implementation of *koinopoliteia* (probably despite the bureaucracy and procedural difficulties that it must have entailed) supports the view that this recognition gave him important rights (?) within Aitolia and therefore in Amphissa.

We do not know when Aitolia and (V)axos had established potential citizenship: both documents that mention it refer to an agreement that had already been signed. Our document (45) indicates that the institution of *isopoliteia*

---

81   See BIELMAN 1994, pp. 268–271.
82   GAUTHIER 1972, pp. 369–371 comments extensively on this text and concludes that Epikles's case is extraordinary also because he sought to attain the rights and security normally given to short-term visitors as permanent resident. In his Habilitation, Funke treats this document, too, and supports the view that even 'just' the federal grant could allow foreigners to enjoy a highly secure legal status in Aitolia.
83   BOUSQUET 1960, pp. 161–164.

was in place. In association with *syngeneia*, it helped to establish the military alliance that the fragmentary text from (V)axos appears to contain.

(46) *Aitolian League and Magnesia on the Meander*

In 1897 a limestone stele was discovered in Thermon. The document inscribed on it testifies to a grant of *asylia* for Magnesia on the part of the Aitolian League. Another copy of the document was found later in Delphi. These texts probably date to 221/0 BC.

The stone from Thermon preserves part of another document with which Aitolia granted Magnesia potential citizenship, *IG* IX 1² 1 4d, in response to a similar, but completely restored grant of the Magnesians, L. 29.[84] Only the left side of the stone is preserved. Klaffenbach tentatively restored the text; the result must therefore only be considered speculative. The Aitolian concession (perhaps the reciprocation of the grant?) of potential citizenship should appear in L. 33 where we read: ... εἶμεν αὐ]/τοὺς Αἰτωλοὺς ἴσου[ς καὶ ὁμοίους.... This formula can indeed signal that a grant of potential citizenship was included, but no more can reasonably be said.[85]

We have very little evidence from the Peloponnese for the use of the award of potential citizenship, but in central Greece we find that the Aitolian League used it extensively. More importantly, with one exception, this grant was consistently adopted at a federal level, which leads to two conclusions. First, Aitolian federal citizenship must have *per se* brought considerable advantages in its territory to those who could claim it. Second, since these grants have been interpreted as a way to draw distant communities into the league, a separate, historical analysis of each concession is necessary to avoid simplistic generalizations. But we must be cautious because even scholars who have contributed very good work to Aitolian history have privileged this reading. When we evaluate the conclusions that can be drawn from this historical and institutional study, however, we realize that Aitolia actively and passively used

---

84   RIGSBY 1996, p. 191 and n. 62. With this decree the Aitolians also grant the Magnesians a vote in the Amphictyony, just like they granted to the Chians.

85   This document is a later addition to the grant of *asylia*. In it we find the name of king Philip, L. 39, that sets its *terminus ante quem* to 179 BC. Philip was involved in the Magnesian quest, as we can infer from the Chalchis's decree where his exhortation to the city to grant what Magnesia had requested in 208 BC is recorded. On Chalchis see RIGSBY 1996, pp. 233–235 no. 97. In his comment to *IG* IX 1² 4d, KLAFFENBACH tried to establish the *terminus post quem* for this inscription by referring to a citizenship grant *ad personam* for two Magnesians on the part of Aitolia in 194 BC. GAWANTKA 1975, p. 58 n. 41 has already noted that this criterion cannot date grants of potential citizenship: these two forms of citizenship concessions do not exclude each other, since they are and imply different institutional forms operating at different levels.

this tool to its full potential. The concession of potential citizenship could reinforce diplomatic relationships, but it could also have the opposite effect on these relations than the one scholarship normally hypothesizes. By establishing a strong diplomatic tie, the partners defined boundaries and reinforced their diplomatic, autonomous status. In other words, in establishing a connection meant to create a stronger relationship, *isopoliteia* actually divided the communities that adopted it.

CHAPTER 7

Crete

The island of Crete has yielded numerous agreements that contain a grant of potential citizenship mainly with neighboring towns. To this evidence we must add *isopoliteia* treaties that involve Cretan cities and non-Cretan communities. The overall number of Cretan agreements that contain some form of *isopoliteia* is indeed impressive and, quantitatively, can be compared with the testimonies from the Ionian city of Miletos. Yet Cretan communities used this tool slightly differently, most often privileging the second type of grants of potential citizenship over the first.

Within Crete, as Chaniotis has shown,[1] the concession of grants of potential citizenship pursued mostly practical goals. It was routinely inserted in agreements that also aimed to better regulate the use of land, especially pasturage land, and perhaps even commerce within the Cretan economic system.[2] At the same time, this institution could be used diplomatically to shape and strengthen relationships between communities, often this happened within broader political frameworks such as military alliances. In these treaties *isopoliteia* can be inserted into a string of other grants, especially with *epigamia* and *enktesis*, which occur infrequently anywhere else. Texts rarely elaborate on these awards and instead move to other issues that quickly become the focus. These factors suggest that this tool was routinely used in Crete less for the exceptionality of its (legal) content and more as a necessary addition to the diplomatic process underway. Here one can well perceive how isopolity had become a cornerstone of Hellenistic diplomacy. The fictitious decree for the colonists who were leaving Crete to found Magnesia can serve as an illustration: the authors of this document were careful to reproduce Cretan language, institutions, and grants, among which the concession of potential citizenship also appears.[3] In this context, another piece of evidence that comes from ancient literary sources, namely, POLYB. XXVIII.14, highlights the importance of the tie created by this tool.[4] The passage recounts the destruction of the city of Apollonia by Kydonia. It was an impious act because … ὑπαρχούσης γὰρ αὐτοῖς

---

1 See CHANIOTIS 1996, esp. 101–104 on *isopoliteia*. In his work he includes new editions and detailed commentaries of the relevant inscriptions.
2 For a detailed study of this aspect, see CHANDEZON 2003, esp. pp. 176–181 and also pp. 370–389.
3 *I.Magn.* 20 = no. 14.
4 For the passage and a brief discussion, see *infra* appendix 2.

οὐ μόνον φιλίας, ἀλλὰ συμπολιτείας πρὸς Ἀπολλωνιάτας καὶ καθόλου κοινωνίας πάντων τῶν ἐν ἀνθρώποις νομιζομένων δικαίων, καὶ περὶ τούτων κειμένης ἐνόρκου συνθήκης παρὰ τὸν Δία τὸν Ἰδαῖον, παρασπονδήσαντες τοὺς Ἀπολλωνιάτας κατελάβοντο τὴν πόλιν καὶ τοὺς μὲν ἄνδρας κατέσφαξαν …

Polybios uses the term *sympoliteia* to describe a relationship that must have been one of *isopolitea* between the cities of Apollonia and Kydonia. If this interpretation is correct, the text shows the high regard for *isopoliteia* within and outside of Crete. It was certainly more valuable inside this island because it was often related to issues vital to the survival of the communities and therefore served almost as a diplomatic requirement for cities to define their relationships with other communities.

One more topic that emerges in the study of Cretan-Cretan *isopoliteiai* is procedure. Few Cretan texts describe the procedures that applicants had to follow in order to change citizenship. When the procedures are included, they are extremely detailed. However, we should not assume that these procedures were unique to Crete: potential citizenship was a widely and internationally recognized diplomatic tool and, although it was used variously across the Mediterranean, within the limits and respect of the legal procedures for the admission of new citizens specific to each community, the basic rules governing this tool (and therefore the basic rules underlying a change of citizenship status) were shared and recognized everywhere. For this reason, *I.Cret.* III.iv 1 = Chaniotis 1996, pp. 185–190 no. 5 = no. 47 (agreement between Hierapytna and Praisos), with its detailed description of the admission procedure, should not be considered an exception from the 'procedural' point of view *a priori*; details must have differed from city to city, but not the essence of a procedure.[5] The text is exceptional because it describes what was routinely omitted in texts engraved on stone—probably because these rules constituted a normal aspect of the grant-giving practice. General procedural requirements, such as the renunciation of a person's active citizenship in case he switched his legal citizenship status, were not exceptional, but must have been a standard practice in the implementation of any citizenship grant.

---

5 An anonymous reviewer has drawn my attention to the Athenian procedure for the enrollment of younger members of the community in the citizen body, *Ath. Pol.* 42. 1–2, as a possible parallel.

Treaties between Cretan *Poleis*

(47) *I.Cret. III.iv 1* (ph) = *Chaniotis 1996, pp. 185–190 no. 5 (Hierapytna and Praisos), Now Stored in the Museum of Heraklion (Inv. No. E94)*

Paleography provides the only dating criterion we can rely on to date this text to the early 3rd century BC. The surviving portion of the text must have belonged to a more comprehensive agreement between Hierapytna and Praisos probably including an alliance and declaration of friendship to which a reciprocal grant of potential citizenship was attached. The very detailed procedural clauses in Frag. B, LL. 1–33 must especially receive a brief comment:

[—] / διαθέμε/νος τὰ ἴδια / ἑκάτερος / ἑκατερῆ, ὅ[ς] / κα ἦι ἔνφυ/λος, καὶ οὔ/τω πολιτ/ευέσθω μ/[ε]τέχων κ/αὶ θίνων κ/αὶ ἀνθρωπί/νων πάντ/ων, παραιτ/ησάμενος / τὰν αὐτῶ π/όλιν· ἐς ὁπ/οτέραν δέ / κα πόλιν ἔρ/πηι πολιτε/ύσων, δια[ψ]/αφιζέσθω/ν ἐν κυρ[ία]/ι ἐκκλησ[ία]/ι πότερ[ον δ]/οκεῖ πολ[ιτεί]/αν δε[δόσθ]/αι ἢ μή· κα[ὶ α]/ἴ κα ἀντίθε/τοι ψᾶφοι γένωνται τ/ρεῖς, μὴ ἔσ/τω πολίτα/ς.

Chaniotis, whose edition I use, translates these lines as follows: "[—] nachdem jeder sein Eigentum in der jeweiligen Stadt geordnet hat, wer Mitglied einer Phyle ist; und so soll er Bürger sein und an allen sakralen und profanen Dingen teilhaben, nachdem er seine eigene Stadt verlassen hat (?). Und in der Stadt, in die er kommt, um sich niederzulassen, soll eine Abstimmung in einer der Hauptvolksversammlungen abgehalten werden, ob es gut scheint, ihm das Bürgerrecht zu verleihen oder nicht; und wenn es drei Gegenstimmen gibt, darf er nicht Bürger werden...."[6]

There is another possible translation: "... after each person has arranged his personal affairs, (he) who is member of a *phyle* (i.e., a full citizen), shall live as a citizen taking part in all human and divine things, after having obtained permission from his *polis*. In whichever city (of the two) he goes to, in order to live as a citizen, a vote should be held in a lawful assembly on whether he should be a citizen or not; if there are three votes against him, he shall not be a citizen...."

---

6 CHANIOTIS 1996, p. 186.

The clause παραιτ/ησάμενος / τὰν αὐτῶ π/όλιν, whose interpretation Chaniotis accompanies with a question mark, is the crux of the matter. I understand it as "after having obtained permission from his *polis*."[7] The applicant had to "obtain permission" from his native city, probably in the form of a document, as it happens in Kios or is attested in the agreement between Xanthos and Myra.[8] This permission must be a way to confirm the applicant's citizenship status, which relates also to the wish of cities to make sure that people did not leave behind any troubled or illegal situation and that the grant of potential citizenship was not abused.

The other matter to be discussed is the very nature of this text. Like Chaniotis, Gawantka, and other scholars, I believe this decree contains an exchange of potential citizenship.[9] Willetts (followed by Guizzi), however, refuses this interpretation.[10] At the heart of this belief is a basic misunderstanding of potential citizenship: Guizzi for example says: "... (Chaniotis 1996, pp. 185–190 no. 5) viene considerato il piú antico trattato di *isopoliteia* cretese. Tale interpretazione è da escludere in presenza della clausula sul voto per l'ammissione di ogni singolo nuovo cittadino nel corpo civico, invece della concessione

---

[7] CHANIOTIS 1996, p. 102, n. 612 discusses the possible translations of the verb παραιτοῦμαι, among which he includes "to obtain permission." But he prefers the meaning of "to leave," along with GUARDUCCI, *I.Cret.* III.iv 1, and GAWANTKA 1975, p. 70 thus following L. Robert. Robert, however, established this meaning for παραιτοῦμαι in texts related to sport. Chaniotis explains his choice and states "ich kenne jedoch keine Parallele dafür, dass ein Bürger die Erlaubnis seiner Stadt erhält, sich in einer anderen niederzulassen." Another note pertains to (LL. 20–21) πολιτε/ύσων vs. (LL. 7–8) πολιτ/ευέσθω. CHANIOTIS 1996, p. 102, n. 613 translates πολιτε/ύσων as "sich niederlassen," πολιτ/ευέσθω as "Bürger sein." He holds that since both middle and active voice appear within the same text, they must have different meanings. He ascribes the meaning of "living" to the active voice because residency was a requirement for becoming a citizen. While certainly true, the text says that if one moves to the other city *to become a citizen* (future participle), he has to undergo the procedure that the text describes. My point is that the logical link between moving and the procedure for becoming a citizen disappears if we read πολιτε/ύσων as describing the simple move without the intention to become a citizen of the other city. Chaniotis refers to *BE* 1958 79 for the meaning of *politeuo* as "inhabiting/residing," but in that text the context, institutional and historical, differs significantly. Finally, Chaniotis translates ἐν κυρ[ία]/ι ἐκκλησ[ία]/ι as *Hauptvolksversammlung*, as in Athens. GUIZZI 2000, p. 326 thinks that here *kyria* means "valida, regolare" and he is probably right. On the *kyria ekklesia* in Crete see also ERRINGTON 1995, pp. 34–36, for whom the expression refers to an assembly with mandatory quorum, *contra* GAUTHIER *BE* 1996 121.

[8] *Milet* I 3 141 = no. 4, LL. 39–41; BOUSQUET and GAUTHIER 1994 = *SEG* XLIV 1218 = no. 8, LL. 23–27.

[9] CHANIOTIS 1996, p. 186 suggests that it was part of a broader agreement including also an alliance and *philia*, as routinely happened in Crete. He is probably correct.

[10] GUIZZI 2000/1, esp. p. 359 where he refers to Willetts.

collettiva da attivare poi singolarmente." Guizzi seems to believe that a concession of potential citizenship entails a passive mass grant of citizenship that individuals then would simply 'activate' at their will.[11] What this 'activation' entails, however, he does not say, but it seems to me that he implies that there was no further screening.[12] But cities had the right and duty to check that applicants were eligible to obtain their citizenship, whether *isopolitai* or not. These applicants had to undergo whatever procedure (perhaps simplified?) a city had in place in order to determine if they met the necessary requirements to change citizenship. It is possible that their applications could fail.

To think that cities gave up their means of screening potential new citizens only because decrees do not routinely list procedural aspects is to assign to epigraphic documents an informational purpose for which they were not intended. The procedure included in our agreement (LL. 16–33) is exceptional only because it is described in detail, not because it exists.

The most striking feature of the procedure is the low number of contrary votes that could stop the implementation of the grant. For Chaniotis it would help to guard the closed nature of the community, but it also signals the interest the grant must have raised among the members of the two cities—in his view mostly Hierapytna.[13] Gawantka thinks, too, that these clauses *de facto* limited the actual adoption of isopolity and confirmed his theory of the limited application and actual use of this tool.[14] These drastic conclusions, however, have been drawn without a sufficient basis of knowledge: three votes are indeed few, but (to begin with) we do not know how many people were allowed to vote or how common it was to vote against an application, namely, a drafted proposal.

This text contains other provisions in addition the grant of potential citizenship: the right of grazing free of charge, ἐπινομά (LL. 33–51);[15] the concession

---

11 GUIZZI 2000/1, pp. 334–335 with a misleading definition and interpretation of this tool.
12 Gawantka in a way has encouraged this reading by speaking of "Aktivierung" for the grant and reducing to simple bureaucratic acts the known (and unknown) implementation procedures, see for example GAWANTKA 1975, pp. 14–16 on the agreement between Miletos and Seleukeia-Tralles, or pp. 73–74 where the inscription from Crete under discussion is treated as an exception. But see HELLER and PONT 2012, p. 11 referring to GAUTHIER 1985, p. 150.
13 CHANIOTIS 1996, p. 187.
14 GAWANTKA 1975, esp. pp. 70–71. Both scholars, Gawantka and Chaniotis, follow Guarducci's view. GUIZZI 2000/1, pp. 326–327 considers only the constitutional side to conclude that a moderate democracy ruled Hierapytna.
15 On the right to *epinomia* see CHANIOTIS 1996, p. 187 and IDEM 1999(c), p. 198, n. 24 correcting his previous interpretation. In this treaty *epinomia* is the concession of grazing free of charge in another community's pasture land (also GUIZZI 2000/1, pp. 346–350), but we cannot assume that this applied to every other known instance of *epinomia* grant.

of staying in each other's territory with one's herd (LL. 52–68); and finally the right to participate in festivals and games, (LL. 68 to the (readable) end).[16] It is clear that one of the main issues treated by the text is the use of pasture land, whether occasional (LL. 33–51) or seasonal (LL. 52–68).[17] Chaniotis suggests that in this region grants of potential citizenship were introduced in broader agreements to facilitate finding a solution to economical and political issues, such as regulating the use of public pasture land that could have (and must have) otherwise led to conflicts between individuals and, eventually, neighboring states.[18]

According to Chaniotis and Guizzi, the treaty between Hierapytna and Praisos is 'unbalanced' because it would show Hierapytna's greater interest for the agreement (i.e., Praisos's territory). This city's growing population should have put the authorities under pressure to find new land and living opportunities for its citizens. Praisos's leadership instead emphasized defending its territory, for example by setting strict limits on the areas that Hierapytnans could access and use (LL. 38–43).[19]

Chaniotis suggests that Hierapytna tried to systematically acquire new options for the livelihood of its citizens by establishing *isopoliteia* treaties that, by giving the option of switching citizenship or simply by allowing the members of both cities to enjoy additional grants, gave them access to new land— for both pasture and cultivation.[20] But Hierapytna also pursued an aggressive and expansionistic policy that led to radical events, such as Praisos's destruction in the middle of the 2nd century BC.

Perhaps we should pay more attention to Praisos's interests: this town was probably just as keen as Hierapytna to stipulate the treaty, since it served as a way to regulate, if not to stop, Hierapytnan behavior. LL. 20–33, i.e., the three votes limit, must not be seen as a way to curb the use and effects of potential citizenship, but instead it could be seen as a means to discipline Hierapytnan acquisition rights. In this text the concession of *enktesis* does not appear, but rather the right of *epinomia*, namely, here the concession of grazing free of

---

The interpretation of this grant, its meaning, and implications has generated a long scholarly debate that is well synthetized and discussed in CHANDEZON 2003, esp. pp. 370–379. This scholar rightly prefers to leave the question of the exact definition of *epinomia* open, as the evidence does not allow a conclusive interpretation.

16 According to Chaniotis, LL. 78–80 could have contained Rechtshilfe clauses.
17 CHANIOTIS 1996, n. 5; and IDEM 1999, esp. pp. 199–205 has already treated this topic exhaustively.
18 CHANIOTIS 1996, p. 104.
19 See esp. GUIZZI 2000/1, pp. 371–372.
20 CHANIOTIS 1996, pp. 102–104 and GUIZZI 2000/1, pp. 370–372.

charge in another community's pastureland. Switching citizenship, and therefore acquiring the right to buy possessions in another town's territory, was the only chance to take away land legally. It is possible that for Praisos the imposition of the three- vote- limit was not a matter of naturalizing too many foreigners, but a way to halt, also symbolically, both a dangerous presence in its territory and the alienation of its land.

(48) I.Cret. *III.iii 1b* = *Chaniotis 1996, pp. 217–221 no. 14* (Hierapytna and the Arkades—) (isopoliteia?), Now Lost

(49) I.Cret. *III.iii 5* = *Chaniotis 1996, pp. 432–439 no. 74* (Hierapytna and the Hierapytnans at ?), Now Lost

The text of *I.Cret.* III.iii 1b = Chaniotis no. 14 is engraved on the back of a stele that contains also an agreement between Hierapytna and Antigonos Doson. The latter document and paleography help to date the inscription to ca. 227/21 BC, just before the Lyttian war began. If Chaniotis's historical interpretation is correct, this document might belong to an attempt to partly unite the Gortynian and the Knossian factions.

In this fragmentary text Chaniotis recognizes a grant of potential citizenship between Hierapytna and the Arkades, but an unusual detail, LL. 5–6, raises doubt about this identification.[21] The first lines are fragmentary, but after a grant of *ateleia* (in restoration), of the right to graze and *epigamia*, LL. 5–6 read as follows:

(...) εἰ δέ τίς κα λῆ[ι κατοικὴν Ἱεραπυτνίων ἐν Ἀρκάσι ἢ Ἀρκάδων ἐν Ἱ]/εραπύτναι, κατοικήτω δ[ικαιοπραγήσας τοῖς ἰδίοις. κτλ[22]

The restorations are heavy, but likely, except perhaps for the last participle that relies only on the uncertain reading of "δ" and imperfect parallels. The verb *dikaiopragein* appears normally in connection with concessions of citizenship

---

21 GAWANTKA 1975, p. 217 includes the inscription in his catalogue as K13 and comments: "die Isopolitie ist nicht ganz sicher." The actual concession does not appear. CHANIOTIS 1996, p. 219 rightly points to the existing parallelisms with other treaties but lacks a final confirmation.

22 CHANIOTIS 1996, p. 219 translates the text as follows: "und wenn [ein Hierapytnier es vorzieht, bei den Arkadern zu wohnen, oder ein Arkader in] Hierapytna, darf er wohnen, nachdem er [die eigenen Rechtsgeschäfte geregelt hat ...]." The text, which is still fragmentary, is then concerned with festivities and sacrifices, the swearing of an oath once a year, and finally treats trials and the concession to import and export.

and the *metechein* clause,[23] but in this sentence we find the verb *katoikein* used to describe possibly a long-term move; the implications are different.[24] Moreover, from the point of view of the content, the clause of LL. 5–6 has few parallels, with none from Crete. The concession to move (*katoikein*) into another city's territory without an apparent emergency and without switching citizenship is extremely unusual. The agreement between Magnesia and Phokaia, which I do not believe contains a grant of potential citizenship, is similar for example.[25]

As it stands, this fragmentary document does not preserve a concession of potential citizenship: it could be lost, or perhaps it was never there. Chaniotis rightly notes that this text seems to contain concessions typical of Cretan agreements that include *isopoliteia*, such as, for example, *epigamia*. But in this text the concession of the right to intermarriage is treated and regulated separately, LL. 4–5, and does not appear together with potential citizenship, as is often the case especially in Crete.

I.Cret. III.iii 1b = Chaniotis 1996, pp. 217–221 no. 14 (48) is often discussed together with another inscription (*I.Cret.* III.iii 5 = Chaniotis 1996, pp. 432–439 no. 74 = no. 49) which dates to the 2nd century BC and preserves part of the word *isopoliteia*, LL. 3–4, and an oath, LL. 11–26. From these lines we learn that Hierapytna granted potential citizenship to the κατοικόντες Ἱεραπύτνιοι [...].

Numerous interpretive problems surround these lines, starting with the identification of the area where the κατοικόντες Ἱεραπύτνιοι [...], LL. 6–7, lived as well as their very identity. Scholars have proposed several locations for this *katoikia*, from Gortyn to Larisa.[26] Muttelsee's proposal, that the Hierapytnans created a colony in the territory of the Arkades, is still the most popular, but Rigsby and Chaniotis warn against the idea of a colony.[27] As I noted in the

---

23   Here I cite one of the two examples that CHANIOTIS 1996, p. 220, 1288, provides: his 37 (*I.Cret.* I.xvi 17 = no. 54, the alliance and potential citizenship between Eleutherna and Latos, end of the 2nd century BC), LL. 7–11: ἦμεν δὲ καὶ πολι/[τεύεσθαι ⟨τὸν⟩? Ἐλευθερναῖον Λ]ατοῖ, καὶ τὸν Λάτιον Ἐλ[ευ]/[θέρναι, μετέχοντα θίνω]ν καὶ ἀνθρωπίνων πάν/[των ------]Ι δικαιοπραγήσαντα τοῖς ἰδίο/[ις παραιτησάμενον?] τὰν ἰδίαν πόλιν (κτλ)

24   For other parallels see GAUTHIER 2000, pp. 109–114.

25   *I.Magn.* 7b = no. 19.

26   GUIZZI 2000/1, p. 367 provides a summary of the various suggestions made over the decades.

27   See CHANIOTIS 1996, p. 438; RIGSBY 1986, pp. 357–358; GUIZZI 2000/1, p. 369 instead speaks of colonists: he thinks that the aftermath of the Lyttian War led to this foundation. But a colony implies the birth of an independent *polis* with its own territory; it would therefore be unclear why colonists would retain the identity of κατοικόντες Ἱεραπύτνιοι [...]. Guizzi's hypothesis relies on the difficult belief that mother city and colony shared citizenship.

introduction, Chaniotis suggests that these κατοικόντες Ἱεραπύτνιοι [...] were an external community of Hierapytnans that had moved to some other territory because of a previous treaty that could be for example *I.Cret.* III.iii 1b = Chaniotis 1996, pp. 217–221 no. 14 = no. 48.[28]

These two agreements (48 and 49) have been artificially connected. I suggest that we sever that connection.[29] Even if this link had existed, it does not explain what the term *isopoliteia* as it appears in no. 49 should mean. Chaniotis has suggested that *isopoliteia* here was granted to give these κατοικόντες Ἱεραπύτνιοι [...] the option to move back home, but this cannot be right: these individuals had never ceased to be citizens of Hierapytna. My position instead is that here *isopoliteia* does not describe the institution but rather it indicates an 'equality of rights' for both the Hierapytnans who lived outside their *polis* of origin and the Hieraytnans at home. The word *isopoliteia* appears again in the oath, L. 20, and refers to the document that was identified here as the *isopoliteia* document, which does not need to have a technical-institutional meaning.

(50)   I.Cret. *II.v 20* = *Chaniotis 1996, pp. 221–222 no. 15 (Axos and Tylissos) End of the 3rd Century BC, Now in Rhetymno (Inv. No. E 29)*

This extremely fragmentary text has been identified as an *isopoliteia* agreement because it contains key words such as a reference to πολιτεύεσθαι (L. 5) and part of a *metechein* clause (L. 6). This text must refer to a grant of potential citizenship that, here, too, must have been inserted into a broader agreement (perhaps one pertaining to an alliance). Nothing else, however, can be said.

(51)   I.Cret. *III.iv 6* (ph.) = *Chaniotis 1996, pp. 234–235 no. 20 (Hierapytna and Itanos) 3rd Century BC, Now in Heraklion (Inv. No. E66)*

The inscription preserves a very brief text that includes the concession of potential citizenship with a clause that accounts for the possibility to change parts of the agreement. A reference to the magistrates under whom the treaty had become applicable appears. However, it is unclear whether this agreement is complete (Guarducci) or is rather the end of a longer text or an emendation

---

28   See the introduction supra, pp. 26–27.

29   CHANIOTIS 1996, esp. p. 438 supports the thesis that the *katoikoi* had created their own community within the territory of Arkadia and cites the case of the *Eleutheronoi* in Sipilos (*I.Cret.* II.x 4) as a parallel. While I believe that Chaniotis is right in envisioning an external community for these *katoikoi*, I do not share his joint reading of my nos. 48 and 49. Probably neither inscription records an exchange of the institution of *isopoliteia*.

to another agreement (Chaniotis).³⁰ Chaniotis must be right: the text is too short and the disposition of the elements it contains is unusual.

The document does not enrich our knowledge on the mode of granting potential citizenship, but Hierapytna here uses the grant with a city with which it shared no border, at least until after the destruction of Praisos around 145 BC. This circumstance is, for Hierapytna and for our evidence in general, unusual and reveals the fact that in Crete, too, this tool might have been used for purposes that went beyond the regulation of land-related and immediate war matters. It is a (possible) rare attestation for the use of the first type of a grant of potential citizenship between Cretan communities.

(52)   I.Cret. *III.iii 4* (ph.) = *Chaniotis 1996, pp. 255–264 no. 28 (Hierapytna and Priansos) End of the 3rd Century BC, Oxford, Epigraphic Collection*

Shortly after 205 BC, Hierapytna and Priansos signed an agreement that must have been the third in a series of treaties that also involved the city of Gortyn (LL. 6–12).³¹ This agreement's excellent state of preservation and the numerous details that it contains make it an invaluable document. However, scholars have used this document as a template for Cretan potential citizenship, even if its concession is hardly the focus of the agreement.

The abstract noun *isopoliteia* appears in L. 13 of the text in a paratactic clause that lists several grants: ἰσοπολιτείαν καὶ ἐπιγα/μίαν καὶ ἔνκτησιν. All these awards seem to be equally important and the sentence ends with a *metechein* clause. The text specifies that the grantees include all those who are *emphyloi*, but does not elaborate on the procedures for switching citizenship.³²

---

30   For Chaniotis this agreement completed the alliance between the two towns that is partly preserved as *I.Cret.* III.V 5 = CHANIOTIS 1996, pp. 231–234 no. 19 ca. 219–204 BC.

31   The treaty between Gortyn, Hierapytna, and Priansos: *I.Cret.* IV 174 = CHANIOTIS 1996, pp. 245–255 no. 27. Chaniotis (at p. 250) hypothesizes that these agreements had been concluded during wars—or their immediate aftermath—in eastern Crete.

32   CHANIOTIS 1996, pp. 255–264, no. 28, LL. 12–15: Ἱεραπυτγ[ίοις] / καὶ Πριανσίο(ι)ς ἦμεν παρ'ἀλλάλοις ἰσοπολιτείαν καὶ ἐπιγα/μίας καὶ ἔνκτησιν καὶ μετοχὰν καὶ θείων καὶ ἀνθρωπίνων πάντων, ὅσοι κα ἔωντι ἔμφυλοι παρ'ἑκατέροις (κτλ) ... GAWANTKA 1975, pp. 30–35 devotes his attention to the difficult question of the 'additional' grants. He is undecided on their meaning and function and suggests, just as it happens with ἀρχεῖα in other *isopoliteiai*, that sometimes *Privatrechte* have the role: "die materielle Rechtswirkung zu beschreiben, die das verliehene Bürgerrecht *im Falle seiner Aktivierung* zeitigen würde" (p. 38). But he also notes, p. 38, that in some texts they are independent of the concession of citizenship. He holds that there is no fixed rule, but I argue that the existing evidence supports Chaniotis's interpretation that these additional grants were available to all citizens of the partner *polis*, and that the switching of citizenship did not play any part in their applicability; see CHANIOTIS 1996, p. 103.

This concession precedes several other provisions meant to regulate behaviors and policies of the two cities,[33] and illustrates that the cities shared economic interests that encompassed financial affairs (LL. 15–18) and land problems deriving from grazing and cultivating.

Chaniotis has called this text an agreement of *isopoliteia*. The synthetic but not very precise description of the agreement does not account for the complex and numerous aspects of the daily interactions between these cities that are here regulated in detail. The cities use the award, along with *epigamia* and *enktesis*, to set the tone of the agreement and introduce clauses that regulate practical issues. None of the additional rights and agreements concerning pasturage and agriculture are in fact directly related to the grant of potential citizenship. Instead they are simply attached to it: a friendly setting for a complex negotiation.

While the agreement between Hierapytna and Priansos is a unique source of information for students of Cretan cultural history,[34] it does not add much

---

33 A detailed commentary on the clauses that this text includes can be found in CHANIOTIS 1996, pp. 258–264. For the sake of clarity, I list here the different provisions following this scholar's schema: LL. 15–18 financial facilitations; LL. 18–21 right of cultivating each other's land; LL. 21–27 transportation and temporary storage of goods (see *supra*); LL. 27–30 right of grazing; LL. 30–33 reciprocal help for ambassadors; LL. 34–38 invitation to the *kosmoi*; LL. 38–40 participation in each other's festivals; LL. 40–47 provisions against those who act against the agreement; LL. 47–58 division of booty; LL. 58–74 judicial provisions for causes started before the signing of the treaty as well as in the future. This last section is hotly debated: the nature of the offenses and the parties involved in the legal activities that is here described is controversial, see MAGNETTO 1997, pp. 426–434 no. 72; LL. 74–77 include clauses on the possibility to modify the agreement; LL. 77–83 final provisions on the inscription and its publication. All these provisions are not legally related to the grant of potential citizenship, which (together with *enktesis* and *epigamia*) instead sets the pace and the general conditions inside which the agreement operates.

34 A clause devoted to the storing of goods stands out and deserves a bibliographic note: LL. 21–27: εἰ δέ τί / κα ὁ Ἱεραπύτνιος ὑπέχθηται ἐς Πριανσ{ι}ὸν ἢ ὁ Πριανσιεὺς / ἐς Ἱεράπυτναν ὁτιοῦν, ἀτελέα ἔστω καὶ ἐσαγομένωι καὶ / ἐξαγομένωι αὐτὰ καὶ τούτων τὸς καρπὸς καὶ κατὰ γᾶν / καὶ κατὰ θάλασσαν· ὧν δέ κα ἀποδῶται κατὰ θάλασσαν ἐώ/σας ἐξαγωγᾶς τῶν ὑπεχθεσίμων ἀποδότω τὰ τέλεα / κατὰ τὸς νόμος τὸς ἑκατερῆ κειμένος. I translate the sentence as follows: "If a Hierapytnan brings something to store in Priansos or a Priansian does so in Hierapytna, these things and their fruits shall be exempted from taxes for him whether importing or exporting, whether by land or sea. If, however, he sells any of the stored goods by exporting them by sea, he shall pay taxes according to the laws of each city." The crux of the matter is the verb ὑπεκτίθεναι and its derivatives, which CHANIOTIS 1996, p. 257 translates as "in Sicherheit bringen." The general meaning is not disputed, but rather its specific significance and implications. In his commentary of the inscription, *CIG* II 2256, Böckh gives two interpretations that have prompted scholarly debate. He suggests that ὑπεχθέσιμα could be the booty of piratical raids that were temporarily stored to be sold later, or could be the surplus of some product to be sold for profit outside the

information about the use of the grant of potential citizenship in Crete. This rich text does not present details on themes that concern the award of potential citizenship, such as the nature of its procedures, the eventual implementation of the grant, its limits, or the goals pursued by cities with this institution.

(53) I.Cret. *III.iii 6* = *Chaniotis 1996, pp. 273–274 no. 35* (*Hierapytna and Unknown City*) *3rd/2nd Century* BC

Chaniotis's suggestion that this fragmentary inscription contains a grant of potential citizenship relies on L. 6, ... ἀν[θρωπ]ίνων [- -, which he interprets as belonging to a *metechein* clause. Chaniotis has discussed also the potential partner cities for the stipulation of this agreement and has suggested Biannos as a possibility. Guarducci, however, had read "P" in L. 5; but there is no candidate for it. Chaniotis thinks "P" could be in fact "B." The stone is lost and we have no means to double check Guarducci's reading.

(54) I.Cret. *I.xvi 17* (ph) = *Chaniotis 1996, pp. 276–278 no. 37* (*Eleutherna and Latos*) *Beginning of the 2nd Century* BC, *Now Stored in the Museum of Heraklion* (*Inv. No. E134*)

The inscription, found in Hagios Nikolaos, ancient *Latos pros Kamara*, contains an alliance between the city of Eleutherna (located in western Crete) and Latos. This inscription includes an exchange of potential citizenship.

---

market created by these two *poleis*. In her commentary, Guarducci prefers the second option. This view was criticized first by J. and L. Robert *BE* 1942 142 and later by Müller 1975, p. 143: she deprives the verb of the urgency it implies. In this inscription no direct reference to a state of emergency appears, but it may be a reference to a concrete, general danger. MÜLLER 1975, p. 146 mentions (recalling Böckh), a state of war and, see his n. 64, Cretan piratical raids. Recently GUIZZI 1999, p. 240 and 2000/1, pp. 350–351 has returned to Guarducci's interpretation, refuting the hypothesis that the verb implies urgency. But he does not seem to fully appreciate the strength of Müller's arguments, who puts together several examples of similar content and context, which were not meant to be direct parallels to LL. 20–22 of the Skepsis-Parion agreement (J. and L. Robert *BE* 1972 371 = here no. 23: ἢν δέ τις χρήματα μεταβάληι φυγῆς ἕνεκεν, ἀτελῆ εἶναι ἕνα ἐνιαυτόν), as Guizzi thinks. Rather the evidence collected by Müller is representative of the practice of storing goods in an ally's territory. This practice was not unusual. CHANIOTIS 1996, pp. 120–121 has read the clause within the economic context of the area (in case of emergencies), proposing that this articulated provision referred to livestock and ensured that shepherds were thus spared from a form of taxation that was instead only imposed on those who imported the animals by sea.

The beginning of the text is lost and the lines recording the alliance are extremely fragmentary. Their restoration relies on formulae and clues provided by the content of the second part of the agreement (LL. 14–21). The stipulation of potential citizenship, between the beginning and the second part, however, itself presents a restoration problem in LL. 10–12.

                    ... ἦμεν δὲ καὶ πολι-
8   [τεύσθαι ⟨τὸν⟩? Ἐλευθερναῖον Λ]ατοῖ καὶ τὸν Λάτιον Ἐλ[ευ]-
    [θέρναι, μετέχοντα θίνω]ν καὶ ἀνθρωπίνων πάν-
    [των----------------]Ι δικαιοπραγήσαντα τοῖς ἰδίο-
    [ις----------------] τὰν ἰδίαν πόλιν, ἔγκτησιν δημο-
12 [σίαι ...]ι θνατῶν καὶ ἀθανάτων κατὰ τ[ὸς]
    [Λατίων νόμος· κατὰ ταὐτ]ὰ δὲ καὶ τῶι Λατίωι Ἐλευθέρνα[ι]
    [κατὰ τὸς Ἐλευθερναίω]ν νόμος· (...)

Several possible restorations have been proposed, but here I limit my discussion to the proposals of Chaniotis, Hennig, and Guarducci (*I.Cret*).[35]

Chaniotis restores the text as follows:

                  ... δικαιοπραγήσαντα τοῖς ἰδίο-
    [ις παραιτησάμενον?] τὰν ἰδίαν πόλιν, ἔγκτησιν δημο-
12 [σίαι καὶ ἰδία?]ι θνατῶν καὶ ἀθανάτων κατὰ τ[ὸς]
    [Λατίων νόμος·[36]

For the restoration of L. 11 Chaniotis relies on a similar expression found in the agreement between Praisos and Hierapytna, *I.Cret.* III.iv 1 = Chaniotis 1996, pp. 185–190 no. 5 (no. 47), LL. 13–16 and restores ἰδία?]ι in contrast to δημο/[σίαι L. 12, which, however, is unusual in this context and its meaning difficult to explain.

---

35 CHANIOTIS 1996, p. 276; HENNIG 1994, p. 332, n. 82.
36 CHANIOTIS 1996, p. 277 translates the section referring to the grant as follows: "[Der Eleuthernäer] darf Bürger in Lato sein und der Latier in Eleutherna, [indem er an] allen [göttlichen] und menschlichen [Dingen teilhat —], nachdem er (der Eleuthernäer) seinen privaten Rechtsgeschäfte (in der eigenen Stadt) geregelt hat, und seine eigene Heimat [verlassen hat, soll er] öffentlich [und privat?] das Besitzrecht sowohl der sterblichen als auch der unsterblicher Güter haben, gemäß [den Gesetzten der Latier usw]." On the translation of '... παραιτ/ησάμενος / τὰν αὐτῶ π/όλιν', see *supra* p. 0.

Another possibility would be to return to Guarducci's restoration that Hennig has also partly adopted, namely: δημο/[σίαι πάντων κα]ὶ θνατῶν καὶ ἀθανάτων. Hennig notes that the fragmentary alliance (and exchange of potential citizenship) between Latos and Hierapytna may be a parallel,[37] and this restoration would help make better sense of L. 12.

At this time Gortyn started reasserting its power in a difficult moment for Knossos.[38] But how this agreement fits in is difficult to say. One final note concerns van Effenterre's observation that these two *poleis* were not neighbors, an uncommon fact in Cretan-Cretan concessions of potential citizenship.

(55)   I.Cret. *I.xviii 10* = *Chaniotis 1996, pp. 287–289 no. 42 (Lyttos and an Unknown City, Early 2nd Century BC)*, Stored in the Museum of Heraklion (Inv. no. E219).

The surviving text is extremely fragmentary. Guarducci and Chaniotis have restored LL. 1–2 of fr. A to contain a *metechein* clause.[39] This restoration has led Chaniotis to suggest that the text preserves a grant of potential citizenship between Lyttos and an unknown city.[40] In the restoration the *metechein* clause is repeated twice, LL. 1–6:

[--- ἦμεν τὸν Λύττιον παραιτησάμε]-
[νον τὰν ἰδίαν πόλιν, ἐν Κυδωνίαι? πολιτεύεν μετέχον]-
τα καὶ θίνων [καὶ ἀνθρωπίνων ὅσων Κυδωνιᾶται μετέχοντι?]
4   καὶ πολίτας [ἔστω. Κατὰ τὰ αὐτὰ δὲ ἐξέστω τῶι Κυδωνι?]-
άται πα[ραιτησαμένωι τὰν ἰδίαν πόλιν Λυττοῖ πολι?]-
τεύεν [--- μετέχοντι καὶ θίνων καὶ ἀνθρω]-
πίνων ὅσ[ων Λύττοι μετέχοντι ---]

---

37   HENNIG 1994, p. 332, n. 82. He comments also on the right to own "mortal and immortal (things)," by which is meant herds and land or building property. CHANIOTIS 1996, pp. 338–351 no. 59 = here no. 56 (*SEG* XXVI 1049), LL. 10–13, *app. crit.*

38   CHANIOTIS 1996, p. 278, VAN EFFENTERRE 1948, p. 157, n. 3 and pp. 235–239 who suggests the involvement of a third city, Gortyn.

39   Fragment B records part of an oath, which signals that this text must have contained more than potential citizenship. Perhaps, as Chaniotis suggests, it was part of an alliance.

40   CHANIOTIS 1996, p. 288 tries to identify the second city using L. 4, which contains a few letters that were probably the ending of the *ethnikon*. He seems to prefer Kydonia to Allaria, Tegea, or Apollonia, which he offers as another likely candidate.

Chaniotis describes a "nicht völlig befriedigende Rekonstruktion des Textes"[41] and the restoration is indeed a bit redundant. *I.Cret.* III.iv 6 = Chaniotis 1996, pp. 234–235 no. 20 (no. 51) could be a parallel for the double *metechein* clause, but the order of the statements that here pile up on top of the two *metechein* clauses and the grammar are uncommon.

Chaniotis ascribes again the meaning of "living in; inhabiting"[42] to πολιτεύεν, while καὶ πολίτας [ἔστω would mean "be citizens in the partner *polis.*" But the concept of inhabiting without citizenship is normally expressed differently, with verbs like *katoikein, oikein,* and others,[43] which should be present in the restoration of L. 3.

But too little text is left to restore these lines; this text is only a tiny portion of a diplomatic exchange that, for the section on potential citizenship, was probably rather standard.

(56)   *Chaniotis 1996, pp. 338–250 no. 59 (Hierapytna and Latos III/10 BC)*
This inscription, which Gawantka does not include, preserves an alliance and probably an exchange of the grant of potential citizenship between Hierapytna and Latos. Its focus concerns, among other things, the definition of the borders between these cities and their respective alliances: Gortyn and Olous (allied with Hierapytna), and Knossos and Itanos (allied with Latos).[44]

LL. 10–13 probably contain the exchange of a grant of potential citizenship, but the text is hardly readable; Chaniotis, who saw the stone, agrees. The restorations are heavy and include a *metechein* clause that is preceded by the requirement of arranging one's affairs in the mother city before moving. The grant of *epigamia* and *enktesis* are completely restored, although the second is to be expected since it is followed by the expression πάντων θνατῶν καὶ ἀθανάτων and the reference to the laws of both cities.

---

41   CHANIOTIS 1996, p. 289.
42   CHANIOTIS 1996, p. 289; so already in *I.Cret.* III.iv 1 = CHANIOTIS 1996, pp. 185–190 no. 5 = no. 47 here.
43   GAUTHIER 2000, pp. 109–114.
44   CHANIOTIS 1996, A II 7 offers a reconstruction of the historical events of this poorly known period. A brief discussion is also included in GUIZZI 2000/1, pp. 314–317.

Chaniotis has drawn attention to LL. 68–69, which establish that a strip of land that must have belonged to Lyttos be given to Latos; both cities had to keep their alliance and friendship with Lyttos as a condition.[45] This detail makes clear that the agreement was part of a wider effort to stabilize and pacify a local, tense situation. In such a context the exchange of a grant of potential citizenship is a means to create a diplomatic platform for dialogue and setting the tone for a broader agreement.

(57)   I. Cret. *I.xviii 9* = *Chaniotis 1996, pp. 352–358 no. 60* (*Lyttos and Olous*) *Surviving in Two Fragmentary Copies, One Found in Athens (EM 7718a; 7716b; 7717c) and One in Rhodes. 111/10 BC*

Two copies of this agreement survive, both very fragmentary. The first, found in Athens and comprising three different fragments, contains a reference to an embassy that was sent by Olous to establish *philia, isopoliteia*, and an alliance with Lyttos (A LL. 8–9). B contains parts of the agreement, but does not mention potential citizenship. The final oath (C) almost recapitulates the essential elements of the agreement and mentions *isopoliteia*, too (C LL. 7–9), which curiously appears with *philia, symmachia*, and *epigamia*.[46] While it is not unusual to find isopoliteia associated with the first two *or* the third term separately, it is quite unusual to find all joined together in a sentence, which leads one to question the relative meaning and value of each term.

This treaty can also be connected with an effort to bring peace to this part of the island. Lyttos's role is unclear, but, according to Chaniotis it ensured the political equilibrium of the area.[47]

(58)   I. Cret. *I.xvi 5* = *Chaniotis 1996, pp. 358–376 no. 61* (*Latos and Olous*) *Venice, Museo Archeologico (Inv. No. 372) 110/9 BC*

This inscription testifies to a long territorial controversy between Latos and Olous and, more specifically, to its solution.[48] The inscription is now in Venice (Copy A), but it is not the only known copy of this text: in the 18th century,

---

45   ... ἐ[μμε]ν[όν]των Λατίων ἐν τᾶι Λυττίων καὶ Ἰαραπυτνίων φιλίαι καὶ συμμαχίαι / ἇς ἔντι οἱ ὑπ[ογε]γραμμένοι ...
46   The Rhodian copy contains only the oath; KONTORINI 1983, pp. 31–37.
47   CHANIOTIS 1996, p. 358.
48   CHANIOTIS 1996, esp. pp. 51–56 on this conflict and the connected arbitrations, partly also in AGER 1996, pp. 466–475 no. 164. Chaniotis revises and corrects the historical reconstruction in BOWSKY 1989, pp. 338–341.

another stone now lost, was seen and copied.⁴⁹ Although the copy apparently contained many mistakes, it significantly included a section that is not otherwise recorded in Copy A (Copy B LL. 206–222). After the dating formulae and the clauses outlining the military help that the two cities were obligated to give each other in case of danger, Copy A mentions a fragmentary exchange of potential citizenship, LL. 10–14, that Chaniotis has thus restored: ἐξέ]/στω δὲ τῶι βωλ[ο]μέ[νωι Λατίων δικαιοπραγήσαντι τοῖς ἰδίοις ἐν Ὀλόντι πολιτεύεσθαι] / μετέχοντι θίνων κ[αὶ ἀνθρωπίνων πάντων ὧν καὶ οἵ ἄλλοι Ὀλόντιοι μετέχοντι, κα]/ τὰ ταὐτὰ δὲ ἐξέστω [Ὀλοντίων τῶι βωλομένωι δικαιοπραγήσαντι τοῖς ἰδίοις Λατοῖ πολιτεύεσθαι με]/τέχοντι θίνων καὶ ἀ[ν]θρ[ωπίνων πάντων ὧν καὶ ἄλλοι Λάτοι μετέχοντι].⁵⁰

The mention of the concession, and the duty to stand by it, appears again in the closing of the oath, Copy A, L. 76; Copy B, LL. 186–190 and, finally, it appears again in the addition to the oath (?) as known only through Copy B, LL. 211–220: ... ἔδοξε Λατί/οις καὶ Ὀλοντίοις κοινᾶι / βωλευσαμένοις προσθέμεν / ‡ πρὸς τὰν φιλίαν καὶ συμμα/χίαν καὶ ἰσοπολιτείαν καὶ πρὸς τἆλλα φιλάνθρωπα / τὰ γεγονότα ταῖς πόλεσι ‡ / καὶ τὰν νῦν δόξαντα προσγρά/ψαι πρὸς τὰς προϋπαρχώσας παρ' / αὐτοῖς στάλας, χρήσιμα ὄν/τα καὶ συμφέροντα, ὅπως μᾶλ/λον αὔξηται ἀ φιλία.

For Chaniotis this concession serves as the rider to a decision that was taken before the actual agreement was subscribed and inscribed: The two *poleis* had decided later to add the alliance and the exchange of potential citizenship to a first treaty of 'friendship.' Therefore, Chaniotis suggests that a first *philia* agreement was reached in 110/9 BC and later *isopoliteia* and *symmachia* (109/8 BC) were added to it. But such an important afterthought seems suspicious. Given the uncertain textual tradition, I tend to dismiss this last section as evidence for the diplomatic process.

Be that as it may, these lines emphasize the weight potential citizenship had within diplomatic transactions even at the very end of the 2nd century BC in Crete, when more 'practical' sides to this grant seem to have been less common.

---

49   See CHANIOTIS 1996, p. 362. The lost text was published in 1728 and 1732 by Chishull and Maittaire, respectively.

50   Following previous editors, Guarducci restored an unlikely concession of *enktesis* in LL. 11 and 13 implying that only those who actually used potential citizenship could benefit from it. CHANIOTIS's comment on p. 373.

Treaties between Cretan and Non-Cretan *Poleis*

(59) *Allaria and Paros*

The stone was found in Crete in the 16th century and later moved to Venice. Now the inscription is stored in Berlin (inv. 1547). M. Guarducci describes the stone as broken on top with the upper part missing. The text dates to the 2nd century BC.

Ed.: *I.Cret.* II.i 2 (*ph*).
Cf.: J. and L. Robert *BE* 1940 117 on L. 4 (B); Bravo 1980, esp. p. 855 on L. 4 (B).

B

Ἀλλαριωτᾶν οἱ κόσμοι καὶ ἁ πόλις Παρίων τᾶι βουλᾶι
καὶ τῶι δάμωι χαίρεμ. παραγενομένων τῶν πρεσβευτᾶν ποτ' ἀμὲ, Φάνιός τε καὶ Δόρκω, οὓς ἀπεστείλατε
4   πρεσβεύσοντας περὶ τὠσύλω ποθ' ἁμέ, καὶ ἀνανε-
ωσαμένων αὐτῶν ἐν τᾶι πρεσβείαι κατὰ τὸ ψάφισμα
τὸ παρ' ὑμῶν τάν τε φιλίαν καὶ τὰν εὔνοιαν τὰν ὑ-
πάρχουσαν ταῖς πόλεσι ποτ' ἀλλάλας διαφυλάτ-
8   τεν, ἐπὶ κόσμων τῶν περὶ Φιλόνβροτον τὸν Εὐθυ-
μάχω, ἀγαθᾶι τύχαι δεδόχθαι Ἀλλαριωτᾶν
τοῖς κόσμοις καὶ τᾶι πόλι· ἐπαινέσαι μὲν τὸν
δᾶμον τῶν Παρίων διότι διαφυλάττει τὰν φιλίαν
12   καὶ τὰν εὔνοιαν πρὸς τὰν πόλιν τὰν ἁμάν, κατὰ
ταὐτὰ δὲ ὑπάρχειν καὶ Παρίοις τὰν φιλίαν καὶ τὰν εὔνοιαν παρὰ Ἀλλαριωτᾶν, ὅπως φαινώμεθα τὰ ὅμοι-
α τοῖς προαιρουμένοις ἀμὲ⟨ς⟩ συντελόντε⟨ς⟩. εἶμεν δὲ
16   Ἀλλαριώταις καὶ Παρίοις ἰσοπολιτείαν, μετέχω-
σιν τῶι τε Ἀλλαριώται ἐμ Πάρωι καὶ θείνων καὶ ἀνθρωπίνων, ὡσαύτως δὲ καὶ τῷ Παρίωι ἐν Ἀλλα-
ρίαι μετέχωσι καὶ θείνων καὶ ἀνθρωπίνων. ἐὰν ⟨δὲ⟩
20   συνδοκεῖ ταῦτα τῶι δάμωι τῶι Παρίων, ἀναγρα-
ψάντων αἱ πόλεις ἀμφότεραι ἐς στάλαν λιθίναν
καὶ ἀνθέντων Πάριοι μὲν ἐς τὸ ἱερὸν τᾶς Δάματρος,
Ἀλλαριῶται δὲ ἐς τὸ ἱερὸν τῶ[[ι]] Ἀπόλλωνος. ταῦ-
24   τα δὲ εἶναι ἐφ' ὑγιείαι καὶ σωτηρίαι τᾶν πόλεων
ἀμφοτερᾶν. ἐὰν δέ τι φαίνηται ὑμε⟨ῖ⟩ν προσθεῖναι
ἢ ἀφέλαι εὐχαριστῶμες. ἔρρωσθε

Text by *I.Cret.* Guarducci unless otherwise noted: L. 4 τὠσύλω as τῶ σύλω Robert, Bravo

Transl.: The *kosmoi* and the city of the Allarians greet the *boule* and the People of Paros. Since the ambassadors, Phanios and Dorkos, have come to us, (those) whom you have sent to report on the right of seizure by us and, since in their embassy, according to your decree, they remind us to preserve the reciprocal existing friendship and benevolence between the two cities, during the term of the *kosmoi* headed by Philombroton son of Euthymachos, to good fortune, it was decreed by the *kosmoi* and the city of Allaria to praise the *demos* of the Parians because it keeps (its) friendship and benevolence toward our *polis*. According to these things the Parians shall enjoy friendship and benevolence on the part of the Allarians, so that it is clear that we reciprocate the same honors for those who give us preference. There shall be isopolity for the Allarians and the Parians, an Allarian shall partake in everything divine and human in Paros, just like a Parian shall partake in everything divine and human in Allaria. If the *demos* of the Parians agrees to this, both *poleis* shall inscribe (the agreement) on a stone stele, the Parian in the sanctuary of Demetra, the Allaria in that of Apollo. These things shall serve to (protect) the health and safety of both cities. If it seems that anything shall be added or taken out we will do it gladly. Be well.

Allaria

Modern knowledge about Allaria is limited.[51] The very location of this town is uncertain. According to the most widespread hypothesis, the city was located in the northwestern part of Crete.[52] Inscriptions concerning this city are few; one text found in Thera relates the dealings between this island and the Cretan city for the liberation of prisoners that had been taken from both sides.[53] The volumes of Cretan inscriptions edited by Guarducci preserve the concession of *asylia* to Teos on the part of Allaria in the first round of inquiries and our text.[54] A few of these documents point already to the possible active participation of this town in piracy-related initiatives.

---

51   See SPYRIDAKIS 1983, pp. 11–13.
52   Guarducci, *I.Cret.* II.i located it around Eleutherna. Other hypotheses in SPYRIDAKIS 1983, p. 11.
53   *IG.* XII 3 328 now BIELMAN 1994, no. 54; middle of the 3rd century BC.
54   RIGSBY 1996, pp. 312–313 no. 151.

Paros

The sources for the history of Paros in the Hellenistic period are mainly epigraphical and very sparse.[55] The island possibly shared in many of the events in which the Cyclades were involved. Paros was a member of the League of the Nesiotai, at least while the league was under Ptolemaic control. It is uncertain whether Paros participated in the league after it came under Rhodes's patronage.[56] The agreement of potential citizenship with Allaria is often cited as a sign of the independence of the island-city in foreign policy, which, however, must not have direct bearing on its membership in the league. Berranger-Auserve has also devoted a few pages to the relationship between Paros and Crete, noting that several inscriptions testify to frequent contacts and probably good relations between the islands.[57]

The stone preserves a dossier containing the end of a cover letter (A, which I have not reproduced here) that establishes that Allaria had to receive a lawful copy of the document and the letter/decree (B) of Allaria that testifies to the grant of potential citizenship.

Paros had initiated the diplomatic contact by sending an embassy to Allaria about τὠσύλω. These letters must be read as τῷ σύλῳ, namely, that Paros must have made a request to the Allarians for personal inviolability. The Allarians' response on this point is extremely generic: they use a rather vague language that becomes precise only with the concession of potential citizenship. This grant is curious, too, because it establishes already reciprocal potential citizenship, to be later ratified by Paros. Other similar instances exist, but in these parallel cases plenipotentiary ambassadors appear who have thus the authority to conclude the exchange of *isopoliteia*, for example *Milet* I 3 150 = no. 7, or

---

55   BERRANGER-AUSERVE 2000, esp. pp. 116–131 tries to reconstruct the events in this period.
56   BERRANGER-AUSERVE 2000, p. 122.
57   BERRANGER-AUSERVE 2000, pp. 124–126. One text in particular has attracted scholarly attention, *SEG* XXXII 825, an honorary decree from Paros for one of its citizens, Timesiphon son of Epianax. According to LL. 2–3: "he led three embassies to Crete on the repayment of the debt that the city owed." The first editor, ORLANDOS 1973, dated the text to the early 2nd century BC and connected it with the grant of potential citizenship to Allaria. He thought that Paros had contracted the debt mentioned in *SEG* XXXII 825 with Allaria. This interpretation was not very compelling even before the new date for the text was suggested by LAMBRINOUDAKIS-WÖRRLE 1983, p. 290, namely, the middle of the 2nd century BC, and NIGDELIS 1989 followed by CANALI DE ROSSI 1997, no. 357 i.e., after the Mithridatic Wars. SPYRIDAKIS 1983 thought that "Crete" referred to the Cretan *Koinon* and to the alleged epidemic in Paros of 188 BC, as Orlandos had also suggested. On the epidemic see BERRANGER-AUSERVE 2000, p. 124. Nigdelis instead argues, I believe rightly, that the text is not related to *I. Cret.* II ii 1, as it belongs to the early Republican period, see EILERS 2002, pp. 214–216.

examples of cities offering the grant with a request of reciprocation *SEG* XXIX 1149 = no. 22 (Temnos and Teos). The closest instance is perhaps Pergamon's embassy to Temnos, *AvP* VIII.I.5 = no. 20, although with a different tone, in which the concession of a grant of *isopoliteia* that figures as the highest grant, among others, also includes plenipotentiary ambassadors who were entrusted with the duty of completing the procedure. The impression that the treaty between Allaria and Paros gives instead, although this is not corroborated by any additional evidence, is that Allaria grants potential citizenship to avoid conceding personal inviolability. It thus avoids granting the one concession that Paros must have requested, perhaps in the attempt to curb Allarian piratical raids, and offers instead a further tie of friendship that was, however, no guarantee against attacks—at least in what we would now call international law.[58]

(60)   *Mylasa and (mostly) Unknown Cretan Cities*

In his work on *asylia*, Rigsby has collected 12 fragmentary decrees that testify to intense contacts between Cretan cities and Mylasa during the 2nd century BC.[59] These texts belong to a wider dossier (23 texts) that Carless Unwin has analyzed in her 2017 book.[60] These two scholars, along with others, have noted the similarities between these texts and the *asylia* dossiers for Teos and Tenos. It is, however, uncertain whether we are dealing with a truly comparable set of documents.[61]

Equally uncertain is whether these texts contain any grant of potential citizenship or mentioned such a relationship as existing in the past. Gawantka has suggested that two of these texts could have included it on the basis of a *metechein* clause. However, before and after the clause, the context is either

---

[58] For possible piratical raids of Allaria in the Cyclades see BIELMAN 1994, no. 54 (Thera and Allaria). GAWANTKA 1975, p. 117 notes the lack of the concession of *asylia* and in n. 56 draws a difficult conclusion for which: "Die Tatsache, daß in diesem Dekret die Asylie formal nicht erhalten ist, beweist nur, daß sie dieses Mal in der Isopolitie inbegriffen gedacht wurde. Wie die anderen genannten Beispiele zeigen, war das keineswegs immer der Fall, zumindest war diese Ableitung nicht selbstverständlich (…)."

[59] RIGSBY 1996, pp. 407–415. The historical context is uncertain; for a possible context see CHANIOTIS 1996, esp. p. 44.

[60] CARLESS UNWIN 2017, esp. pp. 137–160. She collects the texts in her Appendix 2, while esp. at pp. 155–160 tries to better define the chronology and historical context for these documents.

[61] RIGSBY 1996, p. 407 leaves the question open. See also CURTY 1995, pp. 160–163, who rejects the hypothesis that these are *asylia* grants, and tries to define the origins of the alleged *syngeneia* between Mylasa and Crete on which see also MASTROCINQUE 2002, esp. p. 357. BLÜMEL in *I. Mylasa* speaks of "Symmachieverträge und Asyliedekrete."

undetermined or appears unrelated to such a grant.[62] A text that has been discovered later than the others instead contains a *metechein* clause that, for once, could be tied to a grant of potential citizenship.[63] The text, however, is very fragmentary and, on its basis, it is impossible to reach any sound conclusion. That the grant of potential citizenship was included in one or more texts belonging to this dossier is a possibility given the presence of this grant in many other Cretan texts and in many of the Teos-Cretan attested documents. The fragmentary state of the inscriptions, however, is such as to suggest that we stop here.

Conclusions

Numerous pieces of evidence for potential citizenship come from the islands where this tool was used widely and with all the flexibility it allowed. If we consider Crete separately, it is possible to note that in the islands the award of potential citizenship was in use already at the end of the 4th century BC when it mostly served the purpose of establishing diplomatic relations that could have immediate political consequences. Later texts reveal that this tool was used at a 'federal level,' be that inside a federation, to facilitate the relations among its members (Lesbian League), or in international politics (Mytilene and Thessaly). One more piece of evidence from the islands stands out: the grant *ad personam* from Tenos to a man from Kyrene that may be the only actual implementation act of isopolity that has survived in the epigraphic record.

Isopolity in Crete deserves a separate treatment. Its use is indeed exceptional from several points of view. Even if it has been already well studied by A. Chaniotis, it is appropriate to repeat that two traits characterize exchanges of potential citizenship *within* Crete: (1) isopolity was often included in agreements that were military alliances and (2) isopolity was often granted together with additional civic awards such as *epigamia* and *enktesis*. However, a dependency relationship among these grants did not exist, nor was potential citizenship part of other regulations that often follow the grant, as happens for example in the agreement between Hierapytna and Priansos (*I.Cret.* III.iii 4 = Chaniotis 1996, pp. 255–264 no. 28 = no. 52). This treaty is often used as a template for Cretan potential citizenship, but in truth that concession is only briefly

---

62 *I.Mylasa* 643 = GAWANTKA 1975, K 21= RIGSBY 1996, p. 408 no. 189, LL. 13–15: ... καὶ ἦμεν π]ρόξενον καὶ εὐεργέταν / [τᾶς πόλιος -------]Ν πάντων ἀμῶν μετε/[--- ἀνθρ]ωπίνων ἀρετᾶς ἕνεκα κτλ.; *I.Mylasa* 650 = GAWANTKA 1975, K 22= RIGSBY 1996, pp. 410–411 no. 196, LL. 15–17: ἐπαινῆσθαι τὸμ Μυλασ[έων δᾶμον καὶ στεφα/νῶσθαι αὐτὸν μετ᾿ἀνα[γορεύσιος -----]/ καὶ εὐεργεσίαι θείων [τε καὶ ἀνθρωπίνων πάν]/των μέτοχον ἀρετᾶ[ς ἕνεκα κτλ.

63 See RIGSBY 1996, p. 415 no. 209, LL. 10–11. This text is, however, again extremely fragmentary.

mentioned in a text that must be contextualized in a more complex historical scenario (LL. 1–12) that saw Gortyn's involvement, too. Here potential citizenship is granted in association with *enktesis* and *epigamia* within the same line. Immediately follows the clause that establishes that lawful members of these communities could conduct financial transitions according to the law. Starting with L. 18 the text regulates other numerous issues (cultivation, transportation of goods, and so on) for Hierapytnans in Priansos and *vice versa*. These clauses are part of the agreement but do not depend on isopolity; these themes were at stake between these two cities and the concessions of *isopoliteia*, *enktesis*, and *epigamia* allowed the cities to discuss them—and others—on a new level of 'familiarity.' If we want to see this agreement as exemplary then it can only be because it shows that grants such as *isopoliteia*, *enktesis*, and *epigamia* could help establish a new and stronger diplomatic platform.

Another detail worth reflecting upon is the frequent attestation of Hierapytna as a partner in *isopoliteia* agreements. The city mostly signed agreements that included isopolity with neighboring cities, which in fact later came under its control. One of the most common explanations, also within the excellent book by Chaniotis, is that Hierapytna, and maybe other cities (?), used *isopoliteia* to find new lifelines for their population excess. But we know that Hierapytna pursued a rather aggressive policy and took the areas of interest for itself. It is possible that we need to look at these treaties from a different perspective, namely, from that of the partner city: these treaties could indeed appear to be attempts to regulate land control. Isopolity was used a 'defensive' not an 'offensive' tool.

I have also divided the treaties signed between Cretan communities from those signed between a Cretan and a non-Cretan community. While in this chapter I have included only a text from Allaria (*I.Cret.* II.i 2) and a short discussion of a few fragmentary documents that show contact between the city of Mylasa in Karia and several Cretan cities, I here mention other texts that testify to the use, real or alleged, of potential citizenship between a Cretan and a non-Cretan community: the fictional decree concerning the Cretan *Koinon* and Magnesia (14) and the decree between Magnesia and Hierapytna (16) as well as several texts testifying to the concession of *asylia* to Teos.[64] The two texts from Magnesia could be contextualized within the local campaign to obtain *asylia* from several communities of the Greek world, which suggests that the tool of *isopoliteia* was seen as extremely appropriate to deal with the communities of this island. It has been suggested this tool was 'born' in Miletos, but its frequent use in the island and its very adoption even in a fictional decree indicates to me that Crete should be another candidate for the original home of *isopoliteia*.

---

64 See *infra* on *isopoliteia* and *asylia*.

PART 3

Asylia *and* Isopoliteia

∴

CHAPTER 8

Asylia and *Isopoliteia*

The surviving documents attesting to both *asylia* and *isopoliteia* reveal two things: (1) this combination was not as common as it is normally thought and (2) (potential) citizenship can appear as an additional, later grant to 'renewals/reminders' that are associated with older recognitions of inviolability or it can be the starting point for a diplomatic exchange that leads to the concession of inviolability.

In his work Gawantka suggests that potential citizenship 'reinforces' a grant of *asylia*.[1] The evidence that should support this statement comes mainly from the second wave of *asylia* recognitions for Teos on the part of Cretan cities. Here potential citizenship is granted along with other additional concessions and duplicates the general Cretan practice of sealing important agreements by establishing ties that rely on practical concessions, such as *epigamia*, *enktesis*, and even *(iso?)politeia*. While Gawantka's theory is substantially correct, the author focuses on one detail, namely, the prominence of *asylia*, and neglects the larger issue at stake.

In the agreements preserved between Kos and two Sicilian cities, the grant of potential citizenship predates the recognition of *asylia* and is used to legitimize—along with other claims—the Koan request. Here "*isopoliteia*" appears as a long-standing relationship between Kos and Kamarina and Kos and Gela. The Sicilian cities grant *asylia* on the basis of ὑπαρχόντων τε αὐτοῖς παρ'ἀμεῖν τῶν μεγίστων καὶ ἀναγκαιοτάτων, namely, *syngeneia*, *oikeiotes*, and *isopoliteia*. This use of *isopoliteia*, which must have been a long-standing grant, contrasts, in a way, what the Cretan evidence testifies: for the Sicilian cities isopolity worked as basis for the grant of *asylia*; in Crete *asylia* stays and *isopoliteia* helps reinforce the diplomatic process.

---

1 GAWANTKA 1975, p. 164; and on p. 116, after considering the case of the 'second wave' of Cretan texts for Teos and, after defining the meaning of isopolity in these documents writes: "Die Asylie wurde anscheinend gegenüber Leuten, die formal nicht als Fremde, sondern als Bürger (because of isopoliy) galten, als eine bindendere Verpflichtung aufgefaßt." This is not the place to discuss in detail the different views on *asylia*; on the most recent bibliography see SABA 2009/10(b), pp. 294–296; recently P. KATÓ 2014, pp. 97–108 has reminded us again that often these diplomatic and political instruments were flexible and were given with more than one objective.

Another *asylia* dossier that contains evidence for grants of potential citizenship comes from Tenos. These texts are difficult to interpret. The first alleged piece of evidence for the grant of *isopoliteia*, a Phokian grant, does not include potential citizenship at all, while the second probably did, but it is very fragmentary.

Finally, the Teian grant of potential citizenship to three Syrian cities, which I treat first because of its somewhat peculiar nature, stands out in a rather uncomfortable way for the historian. This concession has been interpreted in various ways, but I hold that it should be read within a broader institutional context and diplomatic tradition, rather than with a focus only on the royal context of the grant.

(61)   Teos and the Three Syrian Cities

This long inscription, found in 1963 and published by P. Herrmann soon after its discovery, is recorded on four blocks. It contains at least two Teian decrees, a very fragmentary third text, and a letter of Antiochos III to the city of Teos. The context and content of the dossier have led scholars to date it to ca. 204–202 BC,[2] when the king reestablished his authority in the area.

With the second decree of this dossier Teos voted lavish honors for the king and queen Laodike because of the benefactions they had bestowed on the city.[3] To these honors the Teians attached an unusual announcement of a grant of citizenship.

---

2 There is no universal consensus on the date; for a discussion see VINCI 2008/9.
3 Block I LL. 17–20: (king Antiochos) παρελθὼν εἰς τὴν ἐκκλησίαν αὐτός / ἀνῆκε τὴ[ν] πόλιν καὶ τὴγ χώραν ἡμῶν ἱερὰν καὶ ἄσυλον καὶ ἀφορολό/γητον κ[αὶ] τῶν ἄλλων ὧν ἐφέρομεν συντάξεων βασιλεῖ Ἀττά/λωι ὑπεδέξατο ἀπολυθήσασθαι ἡμᾶς δι'αὐτοῦ (...) text by HERRMANN 1965, on these lines see esp. pp. 51–54. On the dossier see *SEG* XXVI 1307, the complete text in *SEG* XLI 1003, see J. and L. ROBERT, *BE* 1964 495. For *asylia* see RIGSBY 1996, esp. pp. 280–285; on the date see MA 2002, Appendix II. KOTSIDU 2000, no. 239 republished the text with a short commentary; McCabe *Teos* 31. See also GAUTHIER 1985, pp. 169–175 with text and translation in French.

This grant appears almost as an appendix to the second decree, LL. 100–104; I reproduce here Block II, LL. 90–113:[4]

90   ... ἐπεὶ δὲ κ[α]-
[λῶς ἔ]χον ἐστὶν ἅμα ταῖς ἄλλαις ταῖς δεδομέναις παρὰ τῆς πόλε-
[ως τῷ β]ασιλεῖ τιμαῖς καὶ ἀκόλουθον τῇ τε τοῦ βασιλέως καὶ τῶν
[φίλων] εὐνοίαι πρὸς τὸν δῆμον καὶ τῇ παρ' ἡμῶν πρός τε τὸν βασι-
[λέα καὶ] τοὺς φίλους αὐ[τ]οῦ ἐκτενείαι καθάπερ εἰς κοινὸν τεθῆναι τὸ
95 [τῶν ἐ]πωνύμων πόλεων τῶν τοῦ βασιλέως προγόνων τὰ δε[δο]-
[μένα κ]αὶ δοθησόμενα παρὰ τοῦ βασιλέως ἀγαθὰ τῶι δήμωι (ἵνα) ψη[φισ]-
[θείσης] αὐτοῖς πᾶσιν παρ' ἡμῖν τῆς πολιτείας καὶ ἑτοιμότεροι π[ρὸς]
[τὰς εὐ]εργεσίας ὑπάρχωσι σπεύδοντες διὰ παντός, καθά[π]ερ
[καλό]ν ἐστιν, ὑπὲρ τῆς ἰδίας πατρίδος [κ]αὶ [τὴ]ν προϋπάρχουσαν τοῖς
100 [...]οις πρὸς αὐτοὺς ἀνανεωσόμεθα φιλίαν· τύχῃ ἀγαθῇ· τοὺ[ς] στρα-
[τηγο]ὺς καὶ τοὺς τιμούχους εἰσενεγκεῖν εἰς τὰς ἐπιούσας ἀρχαι-
[ρεσία]ς καθότι δοθήσεται πολιτέα τῶι δήμωι τῷ Ἀντιοχέων τῶμ
[πρὸς] Δάφνηι καὶ τῶι δήμωι τῶι Σελευκέων τῶν ἐμ Πιερίαι [κα]ὶ τῶι δή-
104 [μωι τ]ῶι Λαοδικέων τῶμ πρὸς θαλάσσῃ· ἀναγράψαι δὲ [κ]αὶ τὸ ψή-
[φισμα τ]όδε εἰς τὴν παραστάδα τοῦ νέω τοῦ Διονύσω κα[ὶ κ]αθιερώ-
[σαι, τῆ]ς δὲ ἀναγραφῆς τοῦ ψηφίσματος ἐπιμεληθῆνα[ι τ]οὺς ἐνεσ-
[τηκότ]ας τα[μί]ας· ἵνα δὲ ὁ βασιλεὺς Ἀντίοχος καὶ ἡ ἀ[δ]ελφὴ αὐτοῦ
108 [βασί]λισσα [Λ]αοδίκη εἰδήσωσι τὴν εὐχαριστίαν τοῦ [δ]ήμου, ἀποδεῖ-
[ξαι π]ρεσβευτὰς τρὶς ἤδη οἵτινες παραγενόμενοι πρὸς αὐτοὺς τὸ
[μὲν ψ]ήφισμα τόδε ἀποδώσουσι καὶ ἀσπασάμεν[ο]ι ὑπὲρ τοῦ δήμου
[καὶ] συνησθέντες ἐπὶ τῶι ὑγιαίνειν αὐτοὺς [καὶ] πράσσειν ὃν τρόπον
112 [αὐτ]οί τε βούλονται καὶ ἡμεῖς τοῖς θεοῖς εὐχόμεθα καὶ ἐμφανίσαν-
[τες] τὰς [τι]μὰς τὰς ἐψ[η]φισμ[έ]νας καὶ δ[η]λώσαντες αὐτοῖς [-]

---

4 The most recent edition is KOTSIDU 2000, no. 239 who uses Herrmann's text including Merkelbach's and Dunst's restorations, which, however, do not appear in the translation, which is Herrmann's. The incongruities between text and translation have led me to revert to HERRMANN's 1965 text altogether, although I too would prefer καθά[π]ερ / [εἴ γ' ἔ]νεστιν in L. 99 (MERKELBACH 1968, pp. 173–174) to καθά[π]ερ / [καλό]ν ἐστιν as in HERRMANN 1965. I do not think that the restoration by DUNST 1968, pp. 170–173 L. 100 Τηΐ]οις can be accepted, on which see MA 1999, p. 314: "... in these decrees, the Teians refer to themselves in the first person singular or as 'our city'."

Transl.: LL. 90–110: ... since along with the other honors that the city has granted to the king and following the benevolent attitude of the king and his friends toward the *demos* and our zeal toward him and his friends, it seems appropriate to extend to the people of the cities that are named after his ancestors as a common good the privileges that we have been granted and will be granted by the king. This should be so that after citizenship has been voted for all of them, they are more eager to help in everything, according to their possibilities (L. 99: καθά[π]ερ / [εἴ γ'ἔ] νεστιν), just as they do for their own city. Also we renew the preexisting friendship toward them. To good fortune. The *strategoi* and the *timouchoi* shall present to the next assembly a document to vote citizenship for the *demos* of Antiocheia by Daphne, the *demos* of Seleukeia in Pieria and that of Laodikeia by the Sea. The decree shall be inscribed on the *parastas* of the temple of Dionysos and be dedicated. The treasurers in office are responsible for the inscription. So that the king Antiochos and his sister the queen Laodike see that the *demos* is thankful, three ambassadors shall be chosen who will give them the decree and ...

These lines testify to Teos's intent to grant citizenship to three cities whose main sign of distinction (to Teos) was that they were named after Antiochos's ancestors. This unusual text contains the only attested plan to concede potential citizenship that, to some degree and indirectly, involves a king and his friends. In the past these individuals were thought to be the actual targets of the planned concession of potential citizenship.[5]

This text is exceptional from many points of view and, as Gauthier rightly noted, it would be inappropriate to draw general conclusions on (potential) citizenship on its basis, as Gawantka does, by turning this text into the *exemplum* for a political, practical use of grants of potential citizenship.[6] More importantly, Gawantka thinks that the royal involvement would show that kings could also be honored with *isopoliteia*. But neither this text nor other surviving documents allows drawing this inference or thinking that it testifies to an active role of the kings, their friends, or other non-*polis*-related officials in

---

5 GAUTHIER 1985, pp. 153–154 and again pp. 169–175 on the extraordinary character of the grant. On p. 154, in a general context, he hypothesizes the incapacity of the *polis* to find other forms to honor a noncivic partner. For this grant as honor to the *philoi* see already HERRMANN 1965, pp. 79–84.
6 GAWANTKA 1975, pp. 119–127, also p. 46 suggests that this decree shows that this tool could have been used (routinely?) to honor kings, but see GAUTHIER 1985, esp. pp. 153 and 169–171.

agreements that include a grant of potential citizenship. This view would be unacceptable, since its concession was a city's prerogative.[7]

With this document Teos does not (yet) grant potential citizenship but only announces that it would soon vote citizenship for three prominent cities of northern Syria, namely, Antioch, Laodikeia, and Seleukeia.[8] *For Teos* these distant communities did not play a direct role in the events taking place in Teos or its region. This simple consideration prompts the question of why Teos planned to concede this grant.

Herrmann and Gauthier suggest that it was Teos's way to praise Antiochos's *philoi* and, indirectly, the already lavishly honored royal couple.[9] The inscription mentions *philoi* twice, in Teos with the king (Block I, L. 23 and L. 94), but who they were and where they came from, remains unknown. While it is possible that some friends came from these Syrian cities, this origin is far from certain.[10]

As I mentioned, Gawantka speaks of a practical/political scope for the planned grant of potential citizenship, because the Teians say that they would seek further benefactions from the Syrian cities, LL. 97–98.[11] But this generic

---

7   In an article devoted to royal *philoi*, SAVALLI 2001(b), p. 293 states "essi (*viz. philoi*) promuovono lo sviluppo urbano, sia attraverso la fondazione di πόλεις o di κατοικίαι, sia attraverso il rafforzamento, tramite isopoliteia o simpoliteia, di città già esistenti." Neither king nor *philoi* used 'isopolity' to further their plans. Savalli surely refers to the case of Arsinoe and Nagidos, pp. 283–284, and shares the view for which the even the alleged 'isopolity' was Thraseas's initiative; but see SABA 2012, pp. 159–170 on this inscription and the introduction, pp. 25–27.

8   Here I only attempt to stress the distant relationship these cities had with Teos. These cities formed, together with Apameia on the Axos/Orontes, the Syrian Tetrapolis. STRAB. XVI.2.4. On the Tetrapolis see COHEN 2006, pp. 28–30; pp. 80–93 on Antioch; pp. 111–116 on Laodikeia; pp. 126–135 on Seleukeia. On Hellenistic Syria see MILLAR 1987, pp. 110–133. The reason for Apameia's exclusion is unknown and a matter for speculation. HERRMANN 1965, p. 82 suggests that since this privilege was extended only to eponymous cities of the king's ancestors, L. 95, Apameia was excluded because Apame, bride of the founder Seleukos, was Achaemenid by blood. On the importance of eponymy see RIGSBY 1996, pp. 257–260 no. 111. According to another hypothesis, HERRMANN 1965, p. 84, esp. n. 77, with the comment by SAVALLI 1998, pp. 220–221, since Apameia began as a military center, this community may not have had *polis* status from the beginning. But by the end of the 3rd century BC Apameia was the capital of a satrapy. STRAB. XVI.2.4; see COHEN 2006, p. 98, n. 6. On Apameia see EL-ZEIN 1972, esp. pp. 15–77.

9   HERRMANN 1965, esp. pp. 79–84 and later also GAUTHIER 1985, pp. 169–175.

10 SAVALLI 1998, pp. 102 and 217. The slim prosopographic data on royal *philoi* confirm that this is a viable option, but nothing more.

11 GAWANTKA 1975, pp. 127–132 claims that this practice can be found as early as the 5th century BC in Athens, but see GAUTHIER 1985, pp. 152–153. He goes too far when he asks how the relations among the Syrian cities would have changed in light of potential citizenship with Teos, GAWANTKA 1975, p. 46, n. 13.

claim is expressed in a language that refers to a diplomatic operation rather than to actual goals.

Context, *Asylia*, and *(Iso?)politeia*

The two long Teian decrees for Antiochos III were passed at different, but close, times as responses to the benevolent attitude that the king had shown the city, ultimately by recognizing Teos and its territory as *hieros kai asylos*. Rigsby has discussed the royal origin of this recognition by noting that it is unlikely it came unprompted.[12] When it did come, however, together with the exemption from heavy Attalid tributes, it was celebrated lavishly with the creation of a new festival for the royal couple, including a cult image of the king and a fountain for the queen.

In 1985 Gauthier stressed that the surviving decrees do not contain any honor for the *philoi* and that the Teians might have faced the problem of how to remedy this circumstance: a possible solution then was to honor them indirectly by using civic grants for their cities of origin. Gauthier must be right when he excludes a more political/pragmatic use of the grant, but to support his interpretation, namely, that this concession was an indirect way to honor the *philoi*, one must assume their Syrian origin.

Perhaps another approach to this concession is possible: the matter should be put into a broader institutional context. We know that Antiochos had just granted *asylia* to Teos thus prompting the lavish honors to which the proposal to vote citizenship for three eponymous cities was added. Of course, we do not know the terms of the alleged future grant, but this incomplete knowledge is immaterial. My hypothesis is that Teos responded to Antiochos's concessions, and especially to *asylia*, a typically Hellenistic tool, with an equally important concession, *politeia*, typical of the Hellenistic period in its 'isopolitical' form and unique because only cities could bestow it. This suggestion in a way resembles that of Gauthier, but with a positive connotation for the grant.

In the text, the Teians could have used the term *isopoliteia*, since this grant is not the actual concession, but rather the announcement of a project. But they did not.

Asylia and *(iso)politeia* appear together in other instances and their relationship must be explored further.[13] Following a roughly geographical arrangement, I start with Teian documents.

---

12   RIGSBY 1996, p. 283. MA 2002, appendix II also discusses the origin of this concession.
13   The type of *asylia* I refer to is territorial, but some of the decrees here included mention personal inviolability, too. On this see RIGSBY 1996, esp. pp. 19–22; GAUTHIER 1972, pp. 266–282; SCHLESINGER 1933, esp. p. 53.

Asylia for Teos: the Decrees of the Second Series (Crete)

After Antiochos granted *asylia* to the city and territory of Teos in ca. 203 BC, Teian embassies were sent to several communities to obtain the same recognition. Later, a new mission was sent to 'renew' or (better) remind the grantors of the existing *asylia*.[14] No internal data can help determine the exact date of these reminders. Both Guarducci and Rigsby think that the lettering of the documents attesting to them, belongs to the first rather than to the second half of the 2nd century BC. Several decrees come from Crete, and possibly one from Knidos; five testify to (potential) citizenship.[15] I limit myself to reproduce very small parts of the decrees by using Rigsby's recent and reliable editions to which I refer the reader.[16]

(62)   Teos and Eranna

Rigsby 1996, pp. 318–319 no. 155 presents this text that was originally inscribed on a block found at Tepecik and later transported to Ireland.

The city of Eranna (or Erannos) has not been located securely; Faure suggests that it was in the center of the modern district of Lasithi, in eastern Crete.[17] We know very little about this town, which figures among the allies of Eumenes in the agreement signed in 183 BC along with 30 other Cretan communities.[18]

The decree by Eranna begins with a declaration that the *demos* of the Teians, which was *syngenes* and *philos*, had sent an embassy to Eranna. LL. 6–13 of the decree specify that the Teian ambassadors asked that Eranna inscribe its old decree on *asylia*, which is lost to us and must have never been published by the Cretan city.[19] Eranna agreed to the request, declared it would "stand by

---

14   RIGSBY 1996, pp. 158–159 says the status of the city as *asylos* never elapsed. Teos mainly asked the Cretan cities to inscribe and display these old grants.

15   RIGSBY 1996, esp. pp. 281–292 on Teos's *asylia*. It would be easier to cite bibliography that has not commented on these documents than the bibliography that has. Here I limit myself to the works that are most relevant to my topic.

16   This *asylia* dossier was inscribed on different blocks that, MICHEL, *Rec.* esp. p. 63 said, "sont maintenant disperses dans les villages des environs" and probably followed a geographical order in their original arrangement. For a history of their publication and, at least for RIGSBY 1996, pp. 307–322 nos. 147–157, location, see VINCI 2008/9, pp. 190–192. The blocks containing these inscriptions were moved to Ireland, where they remain today.

17   FAURE 1993, p. 69.

18   *I.Cret.* IV 179.

19   Ἐραννίων / [ἐπειδ]ὴ ὁ δᾶμος ὁ Τηΐων ἐκ παλαιῶν / [χρόνων] συγγενὴς ὑπάρχων καὶ φίλος / [δι]ὰ προγόνων τᾶς τῶν Ἐραννίων πόλιος / ἐξαπέσταλκεν ψάφισμα καὶ πρεγ/γευτὰς Ἡρόδοτον καὶ Μενεκλῆν, πα/ρακαλίων ἀμὲ συντηρεῖν τὰ δεδομέ/να τίμια ὑπὸ τῶν προγόνων ἀμίων καὶ / ἐπὶ πλεῖον αὔξειν, καὶ ὅπως ἀναγρα/φῇ τὸ πρότερον δόγμα ὃ κατεβάλοντο / οἱ πρόγονοι περὶ τᾶς ἀσυλίας καὶ καθιε/ρώσιος τᾶς τῶν Τηΐων πόλιος καὶ τᾶς / χώρας, ἐν ὁποίωι κα κρίνωμεν ἱερῶι ...

its old decision" (LL. 24–31), and added defense clauses in favor of Teos along with other grants. Among them, in LL. 37–40, figures the concession of potential citizenship: ὅπως δὲ εἴδωντι Τήϊοι / τὰν Ἐραννίων εὔνοιαν ἂν ἔχοντι πο/τ'αὐτός, δεδόχθαι ἦμεν Τηΐους πολίτας / Ἐραννίων, εἶναι δὲ αὐτοῖς καὶ ἀτελείαν καὶ ἔνκτησιν γᾶς καὶ οἰκίας.[20] These lines contain standard clauses affirming that the Teians are to be citizens of Eranna and have *ateleia* and *enktesis* of land and house, as can often be found in Crete.

(63) *Teos and Biannos*
The last complete publication of the decree can be found in Rigsby 1996, pp. 319–321 no. 156 = *I.Cret.* I.vi 2, who reports that the text was inscribed underneath the text of Eranna.

Biannos was located in the hinterland of southeast Crete, west of Hierapytna. Historical data on this town are few. In her introduction to the history of the cities in *I.Cret.*, Guarducci notes that Biannos also figures among Eumenes's allies of 183 BC.

Both *asylia* decrees from Biannos to Teos survive and Rigsby points out that the first decree (p. 307, no. 146 = *I.Cret.* I.vi 1) already contains the clause pertaining to its engraving and therefore its publication, LL. 10–11. It is unclear what the Teian ambassadors asked with the second embassy, since in LL. 10–13 one can read the statement of the ambassador on Teos's status as *asylos* to Biannos's authorities. The latter answer with claims of friendship, the promise to inscribe the decree (again?), and to make the Teians "*isopolitas* and *ateleis* in war and peace" (LL. 24–26).[21] To this statement follow provisions for providing help to Teos, if under attack.

As Rigsby has suggested, it is possible that the first decree had never been inscribed and the Teians request it would. The text does not elaborate on the grant of potential citizenship, but generally refers to the award and uses the noun *isopolitas* to describe the future status of the grantees. This term and its derivate are more common in Crete than in the rest of the Greek world, but, when it refers to the institution, it has the same meaning: the term can indicate

---

20 LL. 37–43: (…) So that the Teians see the benevolence that the people of Eranna have for them, it has been decreed that the Teians be citizens of Eranna, they shall have *ateleia* and the right to own land and house.

21 LL. 22–32 … ἀναγράψομεν δὲ τό τε πρότερον / δόγμα ἐστάλαι λιθίναι καὶ ἀναθήσο/μεν ἐς τὸ τοῦ Ἄρεος ἱερόν, ποιοῦμεν / δὲ ὑμᾶς καὶ ἰσοπολίτας καὶ ἀτελεῖς / καὶ πολέμω καὶ εἰράνας, καὶ ἐάν τινες / ἐπὶ τὰν χώραν τὰν καθιερωμέναν / καὶ ἐπὶ τὰν πόλιν ἐπερχόμενοι πολεμῶ/σιν ἢ ἀφαιρῶνταί τι ὑμῶν, βοαθήσο/μεν καθότι ἄν ὦμεν δυνατοί· ἔν τε / τοῖς λοιποῖς πειρασόμεθα αἰεί τινος / ἀγαθῶ ὑμῖν παραίτιοι γίνεσθαι· (…)

a project, the promise to grant potential citizenship, or simply describe a legal status in abstract terms. Here we have an example of the last use.

(64) Teos and Mallia

Rigsby 1996, pp. 321–322 no. 157 = *I.Cret.* I.xix 2 reports that the text was inscribed underneath that of Biannos. The stone was later moved to Ireland; its original location, within a modern structure, made it impossible to read the last five lines.

Mallia was located on the south of the Lasithi. We know very little about the history of this town, and only through very sparse epigraphic material. This decree is indeed one of two preserved from this town. The first known decree contains an agreement that Mallia signed with the city of Lyttos, which possibly dates to the 3rd century BC. Mallia too figures among Eumenes's allies.[22] Rigsby stresses that this text alone mentions oracles for Teos.

The Mallians, like the cities of Eranna and Biannos, describe the *demos* of Teos as *syngenos* and *philos* and then address the issue of the grant of *asylia*. Mallia likewise promises to inscribe and display the agreement (LL. 11–14) and then asserts concisely that it will award to the Teians grants of *ateleia* and *isopoliteia* (LL. 14–15) followed by a defense clause.[23] Just as I noted in other instances, this text too does not dwell on the grant of potential citizenship but only briefly refers to it by using the term *isopoliteia*.

(65) Teos and the Arkades

The block containing the inscription was found in the cemetery at Gesusler. The text is inscribed under the closing lines of a decree possibly enacted by Knidos, through which, according to Rigsby, the two ambassadors travelled

---

22 The agreement with Lyttos can be found in *I.Cret.* I.xix.1 now also in CHANIOTIS 1996, pp. 208–213 no. 11; Eumenes's alliance is *I.Cret.* IV 179.

23 LL. 6–18: αὐτοὶ διελέγην ἀκολούθως τοῖς ἐν [τῶι ψαφίσματι κατακε]/χωρισμένοις, ὑπέρ τε τοῦ εἶναι ἱερὰν κα[ὶ ἄσυλον τὴν πόλιν, καὶ ὃ] / συνέστησαν διά τε τῶν χρησμῶ[ν τῶν δοθέντων τὰ μαντεῖα τὰ ἐν] / Δελφοῖς καὶ ἐν Διδύμοις, (LL. 9–10 on the content of the embassy) / ἔδοξεν ⟨Μ⟩αλλαίων τοῖς κόσμοις καὶ τᾶι πόλει ἀ[ποκρίνασθαι] / Τηίοις διότι καὶ ἐν τοῖς πρότερον χρόνοις δεδωκό[των τῶν προ]/γόνων ἡμῶν τὴν ἀσυλίαν καὶ καθιέρωσιν, εἰς στή[λην γράψαντες] / ἀναθήσομεν ἐς τὸ ἱερὸν τῶ Ζηνὸς τῶ Μοννιτίω· δ[ίδομεν δὲ αὐτοῖς] / καὶ ἀτέλειαν καὶ ἰσοπολιτείαν· (clauses on protection and personal inviolability follow). "They spoke (...) of their city being *hiera* and *asylos* and showed the response obtained through the oracles of Delphi and Didyma. (...). (L. 11) It was decided by the *kosmoi* and city of the Mallians to answer the Teians that since in the past our ancestors had recognized *asylia* and sacredness to their city, we will display the stele after it has been inscribed in the sanctuary of Zeus Monnitios. We give them *ateleia* and *isopoliteia* (15) ..."

on their way to Crete (Rigsby 1996, pp. 322–324 no. 159 = *I.Cret.* I.v 53, also *IKnidos* 802).

The Arkades formed a *koinon* of several villages in a mountainous area in south Lasithi. Both Teian embassies to this *koinon* that concern the recognition of *asylia* are attested epigraphically. From the town we have a few other documents testifying to (possibly) Gortyn's influence in the middle of the 3rd century BC.[24] This city is also among Eumenes's allies known for the year 183 BC.

Rigsby notes that this agreement spells out that the Teian embassy did not request only to publish again the old decision on *asylia*, but also other grants that the Arkades decided to concede, namely, the grants of *isopoliteia*, *enktesis* of land and house, and *ateleia*, LL. 35–38.[25] It is possible to assume that the Teians made the same request to all other communities they reached, but then this wish may have gone unfulfilled twice (or more, since our record is not complete).[26]

(66)   Teos and Hyrtakina

Rigsby 1996, p. 324 no. 160 = *I.Cret.* II.xv 2 reports that this block was found by the acropolis in 1924. I reproduce here LL. 3–10:

> [... ποιῆσαι Τηΐος] ἰσοπολίτας [καὶ] / [ἀτελεῖς καὶ πολέμω καὶ εἰρ]άνας, καὶ αἴ τίς
> [κα ἀδικήσηι αὐτὸς] συγγενέας καὶ ἱερὸς / [ἐόντας ἢ πολε]μῆι ἢ κατὰ γᾶν ἢ κατὰ θάλα-
> [σσαν καὶ παραιρῆ]ται τὰν χώραν τὰν καθιερωμέ[ν]αν, βοα[θή]σει ὁ δᾶμος ὁ Ὑρτακινίων καθὼς ἂν / δύναται μάλιστα· ἀναγράψαι δὲ τὰν ἀνανέ/ωσιν εἰς τὸ ἱερὸν τὸ τᾶς Ἥρας· (...)

---

24   See CHANIOTIS 1996, esp. no. 10 and no. 15 with commentaries.

25   LL. 29–38: ... βωλόμενοι οὖν καὶ ἡμεῖς τοῖς εὐνόως / διακειμένοις ἐν χάριτος μέρει μὴ λείπεσθαι, τό / τε πρότερον δόγμα ὃ ἔχετε παρ'ἡμῶν περὶ τᾶς / ἀσυλίας καὶ τᾶς καθιερώσιος τᾶς τε πόλιος καὶ τᾶς / χώρας ἀναγράψομεν, καθότι παρακαλεῖτε διὰ τοῦ / ψαφίσματος, εἰς τὸ ἱερὸν τοῦ Ἀσκλαπιοῦ, καὶ συν/τηρήσομεμ τὰ δεδομένα ὑμῖν φιλάνθρωπα· πα/ρακαλεσάντων δὲ ἀμὲ τῶν πρεσβευτᾶν δοῦναι / ὑμῖν ἰσοπολιτείαν καὶ ἔνκτησιν γᾶς καὶ οἰκίας καὶ ἀτέ/λειαν, ταῦτά τε δίδομεν ὑμῖν, (inviolability and defense clauses follow) ... "Since we also do not want to fall behind on what has been laid before us benevolently, we shall inscribe the former decree that you have from us on *asylia* and the consecration of the city and the land, as you ask with your decree, and display it in the sanctuary of Asklepios and we shall care for the *philanthropa* granted to you. Since the ambassadors have asked us to give you *isopoliteia* (37), right to own house and land and *ateleia*, we grant them to you."

26   RIGSBY 1996, pp. 316–318 no. 154 = *I.Cret.* II iii 2; RIGSBY 1996, p. 325 no. 161.

Hyrtakina was located on the southwest of Crete, on a hilly area away from the coast. This town, also ally to Eumenes II, must have granted *asylia* to Teos already at the end of the 3rd century BC, but the document has not survived. This fragmentary text preserves the second Teian embassy, to which Hyrtakina answers by bestowing *isopoliteia* and *ateleia* in war and peace, as Biannos did, to the Teians and adds protection clauses that mix personal with city-wide rights to inviolability.

Teos—Crete and the Awards of *Isopoliteia-Asylia*

The debate on the Teian dossier on *asylia* normally surrounds two points: the role of piracy and the meaning of *asylia*. It is often held that the Teian initiative was part of an effort directed to stop the piratical attacks that plagued Teos's life.[27] Even if we do not have proof to overrule this hypothesis, as Rigsby notes, piracy does not appear anywhere and it is probably best to suspend judgment.

Scholars have also interpreted variously the grants of *isopoliteia* that appear in these texts. Brulé thinks that these concessions automatically granted Teians access to Cretan courts, i.e., another form of judicial protection.[28] This view is doubtful: whether *symbola* were 'included' is unknown and highly unlikely. Additional privileges—especially if they pertained to such delicate a sphere—were always spelled out.

The text of the Arkades testifies to the Teians' explicit request for potential citizenship, and possibly also for *enktesis* and *ateleia*. One can assume that the Teians made the same requests to all the cities they visited, but two decrees of

---

27   BRULÉ 1978, pp. 94–105; GAWANTKA 1975, esp. p. 115; GAUTHIER 1972, esp. p. 280. KVIST 2003, on which see *SEG* LIII 932, devoted her contribution to the discussion of this topic, esp. pp. 208–212, on the second series. She discusses older bibliography and, by and large, shares the opinion that piracy played a central role in Teos's initiative. She holds, however, that between the first and the second request Teos's attitude had changed and so Crete's interpretation and use of piracy. A new, different way of marketing the same product emerged: at the time of the second series the Cretans offered 'protection' from piracy rather than being themselves the threat. Over the topic of Teos and piracy looms the well-known inscription that SAHIN published in 1994, pp. 1–40, which has been recently revised in text and interpretation by MEIER 2017, pp. 115–188 in what must be now considered an essential study on this text. Meier indeed presents not only a new edition, but redates and reinterprets this text. In 2018 HAMON, pp. 334–374 presented his contribution to the edition of the text. The *communis opinio* holds that Cretan and Aitolian piracy were extensive and much feared. PERLMAN 1999 has tried to reevaluate the truthfulness of these testimonies by analyzing the ancient stereotypical representation of the Cretans, but evidence is thin. GUIZZI's 2001 similar attempt, in his monograph on Hierapytna, meets the same problem.

28   BRULÉ 1978, p. 99.

the second series, from Aptera and an unknown city, do not contain potential citizenship.[29] Did these cities deny the request?

Cretan communities were well acquainted with this tool and used it among themselves often in association with military alliances and friendship.[30] They also tended to add other grants to potential citizenship. This circumstance makes the Teian request and the answers it obtained not at all extraordinary from an institutional point of view. But the texts also show that *isopoliteia* was valued as a seal in association with other grants that confer to it a more practical status. Potential citizenship to Teos—or other towns outside Crete—was certainly less charged than it was when it was granted among Cretan communities, but even there it was a diplomatic tool to seal mainly *symmachiai*. Interestingly, when Crete is involved in a grant of potential citizenship, more 'tangible' grants figure in the texts. This is not to say that potential citizenship had always an immediate and practical function in Crete, but rather that Cretan communities had a less abstract way to conduct their diplomatic dealings probably as a habit derived from inter-Cretan dealings.[31]

(67–68)   *Kos and Kamarina; Gela/Phintias*

In 242 BC Kos obtained inviolability for the temple of Asklepios and its games were declared panhellenic.[32] Two documents of this dossier stand out because they preserve a reference to *isopoliteiai* that predates the concession of *asylia*[33] and they provide indirect pieces of evidence for potential citizenship between Kos and two Sicilian towns, Kamarina and Gela/Phintias.[34] According to the texts, groups of Koans participating in the refoundation of these two cities encouraged the concession of potential citizenship.[35]

---

29   RIGSBY 1996, pp. 316–318 no. 154 = *I.Cret.* II.iii 2; RIGSBY 1996, p. 325 no. 161.

30   Again CHANIOTIS 1996 and *supra*.

31   It is inaccurate to portray Cretan potential citizenships as only devoted to establishing sets of regulations pertaining to the pastoral and rural economy of the island. The surviving grants of potential citizenship from Crete are often more generic and 'multi-purpose': potential citizenship in Crete had a diplomatic meaning as well as more practical scopes.

32   RIGSBY 1996, p. 106 notes that this example preserves our oldest archive of *asylia*.

33   RIGSBY 1996, pp. 149–150 no. 48 and pp. 150–152 no. 49 (*SEG* XII 379 and 380), now *IG* XII 4.1 222 and 223.

34   RIGSBY 1996, p. 110 notes that Kamarina and Gela must have received the same letter from the Koans as "(their) responses are quite similar to each other but not to those of other cities."

35   DIOD. XVI.82.7 testifies that under Timoleon, colonists, among whom figured Koans, were sent to Kamarina to enlarge the city. If we accept Herzog's emendation correcting the provenance of the ecist from Keos to Kos, HERZOG and KLAFFENBACH 1952, esp. p. 24, PLUT. *Tim.* 35.2 would testify to Gela's second foundation with colonists led by a Koan *oikistes* (?). See the discussion by MANGANARO 1990, p. 400.

I reproduce only LL. 8–23 from the Kamarina decree as published in the *IG*. Using this decree, scholars have restored the first part of the document from Gela/Phintias:[36]

... βουλᾶς φερούσας ἔδοξε τᾶι ἁλ[ίαι·]
ἐπειδὴ οἱ Κῶιοι συνοικισταὶ ἐγένοντο τᾶς πόλιος
ἁμῶν ὑπαρχόντων τε αὐτοῖς παρ'ἁμεῖν τῶν μεγίστων καὶ
ἀναγκαιοτάτων, συγγενείας τε καὶ οἰκειότατος καὶ ἰσοπο-
12   λειτείας, ἀποστείλαντες ἀρχιθέωρον Ἐπιδαύριον Νικάρχο[υ,]
θεωρὸν Σωσίστρατον Καφισίου ἐπαγγέλοντι τὰν θ[υ-]
σίαν ἃν θύοντι τῶι Ἀσκλαπιῶι καὶ τοὺς ἀγῶνας
οὓς τίθεντι μουσικὸν καὶ γυμνικὸν κατὰ πενταετηρ[ί]-
16   δα, καὶ ἀξιῶντι δεῖν κοινωνεῖν τὰν ἁμὰμ πόλιν ἐμφανί-
ζοντες τὰν οἰκειότατα καὶ εὔνοιαν ταῖς πολίεσσι, καλῶς
δὲ ἔχον ἐστὶ τάν τε ἐπαγγελίαν παρ'αὐτῶν δέχεσθαι κα[ὶ]
φανερὸν ποιῆσαι αὐτοῖς διότι μνάμαν ἔχοντες δια-
20   τελοῦμες τᾶς ὑπαρχούσας ποτ'αὐτοὺς συγγενείας [ἔν]
ταῖς πατρίοις θυσίαις ἃς παρελάβομες παρ'αὐτῶν κ[αὶ]
ἐν ταῖς παναγυρίεσσι κατακαλοῦντες αὐτοὺς καθ[ὰ]
καὶ τοὺς ἄλλους οἰκιστάς ...

Transl.: ... proposal of the *boule*, it was enacted by the *halia*: since the Koans were co-founders of our *polis*, having the biggest and most important recognitions by us, *syngeneia, oikeiotes*, and *isopoliteia*, after they have sent the *architheoros* Epidaurios son of Nikarchos, the *theoros* Sosistratos son of Kaphisios who announce the sacrifice that they sacrifice to Asklepios and the pentaeteric musical and gymnic competitions, and they think it appropriate that our city participate thereby showing the kinship and benevolence between (our) communities, it seems well to accept their announcement and show them that we keep memory of our kinship in our ancestral sacrifices that we derive from them and that in our festivals we mention them like the other cofounders ...

A possible textual difference appears in the decree of Gela, LL. 9–10,[37] which reads οἰκιστ[εί]/[ας, out of lacuna, instead of οἰκειότατος, L. 11, of Kamarina's

---

36   Rigsby 1996, pp. 149–150 no. 48 and pp. 150–152 no. 49 now also *IG* XII 4.1 222 (Kamarina) and 223 (Gela).

37   The two decrees differ greatly in their second part, on this, see Rigsby's comments with bibliography.

decree. Klaffenbach thinks, probably rightly, that the spelling is a mistake; Manganaro has tried to explain οἰκιστ[εί]/[ας by establishing a stronger tie between Kos and Gela in the recolonization.[38] This clause, however, would be highly unusual.

In any case, both inscriptions testify to preexisting ties, listed as belonging to the ὑπαρχόντων τε αὐτοῖς παρ' ἁμεῖν τῶν μεγίστων καὶ ἀναγκαιοτάτων, namely, *syngeneia, oikeiotes*, and *isopoliteia*, three pillars of Hellenistic diplomacy. Once more we find the ancient term *isopoliteia* used to indicate an abstract concept and here it particularly refers to an older agreement of potential citizenship.

It is unknown when, how, and why potential citizenship was established between these communities. This lack of information makes the theory asserting that colony and mother city, broadly understood, had reciprocal citizenship rights certainly far-fetched. Instead we should note that here this status worked, together with the other two ties of *syngeneia* and *oikeiotes*, as the basis for the diplomatic discourse. In its turn this evaluation shows the grant's tremendous meaning and diplomatic value in the Hellenistic period.

Tenos

According to Rigsby, "the evidence for *asylia* at Tenos presents grave difficulties."[39] Both the chronology and content of this dossier are indeed difficult to establish: two of the texts this dossier includes may testify to potential citizenship.[40]

---

38 HERZOG and KLAFFENBACH 1952, pp. 23–24 and on this, see MANGANARO 1990, p. 400.
39 RIGSBY 1996, p. 154.
40 The chronology of Tenos's quest is difficult to determine. Scholars have assigned the decree of the Phokian League (*IG* IX 1.97 = RIGSBY 1996, pp. 154–156 no. 53) to the first half of the 3rd century BC on the basis of textual and historical considerations that are, however, disputable; see RIGSBY 1996, esp. p. 156. If this date were to be confirmed, this text would be the first recognition for Tenos and the oldest known *asylia*. The fragmentary Aitolian text (*IG* XII.5 857 = RIGSBY 1996, pp. 156–157 no. 54), which may be a response to the quest or not, and the response of Cretan Phaistos (*I. Cret.* I.xvii 1 = RIGSBY 1996, pp. 157–159 no. 55) date to the middle of the 3rd century BC or soon afterward. A fragmentary dossier that includes responses of several Cretan cities (RIGSBY 1996, pp. 159–162 nos. 56–60) from the 2nd century BC completes the early evidence. Finally, a fragment in Latin testifying to Rome's recognition along with other indirect pieces of evidence add to the problematic picture of this grant, see RIGSBY 1996, esp. pp. 162–163. Rigsby suggests that the Phokian decree is later than it is normally assumed, possibly as late as 200 BC, while the Cretan renewals belong to a generation later. The content of the texts of this dossier is also difficult to interpret. The most serious difficulty pertains to the object of the so-called Cretan renewals, presumably *asylia*. This interpretation would be very unusual and relies only on very fragmentary texts and uncertain restorations, see RIGSBY 1996, pp. 156–163 nos. 56 to 60. Rigsby points out that normally cities renew friendship

(69) Tenos and Phokis[41]

The beginning of this document found in Elatea is lost. What survives contains the recognition of the sanctuary and island as *asyla*. The Phokians also gave a gift of five minas to the Tenians and promised more money at the end of a war. This agreement, say the Phokians, seemed appropriate to the temple and the *oikeiotes* that existed between them, LL. 3–11.[42]

LL. 11–15 record a grant of *isopoliteia*: ἐπαινέσαι δὲ καὶ / τὰν πόλιν Τηνίων ὅτι τοῦ τε ἱεροῦ τὰν ἐπιμέ/λειαν ποιεῖνται καὶ τὰν ποτὶ Φωκεῖς οἰκειό/τατα ἀνανεοῦνται, καὶ εἶμεν Τηγίοις ἰσοπολι/τείαν πᾶσι δεδομέναν ἐμ Φωκεῦσι· (...)[43] The rest of the document contains provisions for the Tenian *theoros* and the engraving and displaying of the stone.

Szanto suggests that this grant was a 'federal' concession of potential citizenship.[44] McInerney, who dates the decree well back into the 3rd century BC because of the financial difficulties claimed by the Phokians with indemnities still to be paid after the Third Sacred War,[45] draws far-reaching conclusions:

> The Phokians vote to grant *isopoliteia* to the Tenians, stipulating that the Tenians are to possess the *isopoliteia* 'that has been given to everyone in Phokis'. This clause assumes that the Phokian *koinon* was fashioned as a political union constituted by the recognition of each state's reciprocal rights.[46]

This conclusion is ambitious, especially because it is drawn from a secondary, participial clause, which the author misreads. McInerney assumes that here

---

or kinship, not *asyla*, which is often the object of a different request within 'renewal' decrees. Finally, BURASELIS 2003, pp. 147–149 uses the two questionable attestations of potential citizenship in Tenos's decrees to support his view on the political weight of this instrument. His comment, however, is too cursory to be accurate.

41 RIGSBY 1996, pp. 154–156 no. 53.
42 On Phokis see STOBER *RE* XX, esp. 490–494; DAVERIO ROCCHI 1999, pp. 15–30 with further bibliography; see also LARSEN 1968, pp. 300–302. A more recent contribution is the book by MCINERNEY 1999, which is sometimes less accurate than one wishes.
43 "(the *koinon* decided) to praise the city of the Tenians because they take care of the sanctuary and renew (remind of) their kinship tie to the Phokians, and to the Tenians (shall be given) *isopoliteia*, given to all those (the Tenians) who are among the Phokians."
44 SZANTO 1892, p. 74. Apparently, this *koinon* had a system of dual citizenship that could be traced back to the 4th century BC based on *IG* II² 70, on which briefly BECK 1997, p. 115. For the role cities played within the Hellenistic-Roman *koinon* see DAVERIO-ROCCHI 1994, esp. pp. 189–193. GAWANTKA 1975 lists this grant as n. 6 but does not discuss it.
45 MCINERNEY 1999, pp. 237–239, but it is impossible to know to which war the Phokians referred, see for example SCHOLTEN 2000, p. 84, n. 88.
46 MCINERNEY 1999, p. 238.

isopoliteia is the institution of potential citizenship, which he thinks was the institutional basis of the new Hellenistic *koinon* of the Phokians. But he misreads the text and charges it with a meaning that it does not have: the clause εἶμεν Τηνίοις ἰσοπολι/τείαν πᾶσι δεδομέναν ἐμ Φωκεῦσι does not mean that all the Phokians had the right of *isopoliteia* and that they extended it to the Tenians. Instead it indicates that the Phokians conceded *isopoliteia* to all Tenians in Phokis. The clause that includes *isopoliteia* implies then that this grant was to be available to Tenians *in Phokis* only, which is unusual: here *isopoliteia* probably does not refer to the institution, but only indicates that those Tenians who lived in Phokis had equality of rights.[47]

If this text can provide any historical indication it would be that, at the time, the Phokian League must have not been part of the Aitolian *koinon*.[48]

(70) *Tenos and Phaistos*

The stone on which this fragmentary text was inscribed was found reused near ancient Lebena, at Miamu, but is now lost.[49] The first editor restored the text heavily on the basis of a few keywords.[50] The concession of potential citizenship for example relies only on a few letters Graindor thought belonged to a *metechein* clause: LL. 3–5: [... εἶμεν δὲ ἰσοπολιτείαν Φαιστίοις καὶ] / [Τηνίοις καὶ τὸν Τήνιον ἐν Φαιστοῖ καὶ τὸν Φαίστιον ἐν Τήνωι] / [μετ]έχειν θ[ίνων καὶ ἀν-θρωπίνων ... κτλ].[51] This restoration was offered only as an example. If correct, which I doubt, we will have to assume that the decree of Phaistos contained a bilateral grant of potential citizenship that had to be or had been reciprocated. Phaistos alone did not have the authority to grant bilateral potential citizenship and it is possible that Phaistos had given potential citizenship to Tenos, but, since we are dealing with a fragmentary text, I would restore a unilateral grant.

A short dossier of five, later and very fragmentary decrees from Cretan cities, Gortyn, Tylissos, Aptera, Lappa and Axos, also belongs to the evidence for Tenos's quest. Perhaps some of the texts originally contained potential citizenship too, as in the case of Teos, but any evidence for it is lost to us.

---

47 For parallels see the introduction, pp. 25–27 where I discuss other possible meanings of the term *isopoliteia*.
48 See SCHOLTEN 2000, esp. pp. 174–176 *et alia*.
49 See RIGSBY 1996, pp. 157–159 no. 55 = *I.Cret.* I.xvii 1.
50 GRAINDOR 1907, pp. 22–23.
51 The rest of the fragmentary text probably contains the recognition of *asylia* for the temple of Poseidon and Amphitrite followed by a protection clause for the Tenians. After a long gap appear words that signal provisions tied to the inscribing and displaying of the text.

Asylia and Isopoliteia

The association between the recognition of inviolability of sanctuary and place and the grant of potential citizenship is, as I have already noted, not as common as one is normally led to think. *Isopoliteia* appears in decrees that concede *asylia*, never the other way around. But even in the documents attesting to both grants, there is no dependency relationship, as they were mostly offered at different times. Potential citizenship can be granted later than *asylia* was, as in the Teian quest. Or it can pre-date *asylia*, as in the case of Kos and the Sicilian cities of Gela and Kamarina. In this latter case *isopoliteia* represents a relationship to build upon, while in the Teian dossier it is a seal to the agreement that is often accompanied by other additional grants. In the Teian dossier *isopoliteia* appears consistently within documents involving Cretan cities. Here the grant serves less 'pragmatic' ends (at least for those who do not charge *asylia* with a political meaning) than it does when it is exchanged between Cretan cities, where often it helps to build alliances and to regulate land and other problems tied to the territory.

The meaning of the grant of potential citizenship appears nowhere else as clearly as it does in this section devoted to *asylia*. The ultimate consequence of granting *isopoliteia*, i.e., the concession of the greatest good possessed by a community—citizenship—is, in truth, subordinated to its diplomatic role. The concession helps to move forward a diplomatic discourse and assumes a primary role, thus becoming a pillar of Hellenistic interstate politics, like *syngeneia*, *oikeiotes*, and, to a lesser degree, *philia*. This value is clear in the texts coming from Sicily where isopolity is mentioned in one breath with *syngeneia* and *oikeiotes*; these texts contain a grant of *asylia* that confirms and reinforces the diplomatic relationships that were already in place as testified by *isopoliteia*, *syngeneia*, and *oikeiotes*.

Conclusions

This book began with the presentation of a dossier containing two decrees from Miletos and Seleukeia-Tralles, which testifies to their bilateral exchange of potential citizenship in 218/7 BC.[1] Because of that exchange, starting from that very year, lawful citizens of Miletos could decide to move to Seleukeia-Tralles, and *vice versa*. What is more, they could become full and active members of the partner community after going through the prescribed procedure of control and enrollment.

The ultimate consequence of any grant of the Hellenistic institution of potential citizenship was the option for all lawful members of the involved communities to switch their citizenship. But, in reality, prior to any individual's actual implementation of such a grant, this tool had already served an important diplomatic and political task, on top of which came offering potential citizenship to each citizen.

The sphere of the individual's choice is only of marginal interest in the present study primarily for two reasons. (1) Communities, and not individuals, used potential citizenship within the context of interstate, foreign policy. Even if it may sound like a paradox, citizens were only indirectly and marginally involved in this type of diplomatic exchange. (2) No evidence survives that can help to measure the impact of potential citizenship on the population and, even less, on individuals and their choices.[2]

In the Hellenistic period, potential citizenship was granted to a community as a political entity, not as an embodiment of its citizenry. This tool was in the hands of *poleis* and *ethne* to be used for some three centuries.[3] Moreover, the evidence shows that the target of a concession of potential citizenship was always a community that was politically or otherwise related to the polity granting the concession, either at a local or international level, at the time of the stipulation of the agreement. The type of agreements in which the institution

---

1 *Milet* I 3 143 = no. 5.
2 Even the one inscription we have that might possibly attest an individual's request to use the option to switch citizenship, *IG* XII.5.814 = no. 35, is too fragmentary to support the formulation of any secure hypothesis.
3 The very complex case of the announcement by Teos of the grant of potential citizenship to three Syrian cities, *ed. pr.* HERRMANN 1965 then *SEG* XLI 1003 = no. 61, is no exception. In this document the status of Antiochos III as king is irrelevant to the actual grant, which is a proposal for an award that may be potential citizenship by Teos as *polis* to the three Syrian cities of Antioch, Laodikeia, and Seleukeia. In other words, I exclude royal involvement for any concession of potential citizenship; see *supra* pp. 222–227.

of potential citizenship appears varies greatly, ranging from peace treaties to military alliances,[4] to pure concessions of this grant, to recognitions and reminders of *asylia*.

My comprehensive analysis of the available evidence for potential citizenship has identified two types of this institution, or, better, two ways to use it within *interpoleis* agreements.

A brief summary of the main characteristics of the two types of potential citizenship might help to assess whether these definitions were up to the task I envisioned for them, namely, to work as guidelines for the creation of a (mental) diplomatic map of potential citizenship and also as flexible heuretic tools.

The least common type of potential citizenship (which in this book I sometimes call the "second" type) signals that the signing parties subscribed to an agreement that was meant to respond to actual and pressing problems that might even be tied to imminent dangers. It is not by chance that this type of potential citizenship often appears within military agreements. Under such circumstances, communities tended to keep the technical details pertaining to the enrollment of new citizens short, and they normally added other grants or specified additional conditions that were tied to contingent needs or historical events. One example of this type of potential citizenship, found in this instance outside of a military treaty, is contained in the agreement brokered by the Aitolians between Phigaleia and Messene in the 240s BC, which testifies to a proposal of exchanging potential citizenship.[5] Contested boundaries and contested land probably underlaid the controversy between Phigaleia and Messene, which the Aitolians attempted to mediate by recommending the exchange of *isopoliteia*, along with other diplomatic and practical grants such as *epigamia* and *enktesis*. The final oath that seals the agreement refers to the successful mediation in general and not to the specific grants that the cities were supposed to later stipulate.[6]

---

[4] As we have seen, it was common on Crete for grants of potential citizenship to be tied to military agreements, but that combination should not be generalized to other geographical areas. Outside of Crete, military agreements and *isopoliteia* appear together only in three instances: the case of Skepsis and Parion (J. and L. ROBERT BE 1972 371 = no. 23), in the brief alliance between Aitolia and Akarnania (IG IX² 1 3A= no. 40), and in *Milet* I 3 150 = no. 7 where the grant is embedded in the peace treaty between Miletos and Herakleia under Mt. Latmos.
[5] *IPArk*. 28 = no. 39 and see also the introduction, pp. 19–20.
[6] Oaths never have the function of sealing potential citizenship but are attached to agreements that contain broader contexts; see my comment p. 73 on the oath appearing in the agreement between Skepsis and Parion, J. and L. ROBERT *BE* 1972 37 = no. 23.

A very different spirit and intent animate the most common type of potential citizenship. Although its use is concentrated in Asia Minor, Athens, and the islands, it is well attested in all regions of the Greek world. All examples of this type are contained in agreements that stipulate an exchange or grant of potential citizenship and are concerned with diplomatic matters to which a grant of *isopoliteia* was then attached. One example of this type is found in the dossier of decrees by Miletos and Seleukeia-Tralles, which I have mentioned in the introduction.[7] The actual goals or requests that these *poleis* brought forward are not known, in part because they are deeply embedded in the diplomatic language that is used in these decrees. But it should not go unnoticed that the participating cities stressed various aspects of their diplomatic exchange, a formulation that indicates that the bilateral concession of potential citizenship was part of a bigger political plan.

Occasionally the documents in which we find this type of potential citizenship may include additional grants and, when they do, these are mostly trade oriented. These additional grants seem to favor the temporary presence of foreigners in the partner city or to establish rules for taxation that are extremely convenient for foreign merchants.[8]

The communities that agree to the stipulation of these treaties could be large or small cities, close or distant neighbors.[9] These criteria were irrelevant to the purposes of this type of potential citizenship, as long as each community was somehow politically and diplomatically important for its partner.

Our evidence for these two types of potential citizenship reveals that both provided a powerful diplomatic seal to agreements and opened the door to actual collaborations, exchanges, and other relationships. In the immediate diplomatic and political context in which the agreement had been signed, it was irrelevant whether the citizens of the involved communities would decide to implement the grant.

Hence, the practical value of potential citizenship in the ancient Greek world was far removed from the contemporary one. In brief, the practical value was that a grant of potential citizenship conveyed the most important

---

7 *Milet* I 3 143 = no. 5.
8 For a discussion on tax regulations see the treatment of the agreement between Skepsis and Parion, J. and L. ROBERT *BE* 1972 37 = no. 23. J. and L. Robert have suggested that one of the two goals of potential citizenship favored the movement of things; the other was the freer circulation of people, i.e., migratory movements. The ancient evidence seems to substantiate their first assumption, the second is also quite to the point except that I do not think it favored migrating movements as much as the 'circulation' of people in the short term.
9 Instead closely neighboring communities stipulated the second type of potential citizenship.

recognition a community could ever give to other cities and federal states, and enabled the granting community to pursue different goals. Use of this institution promoted further and better relations, which, in their turn, must have served other purposes.

A general study of this tool provides some insight into long debated and ongoing topics that pertain to the nature and form of Greek citizenship. Two of the most prominent of these topics, which recur in discussions on citizenship and also on *isopoliteia*, concern multiple citizenship in the Hellenistic period and the so-called dual citizenship within *koina*.

The complex topic of multiple citizenship was addressed in 2012 in a collection of papers edited and published by A. Heller and V. Pont. The contributions in that volume adopt varied points of view and cover a broad span of time and political culture(s) that make this work an excellent reference and starting point for further discussions on multiple citizenship. The closing remarks of the volume by O. Picard are particularly illuminating for ancient studies. Having observed that no Greek city ever prohibited individuals from having more than one citizenship, and asking why that might be so, he proposes that the possession of more than one citizenship was, for the ancient Greeks, inconceivable.[10]

Elsewhere, scholars have observed that the decrees through which communities exchanged or granted potential citizenship sometimes include *ethnica* of the grantees, and some have concluded, on the basis of this evidence, that the concession of potential citizenship implied a dual citizenship status. But this interpretation of the evidence ascribes to *ethnica* a legal value that they did not possess.[11] For example, at the end of the 4th century BC the cities of Miletos and Kyzikos exchanged potential citizenship as follows, LL. 13–16: εἶναι δὲ τὸν / Κυζικηνὸν ἐμ Μιλήτωι Μι/λήσιον καὶ τὸν Μιλήσιον ἐν / Κυζίκωι Κυζικηνόν.[12] The text, however, is not establishing that Milesians and Kyzikenes were each other's citizens, but that they were *potential* citizens of each other's cities: they did not possess *a priori* the rights and duties that would derive from the status

---

10 PICARD 2012, p. 342. Picard's comments and the other contributions in the collection are concerned primarily with the granting of multiple citizenship to individuals in honor of their actions or status. HELLER and PONT 2012, esp. p. 11 with reference to Gauthier's work, touch only briefly on the question of the relationship between multiple citizenship and grants of potential citizenship to entire communities. In that discussion, they rightly note that *isopoliteia* did not open the door to multiple citizenships and that it was not itself a way to acquire additional citizenships.

11 See my introduction and SAVALLI 2012, esp. p. 40, n. 5. For this interpretation of *ethnica* regarding the exchange of citizenship between federal states and *poleis* see GAUTHIER 1972, pp. 256–258.

12 *Milet* I 3 137, LL. 13–16 = no. 2.

of holding active citizenship of another city, but they had the option to switch citizenship.[13]

Like the topic of multiple citizenship in the Hellenistic period, the topic of dual citizenship in federal states appears often in connection with potential citizenship.[14] On the basis of our certainly incomplete record, Aitolia was the only *koinon* that used the institution of potential citizenship somewhat regularly. What the Aitolian *koinon* granted was potential federal citizenship, while the *polis* of Naupaktos provides the only example of a *polis* within that federal state that is known to have given a grant of local citizenship, in this case to Keos.[15] We do not know what these local and federal 'citizenships' implied, whether they coexisted or 'completed' each other, and we have little secure evidence of the nature of these two forms of citizenship. The evidence seems to suggest that they coexisted, but this view is still hotly debated, at least in Aitolia. Each federal state and federation must have had its own specific terms.[16]

Aitolia's use of potential citizenship has been widely perceived to have had a political scope,[17] namely, that potential citizenship was a tool of Aitolia's

---

13   In her contribution to the volume of Heller and Pont, SAVALLI 2012, p. 42 wonders whether the process of changing citizenship was reversible in the case of concessions to individuals. One could ask the same question for potential citizenship, but the evidence is too sparse to afford a reliable answer. On a theoretical level, I do not see why it should not have been possible to reverse the process of changing citizenship, but actual circumstances might have made such a reversal more complicated. The affair of the Cretan mercenaries whose native cities refused to take them back because they had taken up Milesian citizenship is instructive, see MAGNETTO 1997, pp. 262–271 no. 43 and AGER 1996, pp. 350–355 no. 127.

14   For bibliography on dual citizenship, see *supra*. The volume of HELLER and PONT 2012 contains a relevant contribution to the topic, that of RIZAKIS who focuses on the status of Achaian citizens within the *koinon*. He questions other aspects and analyzes other types of consequences of federal citizenship than I do here. While I look at consequences on the 'outside' of the federal state, Rizakis looks at those on the 'inside' of the federal state.

15   *StV* III 508, III = no. 41.

16   See LASAGNI 2011, esp. pp. 215–238 in general on this topic with bibliography, also *supra* the section on Aitolia, on the Lesbian *koinon*, and on the Lykian *koinon*.

17   LARSEN 1968, esp. pp. 206–208 on the use of potential citizenship in Aitolia. For further bibliography see the section on Aitolia, pp. 107–121. Gawantka's interpretation on the Aitolian use of potential citizenship is difficult to reconstruct as he does not offer a general interpretation, but mostly considers separate inscriptions. He focuses especially on the treaty between Aitolia and Akarnania, GAWANTKA 1975, esp. pp. 146–149, but suggests that the fear of Akarnania toward Aitolian ambitions of annexation can explain the terms for that treaty, although the known historical circumstances do not match that interpretation of the treaty's terms.

Machtpolitik used to tie to itself to cities that were too geographically distant to become partners in the *sympoliteia*. That interpretation relies too heavily on Polybios's testimonies, which contain institutional terminology that remains open to interpretation.[18]

The epigraphic evidence seems to show, instead, that Aitolia had a 'total' approach to potential citizenship as it used both types of this institution to pursue different goals. For example, in the peculiar military alliance between Akarnania and Aitolia, the two communities added a grant of potential citizenship that reflects the use typical of the first type of potential citizenship.[19] But we see Aitolia in other instances granting potential citizenship in the context of glaringly diplomatic acts, such as, for example, in the decree with which Aitolia granted potential citizenship to Herakleia under Mt. Latmos, in direct response to a curious embassy that this *polis* had sent to the *koinon* seeking Aitolian intercession with the Ptolemies.[20]

Although a grant of potential citizenship by Aitolia was a grant by a *koinon*, and in this respect was dissimilar to the potential citizenship that *poleis* could offer, we can expect that the use of the grant by the *koinon* was like that of other communities in the Greek world. We lack the evidence to identify potential citizenship as an instrument of Aitolian expansionism.

At the beginning of this work I stated that it is possible to offer a general definition of potential citizenship. In the intervening pages, I have tried to characterize the results of my detailed study of all available evidence by identifying two descriptions that can convey general attitudes toward the use of potential citizenship. The evidence at our disposal, however, also shows that rigid categories and generalizations cannot contain all the information available to us on potential citizenship. If my interpretation of the evidence is sound, we can recognize two main uses of potential citizenship, which appear within very different historical and diplomatic contexts in a rather consistent fashion. It is clear, however, that potential citizenship was perceived as a widely applicable tool, known, used, and 'recognized' at an international level. It was a flexible instrument in the hands of communities that were still capable and willing to shape the international or local diplomatic landscape by making connections based on traditional and shared values of the Hellenistic age. *Isopoliteia* or (as I prefer to call it) potential citizenship must be therefore read in context and at

---

18   POLYB. XV.23.8–9 and XVIII.3.11–12. See the appendix on this author.
19   *IG* IX² I 3A = no. 40, LL. 12–13: καὶ πολίταν εἶμε/ν τὸν Αἰτωλὸν ἐν Ἀκαρνανίαι καὶ τὸν Ἀκαρνᾶνα ἐν ⟨Α⟩ἰτωλίαι ἴσογ καὶ ὅμοιον.
20   *IG* IX I², 1, 173 = no. 45.

best treated together with and like the pillars of the Hellenistic diplomacy, such as kinship or *philia*, more than as an instrument comparable with, for example, *sympoliteia*. The tool it most resembles is *asylia*. Both, *asylia* and *isopoliteia*, are difficult to grasp in their meaning and function, but were clearly advanced and high-profile products of Greek diplomacy. Possibly for this very reason that we find them associated, and, in a way, as complements to each other.

APPENDIX 1

The Origins of Potential Citizenship

Grants of potential citizenship are attested epigraphically for a limited time only, from the 4th to the end of the 2nd century BC, which suggests that this institution was a diplomatic experiment whose success was determined by specific political and social conditions. When cities' policies changed, mainly because of Rome's coming, communities must have felt that this tool was no longer effective and potential citizenship fell in disuse. Rome had indeed shown on several occasions that it was not always receptive of the diplomatic forms that were typical of Greek diplomacy.[1] This fact renders the question pertaining to the cessation of potential citizenship less problematic than its origins,[2] whose search has assumed a disproportionate importance in the admittedly short debate on this topic. Explaining the historical development of an institution that derives from a common diplomatic practice, granting citizenship, is, however, a daunting task: the documents we have are finished products of a legally and politically defined procedure that can only show the evolution of the tools, but they do not tell us how and why this very evolution occurred.

In modern scholarship Ph. Gauthier and W. Gawantka have devoted the most attention to the topic of the origins of *isopoliteia*. In their studies they analyzed different sets of evidence that they believed could testify to early forms of the institution of potential citizenship,[3] but their approaches and conclusions are quite distinct.

In his analysis of the literary and epigraphic evidence that dates to a time earlier than the 4th century BC, Gawantka employs a difficult methodology, as he applies his defining criteria for *Hellenistic* potential citizenship to grants that were conceded in the Archaic and Classical periods. Thus, he has been able to detect superficial similarities between grants of different time periods

---

1 In his work on *asylia* RIGSBY 1996, p. 22 notes that Rome had difficulties in grasping the 'meaning' and therefore the use of Greek inviolability for cities and sanctuaries; more on the 'misunderstandings' occurring between these two cultures in GRUEN 1984, who devotes a long chapter to "Attitudes and Motivations," but see esp. pp. 270–272. For an analysis of the changed conditions in which Greek cities had to operate see now also MACK 2015, esp. pp. 233–281.
2 On this GAWANTKA 1975, pp. 198–199.
3 GAUTHIER 1972, esp. pp. 347–358 and pp. 364–365; GAWANTKA 1975, pp. 165–199 on the origins, a summary of his theory at pp. 178–179.

which led him to conclude that the institution of potential citizenship, with its typically Hellenistic traits, existed already in the middle of the 6th century BC.

Gauthier's approach derives from the different focus of his 1972 work, namely, *symbola*. The greatest difference between his work and Gawantka's, however, is Gauthier's more flexible definition and understanding, of 'isopolity': he does not try to establish a monolithic definition that uses specific and detailed criteria applicable to all epochs. He does not search for *isopoliteia* in the Archaic and Classical periods, but instead he analyzes the relationship between communities that exchanged citizenship and that dated to a time before the Hellenistic period. In other words, Gauthier studies a diplomatic phenomenon, that of conceding citizenship, and its development; Gawantka studies *isopoliteia* in all historical periods.

In general, the search for the origins of the institution of potential citizenship relies on problematic evidence that roughly belongs to one of two main categories: (1) Hellenistic documents testifying to claims of preexisting grants of citizenship that supposedly derive from a colonial relationship or that rest on differently motivated kinship claims and (2) 5th century BC—or earlier—mass grants of citizenship for lawful members of *poleis* that found themselves in dire circumstances.

The first category of evidence has been the object of several recent studies showing that the frequent kinship claims attested in the Hellenistic period responded to the logic of Hellenistic diplomacy and helped to create the basis for a diplomatic discourse.[4] But kinship alone, whether fictitious or real, cannot be considered *the* sign of the existence, or even the reason, for the stipulation of an agreement of potential citizenship *ab antiquo*. More generally, kinship claims attest to the effort of a society to trace back in time a shared past with another community; such a process and reelaboration of its own history may be productively considered with the help of the heuristic tool of intentional history, for example.[5]

The other pieces of evidence that I identify here as belonging to the second group include well-known documents, such as those attesting to the agreement between Samos and Athens that was passed at a most tragic historical passage, such as the end of the Peloponnesian Wars. Or the equally tragic case of Plataia that took place at the time when Sparta had taken and destroyed

---

4 For a review of the most recent studies on kinship see SABA 2009/10(b), pp. 276–279.
5 The illuminating work by GEHRKE, now well illustrated in his 2014 book, moves from principles of ethnosociological studies to help historians interpret perceptions of one's 'own' history.

this old Athenian ally. I will return to both treaties later in this appendix. The concessions that these agreements entail, however, differ from Hellenistic potential citizenship, even if they can certainly be considered grants that in a way anticipate the creation of this tool. In other words, while the logic behind these concessions differs from that which will regulate the Hellenistic institution of (potential) citizenship, the 'object' of the exchange is the same. It certainly anticipates the Hellenistic institution even if it cannot be considered identical. Two main reasons account for this difference: first, these earlier concessions were meant for the people of a community, not the community as a political entity. Second, the grantees mostly happened to be survivors of traumatic events that impacted their cities to the point of changing their form of government or even threatening their existence. The mechanisms and, most importantly, the mindset that regulate the grants of potential citizenship in the Hellenistic age differ in that they have been reformulated to respond to different historical conditions and diplomatic needs and codes.

Starting from the early Hellenistic period, the practice of granting citizenship to wider groups of people whose existence was *framed within a well-defined institutional setting* was redefined as a diplomatic tool and acquired new contents and meaning. Potential citizenship as an *institutionalized* diplomatic tool is a Hellenistic invention and practice. Hellenistic potential citizenship was the ultimate result of the evolution of general norms regulating citizenship's grants as prompted by historical circumstances. The object of the concession, *politeia*, did not change: how and why it was exchanged (the institutional frame and its goals) did. Finally, I must note here that even in the Hellenistic period not every concession of '*isopoliteia*' is a concession of the institution of potential citizenship as I define it in this work.[6]

Even if I do not perceive the pre-Hellenistic evidence of wider grants of citizenship as essential to understanding the Hellenistic practice of granting potential citizenship between communities, I cannot dismiss all this evidence as irrelevant. I have therefore selected a few cases that date to the 6th and 5th centuries BC, which are often described as early evidence for *isopoliteia* because of their historical importance as they appear as crucial agreements within difficult historical events.

I argue that these pieces of evidence testify to grants of citizenship meant to address problems posed by specific historical circumstances.

---

6 See the introduction, pp. 24–27.

Delphi and Sardis

The grant of πολιτεία for the Lydians on the part of Delphi, HDT. 1.54.2, deserves a note.[7]

According to Herodotos, in the 6th century BC the Delphians ἔδωκαν Κροίσῳ καὶ Λυδοῖσι προμαντηίην καὶ ἀτελείην καὶ προεδρίην καὶ ἐξεῖναι τῷ βουλομένῳ αὐτῶν γένεσθαι Δελφὸν ἐς τὸν αἰεὶ χρόνον (…). These words summarize the Delphians' response to the enthusiastic gifts that Kroisos made after obtaining the oracle he misunderstood, thereby causing the end of his own reign. Gawantka interprets the words as testifying to the earliest known stipulation of *isopoliteia*, because this sentence fits well his definition of *Hellenistic* potential citizenship. Namely, the concession was potential (like all grants of citizenship), perennial, it was directed to all who wanted to take up this option, and it was hardly meant to be implemented.[8]

But, in truth, we are ignorant of the grant, its terms and its nature: the text preserves only a sentence stating that the Delphians conceded what was considered already at the time of Herodotos the greatest concession a community could make, namely, *politeia*, to a group of people defined by their appartenance to a land, that was, however, no *polis*. The first inescapable observation is that this text is unparalleled, and Herodotos writes a long time

---

7 This grant is sometimes associated with two other inscriptions that testify to later diplomatic relations between Delphi and Sardis. I have already treated this topic in print, SABA 2009/10(a), pp. 171–180, on which the comment in *SEG* LIX 522 is not completely accurate. The lemma attributes to me the statement that *FD* III.3 241 contains a unilateral grant of citizenship to Sardis in ca. 166 BC, which is untenable. The issue is not whether citizenship was granted, instead I discuss the 'reminders' of LL. 5–6. The article is concerned with terminology and, partly, with the flexibility of the diplomatic discourse in the Hellenistic period. There I argue that *FD* III.3 241 does not contain indirect evidence for the institution of potential citizenship, because, had it been so, this relationship—no matter when it had been established—would have been formulated differently (terminology). Another inscription from Delphi, *Syll.*³ 548 (215–210 BC), helps to prove this point. In it *politeia* does not appears, but it does include all other concessions that are also present in *FD* III.3 241, do (ca. 166 BC), LL. 5–6. In an additional comment to *SEG* LIX 522, Chaniotis suggests that *isopoliteia* between Delphi and Sardis could have been established after 215–210 BC but before 166 BC, only the record is lost to us. Although certainly possible, it does not explain *FD* III.3 241, LL. 5–6. I am not suggesting that our record for the diplomatic relationship between Delphi and Sardis is complete but that, if these communities had had potential citizenship in place, this would have appeared in LL. 1–2 of *FD* III.3 241, i.e., in another part of the text and with a different wording (terminology). The concession of potential citizenship would have indeed created a tie comparable to *oikeiotes*, *philia*, etc. (diplomatic discourse).

8 GAWANTKA 1975, pp. 169–170.

after the events. With it we face a cultural and historical *aporia*: the grant is probably an interpretation and, what troubles me, is that it is a concession to a non-Greek grantee. Was this even possible?

This piece of information by Herodotos resists any modern taxonomy of grants and I hold that in this case it is wiser to leave it without a more precise definition.

The 5th Century BC

Evidence dating to this century contains news of mass grants of citizenship that scholars occasionally interpret as early cases of the institution of potential citizenship.

One of the best-known and most discussed cases is the Athenian grant of citizenship to the citizens of Plataia, for which exists abundant but contrasting literary evidence. During the early phases of the Peloponnesian Wars, Spartan and Peloponnesian contingents besieged Plataia, a traditional Athenian ally. After a two-year siege, the exhausted city gave up. The few Plataians who could escape fled to Athens, where they were granted citizenship and lived, apparently, as a separate group.[9]

One of the questions that has been asked of the sources is whether they describe a case of protopotential citizenship (i.e., the institution). Gawantka rightly holds it was not this case, but for the wrong reasons.[10] He argues his case concerning the timing of the concession: it is unclear whether the survivors from Plataia received Athenian citizenship before or after Plataia fell (before 429 or in 427 BC). For Gawantka, had it happened before, the grant *could* be potential citizenship. But, if this concession had been granted after Plataia had surrendered, the grant of citizenship could not be one of *isopoliteia*. This circumstance would indeed have meant that the community had ceased to exist and the 'risk' of implementation would have increased exponentially. In other words, citizenship would have no longer been 'potential.'[11]

---

9   I simplify here the events on which see SABA 2011, esp. pp. 94–95 with bibliography.
10 GAWANTKA 1975, pp. 174–178.
11 THUC. III.53–59 and 61–67 says the grant was given before the destruction of Plataia. But in "Against Neaira," [DEM.] LIX.104 paraphrases an Athenian decree that says citizenship had been given after the destruction of the city. On the document and its nature see KAPPARIS 1995, CANEVARO 2010, and also BEARZOT 1997, pp. 43–60. Pseudo-Demosthenes sketches briefly the history of the relationship between Plataia and Athens starting from the Persian Wars (par. 94). This excursus is part of his plea to the jury

Still, Gawantka adds, even if Thucydides's account is inaccurate, it reveals that the historian knew the institution "isopolity," which then would indirectly confirm its existence in the 5th century BC.[12]

Gauthier also devotes a short note to the case of Plataia and calls it *isopolitie exceptionelle* because of the historical circumstances.[13] Gauthier, however, does not charge the term 'isopoly' with a particular institutional meaning and does not consider it equal with the diplomatic tool typical of the Hellenistic period. Isopolity is a concession of citizenship with variable traits in history.

Surely Athens granted the people of Plataia Athenian citizenship with equal rights, but the institutional context of the grant, its mode of concession, and the grantee contrast it from the Hellenistic practice. All I suggest, however, is that we abstain from using the expression *isopoliteia* in order to avoid confusion. In modern scholarship this term has become too charged and it automatically refers to institutional forms and diplomatic acts that, as Cataldi notes, were still fluid in 5th-century BC Athens.

Our sources indicate that Athens welcomed refugees from an allied city that had been taken and destroyed by a common enemy. Granting citizen rights to the survivors was a way to recognize the strength of the alliance and the tie Athens had with Plataia. It was a due act after the hardship this *polis* suffered. This episode should not be read 'institutionally' as a case of an early (Hellenistic) grant of potential citizenship, whose mechanisms, logic, and goals developed only later. This concession was a mass grant of citizenship for the people of Plataia that, again, can be considered a predecessor of *isopoliteia*, but not the later institution.

Samos and Athens

At the end of the 19th century four fragments of white marble from different areas in and around the Athenian acropolis were joined to form an inscribed

---

against the defenders who had abused citizenship rights, which, instead, the Plataians had deserved for their loyalty to Athens. Scholars give more credit to Pseudo-Demosthenes's chronology. A good discussion is in HORNBLOWER'S *Commentary on Thucydides*, 1991, Vol. 1, pp. 449–450. On the history of Plataia and these events in particular, see PRANDI 1988, pp. 111–120 and 127–132; OSBORNE 1981(a), esp. vol. IV pp. 181–183.

12 GAWANTKA 1975, p. 175 and 178. On the fluidity of these categories and the concept of isopolity in the 5th century BC see CATALDI 1983, p. 382, n. 64. GAWANTKA 1975, p. 178 n. 31a cites another source, DIOD. XV.46.2 who speaks of "*isopoliteia*" pointing out that Diodoros does not use the word as *terminus technicus*.

13 GAUTHIER 1972, p. 364.

stele. A relief with a *dexiosis* between Athena and Hera surmounts and completes the same stele.[14] The stone, *IG* II² 1, contains three decrees passed at different times: II and III date to the archonship of Eukleides in 403/2 BC, while I (now published as *IG* I³ 127) dates to 405/4 BC when Alexias was archon and Athens lost the battle of the Aegospotamoi. *IG* I³ 127 must have been passed shortly after this devastating clash for Athens and, perhaps, had not been engraved at the time. Another possibility is that, had the inscription been engraved, the original stele was destroyed under the Thirty Tyrants and later reinscribed with II and III.[15]

The superscript Σαμίοις ὅσοι μετὰ τõ δήμο τõ Ἀθηναί/ων ἐγένοντο that opens *IG* I³ 127 illustrates that the decisions contained in the stone apply to the Samians who sided loyally with Athens during the entire war. This document is highly politicized.[16] Athens praises the ambassadors of the two Samian diplomatic missions that had reached Attica and then states in LL. 12 to 17:

> (…) δεδόχθαι τῆι βολῆι καὶ τῶι δήμωι· Σαμίος Ἀθηναίος ἐ̃ναι,
> πολιτευόμενος ὅπως ἂν αὐτοὶ βόλωνται· καὶ ὅπως ταῦτα ἔσται ὡς ἐπιτηδειό-
> τατα ἀμφοτέροις, καθάπερ αὐτοὶ λέγουσιν, ἐπειδὰν ἐρήνη γένηται, τότε περὶ
> τῶν ἄλλων κοινῆι βουλεύεσθαι· τοῖς δὲ νόμοις χρῆσθαι τοῖς σφετέροις αὐτῶν
> αὐτονόμος ὄντας, καὶ τἆλλα ποιε̃ν κατὰ τὸς ὅρκος καὶ τὰς συνθήκας καθάπερ
> 16   ξύνκειται Ἀθηναίοις καὶ Σαμίοις·[17]

A rider, LL. 33–34, completes the decree granting citizenship to the ambassadors who had reached Athens and distributes them in the local tribes. Several important provisions follow L. 16. They are meant to regulate the (legal) behavior of Athens and Samos and to confirm the *status quo* of their relationship (LL. 16–22).[18] Additionally, they regulate the use of the equipment and manpower in Samos in case of further war activities, and assert the Samian right

---

14   See LAWTON 1995, pp. 88–89. BLANSHARD 2007, pp. 19–37 has reinterpreted the relief and text with a comment in TYBOUD 2011, esp. pp. 123–124.
15   OSBORNE 1981(a), D 4–5.
16   For the events of those years see SHIPLEY 1987, esp. pp. 130–131 who considers the actual consequences to this grant; CARGILL 1983, pp. 322–325; CATALDI 1983, pp. 349–390.
17   Transl.: "It should be decided by the *boule* and the *demos* that a Samian shall be Athenian, running the state according to the form of government they choose. Also, so that everything is as convenient as possible for both parties, just as they say, decisions on different issues shall be made together, once there is peace. They shall use their own laws, because they are autonomous, and everything else shall be done according to the oaths and the agreements that are already in place for Athenians and Samians."
18   On the clauses regulating the legal aspects of the relationship between Athens and Samos see CATALDI 1983, esp. pp. 360–364.

to participate in Athenian embassies (LL. 22–32). The concession of citizenship of LL. 12–16 has been hotly debated in the past and has been described as an early case of 'isopolity.'[19] But instead of trying to make this 5th-century BC exceptional citizenship project fit into later institutional categories, I suggest that we try to contextualize it within its historical background.[20]

The difficult, post-Aegospotami situation required the signing of an agreement able to reassure the important and loyal ally Samos of Athens's support for its survival and the survival of its lawful, loyal citizens. This support would have continued whether Samos were to be destroyed or continued as a *polis*. The grant of citizenship includes the option of welcoming into the Athenian citizen body allies whose city could be lost to them. Even the rider of LL. 33–34 can be read along the same lines: the Samian ambassadors who had reached Athens—if the restoration is sound—asked and obtained immediately Athenian citizenship because they were loyal allies who could not sail back home. This decree depicts a situation that, at the time, must have felt profoundly similar to that of Plataia a few decades earlier, except that Athens was no longer a safe harbor.

This decree testifies to the project of conceding Athenian citizenship to a group of Samians, with a provision for the separate implementation of the concession for the Samian ambassadors to Athens. Calling it isopolity generates confusion because, as Cataldi reminds us too, this category was still fluid in the 5th century BC; using labels that are appropriate for procedures that are attested centuries later creates confusion. Here too then, I suggest that we avoid using this potentially ambiguous definition. This decree testifies to a mass grant of Athenian citizenship to loyal allies, i.e., the citizens of Samos who stayed by Athens, as the superscript to the decree says.[21] We could call this grant in many ways, even *isopolitie exceptionelle*, by using Gauthier's definition

---

19 To GAWANTKA 1975, pp. 178–197 this example is *isopoliteia* and serves to recognize Samian equality with Athens; CATALDI 1983, p. 358 suggests that this could be called "cittadinanza potenziale," granted that one keeps in mind that at the end of the 5th century BC "è ancora assai poco chiara ad Atene la categoria istituzionale dell'*isopoliteia* nei rapporti tra due stati...." KOCH 1993 offers a different interpretation: to him the (double) mission of the Samians was in preparation for a mass move of Samian people to Athens. This reading is in many ways problematic, as Koch seems aware esp. pp. 73–74, and LL. 12–16 strongly discourage from it. FUNKE 2007, p. 192 reads this agreement as the extreme attempt on the part of Athens to tie itself to an important ally.

20 *IG* I³ 127, LL. 43–44, in restoration, seem to confirm the grant in 403/2 BC, whose memory, however, seems to have later gone lost. SALOMON 1997, pp. 81–85; CARGILL 1993, pp. 322–325.

21 See also PRANDI 1997.

for the case of Plataia. However, it should be clear that this grant foreshadows a later practice.

These few examples of mass grants of citizenship predating the 4th century BC are not concessions of potential citizenship as those that we find routinely in the Hellenistic institution. They are its predecessors, but the concessions of potential citizenship in the Hellenistic period had a different format, frame, and meaning.

As additional examples for early grants of potential citizenship, scholars often cite documents that testify to preexisting ties between communities; I treat some of these in this study, within the context of the geographical chapters. Still I must note that these documents rarely testify to preexisting agreements of potential citizenship. References to, for example, colonial relationships or kinship, were a way to find a common memory of a shared past that could serve as the basis for a new diplomatic discourse. When they include a reference to a preexisting grant of citizenship, we must try to identify this grant. However, we are indeed in the dark as the references are usually brief and without a context.[22] I have insisted on the fact that Hellenistic potential citizenship is granted from a community to a community, while earlier mass grants are for the citizens of a community: the evidence that contains references to citizenship/kinship relations and others seems (of course) to be directed to the community and thus aligns with the Hellenistic practice, but here we must remember that these pieces of evidence date to the Hellenistic period and thus reproduce its diplomatic language and habits. This evidence is flawed because it contains already an interpretation of past relations: just as we are ready to call 'fictitious' certain kinship relations, we should become more critical too of relationships that are based on types of ties that we find more 'acceptable' as they better address our categories of knowledge.

The institution of potential citizenship as it appears in the Hellenistic period cannot be found earlier than the late Classical-early Hellenistic era. Its predecessors are normally mass grants of citizenship for members of a community that can often be explained by taking into account the specific and often rather dramatic historical events that prompted them. This detail likens them mostly to the second type of potential citizenship that I have described here, which was indeed triggered by more compelling and practical circumstances. In terms of 'content,' Hellenistic *isopoliteia* is hardly different from 'mass' grants of citizenship attested in other time periods. The difference emerges in the mode and meaning of the concession. These mass grants could have been the model for the practice that was later replicated but within a different

---

22 See for example the case of Miletos and Phygela *Milet* I 3 142.

institutional framework and meaning. These grants became a tool similar to the pillars of Hellenistic diplomacy, i.e., *syngeneia*, *philia*, and *oikeiotes*, which, however, could be used on a larger scale because their 'institutional' investment was not as high as that which came with the concession of potential citizenship.

Where and when this institution was born is impossible to establish with certainty. The evidence prompts me to identify two main, possible candidates, namely, Miletos and Crete, but does not help us to determine whether either of them truly started on this widespread practice of granting potential citizenship.

APPENDIX 2

Polybios and Potential Citizenship

The evidence for the use of the grant of potential citizenship is mostly epigraphic. Literary sources rarely provide information on it and, when they do, the technical details are foggy and serve their narrative. Using literary sources as actual and factual evidence for this tool is therefore quite complex. As a matter of fact, even when the text truly testifies to an exchange of potential citizenship and we have an historical context for it, we do not have the institutional framework.

One ancient source deserves a brief, separate treatment: Polybios. His work preserves a few interesting cases, but his use of terminology makes assumptions that cannot always be substantiated.[1] To these uncertain testimonies I devote the following brief note.

Aitolia and Kios, Lysimacheia, and Chalchedon

Two passages in particular from the Histories of Polybios, POLYB. XV.23.8–9 and XVIII.3.11–12, provide information that, besides relating Philip's controversial attack and conquest of three Propontic cities, Kios, Lysimacheia, and Chalchedon, ca. 200 BC, shed some (confusing) light on the institutional relationship these cities had with the Aitolians. The first passage, POLYB. XV.23.8–9, says that these cities were friends and allies of the Aitolians, but also that Kios had an Aitolian *strategos*. He, however, could not avert the dangers brought by Philip who took the city and enslaved its inhabitants. POLYB. XVIII.3.11–12 testifies that also Lysimacheia had an Aitolian *strategos* and adds that Kios was in *sympoliteia* with this league.

The question is how to interpret these data. Scholars read this last passage, i.e., the *sympoliteia* between Kios and the league, as a proof for *isopoliteia* between Kios and Aitolia. Polybios, so the modern interpretation goes, would only have used the wrong term.[2]

This reading has helped to foster the belief that Aitolia used potential citizenship to unite its league to communities that were too distant to become

---

1 See WALBANK 1957 already in I, p. 234.
2 WALBANK 1967, vol. II, p. 478 who thinks it happened "during the first Macedonian War, when it was a natural reply to the threatening compact between Philip and Prousias."

part of the sympolity. In this instance, however, I am skeptical about this reading and follow Larsen, as I believe that the presence of Aitolian *strategoi* in Kios and Lysimacheia indicates that they had stipulated *symmachia* with Aitolia, which entailed military help.[3] Although one cannot overrule the possibility that *isopoliteia* had been granted within this wider agreement, the fact remains that Polybios does not say anything about shared citizenship.[4] The relationship among these communities must have been regulated by signing broader agreements that could have been sealed (or not) by potential citizenship. This would have served the military agreement and, perhaps be similar in form and intent to the agreement that Aitolia had established with Akarnania (no. 40).

Athens and Rhodes

Polybios XVI.26 presents the situation in Greece in the year 200 BC when king Attalos visited Attica after crossing over from Aegina. A Roman embassy had just arrived in Athens and Attalos wanted to be present. Rhodian representatives, too, came and joined the alliance that was to face Philip V, who had provoked them for too long in his attempt to lead them to break the agreement they still had in place.[5]

According to Livy, the Athenians had entered a conflict against Philip *haudquaquam digna causa* by putting to death two young Akarnanians who tried to take part in the Mysteries of Eleusis without being initiated. This triggered Akarnania's reaction that sought and found Philip's help. It is in the context of this conflict that Athenian ships, which the Rhodians later recovered for Athens, were taken by the Macedonians.[6]

Athens thanked Rhodes and welcomed the Attalid alliance enthusiastically. They voted to enter war against Philip and showered their guests with honors, among which stands out the creation of a new tribe named *Attalis*.[7]

According to Polybios, XVI.26.9, the Athenians ἀπεδέξαντο δὲ καὶ τοὺς Ῥοδίους μεγαλομερῶς καὶ τόν τε δῆμον ἐστεφάνωσαν ἀριστείων στεφάνῳ καὶ πᾶσι Ῥοδίοις ἰσοπολιτείαν ἐψηφίσαντο διὰ τὸ κἀκείνους αὐτοῖς χωρὶς τῶν ἄλλων τάς τε ναῦς ἀποκαταστῆσαι τὰς αἰχμαλώτους γενομένας καὶ τοὺς ἄνδρας. The rescue of the four Athenian ships with their men and the concession of honors to the

---

3 LARSEN 1968, p. 208.
4 CHANIOTIS 2008, pp. 103–145, esp. pp. 112–114.
5 WIEMER 2002, esp. pp. 192–218; BERTHOLD 1984, pp. 125–134.
6 On the chronology see PRITCHETT 1954, pp. 159–164. The Athenians, however, did not declare war against Philip until after the visit of Attalos and the Rhodian embassy in 200 BC.
7 See LIV. XXXI. 15. 6; and HABICHT 1995, esp. p. 219.

Rhodians including citizenship appears also in the work of the Roman historian Livy [LIV. XXXI. 15, 6–7]: *Rhodiorum populus corona aurea virtutis ergo donatus, civitasque Rhodiis data, quemadmodum Rhodii prius Atheniensibus dederant*. Livy here adds that the Athenian concession was, in truth, only a reciprocation of a similar grant of Rhodian citizenship. Either Polybios omits this detail or we have lost the section with its mention, or, as a third option, Livy read too much into his source.[8]

Gawantka defined this evidence, I think rightly, as uncertainly presenting the institution of potential citizenship. Other scholars have preferred to read these texts literally, but they have reached different conclusions. Osborne devotes a short paragraph to this alleged grant mainly focusing on the term *isopoliteia*, which, he says, is unusual in Athenian decrees.[9] Berthold's comment instead is that "… there is no other record of this allegation (*isopoliteia*), and it is extremely unlikely that Rhodes would ever have done such a thing."[10] No other grant of *isopoliteia* from Rhodes is known and Berthold has a point in classifying this exchange as unusual. Wiemer even suggested the occasion for an alliance where the grant of isopolity was included.[11] According to Wiemer Athens and Rhodes signed a *symmachia* to which potential citizenship was attached. However, we lack direct evidence. Moreover, this combination, although common in Crete, is hardly attested in the rest of the Mediterranean.

Was Polybios really using the term *isopoliteia* as a *terminus technicus*? How does Livy extrapolate the information that the Athenians were only reciprocating a grant? Is he following another source or is he only over-interpreting *isopoliteia*? This brief passage would be a unique testimony for the use of potential citizenship in Rhodes and with a community, Athens, that did not make the widest use of it. This argument is, of course, not persuasive, but institutionally this grant appears unlikely.

Kydonia and Apollonia

POLYB. XXVIII.13–14(/5)[12] has been interpreted as another passage testifying to the existence of a grant of potential citizenship. In this case the partner

---

8   So already BRISCOE 1973, p. 99 citing OEHLER *RE*.
9   OSBORNE 1981(a), T 104, p. 96. See my comment on the language of isopoliteia *supra*, esp. pp. 15–20.
10 BERTHOLD 1984, p. 129 n. 9.
11 WIEMER 2002, p. 214.
12 CHANIOTIS 1996, pp. 285–287 no. 41 discusses the passage: … ὅτι οἱ Κυδωνιᾶται κατὰ τὸν καιρὸν τοῦτον ἐποίησαν πρᾶγμα δεινὸν καὶ παράσπονδον ὁμολογουμένως. καίπερ ⟨γὰρ⟩ πολλῶν

cities were the Cretan communities of Kydonia and Apollonia. At some point, the former destroyed the latter thus committing what was considered an impious act.[13]

A. Chaniotis treats the text as a testimony to potential citizenship mainly relying on the clause κοινωνίας πάντων τῶν ἐν ἀνθρώποις νομιζομένων δικαίων that he thinks is a paraphrase for the typical *metechein* clause. In addition, he suggests that the *syntheke* said to have been kept in the sanctuary recorded the grant of potential citizenship along with a possible alliance, as often happens in Crete. Diodoros records this event, too, but he only refers to a tie of *philia*.[14] If an exchange of potential citizenship had existed between Kydonia and Apollonia, he does not mention it. Our ignorance of even the exact location of Apollonia[15] does not help to determine Apollonia's relationship with Kydonia, but it can safely be said that Polybios is using the term *sympoliteia* in a rather 'untechnical' way. While we should contemplate the possibility that an agreement of *isopoliteia* was in place, we have no certainty. The safest course is still to consider this passage as an uncertain piece of evidence.[16]

Locri Epizephiri

The last passage I wish to discuss, POLYB. XII.9.2–4, focuses on Timaeus's version of the foundation legend of Locri Epizephiri. According to Aristotle, whom Timaeus refutes, this city had been founded by runaway slaves and their women, i.e., the wives of their masters who had been in war.[17] Here the origin

---

τοιούτων γενομένων κατὰ τὴν Κρήτην, ὅμως ἔδοξεν ὑπεραίρειν τὴν συνήθειαν τὸ τότε γενόμενον. ὑπαρχούσης γὰρ αὐτοῖς οὐ μόνον φιλίας, ἀλλὰ συμπολιτείας πρὸς Ἀπολλωνιάτας καὶ καθόλου κοινωνίας πάντων τῶν ἐν ἀνθρώποις νομιζομένων δικαίων, καὶ περὶ τούτων κειμένης ἐνόρκου συνθήκης παρὰ τὸν Δία τὸν Ἰδαῖον, παρασπονδήσαντες τοὺς Ἀπολλωνιάτας κατελάβοντο τὴν πόλιν καὶ τοὺς μὲν ἄνδρας κατέσφαξαν, τὰ δ'ὑπάρχοντα διήρπασαν, τὰς (δὲ) γυναῖκας καὶ τὰ τέκνα καὶ τὴν πόλιν καὶ τὴν χώραν διανειμάμενοι κατεῖχον.

13 CHANIOTIS 1996, pp. 45–48; on Polybios's judgement see ECKSTEIN 1995, p. 24 where the author speaks, too, of joint citizenship.
14 DIOD. XXX.13.
15 See CHANIOTIS 1996, p. 286 n. 1537 for its location near modern Hagia Pelagia west of Heraklion on the coast.
16 Chaniotis's comment, 1996, pp. 285–287 no. 41, is too syllogistic in this case. That *sympoliteia* in Polybios means *isopoliteia* is only an assumption that rests on uncertain grounds. The Achaean historian was not using these terms as technical language and, I argue, he was not confusing them either. We are simply dealing with a different language register.
17 Timaeus instead holds that the colonists were free men. The modern debate around the foundation history of Lokri has been just as lively as the debate in antiquity; VAN COMPERNOLLE 1976, pp. 329–400.

of these colonists is irrelevant; the ties Timaeus says existed between mother city (only generally indicated as the Lokrians of Greece) and the colony are worthy of a note.

During his critique to Timaeus, Polybios, who had also criticized Aristotle, and his methodology, says: (Timaeus) φησὶ τοιγαροῦν κατὰ τὴν αὐτὴν βύβλον, οὐκέτι κατὰ τὸν αὐτὸν εἰκότα λόγον χρώμενος τοῖς ἐλέγχοις, ἀλλ'ἀληθινῶς αὐτὸς ἐπιβαλὼν εἰς τοὺς κατὰ τὴν Ἑλλάδα Λοκρούς, ἐξετάζειν τὰ περὶ τῆς ἀποικίας. τοὺς δὲ πρῶτον μὲν ἐπιδεικνύειν αὐτῷ συνθήκας ἐγγράπτους, ἔτι καὶ νῦν διαμενούσας, πρὸς τοὺς ἐξαπεσταλμένους, αἷς ὑπογεγράφθαι τὴν ἀρχὴν τοιαύτην "ὡς γονεῦσι πρὸς τέκνα". πρὸς δὲ τούτοις εἶναι δόγματα, καθ' ἅ πολιτείαν ὑπάρχειν ἑκατέροις παρ' ἑκατέροις.

One of Timaeus's arguments to disprove Aristotle's tradition on the foundation of Lokri was the existence of documents that attested to an agreement (συνθήκας) between the Italian town and the Greek Lokris, along with decrees (δόγματα) with which the parties had exchanged citizenship. As van Compernolle notes, if the agreement had existed, the wording recorded by Polybios would only show that it was archaic.[18] The only reliable document that comes to mind as a parallel to substantiate this claim of 'πολιτείαν ὑπάρχειν ἑκατέροις παρ' ἑκατέροις' is the oath of the Founders (Thera and Kyrene). The institutional relationship between mother cities and colonies cannot be defined *a priori*, it must have been a quite colorful institutional context that we can hardly reconstruct through our fragmentary sources. This consideration should apply also to this passage, on which we ought to suspend any judgment that would otherwise be the result of pure speculation.

---

18   VAN COMPERNOLLE 1976, pp. 350-352.

Bibliography

ABMEIER 1990: ABMEIER A., "Zur Geschichte von Apollonia am Rhyndakos," *Asia Minor Studien* 1, pp. 1–17.
AGER 2001: AGER S.L., "4th Century Thera and the Second Athenian Sea League," *Ancient World* 32, pp. 99–119.
AKALIN 2008: AKALIN A.G., "Der hellenistische Synoikismos in der Troas," *Asia Minor Studien* 55, pp. 1–38.
ALLEN 1983: ALLEN R.E., *The Attalid Kingdom. A Constitutional History*, Oxford.
ALLEN 1971: ALLEN R.E., "Attalos I and Aigina," *ABSA* 66, pp. 1–12.
AMANDRY 1986: AMANDRY P., "Chios and Delphi," in edd. Boardmann and Vaphopoulou-Richardson, *Chios. A Conference at the Homereion in Chios 1984*, Oxford 1986, pp. 205–232.
AMELING 1991: AMELING W., Review of M. HATZOPOULOS, *Une donation du roi Lysimaque (1988)*, *Gnomon* 63, pp. 110–115.
ANEZIRI 2003: ANEZIRI S., *Die Vereine der dionysischen Techniten im Kontext der hellenistischen Gesellschaft*, Stuttgart.
ANTONETTI 1987: ANTONETTI CL., "Le popolazioni settentrionali dell'Etolia: difficoltà di localizzazione e problema dei limiti territoriali alla luce della documentazione epigrafica" in ed. Cabanes, *L'Illyrie méridionale et l'Épire dans l'Antiquité*, Actes du Colloque International de Clermont Ferrand (22–25 octobre 1984), Clermont-Ferrand, pp. 95–113.
ARCHIBALD 1998: ARCHIBALD Z., *The Odrysian Kingdom of Thrace*, Oxford.
AYLWARD 2005: AYLWARD W., "Security, *Synoikismos*, and *Koinon* as Determinants for Troad Housing in Classical and Hellenistic Times," in edd. Ault and Nevett, *Ancient Greek Houses and Households*, Philadelphia, pp. 36–53.
BADIAN 1966: BADIAN E., "Alexander the Great and the Greeks of Asia," in edd. Ehrenber and Badian, *Ancient Society and Institutions. Studies presented to Victor Ehrenberg on his 75th birthday*, Oxford, pp. 37–70.
BAGNALL 1976: BAGNALL R.S., *The Administration of the Ptolemaic Possessions outside Egypt*, Leiden.
BEAN 1971: BEAN G.E., *Turkey beyond the Meander. An Archaeological Guide*, London.
BEAN and COOK 1957: BEAN G.E. and COOK J.M., "The Caria Coast III," *BSA* 52, pp. 58–146.
BEAN and COOK 1952: BEAN G.E. and COOK J.M., "The Cnidia," *BSA* 47, pp. 171–212.
BEARZOT 1997: BEARZOT C., "Ancora sui Plateesi e la fratrie di Atene," *Simblos. Scritti di storia antica* 2, pp. 43–60.
BECK 1997: BECK H., *Polis und Koinon. Untersuchungen zur Geschichte und Struktur der griechischen Bundesstaaten im 4. Jahrhundert v. Chr.* Stuttgart.

BEHRWALD 2000: BEHRWALD R., *Der lykische Bund: Untersuchungen zu Geschichte und Verfassung*, Bonn.
BELIN DE BALLU 1972: BELIN DE BALLU E., *Olbia: cité antique du littoral Nord de la Mer Noire*, Leiden.
BENCIVENNI 2003: BENCIVENNI A., *Progetti di riforme costituzionali nelle epigrafi greche dei secoli IV–II a.C.*, Bologna.
BERGES 1994: BERGES D., "Alt-Knidos und Neu-Knidos," *MDAI* 44, pp. 5–16.
BERNSTEIN 2003: BERNSTEIN F., *Konflikt und Migration. Studien zu griechischen Fluchtbewegungen im Zeitalter der sogenannten großen Kolonisation*, St. Katherinen.
BERRANGER-AUSERVE 2000: BERRANGER-AUSERVE D., *Paros. 2, Prosopographie générale et étude historique du début de la période classique jusqu'à la fin de la période romaine*, Clermont-Ferrand.
BERTHOLD 1984: BERTHOLD R.M., *Rhodes in the Hellenistic Age*, Ithaka.
BERVE 1926: BERVE H., *Das Alexanderreich auf prosopographischer Grundlage*, Vol. 2, Munich.
BIAGETTI 2010: BIAGETTI C., "Ricerche sulle tradizioni di fondazione di Magnesia al Meandro. Un aggiornamento," *Klio* 92, pp. 42–64.
BILLOWS 1990: BILLOWS R.A., *Antigonos the One-eyed and the Creation of the Hellenic State*, Berkeley.
BINGÖL 2005: BINGÖL O., "Neue Forschungen in Magnesia am Mäander," in edd. Işık, Schwertheim, Winter; *Neue Forschungen zu Ionien: Fahri Isik zum 60. Geburtstag gewidmet*, Bonn, pp. 165–170.
BLANSHARD 2007: BLANSHARD A., "The problems with honouring Samos: an Athenian Document Relief and its Interpretation," in edd. Newby and Leader-Newby, *Art and Inscriptions in the Ancient World*, Cambridge, pp. 19–37.
BOFFO 1985: BOFFO L., *I re ellenistici e i centri religiosi dell'Asia Minore*, Pavia.
BOGAERT 1968: BOGAERT R., *Banques et banquiers dans les cités grecques*, Leiden.
BOSWORTH 1993: BOSWORTH A.B., "Perdiccas and the Kings," *CQ* 87, pp. 420–427.
BOSWORTH 1988: BOSWORTH A.B., *Conquest and Empire. The Reign of Alexander the Great*, Cambridge.
BOTERMANN 1994: BOTERMANN H., "Wer baute das neue Priene? Zur Interpretation der Inschriften von Priene Nr. 1 und 156," *Hermes* 122, pp. 162–187.
BOUSQUET 1960: BOUSQUET J., "Inscriptions de Delphes", *BCH* 84, pp. 161–175.
BOUSQUET and GAUTHIER 1994: BOUSQUET J. and GAUTHIER PH., "Inscriptions du Létôon de Xanthos," *REG* 107, pp. 319–361.
BOWSKY 1989: BOWSKY M.W., "Portrait of a Polis: Lato pros Kamara (Crete) in the Second Century B.C.," *Hesperia* 58, pp. 331–347.
BRAUND 2007: BRAUND D., "Greater Olbia: Ethnic, Religious, Economic, and Political Interactions in the Region of Olbia, c. 600–100 B.C.," in edd. Braund and Kryzhic'kij, *Classical Olbia and the Scythian World*, Oxford, pp. 37–78.

BRAVO 1980: BRAVO B., "Sûlan, Représailles et justice privée contre des étrangers dans les cités grecques (Études du vocabulaire et des institutions)," *ASNP* 10, 3, 1980, pp. 675–987.

BRESSON 2010: BRESSON A., "Cnidos: Topography of a Battle," in edd. van Bremen and Carbon, *Hellenistic Karia: proceedings of the First International Conference on Hellenistic Karia, Oxford, 29 june–2 july 2006*, Paris, pp. 435–451.

BRESSON 1999: BRESSON A., "Cnide à l'époque classique: La cité et ses villes," *REA* 101, 83–114.

BRISCOE 1973: BRISCOE J., *A Commentary on Livy (Books xxxi–xxxiii)*, Oxford.

BRULÉ 1978: BRULÉ P., *La piraterie crétoise hellénistique*, Paris.

BRUN 1993: BRUN P., "La stèle des céréales de Cyrène et le commerce di grain en Egée au IV° S. Av. J.C.," *ZPE* 99, pp. 185–196.

BRUN 1989: BRUN P., "L'île de Kéos et ses cités au IVe siècle av. J.C.," *ZPE* 76, pp. 121–138.

BUCHHOLZ 1975: BUCHHOLZ H.G., *Methymna. Archäologische Beiträge zur Topographie und Geschichte von Nordlesbos*, Mainz.

BUCKLER 1998: BUCKLER J., "Epameinondas and the new Inscription from Knidos," *Mnemosyne* 51.2, pp. 192–205.

BUCKLER 1980: BUCKLER J., *The Theban Hegemony*, Cambridge.

BURASELIS 2003: BURASELIS K., "Considerations on Symmachia and Sympoliteia," in edd. Buraselis et Alii, *The idea of European Community in History: Conference Proceedings* vol. II, Athens, pp. 39–50.

BURASELIS 2002: BURASELIS K., Review to Ager 1996 and Magnetto 1997, *Gnomon* 74, pp. 224–231.

BUSSI 1999: BUSSI S., "Attacco di pirati a Teos ellenistica," *Studi Ellenistici* XII, pp. 159–171.

CANEVARO 2010: CANEVARO M., "The Decree Awarding Citizenship to the Plataeans ([Dem.] 59.104)," *GRBS* 50, pp. 337–369.

CARGILL 1983: CARGILL J., "*IG* II^2 1 and the Kleruchy on Samos," *GRBS* 24, pp. 321–332.

CARLESS UNWIN 2017: CARLESS UNWIN N., *Caria and Crete in Antiquity*, Cambridge.

CARLSSON 2010: CARLSSON S., *Hellenistic Democracies. Freedom, Independence and Political Procedure in Some East Greek City-States*, Stuttgart.

CARTLEDGE and SPAWFORTH 2002: CARTLEDGE P. and SPAWFORTH A., *Hellenistic and Roman Sparta. A Tale of Two Cities*, Routledge.

CATALDI 1983: CATALDI S., *Symbolai e le relazioni tra le città greche nel V secolo a.C.*, Pisa.

CHAMOUX 1953: CHAMOUX F., *Cyrène sous la monarchie des Battiades*, Paris.

CHANDEZON 2003: CHANDEZON CH., *L'élevage en Grèce (fin V^e–fin Ier s. a.C.). L'apport des sources épigraphiques*, Pessac.

CHANIOTIS 2008: CHANIOTIS A., "Policing the Hellenistic Countryside: Realities and Ideologies," in edd. Brélaz and Ducrey, *Sécurité Collective et ordre public dans les sociétés anciennes*, pp. 103–145.

CHANIOTIS 1999(a): CHANIOTIS A., "The Epigraphy of the Hellenistic Crete," in *XI congresso internazionale di epigrafia* vol. 1, Rome, pp. 287–299.

CHANIOTIS 1999(b): CHANIOTIS A., "Empfängerformular und Urkundenfälschung: Bemerkungen zum Urkundendossier von Magnesia am Mäander," in ed. Khouri, *Urkunden und Urkundenformulare im klassischen Altertum und in den orientalischen Kulturen*, Heidelberg, pp. 51–69.

CHANIOTIS 1999(c): CHANIOTIS A., "Milking the Mountains: Economic Activities on the Cretan Uplands in the Classical and Hellenistic Period," in ed. Chaniotis, *From Minoan Farmers to Roman Traders*, Stuttgart, pp. 181–220.

CHANIOTIS 1986: CHANIOTIS A., "ἐντέλεια: Zu Inhalt und Begriff eines Vorrechtes," *ZPE* 64, pp. 159–162.

CHARNEAUX 1966: CHARNEAUX P., "Liste argienne de Théarodoques," *BCH* 90, pp. 156–239.

CLAY 1993: CLAY D., "Plato's Magnesia," in edd. Rosen and Farrell, *Nomodeiktes. Greek Studies in Honor of Martin Ostwald*, Ann Arbor, pp. 435–445.

COHEN 2006: COHEN G., *The Hellenistic Settlements in Syria, the Red Basin, and North Africa*, Berkeley.

COHEN 1995: COHEN G., *The Hellenistic Settlements in Europe, the Islands, and Asia Minor*, Berkeley.

VAN COMPERNOLLE 1976: VAN COMPERNOLLE R., "Le tradizioni sulla fondazione e sulla storia arcaica di Locri Epizefiri e la propaganda politica alla fine del V e nel IV secolo av. Cr.," *ASPN* VI, pp. 329–400.

COOK 1973: COOK J.M., *The Troad. An Archaeological and Topographical Study*, Oxford.

CRISCUOLO 2007: CRISCUOLO L., "Erodoto, Aristotele e la 'Stele dei fondatori'," in edd. Gasperini and Marengo, *Cirene e la Cirenaica nell'Antichità. Atti del Convegno Internazionale di Studi*, Tivoli, pp. 187–200.

CRISCUOLO 2001: CRISCUOLO L., "Erodoto, Aristotele e la 'Stele dei fondatori'," *Simblos* 3, pp. 31–44.

CROWTHER 1996: CROWTHER C.V., "I. Priene 8 and the History of Priene in the Hellenistic Period," *Chiron* 26, pp. 195–243.

CULASSO GASTALDI 2004: CULASSO GASTALDI E., *Le prossenie ateniesi del IV secolo a.C. Gli onorati asiatici*, Alessandria.

CURTY 2005: CURTY O., "Un usage fort controversé: la parenté dans le langage diplomatique de l'époque hellénistique," *Ancient Society* 35, pp. 101–117.

CURTY 1999: CURTY O., "Les parentés légendaire à l'époque hellénistique. Précisions méthodologiques," *Kernos* 12, pp. 167–194.

CURTY 1995: CURTY O., *Les parentés légendaire entre cités grecques: catalogue raisonné des inscriptions contenant le terme syngeneia et analyse critique*, Geneva.

DANY 1999: DANY O., *Akarnanien im Hellenismus. Geschichte und Völkerrecht in Nordwestgriechenland*, Munich.

DAVERIO ROCCHI 1999: DAVERIO ROCCHI G., "Identità etnica, appartenenza territoriale e unità politica del κοινόν focese," *Orbis Terrarum* 5, pp. 15–30.

DAVERIO ROCCHI 1994: DAVERIO ROCCHI G., "Strutture urbane e centralismo politico nel 'koinon' focese," in edd. Aigner Foresti et alii, *Federazioni e federalismo nell'Europa antica*, pp. 181–193, Milan.

DEMAND 1990: DEMAND N., *Urban Relocation in Archaic and Classical Greece: Flight and Consolidation*, Bristol.

DEMAND 1989: DEMAND N., "Did Knidos really move? The literary and epigraphical Evidence," *Class. Ant.* 8.2, pp. 224–237.

DEMAND 1986: DEMAND N., "The Relocation of Priene Reconsidered," *Phoenix* 40.1, pp. 35–44.

DEMETRIOU 2010: DEMETRIOU D., "Pistiros and a North Aegean Trade Network," *AntCl.* 79, pp. 77–93.

DEVELIN 1989: DEVELIN R., *Athenian Officials: 684–321 B.C.*, Cambridge.

DIMIPOULOU 2015: DIMIPOULOU A., Λεσβίων πολιτεῖαι: πολίτευμα, θεσμοί καὶ δίκαιο τῶν πόλεων τῆς Λέσβου (ἀρχαϊκοί, κλασικοί, ἑλληνιστικοί, ρωμαϊκοί χρόνοι), Athens.

LE DINAHET-COUILLOUD 1974: LE DINAHET-COUILLOUD M. TH., "Reliefs funéraires des Cyclades de l'époque hellénistique à l'époque impériale," *BCH* 98, pp. 397–498.

DÖSSEL 2002: DÖSSEL A., *Die Beilegung innerstaatlicher Konflikte in den griechischen Poleis vom 5.–3. Jahrhundert v. Chr.*, Frankfurt.

DOBIAS-LALOU 2001: DOBIAS-LALOU C., "Les rapports linguistiques entre une métropole et sa colonie," in edd. Fromentin and Gotteland, *Origines Gentium*, Bordeaux, pp. 357–363.

DOBIAS-LALOU 1994: DOBIAS-LALOU C., "SEG IX 3: un document composite ou inclassable?," *Verbum* 3–4, pp. 243–256.

DUMULIN 1902: DUMULIN H., "Fouilles de Ténos," *BCH* 26, pp. 399–439.

DUNANT and THOMOPOULOS 1954: DUNANT CH. and THOMOPOULOS J., "Inscriptions de Ceós," *BCH* 78, pp. 316–348.

DUNST and MERKELBACH 1968: DUNST G. and MERKELBACH R., "Zu dem neuen epigraphischen Dokument aus Teos," *ZPE* 3, pp. 170–174.

DUSANIC 1978: DUSANIC SL., "The ὅρκιον τῶν οἰκιστήριων and Fourth Century Cyrene," *Chiron* 8, pp. 55–76.

ECKSTEIN 1995: ECKSTEIN A., *Moral Vision in the Histories of Polybius*, Berkeley.

VAN EFFENTERRE 1948: VAN EFFENTERRE H., *La Crète et le monde grec de Platon à Polybe*, Paris.

EHRHARDT 2003: EHRHARDT N., "Milet nach den Perserkriegen: ein Neubeginn?," *AMS* 50, pp. 1–19.
EHRHARDT 1988: EHRHARDT N., *Milet und seine Kolonien: vergleichende Untersuchung der kultischen und politischen Einrichtungen*, Frankfurt.
EHRHARDT 1987: EHRHARDT N., "Die politischen Beziehungen zwischen den griechischen Schwarzmeergründungen und ihren Mutterstädten. Ein Beitrag zur Bedeutung von Kolonialverhältnissen in Griechenland," in *Terra Antiqua Balcanica. Actes du IXe congrès international d'épigraphie grecque et latine*, Sofia, pp. 78–117.
EILERS 2002: EILERS CL., *Roman Patrons of Greek Cities*, Oxford.
EL-ZEIN 1972: EL-ZEIN M., *Geschichte der Stadt Apameia am Orontes von den Anfängen bis Augustus*, Diss. Heidelberg.
ERRINGTON 2006: ERRINGTON R.M., "Chios in the Third Century B.C.," in edd. Malochou and Matthaiou, *Chiakon Symposion eis mneme W.G. Forrest*, Athens, pp. 137–147.
ERRINGTON 1995: ERRINGTON R.M., "Ἐκκλησίας κυρίας γενομένης," *Chiron* 25, pp. 19–42.
ERRINGTON 1989: ERRINGTON R.M., "The Peace Treaty between Miletus and Magnesia (*I. Milet* 148)," *Chiron* 19, pp. 279–288.
ERRINGTON 1969: ERRINGTON R.M., *Philopoemen*, Oxford 1969.
ERSKINE 1990: ERSKINE A., *The Hellenistic Stoa political Thought and Action*, London.
ÉTIENNE 1990: ÉTIENNE R., *Ténos II. Ténos et les Ciclades du milieu du IV siècle av. J.C. au milieu du IIIe siècle ap. J.C.*, vol. II, Athens.
ÉTIENNE 1984: ÉTIENNE R., "Astu et Polis à Ténos (Cyclades)," *Ktema* 9, 1984, pp. 205–211.
ÉTIENNE and BRAUN 1986: ÉTIENNE R. and BRAUN J.P., *Ténos. I, Le sanctuaire de Poseidon et d'Amphitrite*, Athens.
FARAGUNA 2013: FARAGUNA M. (ed.), *Archives and Archival Documents in Ancient Societies. Trieste 30 September–1 October 2011*, Trieste.
FARAONE 1993: FARAONE CH., "Molten Wax, Spilt Wine and Mutilated Animals: Sympathetic Magic in Near Eastern and Early Greek Oaths Ceremonies," *JHS* 113, pp. 60–80.
FAURE 1993: FAURE P., "Nouvelles identifications d'antiques localités crétoises," *Kadmos* 33, pp. 67–74.
FERNOUX 2004: FERNOUX H., "Les cités s'entraident dans la guerre: historiques, cadres institutionnels et modalités practiques des conventions d'assistance dans l'Asie Mineure hellénistique," in edd. Couvenhes and Fernoux, *Les cités grecques et la guerre en Asie Mineure à l'époque héllenistique*, Lyon, pp. 115–176.
FERRARY 1988: FERRARY J.L., *Philhellénisme et impérialisme: aspects idéologiques de la conquête romaine du monde hellénistique, de la seconde guerre de Macédoine à la guerre contre Mithridate*, Rome.

FERRI 1925: FERRI S., "La stele dei fondatori," *Abhandl. Preuss. Akad. Wiss. Berlin* 5, pp. 19–24.

FEUSEN 2009: FEUSEN ST., *Der Hafen von Alexandria Troas*, Bonn.

FLACELIÈRE 1937: FLACELIÈRE R., *Les Aitoliens à Delphes*, Paris.

FONTENROSE 1988: FONTENROSE J., *Didyma. Apollo's Oracle, Cult, and Companions*, Berkeley.

FRASER 1952: FRASER P.M., "Alexander and the Rhodian Constitution," *PP* 7, pp. 192–206.

FREITAG 2000: FREITAG K., *Der Golf von Korinth. Historisch-topographische Untersuchungen von der Archaik bis in das 1 Jh. v. Chr.*, Munich.

FUNKE 2008: FUNKE P., "Die Aitoler in der Ägäis. Untersuchungen zur sogenannten Seepolitik der Aitoler im 3. Jh. v.Chr.," in ed. Winter, *Vom Euphrat bis zum Bosphorus, Asia Minor Studien* 65.1, pp. 253–267.

FUNKE 2007: FUNKE P., "Alte Grenzen—Neue Grenzen. Formen polisübergreifender Machtbildung in klassischer und hellenistischer Zeit," in edd. Albertz, Blöbaum and Funke *Räume und Grenzen. Topologische Konzepte in den antiken Kulturen des östlichen Mittelmeerraums*, Munich, pp. 187–204.

FUNKE 2000: FUNKE P., "Zur Datierung der aitolischen Bürgerrechtsverleihung an die Bürger von Herakleia am Latmos (*IG* IX 1^2, 1, 173)," *Chiron* 30, pp. 505–517.

FUNKE 1997: FUNKE P., "Polisgenese und Urbanisierung in Aitolien im 5. und 4. Jhd. v. Chr.," in *The Polis as an Urban Centre and as a Political Community*, Acts of the Copenhagen Polis Centre vol. IV, Copenhagen, pp. 145–173.

FUNKE 1995: FUNKE P., *Habilitationsschrift zum Aitolischen koinon*, (unpublished) Cologne.

GABRIELSEN 2002: GABRIELSEN V., "The Synoikized City," in edd. by Flensted-Jensen, Nielsen and Rubinstein, *Polis and Politics: studies in ancient Greek History presented to Mogens Hermann Hansen on his sixtieth birthday, August 20*, Copenhagen, pp. 177–205.

GABRIELSEN 1997: GABRIELSEN V., *The Naval Aristocracy of Hellenistic Rhodes*, Aarhus.

GAUTHIER 2000: GAUTHIER PH., "Epigraphica IV," *RPh.* 74, pp. 103–114.

GAUTHIER 1997: GAUTHIER PH., "Compte Rendu: Les cités de Lesbos aux époques hellénistique et impériale," *Topoi* 7, pp. 349–361.

GAUTHIER 1992: GAUTHIER PH., "L'archonte éponyme à Ténos," *REG* 105, pp. 111–120.

GAUTHIER 1985: GAUTHIER PH., *Les cités grecque et leur bienfaiteurs*, Athens-Paris.

GAUTHIER 1977/78: GAUTHIER PH., "Épigraphie et institutions grecques," *EPHE* 110, pp. 373–378.

GAUTHIER 1972: GAUTHIER PH., *Symbola. Les étrangers et la justice dans les cités grecques*, Nancy.

GAUTHIER and BOUSQUET 1994: GAUTHIER PH. and BOUSQUET J., "Inscriptions du Létôon de Xanthos," *REG* 107, pp. 319–361.

GAWANTKA 1975: GAWANTKA W., *Isopolitie. Ein Beitrag zur Geschichte der zwinschenstaatlischen Beziehungen in der griechischen Antike*, Munich.

GEHRKE 2014: GEHRKE H.J., *Geschichte als Element Antiker Kultur*, Munich.

GEHRKE 2001: GEHRKE H., "Myth, History and Collective Identity: Uses of the Past in Ancient Greece and Beyond," in ed. Luraghi, *The Historian's Craft in the Age of Herodotus*, Oxford, pp. 286–313.

GEHRKE 1985: GEHRKE H., *Stasis. Untersuchungen zu den inneren Kriegen in den griechischen Staaten des 5. und 4. Jahrhunderts v.Chr.*, Munich.

GEORGOUDI 1998: GEORGOUDI S., "Les porte-parole des dieux: réflexions sur le personnel des oracles grecs," in edd. Chierassi-Colombo and Seppilli *Sibille e linguaggi oracolari*, Macerata, pp. 315–365.

GORMAN 2002: GORMAN V.B., "Milesian Decrees of 'Isopoliteia' and the Refoundation of the City, ca. 429 BCE," in edd. Gorman and Robinson, *Oikistes. Studies in Constitutions, Colonies, and Military Power in the Ancient World offered in Honor of A.J. Graham*, Leiden, pp. 181–193.

GORMAN 2001: GORMAN V.B., *Miletos Ornament of Ionia*, Ann Arbor.

VON GRAEVE 2000: VON GRAEVE V., "Die Belagerung Milets durch Alexander den Grossen," in *Civilisation grecque et cultures antiques périphériques*, Bucarest, pp. 113–129.

GRAF 1985: GRAF F., *Nordionische Kulte*, Rome.

GRAHAM 2001: GRAHAM A.J., "The Authenticity of the ὅρκιον τῶν οἰκιστήριων of Cyrene," in *Collected Papers on Greek Colonization*, Leiden, pp. 83–112.

GRAHAM 1964: GRAHAM A.J., *Colony and Mother City in Ancient Greece*, Manchester.

GRAINDOR 1911: GRAINDOR P., "Liste d'archontes eponyms Téniens," *Musee Belge* 15, pp. 255–261.

GRAINDOR 1907: GRAINDOR P., "Les fouilles de Ténos," *Le Musée Belge* 11, pp. 5–51.

GRANDJEAN 2003: GRANDJEAN C., *Les Messéniens de 370/369 au 1er siècle de notre ère monnayages et histoire*, Paris.

GRIEB 2008: GRIEB V., *Hellenistische Demokratie*, Stuttgart.

GRUEN 1984: GRUEN E., *The Hellenistic World and the Coming of Rome*, Berkeley.

GUAGLIUMI 2005: GUAGLIUMI B., "Tra esilio e cittadinanza: il caso di Iulis," *Serta Antiqua et Mediaevalia* 7, pp. 419–425.

GUAGLIUMI 2003: GUAGLIUMI B., "Il Racconto di una *Stasis* nel decreto ateniese per Iulis (*IG* II² 111)," *Quaderni del Dipartimento di Filologia A. Rostagni*, pp. 25–47.

GUIZZI 2008: GUIZZI F., "Texts" in ed. Ritti *Museo archeologico di Denizli-Hierapolis: catalogo delle iscrizioni greche e latine: Distretto di Denizli*, Naples.

GUIZZI 2000/1: GUIZZI F., *Hierapytna. Storia di una polis cretese dalla fondazione alla conquista romana*, Rome.

GUIZZI 1999: GUIZZI F., "Private Economic Activities in Hellenistic Crete. The Evidence of the Isopoliteia Treaties," in ed. Chaniotis, *From Minoan Farmers to Roman Traders: Sidelights on the Economy of Ancient Crete*, Stuttgart, pp. 235–245.

GÜNTHER 1998: GÜNTHER W., "Milet und Athen im zweiten Jahrhundert v. Chr.," *Chiron* 28, pp. 21–34.

GÜNTHER 1988: GÜNTHER W., "Milesische Bürgerrechts- und Proxenieverleihungen der hellenisticher Zeit," *Chiron* 18, pp. 383–419.

GÜNTHER 1971: GÜNTHER W., *Das Orakel von Didyma in hellenistischer Zeit*, Tübingen.

HABICHT 2005(a): HABICHT CH., "Notes on Inscriptions from Cyzicus," *EA* 38, pp. 93–100.

HABICHT 2005(b): HABICHT CH., "Datum und Umstände der rhodischen Schlichtung zwischen Samos und Priene," *Chiron* 35, pp. 137–146.

HABICHT 1995: HABICHT CH., *Athen, die Geschichte der Stadt in der hellenistischen Zeit*, Munich.

HABICHT 1991: HABICHT CH., "Milesische Theoren in Athen," *Chiron* 21, pp. 325–329.

HABICHT 1989: HABICHT CH., "Sosikrates von Abdera," *ZPE* 77, p. 94.

HABICHT 1952: HABICHT CH., "Samische Volksbeschlüsse der Hellenistischen Zeit," *AM* 72, pp. 152–274.

HAMON 2018: HAMON P., "Tout l'or et l'argent de Téos: au sujet d'une nouvelle édition des décrets sur les pirates et l'emprunt pour la libération des otages," *Chiron* 48, pp. 333–374.

HANSEN 1947 (1971²): HANSEN E.V., *The Attalids of Pergamon*, Ithaca.

HARTER-UIBOPUU 1998: HARTER UIBOPUU K., *Das zwischenstaatliche Schiedsverfahren im achäischen Koinon: zur friedlichen Streitbeilegung nach den epigraphischen Quellen*, Cologne.

HASLUCK 1910: HASLUCK F.W., *Cyzicus*, Cambridge.

HAUSSOLIER 1902: HAUSSOLIER B., *L'historie de Milet et du Didymeion*, Paris.

HELLER and PONT 2012: HELLER A. and PONT V., *Patrie d'origine et patries électives: les citoyenneté multiples dans le monde grec d'époque romaine*, Bordeaux.

HENNIG 1994: HENNIG D., "Immobilienerwerb durch Nichtbürger in der klassischen und hellenistischen Polis," *Chiron* 24, pp. 305–344.

HENRY 2001: HENRY A.S., "Adolf Wilhelm and *IG* II² 401," *ZPE* 137, pp. 106–108.

HERRMANN 2001: HERRMANN P., "Milet au IIe siècle a.C.," in edd. Bresson and Descat *Les cités d'Asie Mineure occidentale au IIe siècle*, Bordeaux, pp. 110–116.

HERRMANN 1979: HERRMANN P., "Die Stadt Temnos und ihre auswärtigen Beziehungen in hellenistischer Zeit," *Ist.Mitt.* 29, pp. 239–271.

HERRMANN 1965: HERRMANN P., "Antiochos der Grosse und Teos," *Anadolu* 9, pp. 29–160.

HERZOG and KLAFFENBACH 1952: HERZOG R. and KLAFFENBACH G., "Asylieurkunden aus Kos," *ADAW*, 1.

HEUSS 1995: HEUSS A., "Die Freiheitserklärung von Mylasa in den Inschriften von Labraunda," in *Gesammelte Schriften in 3. Bänden*, Stuttgart, pp. 298–310.[1]

HÖLKESKAMP 1993: HÖLKESKAMP K., "Demonax und die Neuordnung der Bürgerschaft von Kyrene," *Hermes* 121, pp. 404–421.

HOLLEAUX 1942: HOLLEAUX M., *Etudes d'épigraphie et d'histoire grecques*, vol. III, Paris.

HORDEN and PURCELL 2000: HORDEN P. and PURCELL N., *The Corrupting Sea. A Study of Mediterranean History*, Oxford.

HORNBLOWER 1991: HORNBLOWER S., *A Commentary on Thucydides*, Vol. I, Books I–III, Oxford.

HORNBLOWER 1982: HORNBLOWER S., *Mausolos*, Oxford.

HOSE 1999: HOSE M., "Post-Colonial Theory and Greek Literature in Rome," *GRBS* 40, pp. 303–326.

HUMANN 1904: HUMANN C., *Magnesia am Maeander: Bericht über die Ergebnisse der Ausgrabungen der Jahre 1891–1893*, Berlin.

ISAAC 1986: ISAAC B., *The Greek Settlements in Thrace until the Macedonian Conquest*, Leiden.

JONES 1999: JONES Ch. P., *Kinship Diplomacy in the Ancient World*, Cambridge.

JONES 1987: JONES N.F., *Public Organization in Ancient Greece. A Documentary Study*, Philadelphia.

KAGAN 1984: KAGAN J., "Hellenistic Coinage at Scepsis after its Refoundation in the Third Century B.C.," *ANSMN* 29, pp. 11–29.

KAPPARIS 1995: KAPPARIS K., "The Athenian Decree for the Naturalisation of the Plataeans," *GRBS* 36, pp. 359–378.

KATÓ 2014: KATÓ P., "Asylie-Variationen. Bemerkungen zu den Entstehungsgründen und Funktionen der hellenistischen Asylie," in edd. Matthaei and Zimmermann, *Stadtkultur im Hellenismus*, Mainz, pp. 97–108.

KIRBIHLER 2009: KIRBIHLER F., "Territoire civique et population d'Éphèse (Ve siècle av.J.–IIIe siècle apr. J.C.)," in ed. Bru, *L'Asie Mineure dans l'Antiquité. Echanges, populations et territoires. Regards actuels sur une péninsule. Actes du colloque international de Tours, 21–22 octobre 2005*, Rennes, pp. 301–333.

KLAFFENBACH 1955: KLAFFENBACH G., "Bemerkungen zu griechischen Inschriften," in ed. Bruns, *Festschrift für Carl Weickert*, Berlin, pp. 93–95.

KNOEPFLER 1997: KNOEPFLER D., "Le territoire d'Erétrie et l'organisation politique de la cite (*dêmoi, chôroi, phylai*)," in ed. Hansen, *The Polis as an Urban Centre and as a Political Community*, Copenhagen, pp. 352–448.

---

[1] Originally in *Le Monde grec: pensée, littérature, histoire, documents: hommages à Claire Préaux*, edd. Bingen, Cambier, Nachtergael, Bruxelles 1975.

KOBES 1996: KOBES J., *Kleine Könige. Untersuchung zu den Lokaldynasten im hellenistischen Kleinasien (323–188 v.Ch.)*, St. Katharinen.

KOCH 1993: KOCH C., "Integration unter Vorbehalt—der athenische Volksbeschluss über die Samier von 405/4 v. Chr.," *Tyche* 8, pp. 63–75.

KÖCHE 2012: KÖCHE L.M., "Milet stirbt aus? Demographische Überlegungen zu Neubürgern in einer hellenistischen Großstadt," in ed. Günther, *Migration und Bürgerrecht in der hellenistischen Welt*, Wiesbaden, pp. 41–50.

KÖNIG 1910: KÖNIG W., *Der Bund der Nesioten. Ein Beitrag zur Geschichte der Kykladen und benachbarten Inseln im Zeitalter des Hellenismus*, Halle.

KOSMETATOU 2003: KOSMETATOU E., "The Attalids in the Troad, an Addendum: an Episode of the Perils of the Aristotelian Corpus," *AncSoc* 93, pp. 53–60.

KRYZHIC'KIJ 2005: KRYZHIC'KIJ S.D., "Olbia and the Scythians in the Fifth Century B.C. The Scythian 'Protectorate'," in ed. Braund, *Scythians and Greeks*, Exeter, pp. 123–130.

KRYZHIC'KIJ 1995 see VINOGRADOV 1995.

KVIST 2003: KVIST K., "Cretan Grants of «asylia»: Violence and Protection as Interstate Relations," *C&M* 54, pp. 185–222.

LABARRE 1996: LABARRE G., *Les cités de Lesbos aux époques hellénistique et impériale*, Lyon.

LABARRE 1994: LABARRE G., "Koinon Lesbion," *REA* 96, pp. 415–446.

LAFFI 2010: LAFFI U., *Il Trattato fra Sardi ed Efeso degli anni 90 A.C.*, (Studi Ellenistici XXII) Pisa.

LAMBRINOUDAKIS and WÖRRLE 1983: LAMBRINOUDAKIS V. and WÖRRLE M., "Ein hellenistisches Reformgesetz über das Urkundenwesen von Paros," *Chiron* 13, pp. 283–368.

LANDUCCI-GATTINONI 1992: LANDUCCI-GATTINONI F., *Lisimaco di Tracia nella prospettiva del primo ellenismo*, Milan.

LANZILLOTTA 1978: LANZILLOTTA E., "Un'epigrafe di Scepsis dell'inizio del II sec. A.C.," in ed. Gasperini, *Scritti storico-epigrafici in memoria di Marcello Zambelli*, Rome, pp. 207–213.

LARONDE 1987: LARONDE A., *Cyrène et la Lybia hellénistique, Lybikai historiai; de l'époque républicaine au principat d'Auguste*, Paris.

LARSEN 1968: LARSEN J.A.O., *Greek Federal States. Their Institutions and History*, Oxford.

LASAGNI 2017: LASAGNI C., "Politeia in Greek Federal States," in edd. Cecchet and Busetto, *Citizens in the Graeco-Roman world: aspects of citizenship from the Archaic Period to AD 212*, pp. 78–109, Leiden.

LASAGNI 2011: LASAGNI C., *Il concetto di realtà locale nel mondo greco. Uno studio introduttivo nel confronto tra poleis e stati federali*, Roma 2011.

LASAGNI 2010: LASAGNI C., "Histiaia-Oreos e l'insediamento ateniese," in *Lemno dai 'Tirreni' agli Ateniesi*, *SAIA* LXXXVIII Ser. III. 10. 2010, pp. 371–390.

LAWTON 1995: LAWTON C.L., *Attic Document Reliefs: Art and Politics in ancient Athens*, Oxford.

LEAF 1923: LEAF E.W., *Strabo on the Troad*, Cambridge.

LE BOHEC 1993: LE BOHEC S., *Antigone Dôsôn roi de Macédoine*, Nancy.

LEFÈVRE 1995: LEFÈVRE F., "La chronologie du IIIe siècle à Delphes, d'après les actes amphictioniques (280–200)," *BCH* 119.1, pp. 161–208.

LERAT 1952: LERAT L., *Les Locriens de l'ouest*, Paris.

LEWIS 1962: LEWIS D., "The Federal Constitution of Ceos," *BSA* 57, pp. 1–4.

LOUKOULOPOULOU and PSOMA 2008: Loukoulopoulou L. and Psoma S., "Maroneia and Stryme revisited. Some Problems of Historical Topography," in *Thrakika Zetemata I*, Athens, pp. 55–86.

LOVE 1973: LOVE I., "A Preliminary Report of the Excavations at Knidos 1972," *AJA* 77, pp. 413–424.

LOW 2007: LOW P., *Interstate Relations in Classical Greece*, Cambridge.

LÜCKE 2000: LÜCKE ST., *Syngeneia. Epigraphisch-historische Studien zu einem Phänomen der antiken griechischen Diplomatie*, Frankfurt.

LUND 1992: LUND H., *Lysimachus. A Study in early Hellenistic Kingship*, London.

MA 2003: MA J., "Peer Polity Interaction in the Hellenistic Age," *P&P* 180, pp. 9–39.

MA 2002: MA J., *Antiochos III and the Cities of Western Asia Minor*, Cambridge 2002.

MACK 2015: MACK W., *Proxeny and Polis. Institutional Networks in the Ancient Greek World*, Oxford.

MACKIL 2013: MACKIL E., *Creating a Common Polity*, Berkeley.

MAGIE 1950: MAGIE D., *Roman Rule in Asia Minor to the End of the Third Century after Christ*, Princeton.

MAGNETTO 2008: MAGNETTO A., *L'arbitrato di Rodi fra Samo e Priene*, Pisa.

MALKIN 2012: MALKIN I., *A Small Greek World: Networks in the Ancient Mediterranean*, Oxford.

MALKIN 2003: MALKIN I., "Tradition in Herodotus. The Foundation of Cyrene," in edd. Derow and Parker, *Herodotus and his World. Essays from a Conference in Memory of George Forrest*, Oxford, pp. 153–170.

MANGANARO 2000: MANGANARO G., "Kyme e il dinasta Philetairo," *Chiron* 30, pp. 403–413.

MANGANARO 1990: MANGANARO G., "Metoikismos-Metaphora di Poleis in Sicilia: il caso dei Geloi di Phintias e la relativa documentazione epigrafica," *ASNP* XX.1, pp. 391–408.

MARASCO 1992: MARASCO G., *Economia e Storia*, Viterbo 1992.

MASON 1995: MASON H.J., "The End of Antissa," *AJPh* 116.3, pp. 399–410.

MASTROCINQUE 2002: MASTROCINQUE A., "Zeus Kretagenes seleucidico. Da Seleucia a Praeneste (e in Giudea)," *Klio* 84.2, pp. 355–372.

MASTROCINQUE 1994: MASTROCINQUE A., Review to Brodersen 1991, *Gnomon* 66, pp. 451–453.

MASTROCINQUE 1984(a): MASTROCINQUE A., "Città sacre e 'asylia' alla fine della Guerra tra Roma e Antioco III," in ed. Sordi, *I santuari e la guerra nel mondo classico*, Milan, pp. 142–163.

MASTROCINQUE 1984(b): MASTROCINQUE A., "Seleucidi divinizzati a Teo (OGIS 246)," *EA*, pp. 83–86.

MASTROCINQUE 1979: MASTROCINQUE A., *La Caria e la Ionia meridionale in epoca ellenistica*, Rome.

MCINERNEY 1999: MCINERNEY J., *The Folds of Parnassos*, Austin.

MCSHANE 1964: MCSHANE R.B., *The Foreign Policy of the Attalids in Pergamon* Urbana.

MEADOWS 2013: MEADOWS A., "The Ptolemaic League of the Islanders," in edd. Buraselis et Al., *The Ptolemies, the Sea and the Nile: Studies in Waterborne Power*, Cambridge, pp. 19–38.

MEIER 2017: MEIER L., "Der sogennante Piratenüberfall auf Teos und die Diadochen: Eine Neuedition der Inschrift SEG 44, 949," *Chiron* 47, 2017, pp. 115–188.

MERKELBACH and STAUBER 1998: MERKELBACH R. and STAUBER J., *Steinepigramme aus dem griechischen Osten*, vol. I, Stuttgart and Leipzig.

MERKER 1970: MERKER I.L., "The Ptolemaic Officials and the League of the Islanders," *Historia* 19, pp. 141–160.

MIGEOTTE 2004: MIGEOTTE L., "La mobilité des étrangers en temps de paix en Grèce ancienne," in ed. Moatti, *La mobilité des personnes en méditerranée de l'antiquité à l'époque moderne*, Rome, pp. 615–648.

MILLAR 1987: MILLER F., "The Problem of Hellenistic Syria," in edd. Kuhrt and Sherwin-White, *Hellenism in the East*, London, pp. 110–133.

MOATTI 2004: MOATTI C., *La Mobilité des personnes en Méditerranée de l'Antiquité à l'époque moderne*, Rome.

MOGGI 1995: MOGGI M., "Emigrazioni forzate e divieti di ritorno nella colonizzazione greca dei secoli VIII–VII a.C.," in ed. Sordi, *Coercizione e mobilità umana nel mondo antico*, Milan, pp. 27–49.

MÖLLER 1996: MÖLLER A., "Überlegungen zur *ktisis* von Maroneia," *Klio* 78.2, pp. 315–324.

MÜLLER 2010: MÜLLER C., *D'Olbia à Tanaïs*, Bordeaux.

MÜLLER 1976: MÜLLER H., *Milesische Volksbeschlüsse*, Göttingen.

MÜLLER 1975: MÜLLER H., "Φυγῆς ἕνεκεν", *Chiron* 5, pp. 129–156.

MUTTELSEE 1925: MUTTELSEE M., *Zur Verfassungsgeschichte Kretas im Zeitalter des Hellenismus*, Hamburg.

NAWOTKA 2004: NAWOTKA K., "Legislation in the Pontic Colonies of Miletus," *Eos* 91, pp. 234–241.

NIELSEN 1999: NIELSEN H.T., "The Concept of Arkadia—The People, their Land, and their Organization," in edd. Nielsen and Roy, *Defining Ancient Arkadia*, Symposium April 1–4, 1998, Copenhagen, pp. 16–79.

NIGDELIS 1989: NIGDELIS P., "Ρωμαίοι πάτρωνες και αναγκαιότατοι καιροί", *Hellenika* 40, pp. 34–49.

NOLLÉ 2003: NOLLÉ J., "Neues von Themistokles! Themistokles' Aufstieg, Fall und Ende: Der Tod eines Helde im Exil," *Antike Welt* 2, pp. 189–198.

NOLLÉ and WARTNER 1987: NOLLÉ J. and WARTNER S., "Ein tückischer Iotazismus in einer milesischen Inschrift," *Chiron* 17, pp. 361–364.

ØDEGÅRD 2005: ØDEGÅRD K., "The Topography of ancient Tegea: New Discoveries and Old Problems," in ed. ØSTBY, *Ancient Arcadia*, Athens, pp. 208–221.

ØSTBY 2005: ØSTBY E. (ed.), *Ancient Arcadia. Papers from the third international seminar on Ancient Arcadia, held at the Norwegian Institute at Athens, 7–10 May 2002*, Athens.

ØSTBY 2002: ØSTBY E., "Recent Excavations in the Sanctuary of Athena Alea at Tegea. Results and Problems," in ed. Hägg, *Peloponnesian Sanctuaries and Cults: Proceedings of the Ninth International Symposium at the Swedish Institute at Athens, 11–13 June 1994*, Stockholm, pp. 139–147.

OHLEMUTZ 1940: OHLEMUTZ E., *Die Kulte und Heiligtümer der Götter in Pergamon*, Würzburg.

OLIVER 2007(a): OLIVER G.J., *War, Food, and Politics in Early Hellenistic Athens*, Oxford.

OLIVER 2007(b): OLIVER G.J., "Citizenship: Inscribed Honours for Individuals in Classical and Hellenistic Athens," in edd. Couvenhes and Milanezi, *Individus, groupes et politique à Athènes de Solon à Mithridate*, Tours, pp. 273–293.

OLIVERIO 1928: OLIVERIO G., "Iscrizioni di Cirene antica" in *Documenti di Cirene antica*, pp. 183–239, Turin.

ORLANDOS 1972: ORLANDOS A.K., Πεπραγμένα τοῦ Γ' Διεθνοῦς Κρητολογικοῦ Συνεδρίου I, Athens, pp. 199–205.

OSBORNE 1981(a): OSBORNE M.J., *Naturalization in Athens*, vols. 3, Brussel.

OSBORNE 1981(b): OSBORNE M.J., "Entertainment in the Prytaneion at Athens," *ZPE* 41, pp. 153–170 (Corrigenda dazu: *ZPE* 42, 1981(b) 294).

PACE 1996: PACE R., "Alabanda e le sue monete," *CN* 81. Dicembre, pp. 60–65.

PADZERA 2006: PADZERA M., *Getreide für Griechenland*, Berlin.

PATTERSON 2004: PATTERSON L., "An Aetolian Local Myth in Pausanias?," *Mnemosyne* 52, pp. 346–352.

PERLMAN 1999: PERLMAN P., "kretes aei leistai? The Marginalization of Crete in Greek Thought and the Role of Piracy in the Outbreak of the First Cretan War," in ed. Gabrielsen, *Hellenistic Rhodes*, Aarhus, pp. 132–161.

PESCHLOW-BINDOKAT 2005: PESCHLOW-BINDOKAT A., *Feldforschungen im Latmos. Die karische Stadt Latmos, mit einem Exkurs von Koray Konuk*, Berlin (Milet, Teil 6).

PETROPOULOU 1985: PETROPOULOU A., *Beiträge zur Wirtschafts- und Gesellschaftsgeschichte Kretas in hellenistischer Zeit*, Frankfurt.

PICARD 2012, PICARD O., "Conclusions," in edd. Heller and Pont, *Patrie d'origine et patries électives: les citoyenneté multiples dans le monde grec d'époque romaine*, pp. 341–346.

PIEJKO 1986: PIEJKO F., "Textual Supplements to the new Inscriptions concerning Temnos", *MDAI* 36, pp. 95–97.

PIERART 1974: PIERART M., *Platon et la cité grecque théorie et réalité dans la Constitution des "Lois"*, Bruxell.

PONTANI 1997: PONTANI, F., "*I. Amyzon* 27 C–D: Teil eines milesischen Isopolitievertrags," *EA* 28, pp. 5–8.

POUNDER 1978: POUNDER R.L., "Honors for Antioch of the Chrysaoreans," *Hesperia* 47, pp. 49–57.

PRANDI 1999: PRANDI L., "La concessione della cittadinanza ateniense ai Sami (*IG* I3 127; *IG* II2 1 b–c). Problemi e proposte," in *Atti del XI Congresso Internazionale di Epigrafia Greca e Latina* I, Roma, 18–24 settembre 1997, Rome, pp. 199–204.

PRANDI 1988: PRANDI L., *Platea: momenti e problemi della storia di una polis*, Milan.

PRÊTEUX 2009: PRÊTEUX F., "Parion et son territoire à l'époque hellénistique. Un exemple d'organisation de la chôra sur les rivages de la Propontide," in ed. Bru, *L'Asie Mineure dans l'Antiquité. Échanges, populations et territoires. Regards actuels sur une péninsule. Actes du colloque international de Tours, 21–22 octobre 2005*, Rennes, pp. 335–350.

PRETZLER 1999: PRETZLER M., "Myth and History at Tegea—Local Tradition and Community Identity," in edd. Nielsen and Roy, *Defining Ancient Arkadia*, Symposium April 1–4, 1998, Copenhagen, pp. 89–129.

PRINZ 1979: PRINZ F., *Gründungsmythen und Sagenchronologie*, Munich.

PRITCHETT 1954: PRITCHETT W.K., "An Unfinished Inscription, *IG* II^2 2362," *TAPA* 85, pp. 159–167.

PSOMA ET AL. 2008: S. PSOMA, C. KARADIMA and D. TERZOPOULOU, *The Coins from Maroneia and the Classical City at Molyvoti*, Athens.

QUAß 1993: QUAß F., *Die Honoratiorenschicht in den Städten des griechischen Ostens*, Stuttgart.

RAGONE 1996: RAGONE G., "Pygela/Phygela. Fra Paraetimologia e Storia," *Athenaeum* 84 I. II., pp. 183–241 and pp. 343–379.

RAMSAY 1881: RAMSAY W.M., "Contributions to the History of Southern Aeolis," *JHS* 2, pp. 271–308.

REGER 2010: REGER G., "Mylasa and its Territory," in edd. van Bremen and Carbon, *Hellenistic Karia*, Pessac, pp. 43–59.

REGER 2004: REGER G., "*Sympoliteiai* in Hellenistic Asia Minor," in ed. Colvin, *The Graeco Roman East*, Cambridge, pp. 145–180.

REGER 2001: REGER G., "The Mykonian Synoikismos," *REA* 103, pp. 157–181.

REGER 1997: REGER G., "Islands with One Polis versus Islands with Several Poleis," in ed. Hansen, *The Polis as an Urban Centre and as a Political Community*, Copenhagen, pp. 450–492.

REGER 1994: REGER G., "The Political History of the Kyklades 260–200 B.C.," *Historia* 43.1, pp. 32–69.

REGER 1992: REGER G., "Athens and Tenos in the early Hellenistic Age," *CQ* 42.2, pp. 365–383.

REGER and RISSER 1991: REGER G. and RISSER M., "Coinage and Federation in Hellenistic Ceos," in edd. Cherry, Devis and Mantzourani, *Landscape Archaeology as Long-Term History*, Los Angeles, pp. 305–317.

REITZENSTEIN 2012: REITZENSTEIN D., "Elite und Mehrfachbürgerrechte im lykischen Bund," in edd. Heller and Pont, *Patrie d'origine et patries électives*, Bordeaux, pp. 153–173.

REITZENSTEIN 2011: REITZENSTEIN D., *Die lykische Bundespriester: Repräsentation der kaiserzeitlichen Elite Lykiens*, Berlin.

RHODES 2001: RHODES P.J., "Public Documents in the Greek States: Archives and Inscriptions," *G&R* 48.1, pp. 33–44.

RHODES 1984: RHODES P.J., "ΞΕΝΙΑ and ΔΕΙΠΝΟΝ in the Prytaneum," *ZPE* 57, pp. 193–199.

RICL 1997: RICL M., "Unpublished Inscriptions from the Troad," *ZAnt* 47, pp. 177–186.

RIGSBY 1996(b):[2] RIGSBY K., "Missing Places," *CPh* 91.3, pp. 254–260.

RIGSBY 1986: RIGSBY K., "Notes sur la Crète hellénistique," *REG* XCIX, pp. 350–360.

RIZAKIS 1995: RIZAKIS A., *Achaie I. Sources textuelles et historie regionale*, Athens.

RIZAKIS 2012: RIZAKIS A., "La double citoyenneté dans la cadre des koina grecs: l'exemple du koinon achéen," in edd. HELLER and PONT, *Patrie d'origine et patries électives: les citoyenneté multiples dans le monde grec d'époque romaine*, Bordeaux, pp. 23–38.

ROBERT *OMS*: ROBERT L., *Opera Minora Selecta* vol. I–VII, Amsterdam 1969–1990.

ROBERT 1989: ROBERT L., *Claros I*, Paris.

ROBERT 1978: ROBERT L., "Documents d'Asie Mineure," *BCH* 102, pp. 395–453.

ROBERT 1937: ROBERT L., *Études anatoliennes; recherches sur les inscriptions grecques de l'Asie Mineure*, Paris.

ROBERT 1951: ROBERT L., *Études numismatique grecque*, Paris.

ROBERT 1946: ROBERT L., *Hellenica* II, Paris.

ROBERT 1966: ROBERT L., *Monnaies antiques en Troades*, Paris.

ROBERT J. and L. 1983: ROBERT J. and ROBERT L., *Fouilles d'Amyzon en Carie*, Paris.

ROBERT J. and L. 1976: ROBERT J. and ROBERT L., "Une inscription grecque de Téos en Ionie l'union de Téos et de Kyrbissos," *Journal des Savants*, pp. 153–235.

---

2 For 1996(a) see *corpora*.

DE ROMILLY 1972: DE ROMILLY J., "Vocabulaire et propagande ou les premiere employs du mot *homonoia*," in *Mélanges de linguistique et de philologie grecques offerts à P. Chaintraine*, Paris, pp. 199–209.

ROSE 2003: ROSE CH. B., "The Temple of Athena at Ilion," *Studia Troica* 13, pp. 27–86.

ROUSSEL 1916: ROUSSEL P., "Notes épigraphiques," *REG* 29, pp. 166–187.

ROY 1999: ROY J., "The Economies of Arkadia," in edd. Nielsen and Roy, *Defining Ancient Arkadia*, Symposium April 1–4, 1998, Copenhagen, pp. 320–381.

RUBINSTEIN 2009: RUBINSTEIN L., "Ateleia Grants and their Enforcement in the Classical and early Hellenistic Periods" in edd. Mitchell, Davies, and Rhodes, *Greek History and Epigraphy. Essays in Honour of P.J. Rhodes*, Wales, pp. 115–143.

SABA 2018: SABA S., "A Problem of Historical Geography: Orthagoreia in Thrace Reconsidered," *Ancient Society* 48, pp. 103–113.

SABA 2014: SABA S., "Isopoliteia in the Hellenistic Polis," in edd. Matthaei and Zimmermann, *Stadtkultur im Hellenismus*, Mainz, pp. 122–132.

SABA 2012: SABA S., "Nagidos, Arsinoe and *Isopoliteia*," *Dike* 15, pp. 159–170.

SABA 2011: SABA S., "*Epigamia* or the Right of Intermarriage in Hellenistic Interstate Agreements," *Ancient Society* 41, pp. 93–108.

SABA 2009/10(a): SABA S., "Delphi, Sardis and Citizenship: a Note," *Dike* 12/13, pp. 171–180.

SABA 2009/10(b): SABA S., "Hellenistic Institutions and Law: A Survey (2000–2010)," *Dike* 12/13, pp. 272–302.

SABA 2007: SABA S., "Temporary and Permanent Housing for New Citizens," *EA* 40, pp. 125–134.

SABA and RENBERG 2011: SABA S. and RENBERG G., *Greek Epigraphy* in OUP Online Bibliographies.

SAHIN 1994: SAHIN S., "Piratenüberfall auf Teos. Volksbeschluß über die Finanzierung der Erpressungsgelder," *EA* 23, pp. 1–40.

SALOMON 1997: SALOMON N., *Le cleruchie di Atene*, Pisa.

SAMMARTANO 2008/9: SAMMARTANO R., "Magnesia sul Meandro e la 'diplomazia della parentela'," *Hormos n.s.* 1, pp. 111–139.

SAMMARTANO 2007: SAMMARTANO R., "Sul concetto di *oikeiotes* nelle relazioni interstatali greche," in ed. Daverio Rocchi, *Tra concordia e pace*, Milan, pp. 207–235.

SAVALLI 2012: SAVALLI I., "Collections de citoyennetés et internationalisation des élites civiques dans l'Asie Mineure hellénistique," in edd. Heller and Pont, *Patrie d'origine et patries électives: les citoyenneté multiples dans le monde grec d'époque romaine*, Bordeaux, pp. 39–59.

SAVALLI 2001(a): SAVALLI I., "Les Attalides et les cités grecque au IIe siècle a.C.," in edd. Bresson and Descat *Les cités d'Asie Mineure occidentale au IIe siècle a.C.*, Bordeaux, pp. 76–91.

SAVALLI 2001(b): SAVALLI I., "Amici del re, alti funzionari e gestione del potere principalmente nell'Asia Minore ellenistica," *Simblos* 3, pp. 263-294.

SAVALLI 1998: SAVALLI I., *Les philoi royaux dans l'Asie hellénistique*, Geneva.

SAVALLI 1985: SAVALLI I., "I neocittadini nelle città ellenistiche. Note sulla concessione e l'acquisizione della politeia," *Historia* 34, pp. 387-431.

SCHIPLEY 1987: SCHIPLEY G., *A History of Samos 800-180 a.C.*, Oxford.

SCHIPPOREIT 1998: SCHIPPOREIT S. TH., "Das alte und das neue Priene. Das Heiligtum der Demeter und die Gründungen Prienes," *MDAI* 48, pp. 193-236.

SCHLESINGER 1933: SCHLESINGER E., *Die grieschische Asylie*, Diss. Gött.

SCHMITT 1964: SCHMITT H., *Untersuchungen zur Geschichte Antiochos' des Großen und seiner Zeit*, Wiesbaden.

SCHOLTEN 2000: SCHOLTEN J.B., *The Politics of Plunder. Aitolians and their* Koinon *in the Early Hellenistic Era, 279-217 B.C.*, Berkeley.

SCHULER 2010: SCHULER C., "Priester πρὸ πόλεως in Lykien," *ZPE* 173, pp. 69-88.

SCHULER 1996: SCHULER C., *Ländliche Siedlungen und Gemeinden im hellenistischen und römischen Kleinasien*, Munich.

SCULLION 2002: SCULLION S., "A Reply to Henry on *IG* II^2 401," *ZPE* 140, 2002, pp. 81-84.

SCULLION 2001, SCULLION S., "Three Notes on Inscriptions," *ZPE* 134, pp. 116-120.

SEIBERT 1963: SEIBERT J., *Metropolis und Apoikie*, Würzburg.

SHEEDY 1996: SHEEDY K., "The Origins of the Second Nesiotic League and the Defence of Kythnos," *Historia* 95, pp. 423-449.

SHERK 1992: SHERK R., "Greek Eponymous Officials in Greek Cities. IV The Register," *ZPE* 93, pp. 223-272.

SHERWIN-WHITE 1985: SHERWIN-WHITE S.M., "The Edict of Alexander to Priene, a Reappraisal," *JHS* 105, pp. 69-89.

SHIPLEY 1987: SHIPLEY G., *A History of Samos 800-188 B.C.*, Oxford.

SICKINGER 1999: SICKINGER J., *Public Records and Archives in classical Athens*, Chapel Hill.

SIPPEL 1986(a): SIPPEL D.V., "The Meeting Place of the Rhodian Nesiotic League," *AncW* 13, pp. 35-40.

SIPPEL 1986(b): SIPPEL D.V., "Tenos and the Nesiotic League," *AncW* 13, pp. 41-46.

SORDI 1994: SORDI M., "Il federalismo greco nell'età classica," in ed. Aigner-Foresti *Federazioni e Federalismo nell'Europa antica. Alle radici della casa comune europea* (Atti del Convegno di Bergamo, 21-25 settembre 1992), Milan, pp. 2-22.

SOSIN 2009: SOSIN J., "Magnesian Inviolability," *TAPA* 139, pp. 369-410.

SOSIN 2002: SOSIN J., "Grain for Andros," *Hermes* 130, pp. 131-145.

SPYRIDAKIS 1983: SPRYRIDAKIS St., "Paros, Allaria and the Cretan Koinon," *Ariadne*, pp. 1-19.

STROBEL 2006: STROBEL K., "Galatien, die Galater und die Poleis der Galater. Historische Identität und ethnische Tradition," *Eirene* XLII, pp. 89–123.

STROUD 1984: STROUD R.S., "An Argive Decree from Nemea Concerning Aspendos," *Hesperia* 53.2, pp. 193–216.

SZANTO 1892: SZANTO E., *Das griechische Bürgerrecht*, Freiburg.

THÉRIAULT 1996: THÉRIAULT G., *Le Cult d'Homonoia dans les cites grecques*, Lyon.

THONEMANN 2003: THONEMANN P.J., "Hellenistic Inscriptions from Lydia," *EA* 36, pp. 95–108.

TYBOUT 2011: TYBOUT R., *Novi libri Iudicia* on BLANSHARD 2007, *Mnemosyne* 64, pp. 123–124.

TZIAFALIAS and HELLY 2007: TZIAFALIAS A. and HELLY B., "Décrets inédits de Larissa," *BCH* 131, pp. 421–474.

TZIAFALIAS and HELLY 2004/5, TZIAFALIAS A. and HELLY B., "Deux décrets inédits de Larissa," *BCH* 128–129, pp. 377–420.

VANSEVEREN 1937: VANSEVEREN J., "Inscriptions d'Amorgos et de Chios," *RPh* 11, pp. 313–347.

VÉRILHAC and VIAL 1998: VÉRILHAC A.-M. and VIAL C., *Le mariage grec du IVe siècle av J.C. a l'epoque d'Auguste*, [Bulletin de correspondance hellenique Supplement 32], Paris.

VESTERGAARD 2000: VESTERGAARD T., "Milesian Immigrants in Late Hellenistic and Roman Athens," in ed. Oliver, *The Epigraphy of Death*, Liverpool, pp. 81–109.

VINCI 2008/9: VINCI M., "Il decreto di Eleutherna e la datazione dei documenti teii di asylia," *Hormos* 1, pp. 189–210.

VINOGRADOV and KRYZHIC'KIJ 1995: VINOGRADOV J.G. and KRYZHIC'KIJ S.D., *Olbia. Eine altgriechische Stadt im nordwestlischen Schwarzmeerraum*, Leiden.

VIRGILIO 1984: VIRGILIO B., "Strabone e la storia di Pergamo e degli Attalidi," in *Studi Ellenistici I*, Pisa, pp. 24–37.

VITUCCI 1953: VITUCCI G., *Il Regno di Bitinia*, Rome.

WALBANK 1957: WALBANK F.W., *A Historical Commentary on Polybius*, Vol. I, Oxford.

WALSER 2009: WALSER A.V., "Sympolitien und Siedlungsentwicklung" in edd. Matthaei and Zimmermann, *Stadtbilder im Hellenismus*, Berlin, pp. 135–155.

WALSER 2008: WALSER A.V., *Bauern und Zinsnehmer. Politik, Recht und Wirtschaft im frühhellenistischen Ephesos*, Munich.

WARREN 2008: WARREN J., "The Framework of the Achaian Koinon," in ed. Grandjean, *Le Péloponnèse d'Épaminondas à Hadrien*, Pessac, pp. 91–100.

WARREN 2007: WARREN J., *The Bronze Coinage of the Achaian Koinon*, London.

WESTERMARK 1991: WESTERMARK U., *Sylloge Nummorum Graecorum, Sweden* 2.3, Stokholm.

WHEATLEY 1998: WHEATLEY P., "The Chronology of the Third Diadoch War: 315–311 B.C.," *Phoenix* 52, pp. 257–281.

WIEGAND UND SCHRADER 1904: WIEGAND Th. und SCHRADER H., *Priene: Ergebnisse der Ausgrabungen und Untersuchungen in den Jahren 1895–1898*, Berlin.

WIEMER 2002: WIEMER H.U., *Krieg, Handel und Piraterie. Untersuchung zur Geschichte des hellenistischen Rhodos*, Berlin.

WILHELM 1974²: WILHELM A., *Akademieschriften zur griechischen Inschriftenkunde* (1895–1951), Vol. 1, Leipzig.

Wilhelm 1897 (*Kl. Schriften* 2000): WILHELM A., *Kleine Schriften. Abteilung II. Teil III.* edd. Dobesch and Rehrenböck, Vienna.

WILL 1995: WILL E., "Syngeneia, oikeiotès, philia," *RPh* 69.2, pp. 299–325.

WILL 1982: WILL E., *Histoire politique du monde hellénistique*, B. 2 Nancy.

WILL 1966: WILL E., *De la mort d'Alexandre aux avènements d'Antiochos III et de Philippe V. Histoire politique du monde hellénistique*. B. 1 Nancy.

WILL 1960: WILL E., "La Cyrenaïque et les partages successifs de l'empire d'Alexandre," *Ant. Class.* 29, pp. 369–390.

WILLETS 1975: WILLETS R.F., "The Cretan Koinon: Epigraphy and Tradition," *Kadmos* 14, pp. 143–148.

WÖRRLE 2004: WÖRRLE M., "Der Friede zwischen Milet und Magnesia. Methodische Probleme einer Communis Opinio," *Chiron* 34, pp. 45–57.

WÖRRLE 2003: WÖRRLE M., "Der Synoichismos der Latmioi mit den Pidaseis," *Chiron* 23, 2003, pp. 121–143.

WÖRRLE 1999: WÖRRLE M., "Epigraphische Forschungen zur Geschichte Lykiens VII. Asarönü, ein Peripolion von Limyra," *Chiron* 29, pp. 353–370.

WÖRRLE 1988: WÖRRLE M., "Inschriften von Herakleia am Latmos I: Antiochos III., Zeuxis und Herakleia," *Chiron* 18, pp. 421–476.

Reference Works

BE: Bulletin épigraphique

Inventory: ed. HANSEN H.M., *An Inventory of Archaic and Classical Poleis*, Oxford 2004.

LEXICON OF GREEK PERSONAL NAMES (Vol. V, B) edd. by Fraser P.M. and Matthews E., Oxford 2010.

OSBORNE M.J. and BYRNE S. 1996, *The Foreign Residents of Athens*, Leuven.

RE: (Paulys) *Realenzyklopädie der classischen Altertumwissenschaft* 1824–2000.

SEG: *Supplementum Epigraphicum Graecum*, Brill.

Corpora and Collections of Inscriptions

AvP: Altertümer von Pergamon: (Band VIII, Band 1–2): *Die Inschriften von Pergamon,* ed. Fränkel M., Berlin 1890–1895.

AGORA XVI: *The Athenian Agora: Inscriptions the Decrees (16)*, ed. Woodhead A., Athens 1997.

AGER 1996: AGER L.S., *Interstate Arbitration in the Greek World, 337–90 B.C.* Hellenistic Culture and Society, 18. Berkeley.

BIELMAN 1994: BIELMAN A., *Retour à la liberté,* Lousanne.

BLASS, *SGDI: Sammlung der griechischen Dialekt Inschriften,* Göttingen 1884.

BOFFO 1994: BOFFO L., *Iscrizioni greche e latine per lo studio della Bibbia,* Brescia.

Inscr. Sardeis VII = BUCKLER W.H. and ROBINSON D.M., *Sardis: Publications of the American Society for the Excavation of Sardis, Greek and Latin Inscriptions* vol. 7, Leyden 1932.

CANALI DE ROSSI 2004: CANALI DE ROSSI F., *Iscrizioni dello Estremo Oriente,* Bonn.

CANALI DE ROSSI 1997: CANALI DE ROSSI F., *Le ambascerie dal mondo greco a Roma in età repubblicana,* Rome.

CHANIOTIS 1996: CHANIOTIS A., *Die Verträge zwischen kretischen Poleis in der hellenistischen Zeit,* Stuttgart.

CHOIX: *Choix d'inscriptions de Delphes, traduites et commentées,* JACQUEMIN A., MULLIEZ D., ROUGEMONT G., Athens 2012.

CRAMPA 1969: CRAMPA J., *Labraunda. Swedish Excavations and Researches.* Vol. III. Part I *The Greek Inscriptions,* Lund.

DUBOIS 1996: DUBOIS L., *Inscriptions grecques dialectales d'Olbia du Pont,* Geneva.

FD: Fouilles de Delphes III. Épigraphie.

IG: Inscriptiones graecae, Akademie der Wissenschaften Berlin 1828.

IGDS: DUBOIS L., *Inscriptions grecques dialectales de Sicile, contribution à l'étude du vocabulaire grec colonial,* Paris 1989.

I.Cret.: Inscriptiones Creticae opera et consilio Friderici Halberr collectae 4 vll., ed. M. Guarducci, Rome 1935–1950.

IK Ilion: Die Inschriften von Ilion, FRISCH P., Bonn 1975.

IK. Kios: Die Inschriften von Kios, CORSTEN Th., Bonn 1985.

IKnidos I: *Die Inschriften von Knidos,* BLÜMEL W., Bonn 1992.

IK Kyzikos: Die Inschriften von Kyzikos und Umgebung, SCHWERTHEIM E., Bonn 1980.

IK Parion: Die Inschriften von Parion, FRISCH P., Bonn 1983.

IK Tralleis und Nysa: Die Inschriften von Tralleis und Nysa, POLJAKOV F.B., Bonn 1985.

IPArk: Prozeßrechtliche Inschriften der griechischen Poleis, Arkadien, THÜR G. and TAEUBER H., Wien 1994.

IThr.Aeg.: Epigraphes tēs Thrakēs tou Aigaiu, LOUKOPOULOU L., Athens 2005.

KONTORINI 1983: KONTORINI V., *Rhodiaka/1. Inscriptions inédites relatives á l'histoire et aux cultes de Rhodes au IIe et au Ier siécle avant Jesus-Christ,* Louvain-La-Nouve.

KOTSIDU 2000: KOTSIDU H., *TIMH KAI DOXA. Ehrungen für hellenistische Herrscher im griechischen Mutterland und in Kleinasien unter besonderer Berücksichtigung der archäologischen Denkmäler*, Berlin.

Milet.: *Inschriften von Milet*, aa.vv. (vv Volumes), Berlin.

ISE: *Iscrizioni storiche Ellenistiche*, MORETTI L. I-II, Rome 1967–1976.

IScM: *Inscriptiones Histriae et vicinia*, PIPPIDI D.M. 1983.

IMagn.: *Die Inschriften von Magnesia am Maeander*, KERN, O. Berlin 1900.

MAGNETTO 1997: MAGNETTO A., *Gli arbitrati interstatali greci*, Pisa.

M&L: MEIGGS, R. and LEWIS D.M., *A Selection of Greek Historical Inscriptions to the end of the Fifth Century B.C.* Oxford 1969.

MICHEL, *Rec.*: *Recueil d'inscriptions grecques*, MICHEL CH., Bruxel 1900.

RIGSBY 1996: RIGSBY K., *Asylia. Territorial Inviolability in the Hellenistic world*, Berkeley.

RHODES AND OSBORNE 2003: RHODES P. and OSBORNE R., *Greek Historical Inscriptions, 404–323 BC*, Oxford.

Syll.3: *Sylloge Inscriptionum Graecarum*, ed. W. Dittenberger, Leipzig (4 vol. 1915–1920).

StV: *Die Staatsverträge des Altertums*, Bengston et al., München—Berlin (I-III).

SUSINI 1963/64: SUSINI G., "Supplemento epigrafico di Caso, Scarpanto, Saro, Calchi, Alinnia e Tilo," *SAIA* XXV–XXVI, pp. 202–292.

TASLIKLIOGLU 1971: TASLIKLIOGLU Z., *Trakya'da epigrafya arastirmalari* II, Istanbul.

Tit. Camirenses: SEGRÈ M. and PUGLIESE CARRATELLI G. in *Annuario* 27–29 n.s. 1949–1951, pp. 141–318.

TOD: Tod M.N., *A Selection of Greek Historical Inscriptions to the End of the Fifth Century B.C.* 2nd edition. Oxford: Oxford University Press, 1962 (1946).

WELLES 1934: WELLES C.B., *Royal Correspondence in the Hellenistic Period. A Study on Greek Epigraphy*, New Haven.

ZIEGLER 1975: ZIEGLER W., *Symbolai und Asylia*, Diss. Bonn.

Index Locorum

Inscriptions

IG I³ 127	79 n. 124, 85, 250–253
IG I³ 261	46 n. 36
I.Priene 45 = *IG* II³ 1 1239	134 n. 5 and n. 7
IG II² 70	235 n. 44
IG II² 111	146 n. 5, 148
IG II² 401	47
IG II² 456	133 n. 1
IG II² 566	134 n. 3, 137 n.15
IG II² 1091	93 n. 19
IG II² 1628	136 n. 10
IG II³ 1 1065	**no. (27)** 133–137
IG V.1 1430	172 n. 19
IG IX² 1 3A	6 n. 10, 101 n. 2, 121, 123, **no. (40)** 175–179, 239 n. 4, 243 n. 19
IG IX.1².1 4d	**no. (46)** 193–4
IG IX.1².I 174	171 n. 16
IG IX.1² 17	60 n. 75
IG IX 1² 172 (= *Syll.*³ 479)	185 n. 56
IG IX² 1 6	191
IG IX² 1 99	191
IG IX² 1 136	**no. (44)** 190–191
IG IX 1² 1 193 = *I.Cret.* II.V. 18A	124 n. 83, **no. (45)** 191–3
IG XI.4 1064 = *Suppl.* 136	143, **no. (36)** 156–9
IG XII 3 328 (= Bielman 1994, no. 54)	213 n. 53
IG XII 5 814	22, 143, **no. (35)** 153–6, 238 n. 2
IG XII 6.1.6	22, **no. (18)** 95–98, 102 n. 9
IG XII 9 218	61 n. 77
IG XII *Suppl.* 3	160–1
IG XII *Suppl.* 312	**no. (9)** 78–79
Ag. XVI 111	134 n. 6
Ag. XVI 172	136 n. 12
I.Cret. I.xvi 5 = Chaniotis 1996, pp. 358–376 no. 61	126 n. 87, **no. (58)** 210–2
I.Cret. I.xvi 17 = Chaniotis 1996, pp. 276–278 no. 37	121 n. 71, 202 n. 23, **no. (54)** 206–8
I.Cret. I. XVIII.9 = Chaniotis 1996, pp. 352–358 no. 60	**no. (57)** 210
I.Cret. II 1 2	**no. (59)** 212–215, 217
I.Cret. I. XVIII.10 = Chaniotis 1996, 287–289 no. 42	**no. (55)** 208–209
I.Cret. II v 20 = Chaniotis 1996, pp. 221–222 no. 15	**no. (50)** 203
I.Cret. II.x 4	203 n. 29
I.Cret. III.iii 1b = Chaniotis 1996, pp. 217–221 no. 14	26 n. 58, **no. (48)** 201–3
I.Cret. III iii 3A and B	92 n. 17
I.Cret. III.iii 3C	84, **no. (16)** 92–95, 99 n. 40
I.Cret. III.iii 4 = Chaniotis 1996, pp. 255–263 no. 28	121 n. 71, 172 n. 19, **no. (52)** 204–6, 216
I.Cret. III.iii 5 = Chaniotis 1996, pp. 432–439 no. 74	26–7, **no. (49)** 201–3
I.Cret. III.iii 6 = Chaniotis 1996, pp. 273–274 no. 35	121 n. 71, **no. (53)** 206
I.Cret. III.iv 1 = Chaniotis 1996, pp. 185–190 no. 5	13 esp. n. 26, 77 n. 115 **no. (47)** 197–201, 207, 209 n. 42
I.Cret. III.iv 6 = Chaniotis 1996, pp. 234–235 no. 20	**no. (51)** 203–4, 209
I.Cret. III.v 5 = Chaniotis 1996, pp. 231–234 no. 19	204 n. 30
I.Cret. IV 174 = Chaniotis 1996, pp. 245–255 no. 27	204 n. 31
I.Cret. IV 179	227, 228
Chaniotis 1996, pp. 338–351 no. 59	121 n. 71, 208 n. 37, **no. (56)** 209–10
SEG IX 3 = Dobias-Lalou 1994	39 n. 6, **no. (15)** 89–91, 259

INDEX LOCORUM

SEG XXIX 1149 = Herrmann 1979		*Milet* I 3 137	38, **no. (2)** 45–8, 241
	6 n. 9, 17 n. 35, 101, **no. (22)** 113–116, 121, 130 n. 106, 215	*Milet* I 3 141	17 n. 35, **no. (4)** 52–58, 62 n. 83, 77, 138
SEG XXIX 1130 and 1130 bis		*Milet* I 3 142	17 n. 35, 38, 46, **no. (3)** 48–51, 253 n. 22
	106 n. 21	*Milet* I 3 143	11–12, 14 n. 30, 44, 57, **no. (5)** 58–63, 73 n. 106, 80, 81, 101 n. 2 and 102, 111 n. 36, 169 n. 12, 174 n. 28, 238, 240
SEG XXXII 825	214 n. 57		
SEG XXXIV 282 = Stroud 1984			
	no. (38) 166–169		
SEG XLI 1003	131, **no. (61)** 222–227, 238 n. 3		
SEG XLIV 1218 = Bousquet and Gauthier 1994		*Milet* I 3 144	**no. (12)** 81
	13, 18, 24–25, **no. (8)** 74–78, 174 n. 28, 198 n. 8	*Milet* I 3 146	14 n. 30, 44, 57, **no. (6)** 64–67, 73 n. 106, 80, 81
		Milet I 3 148	43 n. 31, 71
SEG LII 1462	16 esp. n. 34, 25–7, 225 n. 7	*Milet* I 3.150	8 n. 17, 18, 19 n. 40, 24, 35, 44, **no. (7)** 67–74, 80, 107, 123 and ibid. n. 78, 149 n. 15, 173 n. 25, 174 n. 28, 186 n. 67, 214, 239 n. 4
SEG LV 605 = Tziafalias and Helly 2004–5, pp. 378–402	11 n. 24, 143, **no. (37)** 159–162		
SEG LV 1502	76 n. 110		
SEG LVIII 1541 = Guizzi 2001		*Milet* I 3 155	**no. (13)** 81–2
	102 n. 6, **no. (24)** 124–125	*Milet* V 3 1032	**no. (29)** 137–8
		Milet VI 3 1021	40
		Milet VI 3 1023	40
FD III 3 117	192	*Milet* VI.3 1050	**no. (10)** p. 79–80
FD III.3 144 = *IG* IX 1², 1, 173 = Funke 2000, pp. 506–509	**no. (42)** 184–186	*Milet* VI 3 1051	**no. (11)** 82
		Milet VI 3 1058	60 esp. n. 77
FD III.3 241	248 n. 7	*Milet* VI 3 1065	40
Choix pp. 151–156 no. 77		*StV* II² 232	**no. (32)** 145–6
	no. (43) 187–189	*StV* II² 287	143, **no. (33)** 147–149, 169 n. 12
IPArk 18	99 n. 40	*StV* III 508	121, 144, **no. (41)** 179–183, 242
IPArk. 28	19–20, 24, 123 n. 78, **no. (39)** 170–4, 239	*StV* III 585 = *IG* IX 1², 1, 173	**no. (45)** 191–193, 243 n. 20
Milet I 3 71	47 n. 44		
Milet I 3 33–38	95 n. 27	*StV* III 564	186 n. 66
Milet I 3 33a–50	56		
Milet I 3 34–90	36 n. 1, 54	*Syll.*³ 444E	171 n. 16
Milet I 3 122	38 n. 3, 40	*Syll.*³ 480	171 n. 16
Milet I 3 123	40 n. 15	*Syll.*³ 548	248 n. 7
Milet I 3 124	60 n. 72	*Syll.*³ 461	171 n. 16
Milet I 3 135	38 n. 3, 40	*Syll.*³ 622A and B (now in Choix no. 120)	
Milet I 3 136	14 n. 30, **no. (1)** 37–44, 57, 107		192–3

Rigsby 1996, pp. 149–150 no. 48 (now *IG* XII 4.1 222)	22–23, 102 n. 9, **no. (67)** 232–3, 237
Rigsby 1996, pp. 150–152 no. 49 (*IG* XII 4.1 223)	22, **no. (68)** 232–3, 237
Rigsby 1996, pp. 154–156 no. 53 (*IG* IX 1.97)	155 n. 33, 234 n. 40, **no. (69)** 235–6
Rigsby 1996, pp. 157–159 no. 55 (*I. Cret.* I.xvii 1)	234 n. 40, **no. (70)** 236
Rigsby 1996, pp. 159–162 nos. 56–60	234 n. 40
Rigsby 1996, pp. 204–205 no. 79	185 n. 58
Rigsby 1996, pp. 312–313 no. 151	213 n. 54, 234 n. 40
Rigsby 1996, pp. 316–318 no. 154 = *I.Cret.* II iii 2	230 n. 26, 232 n. 29
Rigsby 1996, pp. 318–319 no. 155	**no. (62)** 227–8
Rigsby 1996, pp. 319–321 no. 156 = *I.Cret.* I.vi 2 228	**no. (63)** 228–229
Rigsby 1996, pp. 321–322 no. 157 = *I.Cret.* I.xix 2 229	**no. (64)** 229
Rigsby 1996, pp. 322–324 no. 159 = *I.Cret.* I.v 53, also *IKnidos* 802	**no. (65)** 229–230
Rigsby 1996, 324 no. 160 = *I.Cret.* II.xv 2	**no. (66)** 230–231
Rigsby 1996, 325 no. 161	230 n. 26, 232 n. 29
Rigsby 1996, pp. 332–334 no. 163 (*IG* II³ 1 1178 and now in Choix pp. 174–177 no. 90)	13 n. 28, 15–16, **no (30)** 139–141

Mylasa – Crete: **no. (60)** 215–7 in particular see:
  I.*Mylasa* 643 = Gawantka 1975, K 21= Rigsby 1996, p. 408 no. 189   216 n. 62
  I.*Mylasa* 650 = Gawantka 1975, K 22= Rigsby 1996, pp. 410–411 no. 196   216 n. 62
  Rigsby 1996, p. 415 no. 209   216

Roberts *BE* 1972 371	8 n. 17, 101, 107, **no. (23)** 116–124, 149 n. 15, 205–6 n. 34, 239 n. 4 and n. 6, 240
Robert *OMS* I, pp. 436–442	106 n. 21
I.Magn. 5	94 n. 21
I.Magn. 7b	84, 85, **no. (19)** 98–100, 202
I.Magn. 17	87
I.Magn. 20	84, **no. (14)** 86–88, 195
I.Magn. 70	92 n. 17
I.Magn. 18–87	84 n. 1
I.Magn. 103	22, 84, 85, **no. (17)** 95–98
AvP VIII.1 5	101 **no. (20)** 103–108, 121, 173 n. 25, 215
AvP VIII.1 156	101–2, **no. (21)** 108–112
AvP VIII.1 157	106 n. 20
AvP VIII.3 268 also *OGI* 437	125 n. 86
I.Priene 1	127 n. 90
I.Priene 5	**no. (28)** 133–137
I.Priene 10	102 n.6, **no. (26)** 126–131
I.Priene 14 and 15 = Welles, no. 44	128 n. 92
I.Priene 17	128 n. 94
I.Priene 18	128 n. 93
I.Priene 47 = *IIasos* 607	22, 26
I.Priene 59	128 n. 93
I.Priene 82	128 n. 93
I.Priene 109	134 n. 5
I.Ilion nos. 1–18	119 n. 67
I.Ilion 5, 6, 10 and 11	120 n. 68
IKnidos 605	121, 143, **no. (34)** 150–2
ILabraunda III.i 8	65 n. 93
Inscr. Sardeis VI.6	102 n. 6, **no. (25)** 125–6

INDEX LOCORUM

ITralles 26	61 n. 81
Tit. Cam. 109 = *IG* XII. 1. 694 and Suppl. p. 237 n. 109	151 n. 21
Ager 1996, pp. 350–355 no. 127	242 n. 13
Ager 1996, pp. 466–475 no. 164	210 n. 48
Bielman 1994, no. 35	106 n. 21
Bielman 1994, no. 54	215 n. 58
Le Dinahet-Couilloud 1974, p. 414	154 n. 31
Magnetto 1997, pp. 262–271 no. 43	242 n. 13
Herrmann 1979, pp. 249–271	106 n. 21
McCabe Kolophon 8, 3rd-century BC?	106 n. 21
McCabe Chios 28 (= *I.Parion* T 59)	119
Moretti *ISE* I 40 = Curty 1995, no. 4	167 n. 6
Rhodes and Osborne GHI, pp. 486–493 no. 96	40 n. 17, 155
Welles 1934, no. 1 = Kotsidou 2000, no. 214	118

Literary Sources

App. *Syr.* 25	99 n. 41
Arr. I. 26	168 n. 7
Arr. I. 18–19	39 n. 9
Arr. I.19.6	39–40
Ath. Pol. 42. 1–2	196 n. 5
Curt. 10.1.44	41 n. 25
Curt. IV. 5.13	40 n. 12
Dem. L. 22	129 n. 98
[Dem.] LIX.104	249 n. 11
Diod. XV.46.2	250 n. 12
Diod. XVI.82.7	232 n. 35
Diod. XVII. 22.4–5	40 n. 10
Diod. XVII.7	46 n. 38
Diod. XVIII 51.52	46 n. 39
Diod. XVIII. 3.1 and 40.1, XVIII 50.1	40 n. 14
Diod. XIX. 75.1	40 n. 14
Diod. XIX. 75.4	40 n. 15
Diod. XXX.13	258
Hdt 1.66.1	110
Hdt IV. 153	91 n. 15
Hdt. 1.54.2	248
Hdt. I.174.2	151 n. 19
Hdt. VII.108–109	129 n. 98 and 100
Just. 2.3.4, 12.2.6, 37.3.2	41 n. 25
Liv. XLV. 31.13	156 n. 40
Liv. XXXI. 15. 6	256 n. 7
Liv. XXXI.15.8	154 n. 28
Liv. XXXVII. 9.1–4	99 n. 41
Liv. XXXVIII.41	129 n. 100
Liv. XXXIX. 25. 3–4	190 n. 76
Macrob. I. 11.33	41 esp. n. 24
Mela 1.78	168 n. 7
Paus. I.10.3–4	130 n. 104
Paus. VII.2.10–11	127 n.90
Paus. VIII.45–54.3	110 n. 29, 111, 112 n. 40
Pl. *NH* 5.112	38 n. 4
Pl. *NH* IV.42	129 n. 98
Pl. *NH* V.32	105 n. 17
Plut. *Tim.* 35.2	232 n. 35
Polyaen. V.44	46 n. 38
Polyb. II. 12.8	142 n. 34
Polyb. II. 45.1	177 n. 35
Polyb. II.46.2	172 n. 21

Polyb. IV.3.6	172 n. 21
Polyb. IV.34.9	171 n. 16
Polyb. IV.6.11	172 n. 21
Polyb. V.77	99 n. 41, 106 n. 19,
Polyb. IX.34.7	177 n. 35
Polyb. XII.9.2–4	258–9
Polyb. XV 21	55 n. 65 and 66
Polyb. XV.23.8–9 and XVIII.3.11–12	
	243 n. 18, 255–6
Polyb. XVI 24	94 n. 23
Polyb. XVI.26	154 n. 28, 256–7
Polyb. XXI.46.7	99 n. 41
Polyb. XXII.7–9	111 n. 35
Polyb. XXVIII.14	195
Ps. Skymnos, LL. 676–680	
	128 n. 97
Steph. *s.v.* Alabanda	140 n. 29
Strab. VII, fr. 43, 44a	128 n. 97
Strab. VII, fr. 47	129 n. 98
Strab. IX.4.7	180 n. 41
Strab. X.5.11	153 n. 25
Strab. X.5.15	151 n. 20
Strab. XII.8.11	46
Strab. XIII. 582, 621	99 n. 41
Strab. XIII.1.14	119
Strab. XIII.1.33	118 n. 54
Strab. XIII.1.52	118 and n. 61
Strab. XIII.3.5	105 n. 17
Strab. XIII.4.1–3	105 n. 13
Strab. XIII.4.1	130 n. 104
Strab. XIII.4.15	81 n. 136
Strab. XIV 1.8	72 n. 103
Strab. XIV.1.12	127 n. 90
Strab. XIV.1.39	84 n. 1
Strab. XIV.2.6	151 n. 19
Strab. XIV.2.23	65
Strab. XIV.2.26	140 n. 28
Strab. XIV.4.2	168 n. 7
Strab. XVI.2.4.	225 n. 8
Strab. XVII.1.43	40 n. 13
Tac. Ann. 3.62.1	94 n. 25
Thuc. III.53–59 and 61–67	
	249 n. 11
Thuc. VIII.107	46 n. 36
Xenoph. *Hell.* I.1.26	79 n. 124
Xenoph. *Hell.* IV.8.5	105 n. 18
Xenoph. *Hell.* I.2–3	50 n. 53
Zonaras VIII 19	141–2

Index of Concepts and Greek Terms

Arbitration 1, 72 n. 104, 106 n. 21, 127, 158, 172 n. 19
Asylia 1, 4 (personal), 7, 13 n. 28, 14 n. 30, 15–6, 18–9, 23, 29, 30, 51, 84, 87, 94, 95, 100, 102 n.9, 114, 121 n. 79, 139–141, 154–5, 180 n. 38 (personal), 185–6, 193, 213, 215, 217 (personal)
(Asylia and isopoliteia Part 3 219–237)

Enktesis 2, 3, 17 n. 36 (ἔνκτησιν), 86 (ἔνκτησιν), 92 (ἔνκτησιν), 94, 103 (ἔνκτησιν), 107–8, 113–4, 115, 116 (ἔνκτησιν), 120–124, 152, 158 n. 47, 175–9 esp. 176 (ἔνκτησιν), 181, 195, 200, 204–5 (ἔνκτησιν), 207 (ἔνκτησιν), 211 n. 50, 216–7, 221, 228 (ἔνκτησιν), 230 and n. 25 (ἔνκτησιν), 231, 239
Epigamia 2, 3, 17 n. 36, 19 esp. n. 41, 20, 21, 24 (ἐπιγαμίαν), 93–4, 103, 113 (ἐπιγαμίαν), 115, 121, 123–4, 158 n. 47, 170 (ἐπιγαμίαν), 173 n. 26 (ἐπιγαμίαν), 176 (ἐπιγαμίαν) and 178, 181, 195, 201–2, 204 (ἐπιγαμίαν), 209, 210, 216–7, 221, 239
Epinomia 199–200

Hieropoioi 53–54, 56

Isoteleia 17 n. 36, 107, 117, 135–6, 167–8
    ateleia (ateleis etc) 37 (ἀτελείας), 43 esp. n. 30, 78 (ἀτέλεια), 79 (ἀτέλεια), 86 (ἀτέλειαν), 92–4 esp. 92 (ἀτέλειαν), 99 n. 40 (ἀτέλειαν), 107, 117 (ἀτελῆ), 122 n. 74, 125 (ἀτέλειαν) and n. 85 (ἀτελεῖ), 190 (ἀτέλειαν), 201, 205 (ἀτελέα), 206 (ἀτελῆ), 228 (ἀτέλειαν), 229 (ἀτέλειαν), 230 (ἀτελεῖς), 231, 248 (ἀτελείην)
    enteles 37 (ἐντελής), 43

Katoikoi 26–7 (κατοικόντες), 202–3 esp. n. 29 (κατοικόντες)
Katoikein 201, 202, 209
Kinship 15, 23, 35, 62–3, 64, 66, 78, 81 n. 133, 82, 87, 93, 96, 102, 109, 111–2, 115, 134, 136, 138, 166, 184–6, 191, 233, 235, 244, 246, 253
Oikeiotes 23 (οἰκειότητος), 50–1, 62–63, 81 n. 133, 87, 96, 108 (οἰκειότητος), 111–112, 132, 137–8 esp. 137 (οἰκειότητα), 153 ([οἰ]κειότητα), 155, 187 (οἰκειότητα), 221, 233–4 (οἰκειότητος - οἰκειότητα), 235 (οἰκειότητα), 237, 248 n. 7, 254
Syngeneia (and derivates) 23, 58 (συγγενείας), 62–63, 81 n. 133 and n. 134 (συγγενεῖς), 82 n. 137, 108 (συγγενεί[ας), 111–2, 132, 134 (συγγενεῖς), 135 (συγγενείας), 136, 138 n. 19, 140 n. 28 (συγγενὴς), 165 and 166 (συγγενέ/[σι), 167–8, 184–5, 191 (συγγεν[ει), 193, 215 n. 61, 221, 227 (συγγενὴς), 229, 230 (συγγενέας), 233 (συγγενείας) and 234, 237, 254
Koinopoliteia 4, 192

Metechein-clause 17 esp. n. 35 and 36, 37 (μετέχειν etc.), 48 (μετέχειν), 50, 53 (μετέχειν), 59 (μετέχειν etc.), 64 (μετέχουσιν), 68 (μετέχειν), 69 (μετέχωσι), 75 (μετέχουσιν), 85, 94, 99 n. 40 (μετέχειν) and 100, 103 (μετεχόντ[ε]σσι etc.), 107, 108 (μετέχουσι) and 109, 112, 115, 125 (μετέχειν etc.), 130, 159 (μετεχό[ντεσ]σι), 179 (μετέχουσιν), 187 (μετέχουσιν etc), 189, 202 and n. 23 (μετέχοντα etc.), 203, 204, 206, 207 (μετέχοντα etc.), 208 (Greek in restoration) and 209, 211 (μετέχοντι etc.), 212 (μετέχωσι etc.), 215–6, 236, 258

Nomos proxenikos 94 n. 26
Nothoi 47–8 n. 44

Oath(s) 73, 85 (oath of the founders), 88 n. 7, 89–91, 92 n. 17, 117, 123, 148–9, 171, 201 n. 22, 202–3, 208 n. 39, 210–1, 239, 251 n. 17, 259 (oath of the founders)

Philia 21–22 esp. n. 47 (philos etc Greek terms, ex. φίλοι), 24 (φίλοι), 38 (φιλία), 45 (φίλας), 47, 48 (φιλία etc.), 50 ([φιλί]αγ) and 51, 52 (φιλίαν), 56, 59 (φίλοι), 64 (φίλοι etc), 67 (φίλοι), 68 (φίλον), 73 n. 108 (φίλοι), 81 n. 134 (φίλοι etc), 86 (φίλοι etc), 92 (φιλίαν), 96 (φίλους and φίλοι), 113 (φίλων), 125 (φίλοι), 132, 135 (φιλίας), 132, 136, 137 (φιλί[αν]), 138, 141 (φιλίαν), 157, 159([φιλ]ία), 170 (φιλίαι) and 171 (ἐν τᾶι φιλί[αι), 172, 174, 176 (φιλίαν etc), 180 n. 38, 183 n. 51 (φιλίαν), 187 (φιλίαν in restoration), 196 (φιλίας), 198 n. 9, 210 and n. 45(φιλίαι) , 211 (φιλίαν), 212 (φιλίαν), 223 (φιλίαν etc), 227 (philos) and n. 19 (φίλος), 229 (philos), 237, 244, 248 n. 7, 254, 258 and n. 12 (φιλίας)
(royal) philoi 225–6
Piracy 14 n. 30, 87, 93, 95, 205–6 n. 34, 213–5, 231–2
Proedria 10 n. 21, 37–8, 59 (προεδρίαν), 66, 92 (προεδρίαν), 93–4, 99, 108–9, 112, 113 (προεδρίαν) and 114, 116 and 117 (προεδρίαν), 123, 125 (προεδρίαν), 135–6, 139 n. 23 (προεδρίαν), 187 (προεδρίαν), 188
Proxenia 5 and n. 7 (proxenoi), 7 n. 15, 40, 92 (προξένοις), 93, 94, 95, 99, 148 n. 11

Rechtshilfe 94–95, 121, 130, 200 n. 16

Sitesis 87–8, 133 n. 1
Sitodeia 40 n. 17
Symbole/a/on 20, 28, 115 n. 51, 131, 154, 157, 170, 231, 246
Symmachia 175 n. 33, 176, 178 n. 37, 210, 211, 215 n. 61, 232, 256
Sympoliteia 1, 6–7, 21 n. 44, 29, 122 n. 75, 146 n. 3 and 4, 166 n. 3, 172 n. 21, 191 n. 78, 122 n. 75, 146 n. 4, 196, 243–4, 255, 258
Synoikismos 96, 118 n. 60

Teileffektivierung 17 n. 36

Index of Places

Acheloos (river)   177
Aegina   256
Aegospotamoi   251–252
Aeolis   105, 108
Agathokleia   130
Aitolia   4, 6, 8 n. 17, 20, 21, 30, 55, 101 n. 2, 121, 123–4, 144, 162, 165, 172–194, 242, 243, 255–256
Aixones   136
Akarnania   6, 8 n. 17, 101 n. 2, 121, 124, 175–9, 185, 239 n. 4, 242–3, 256
Aktion   177
Alabanda/Antioch   13 n. 28, 15, 133, 139–40
Alexandreia Troas   118
Allaria   208 n. 40, 212–5, 217
Amphissa   4, 192
Amyzon   79–80
Antandros   79 n. 124
Antigoneia   118
Antioch on the Meander   78, 81, 95–6
Antiocheia   224 (by Daphne)
Antissa   156, 158
Apameia (agreement of)   60, 114, 119, 130, 140
Apameia on the Axos/Orontes   225 n. 8
Apollonia   195–6, 208 n. 40, 257–8
Apollonia on the Rhyndakos   81–2
Aptera   232, 236
Argos   165–9
Arkadia   26 n. 58, 109–10, 112, 171, 203 n. 29
Arsinoea   6 n. 11, 16 n. 34, 25–27, 225 n. 7
Aspendos   165–9
Athens   8, 13 n. 28, 15, 17, 18, 21, 30, 40 n. 17, 46, 47, 49, 79 n. 124, 85, 127 n. 90, 139–142, 146–9, 179, 198 n. 7, 225 n. 11, 240, 246, 249–52, 256–7
Attica   149 n. 14, 251, 256
Aulon   171
Axos   124 n. 83, 191 (city in Lokris), 203, 236

Bargylia   22, 26, 97
Berezan   41
Biannos   206, 228, 229, 231
Bilkon   86
Borysthenes (river)   41

Chalchedon   55–56, 255
Chalchis   193 n. 85
Chalke   121, 143, 150–153
Chios   30, 119, 187–189
Cyclades   214, 215 n. 58
Cyprus   192

Delos   154 n. 28, 156 n. 37
Delphi   139, 171, 177, 184, 185, 187, 193, 229 n. 23, 248
Demphis   177
Didyma   40, 47, 55, 61, 70, 229 n. 23
Dodona   177

Elatea   99 n. 40, 235
Eleusis   256 (mysteries of)
Eleutherna   202 n. 23, 206–7, 213 n. 52
Ephesos (also Ephesos-Arsinoeia 50)   49–51, 93, 125
Epiros   124, 177
Eranna/Erannos   227–29
Eressos   156
Eretria   143–49
Euboea   143–49

Gela/Phintias   22–23, 102 n. 9, 221, 232–34, 237
Gortyn   95, 202, 204, 208–9, 216, 230, 236

Herakleia under Mt. Latmos   8, 14, 18, 19 n. 40, 24, 35, 44, 67–73, 80, 82–3, 103, 123, 175, 184–6, 239 n. 4, 243
Heraklion   197, 203, 206, 208, 258 n. 15
Hermus (river)   105
Hestiaotis   190
Hierapytna   13, 26–7, 84–5, 92–5, 196–7, 199–209, 216–7, 228, 231 n. 27
Histiaea/Horoi   143–4, 147–8
Histros   81
Hypanis (river)   41
Hyrtakina   230–1

Ilion   106, 120
India   41–2 n. 25
Ipsos (battle of)   127
Itanos   203, 209

Kaikos (river)   111 n. 37
Kalydon   190
Kamarina   22–3, 102 n. 9, 221, 232–4, 237
Kamiros   151
Karthaia   148 n. 11, 179
Kebren   108
Keos   121–2, 143–4, 145–9, 165 n. 2, 169 n. 12, 174, 179–183, 232, 242
Kios   52–57, 77, 82, 198, 255–6
Klazomenai   106 n. 21
Knidia / Knidos   121, 143, 146, 151–2
Knossos   95 n. 27, 208–9
Kolophon   106 n. 21
Kos   22–3, 221, 232, 234, 237
Kouropedion   93, 99, 119, 130
Kydonia   195–6, 208, 257–8
Kyrenaika   154 n. 30
Kyrene   4, 14 n. 6, 40 n. 17, 85, 88–91, 143, 153–6, 216, 259
Kyzikos   38, 45–47, 50, 79 n. 124, 105 n. 15, 138, 241

Labraunda   65
Lampsakos   119
Laodikeia by the Sea   224–5 esp. n. 8, 238
Laodikeia on the Lykos   102 n. 6, 124–5
Lappa   236
Larisa   11 n. 24, 143, 159–161
Latos   126 n. 87, 202 n. 23, 206, 208, 209–10
Lebena   236
Lesbos   158
Lethos (river)   93
Leuktra (battle of)   148
Libya   90, 154
Lokris   180, 191, 259
Lysimacheia   55–6, 255–6
Lyttos   92 n. 17, 208, 210, 229

Magnesia at the Sypilos   94, 105
Magnesia (on the Meander)   22, 30, 71–72, 84–8, 92–100, 101, 193–5, 202, 217
Mallia   229
Maroneia   102 n. 6, 126, 128–130
Marsias (river)   140
Messa   157
Messene   165, 170–174, 178, 239
Methymna   156, 158

Miletos   8–14, 18–19, 21, 24, 30, 35–74, 77–83, 95 n. 27, 100, 101, 102 n. 8, 107, 111, 118, 123, 127, 131, 133, 137–138, 141, 149 n. 15, 186, 195, 199 n. 12, 217, 238–41, 253 n. 22 and 254
Miletouteichos   81–2 n. 137
Mt. Ismaros   128
Mt. Thorax   93
Mykale peninsula   127
Mylasa   14 n. 30, 40, 44, 57 n. 71, 64–67, 73 n. 106, 80–83, 215–7
Myous   54, 71–3, 94, 95 n. 27
Myra   13, 18, 25, 36, 74–75, 174, 198
Mysia   55–6
Mytilene   11 n. 24, 143, 156, 159–162, 216

Nagidos   6 n. 11, 16 n. 34, 25–27, 225 n. 7
Naupaktos   121–2, 144, 165 n. 2, 174, 179–183, 189 n. 75, 242
Neda (river)   171
Nemea   166–168
Nysa   93

Olbia   14 n. 30, 37–44, 46–7, 50, 57 n. 71, 79 n. 124, 107, 138
Olous   126 n. 87, 209–10
Olympia   176–7
Orthagoreia   129 n. 98

Palaiskepsis   118
Parion   8 n. 17, 101–2, 107, 116–123, 149, 205–6 n. 34, 239 n. 4 and 6, 240
Paros   119, 212–215
Pergamon   18, 101–2, 103–108, 108–112, 115, 119, 121, 125
Phaistos   234 n. 40, 236
Phigaleia   19–21, 24, 30, 123 n. 78, 165, 170–174, 178, 239
Phokaia   84–5, 98–100, 202
Phokis   155 n. 33, 235–236
Phygela   38, 46, 48–51, 79 n. 124, 138, 235 n. 22
Pistiros   129 n. 101
Plataia   133, 246, 249–52
Poiessa   146 n. 4
Praisos   13, 196, 197, 200–1, 204, 207
Pras   177

INDEX OF PLACES

Priansos   204–5, 216–7
Priapos   119
Priene   22, 26, 71, 97, 102, 126–131, 133–7, 141
Prousias by the Sea   56

Rome   7, 76, 96, 141–2, 154, 234 n. 40, 245

Sale   129 n. 100
Samos   22, 30, 49, 51, 79 n. 124, 84–85, 95–100, 101, 102 n. 8, 127, 128 n. 92, 133, 134, 136, 246, 250–2
Samothrace   128
Sardis   38, 40, 46, 125–6, 248–9
Seleukeia in Pieria   224–5
Seleukeia-Tralles   9–14, 44, 57 n. 71, 58–67, 73 n. 106, 80, 81, 101 n. 2, 102 n. 8, 111, 169 n. 12, 199 n. 12, 238, 240
Sellasia (battle of)   110
Skamander   118
Skepsis   8 n. 17, 101–2, 107, 116–123, 149, 205–6 n. 34, 239 n. 4 and 6, 240 n. 8
Smyrna   106 n. 61
Soloi   167
Sparta   109–10, 172 n. 21, 246, 249
Stratonikeia   124

Stryme   129
Stymphalos   99 n. 40

Tegea   101 n. 1, 102 n. 8, 108–112, 208 n. 40
Temnos   6 n. 9, 17 n. 35, 18, 101, 103–108, 112, 113–116, 121, 215
Tenos   4, 78, 79 n. 124, 143, 153–155, 215–6, 222, 234–236
Teos   6 n. 9 and 11, 17 n. 35, 94, 101 n. 3, 102 n. 9, 106 n. 21, 113–116, 121, 130 n. 106, 131, 139, 140 n. 27, 213, 215–17, 221, 222–232, 236, 238 n. 3
Thebes   146, 148
Thera   39 n. 6, 88 n. 7, 89–91, 213, 215 n. 58, 259
Thermon   176–77, 193
Thessaly   159–162, 190, 216
Traianoupolis   129 n. 100
Trikka   190–1
Tylissos   203, 236

Vaxos   4, 191–193

Xanthos   13, 18, 24, 36, 74–78, 174, 198